9HEADS

9 Heads — a guide to drawing fashion
by Nancy Riegelman

Published by 9 Heads Media

Copyright © 2000, 2003, 2006, 2012, 2016, 2020, 2022 9 Heads Media Inc.

First edition 2000
Second edition2003
Third edition 2006
Fourth edition, 2012
Revised 2016

Printed in China

Publisher's Cataloging-in-Publication Data

Riegelman, Nancy

9 Heads — a guide to drawing fashion/ Nancy Riegelman 4thedition
576p. 33 x 23 cm
LCCN: 00-106285
ISBN: 0-9702463-3-1

1. Fashion Drawing 2. Drawing — technique I Title

Lib. Cong. Class. No. TT509 DDC 741.672

"This book is dedicated to the memory of my dear friend Paul McDonough and my aunt Ruthann Askey." N.R.

Nancy Riegelman was born in San Francisco. She attended the University of California at Berkeley, UCLA and Art Center College of Design in Pasadena, Ca., where she studied drawing and fine arts.

Nancy teaches fashion drawing at the Fashion Institute of Design and Merchandising (FIDM) in Los Angeles and international style at Art Center College of Design. She has been visiting professor at the University Premila Polytechnic in Bombay, India, Seibu University in Tokyo, Japan, the Paris Fashion Institute and the Central Academy of Art & Design in Beijing, China.

Nancy is also a fine artist who has exhibited in museums in the USA and overseas. Nancy lives in Los Angeles.

a guide to
drawing fashion

Nancy Riegelman

9HEADS

contents

Girl with turkey
Demetrios Psillos 2003

preface

This fourth edition of 9 Heads is overdue for a number of reasons. One of the most important of these is that while the methods and techniques used in modern fashion drawing have not changed much in the last fifty years, fashion itself, by its very nature, changes constantly. Change of course takes place from one season to the next, but beyond the seasonal variations there is usually a longer-term evolutionary process at work such that, given the accelerated modern pace of change, the fashion of just 5 or 6 years ago can begin to look distinctly dated. To keep the attention of young students of fashion, who are extremely trend-conscious and sensitive to what is and what is not fashionable, it is best to avoid association with any fashion item that might look dated!

And fashion, of course, is not just about "the garments". Garments are worn on the figure, and all the other factors that make up the overall "look" of an outfit on the figure —how the garments are worn, how they are combined with other garments, the hair, the makeup, the accessories, the poses and facial expressions, the context and environment they are displayed in (in other words, the way in which the garments and figure are *styled*)—change with the same rapidity and unpredictability as trends in the garments themselves. To show *new* garments outside the styling context of their time would be, to highly attuned fashion sensibilities, more jarring than to show dated garments with contemporary styling. (In fact TV and cinema increasingly produce "period" costume dramas that include many elements of contemporary styling, presumably so the audience will find it easier, even if it works only on a subconscious level, to "relate" to the characters.)

So, both the fashion garments *and* the styling begin to look dated over time. But the reason why a book on fashion drawing (or indeed books on any technical aspect of fashion) needs to be updated to show *new* garments displayed in a *new* styling environment is not just to avoid charges of being unfashionable: New students of fashion learn the skills of the industry as it is *today*. This means that not only do they work with contemporary garments and styles but they are also conduct their studies in the context of the larger historical social and cultural trends—the zeitgeist—that dictate what types of garments are worn and the occasions for which they are appropriate. For example, since the last edition of this book was published, active sportswear has grown considerably as a share of the total market and is worn frequently in situations where until recently "casual wear" was the norm. This type of "category change" has to be recognized, and it is reflected in this new edition in the numbers of drawings for that category. Besides activewear, other categories that have grown quickly in relative importance include accessories, lingerie and swimwear and the sections on those garments have accordingly been expanded with numerous new drawings.

Over my many years of teaching fashion drawing, one of the beliefs I have come to hold most strongly is that *as clothes mostly take their shape from the figure underneath, the foundation for good fashion drawing is the ability to draw the human figure*, in the simplified and slightly idealized way appropriate for fashion. Drawing the figure is an act, as I frequently point out, that is a challenge even for fine

artists specialized in that area, so it is not surprising that students of fashion, interested in drawing usually only as a tool for expressing their fashion ideas, find it particularly difficult. One of the principal motivations for writing this book at the outset was to address this difficulty, to provide students and teachers with a method for learning to draw, in as simple a way as possible, realistic and attractive fashion figures that would serve as firm foundations for fashion design sketches. That was the origin of the nine-head system I developed which reduced, as much as possible, the basic component parts of the figure to simple commonplace shapes and simple measurements of the parts against each other (or, more accurately against the length of the head). This goal of simplifying how to draw good fashion croquis remains one of the most important of the book and a new edition afforded an opportunity to refine and improve it, based on my classroom experience since the previous edition.

I have found in fact that students often still have difficulty drawing fashion croquis in a number of areas. I have addressed these areas of continuing difficulty by expanding the sections on some of the different views of the croquis into full step-by-step explanations. This is the case for example with the new explanation of the S curve figure, a key fashion pose, where a new step-by-step diagrammatic treatment is included before showing how to draw the regular figure, the inclusion of the three-quarter back view breakdowns and more diagrammatic explanations for drawing hair, something that students often find difficult.

As mentioned, the drawings of fashion garments throughout the book have been comprehensively updated. There is now a greater emphasis on daywear, and there more street wear is shown. A wider selection of fashion silhouettes is included and, as with the explanations of drawing the human figure in Chapter One, more step-by-step explanations for drawing the basic garments such as skirts and dresses have been added. The chapter on Accessories has doubled in size and additions have been made to the Encyclopaedia of Details to expand its scope. The chapter on Flats has been updated to include more contemporary looks, as has the chapter on Men. The chapter on Fabrics has been updated and expanded to show a wider range of garments.

A new chapter has been added to the book, *Composition and Fashion Shorthand*, also largely resulting from my classroom experience of areas where students still need guidance and sources of inspiration. This chapter deals with two more advanced types of fashion drawing: The first, *Composition*, makes suggestions as to how students should decide what final refinements to make to their drawings to ready them for display to clients or to include in their portfolios. This is the step that comes after the production of the artwork, a step that students of fine art learn about early in their careers but one that often goes neglected in the teaching of fashion drawing, with the result that students are able to draw isolated fashion figures well but are at a loss as to how to present them in groups, or how to make a single figure command attention. A number of examples of what constitutes "good" composition are included.

The other area of more advanced fashion drawing tech-

ALL THE VASTNESS OF THE UNIVERSE
WAS IN THE CIRCLE OF HER PUPILS.

OPEN WIDE.

NEVER WAS
IMMENSE LOVE MORE POWERFULLY
SIGNIFIED BY ANY EARTHLY
CREATURE.

BUT SHE SMILED HER SLIGHT, CONCEALING SMILE.

No title (All the Vastness)
Raymond Pettibon, 1990

say that the techniques employed in fashion drawing should be less than *any* type of drawing, technical or otherwise. As this book shows, it is possible to communicate in a drawing a large amount of information about a garment, including shape, fit and drape and fabric type, as well as mood, market, age range and so on. If this amount of information about a garment that as yet only exists in the designer's mind's eye can be effectively communicated in a drawing, then drawing becomes a very powerful design tool: quick, effective, versatile and economical. This "enhanced" type of drawing takes drawing beyond the diagrammatic: it communicates with an immediacy and realism that is the next best thing to seeing the finished garment on a model.

When drawing garments on the figure is introduced in the second chapter of the book, again, as with learning to draw the figure itself, wherever possible systems and techniques that facilitate the learning process have been introduced. For a drawing to be effective it has to be accurate and realistic, and experience shows this means accuracy and realism in every aspect of the representation of the garments. All the basic garment types are analyzed, and focus is brought to bear on the defining properties that make each garment unique: silhouette; fit and drape, and fabric. For a drawing to be most effective, and for the garment to appear its most realistic and convincing, each of these properties has to be represented (given the limitations of the medium) as accurately and realistically as possible.

Much modern fashion drawing, for example, is accurate in its depiction of silhouette and fit, but is often curiously negligent when depicting drape and fabric type. How the fabric of a garment fits the body and how, when it is not close to the body, the fabric falls away from the body in folds and drape, whether the body is in motion or in a fashion pose, is crucial information about the appearance and the very essence of the garment. *9 Heads* shows how to represent all these defining properties of a garment in a drawing in chapters on women's, men's and children's clothes. A separate chapter provides a more detailed treatment of how to draw fabric types so they are instantly recognizable.

THE FASHION CROQUIS—THE FOUNDATION FOR ALL GOOD FASHION DRAWING

Fashion drawings, whether new designs or stylings that use existing designs, have as their subject matter, garments and accessories. Accessories are usually solid freestanding objects with forms that are independent of the figure that can mostly be drawn in the same way as things such as buildings or cars. (There are a number of obvious exceptions, such as hair, the most important of accessories, which requires a special approach of its own.) Garments, however, designed with the sole purpose of being worn, take their shape (in differing degrees but overwhelmingly more so than not) from the body underneath, and the way fashion designers intend their designs to appear can only be fully appreciated when they are shown on the figure. In fashion drawing, then, particularly when presenting original new clothes where cut, drape, fabric and details must be clear, it is usual to show the clothes on a figure. This is why when starting to learn to draw fashion we begin by learning to draw the figure the garments will be displayed on; this figure is the foundation underlying all good fashion drawing:all the

elements of a fashion drawing are designed to emphasize and show off the clothing, and the figure in the drawing is also chosen specifically for this task. The type of figure best suited, and that is most commonly used in fashion drawing is an elongated one called the *croquis* (the French word for "sketch"). The croquis figure is equivalent in length to nine heads, as opposed to the natural figure that is closer to eight.

While the croquis is essentially a mannequin to show off the garments, and should never dominate the clothes in the drawing, it is important that it is drawn accurately. The simple reason for this is that, as mentioned, how clothes look on the figure is to a large extent determined by the figure underneath. At the extreme—snug-fitting swim-wear, or bodysuits for active sports, for example—the clothes take on almost exactly the same form as the body underneath, like an additional layer of skin; for other less-fitted clothes the shape (or silhouette, as it is known) is determined by where the clothing *touches* the body underneath, and in the parts where it does *not* touch it, how the fabric follows the shape of the figure and then falls away in drape and folds. If the figure can be correctly drawn and the garments to be displayed then correctly aligned on that figure, then the difficult part of the fashion drawing will have been accomplished. Because it provides the essential foundation to all good fashion drawing, the croquis is the first element to be learnt and is the subject of the first chapter of this book.

MODERN CROQUIS AND POSES

It is almost always the case that a poorly drawn croquis will detract from garments and can give an unrealistic representation of the clothing. A well drawn croquis, on the other hand, will bring flair and realism to the clothes and, often, important information on the type of person they are designed for and how they should be marketed. It is not sufficient, though, simply to draw the croquis *accurately*. In order for the portrayal of the garments to be most effective they have to be shown convincingly, in a pose that is modern and fashionable and appropriate for the subject matter. This will often involve the choice of a three-quarter view pose, and also often a modern pose that is a variation of the classic S curve pose. A variety of poses of this type is also included in the chapter and every attempt is made throughout the book to make the poses fresh and modern and to suit the clothes on display.

DRAWING CLOTHES ON THE FIGURE

The chapter on drawing clothes on the figure—the female figure—is at the core of the book. Each of the main garment categories is reviewed, in a sequence that corresponds approximately to their order of difficulty, beginning with skirts and ending with necklines and collars. Examples of silhouette, drape and fit, and details are presented and analyzed, and how to draw the garments is explained in step-by-step detail in the text and images. In most cases drawings of varying degrees of complexity, which might correspond to different amounts of time available, or how advanced the design is, are included, ranging from simple silhouettes to fully rendered concept drawings. Often multiple examples of details or basic style variations of the garment are included. The emphasis is on showing effective methods for showing each garment and indicating what is and what is not good practice and technique in drawing them. **Chapter Three**

introduction/fabrics/flats/ good fashion drawing

on **Accessories** and **Chapter Five**, the **Encyclopedia of Details** are intended as comprehensive—though not exhaustive—sources for detailed information on garments that will complement the information of the other chapters the appendix and can be used for inspiration or direct incorporation into new design drawings.

MEN AND CHILDREN
Although the principles of garment design and construction are similar between the sexes and among the ages, there are strong physical differences between men and women, adults and children and between children of different ages. These make for significant differences in design, how the clothes fit and how they are drawn on the figure between these different groups.

.Much of the emphasis in these chapters is on drawing the croquis and face , particularly the way the features are differentiated by age and sex, and also showing how to choose poses appropriate to age and activity. A range of modern garments is shown, both on the figure and as flats.

FABRICS
Those who have followed the arguments in this introduction this far will appreciate that the underlying approach and philosophy of this book is one of striving for accuracy and realism in fashion drawings. This extends to the fabric of the garment as well as its other defining elements. Although this book deals only with black and white drawing, and color is unquestionably one of a fabric's major features, much can be achieved in the accurate representation of a fabric using only black and white/ greyscale. Indeed, to be able to achieve success in depicting fabrics in color it is important first to learn how to depict fabrics in greyscale, without the use of color. In this chapter of the book fabrics are examined according to weight and texture, and a range of garments typical of the type made of those fabrics are presented.

FLATS
Flats—the two-dimensional drawings that serve as the basis for the manufacture of (mainly mass-produced) garments have evolved into the single most important device for communicating information about modern garments. For anyoneworking in, or contemplating a career in the fashion industry, it is important to become familiar with flats and to be able to draw them. The treatemtn of flats in this book is divided between **Chapter Four: Flats**, and **Appendix b**, which contains hundreds examples of women's flats to be used as learning aides or as the basis for new designs. A description of "specs"—the precise measurements used in the manufacture of garments—is also included with the appendix.

GOOD FASHION DRAWING: DISCIPLINE AND AN ATTENTION TO DETAILS
The opinion I have formed, over the years of both drawing fashion and teaching how to draw fashionto both undergraduate and graduate students at colleges of fashion and design, is that the key to successful fashion drawing, as is the case with many other areas of design, art and indeed human enterprise in general, lies in discipline. In the case of fashion drawing this discipline consists of developing a sensitivity to, and continually paying attention to, detail, in all areas. Developing powers of observation and the ability to perceive the details is part of the

larger process of learning to understand and appreciate fashion, which is also key in developing drawing and design skills.

The importance of careful observation at all levels cannot be over-emphasized: the imagination is a powerful tool, but it is important, for example before adding a modern hairstyle or makeup to a drawing, or before deciding how loose or tight the fit of a garment should be, to look around oneself to see what hairstyles, makeup or fits are actually being worn. Related to this need for careful observation at all levels is the importance of avoiding inappropriate generalization and abstraction in fashion drawing: Where the clothes in the drawing are elaborate it is often effective to divert attention from the *figure* and reflect it back onto the clothes by making the figure, or part of it, an abstract or generalized form. (For example, I often omit the croquis' faces or heads or exclude detailing on hands or hair when showing complex garments.) This does not work when drawing the garments themselves, though: shoes should be drawn not as "shoe-shapes" but as faithful representations of the actual complexity of shapes and details that make up the shoe. Again, detailed observation is critical to the success of the drawing.

As when learning any new set of skills, learning to draw takes time, and there will be some frustrations along the way. Drawing skills usually develop hand- in-glove (and drawing hands in gloves itself takes some time to perfect) with the increasing knowledge of and a developing eye for fashion itself. Hand/eye coordination improves with constant practice, the trajectory of one's line and one's shading technique become more confident and instinctive and a lighter and more controlled touch evolves. When this starts to happen drawing becomes a pleasurable and rewarding activity; until that point is reached, though, (and also in order to reach that point as quickly as possible) a conscious effort should be made to make every mark on the page meaningful, clear and precise. Work slowly and deliberately and progress will come.

As one's skills improve, the rewards are ample: as well as being a powerful tool of communication (and a potential way to earn one's living), drawing is a wonderfully relaxing and fulfilling activity. To be able to express one's creative ideas in such a clear and immediate form is highly satisfying and can be a great source of personal pride.

Now let's begin to draw.

MATERIALS

Fashion drawing is a precise type of drawing, involving the depiction of garments with exact measurements and a clear depiction of often-complex detail; the materials chosen are those that can best reproduce this exactness and detail.

The materials required for drawing the croquis are few: pencils, paper and an eraser (a few other materials are used when drawing flats and are discussed in that chapter).

When beginning to draw it is not necessary to use expensive paper—a bond paper is the best choice. Begin by using a fairly hard pencil—an HB lead is ideal—to give a crisp and precise line. Either a regular graphite or a mechanical pencil can be used.

MATERIALS

Graphite pencil HB, 2B, 4B
Mechanical pencil and leads
.005 pen
10% grey marker
Brush
Eraser
Drafting tape
Ruler
11" x 18" or 14" x 17" newsprint
11" x 18" white layout pad
Tracing paper

| 1885 | 1892 | 1907 | 1912 | 1914 | 1927 |

| 1931 | 1939 | 1947 | 1950 | 1950 | 1951 |

1959   1968   1971   1983   1984   1989

2000   2003   2005   2007   2010   2012

chapter one: proportions of the croquis

introduction

INTRODUCTION: FASHION DRAWING, THE KEY TO CREATIVITY IN FASHION

Fashion drawing is one of the most important skills used in creating fashion, a skill anyone planning for a career in fashion should make every effort to acquire. Fashion drawing allows us to express and communicate our fashion ideas, to develop and refine those ideas and to explore and discover our own fashion preferences.

Fashion is overwelmingly visual, concerned with the visual appearance of garments, fabrics and other materials. Practically everything in fashion can be drawn, so drawing is the single most important tool for *communicating* fashion ideas, and studying and copying drawings is one of the most effective ways to *learn* about fashion.

For most of us our main area of interest in fashion is not fashion drawing as an end in itself (except for the small numbers who become professional illustrators) but on other areas of fashion—design, merchandising, buying or manufacturing, for example. The fact that fashion *is* so visual though, means that if we *can* draw we will have an enormous advantage throughout our careers. Everyone involved in fashion should seize this advantage and make an effort to draw well—to a standard where drawings appear correct, accurate and clear as well as attractive and pleasing to view, both to others and to ourselves. Being able to draw well is also rewarding on a personal level, becoming, the more we advance, a highly enjoyable, stimulating activity.

Learning to draw well involves making an investment of time and effort. That investment, though, particularly if made early on, gives an enormous payback through one's entire career in fashion. If we decide to make the commitment to learn fashion drawing—and like learning any valuable skill it does require a commitment— then it is important to commit to learn to draw *well*. Learning to draw *well* takes a little more time and effort than learning to draw *"so so"*, but not *that* much more; the little more time and effort it requires is repaid many times over in the impact and value of one's drawings. This book teaches how to draw fashion well, in a clear, easy and systematic way so the investment of time and effort will be as efficient and productive as possible. It uses methods based on many years of classroom experience teaching thousands of students of fashion (most of whom have gone on to successful careers in fashion and design).

As garments take their shape and appearance from the body underneath the first step to learning how to make beautiful complex fashion design drawings like this is to learn how to draw the fashion figure—the croquis..

introduction/the nine head fashion croquis

This book starts right at the beginning, making no assumptions about existing drawing skills, and takes the student from complete beginner to an advanced level, covering all the skills needed to master the subject. If the whole book is studied, either by itself or as part of a course built around it, one will be well-equipped and ready to start out on one's career in fashion. So let's start to explore the wonderful world of fashion—with a pencil! Good luck!

DRAWING THE BODY CORRECTLY IS THE KEY TO GOOD FASHION DRAWING

Clothes are made for the body. Most of our fashion drawings will show clothes on the body so it is important that our drawing of the body underneath is *correct*, in order that the clothes are also drawn in the correct proportions. Unless we can draw the body correctly our fashion drawings will not look right: clothes take their proportions from the body underneath, so it is essential that the body itself is drawn in the right proportions or the whole drawing will look wrong. Even when we draw clothes by themselves, not on the body, we have to have a good understanding of the proportions and shape of the body that will fit into them. Because of the importance of the body in fashion and fashion drawing we start out by learning to draw the figure, or, as it is commonly known in fashion drawing, the *croquis*, the French word for a sketch.

THE NINE HEAD FASHION CROQUIS

In fashion drawing the focus is on the clothes, which we wish to present in as beautiful and appealing a way as possible. The figure is always present under the clothes— it is the underlying foundation that gives clothes their shape, and must itself be beautiful and striking to display the clothes to best effect. The figure that is used in fashion drawing is one that is a little different from the natural figure: it is an idealized figure, with longer legs, thinner hips and torso and a slightly smaller head. Using this longer, thinner figure makes the clothes appear larger and more dramatic.

If we take the length of the head as one unit, the overall length of the natural figure is approximately equal to seven and one half to eight units–eight heads from the top of the head to the ankles, as seen in the drawing on the right. The fashion figure is nine heads as seen in the figure on the next page.

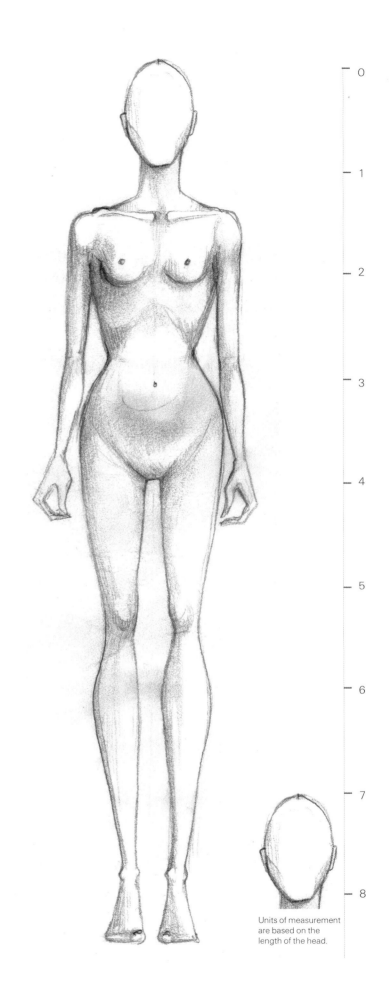

Units of measurement are based on the length of the head.

The natural figure is approximately equal to eight heads in length.

drawing the croquis/
the nine heads system

LEARNING TO DRAW THE CROQUIS—THE NINE HEADS SYSTEM.

Unless we can draw the fashion figure—the croquis—and understand its shapes and proportions we will not be able to draw fashion well. Not everyone, though, is a natural artist with an ability to draw the difficult human form. Luckily, this is not of concern to us: *fashion drawing is not about art, it is a tool for communicating design, a means to an end, with the end product being designs for new fashion garments.* We *do* need to be able to draw to express our fashion ideas well, and to do so quickly and easily, but we *do not* need to acquire the advanced set of skills that figure or portrait artists acquire in order to portray the detailed features (not to mention the characters and souls) of their subjects on the canvas. In fact, we wish to invest as little time as possible to acquire our drawing skill set and for that skill set to be closely tailored to our needs as designers so that we can get on with the main work of designing.

In order to make learning to draw the croquis as quick and easy as possible, and also because in fashion drawing we do not want the attention to focus on the figure but on the garments, the figure we learn to draw is, besides being idealized, *simplified*. We do not need to show all the muscles and lines and wrinkles of the natural figure in our drawings—more often than not to show those details distracts from the garments and makes the drawing weaker. What we need to be able to draw is a figure that looks like an anatomically correct (even though it is slightly longer and thinner than is natural), correctly proportioned, slim, attractive fashion figure. Our drawing will look somewhat like a mannequin, and, like a mannequin, it will be an excellent way to show off beautiful garments.

This chapter demonstrates a system for learning to draw this simplified fashion figure based on a simple form of geometry of *measuring the proportions and the locations of the different parts of the body in relation to one another and comparing their shapes, as much as possible, to simple geometric shapes. The unit we use to measure the different parts of the body by comparing them to each other is the head. The figure itself is equal to 9 heads in length*

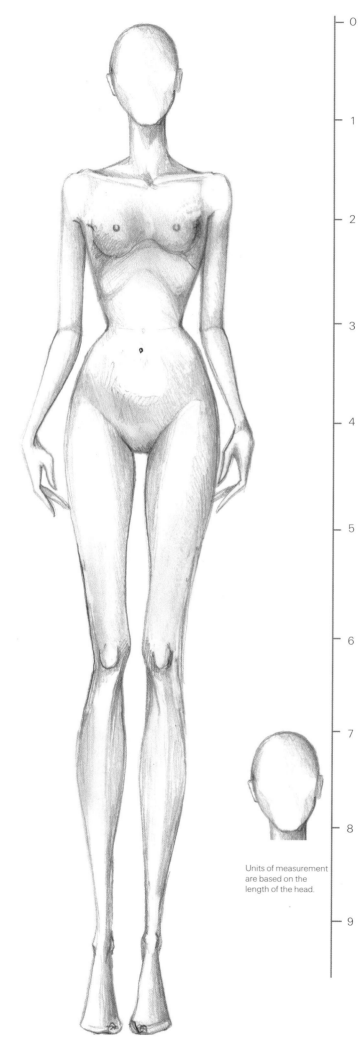

Units of measurement are based on the length of the head.

The fashion figure is nine heads in length—longer in the legs and thinner in the hips and torso than the natural eight head figure.

preparing to draw

*and the sizes of the different parts are express-
ed as multiples or fractions of the length of a
head.* When learning to draw this system
shows beginners how to draw anatomically
accurate figures within a very short period of
time. Soon, when we have acquired the habit
of drawing fashion figures we will come to rely
on measuring less and less and will be able to
draw beautiful figures quickly and easily at will.
This system has been used extensively in class-
rooms around the world and many fashion professionals learned to draw their croquis this
way.

REALISM AND ACCURACY ARE
IMPORTANT

Before we begin, it is important to understand
that although the figure we are learning to
draw is a simplified and slightly altered version
of the natural figure, what we are aiming for in
drawing the figure (as well as later on when we
start to draw clothes) is a high degree of accuracy and realism. If the shape, size and position
of one or more parts of the body are drawn
incorrectly in even a very small way then the
eye very often immediately detects the mistake—the drawing looks distinctly "odd", though
we might not be able to say exactly why. While
we can vary the size of legs, arms or the bosom
bringing our own style to the drawing, we cannot, for example, vary the position of the features of the face by much at all, and certainly
cannot draw them aligned incorrectly or out of
proportion to the others. With this in mind, let
us begin:

PREPARING TO DRAW

Sit comfortably in a chair with the back
straight. Keep the weight on the elbow and rest
it on the desk (or other flat surface) so that the
forearm and wrist are free to move on the page.
If the hand shakes when beginning to draw
(this is very common),try the following exercise: Place two dots randomly on a sheet of
paper about three inches apart. Place the pencil on one dot and, without removing the pencil
from the paper, rapidly draw a line to the other
dot. Repeat this excercise until the action of
making the line feels smooth and the shaking
disappears.

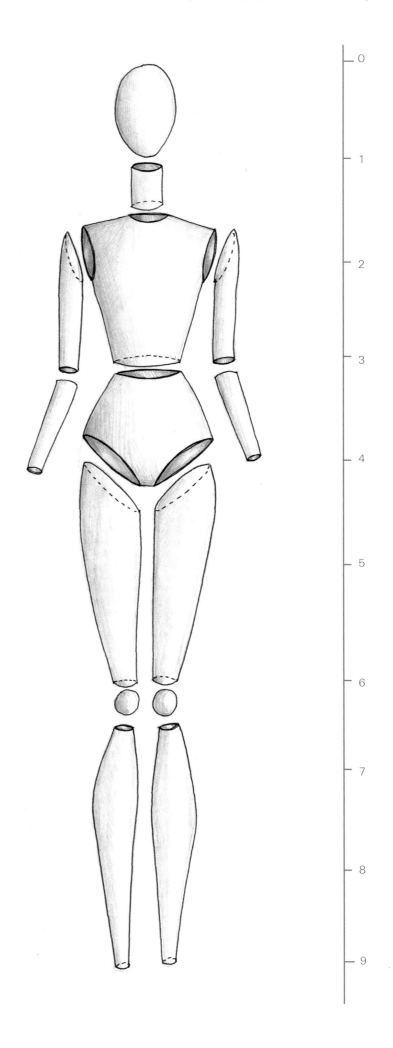

Most of the parts of the body are similar in shape to common geometric shapes and forms—ovals, cylinders, spheres, rectangles,
ellipses, trapezoids and others. Thinking of the corresponding geometric shape and then making adjustments will make it easier to
draw the parts of the body.

planning the figure on the page

PLANNING THE FIGURE ON THE PAGE

To begin drawing the fashion croquis it is necessary first to plan out the placement of the figure on the page. As a rule, the figure will be placed in the center and fill up the page so that all the details can be clearly seen. Our figure will be equal to 9 heads in length, so a head of one to one and a half inches is a good size for a sheet of 14" x17" paper; make the figure smaller if using a smaller sheet of paper. For the front view croquis, the position of the figure on the page is fixed by drawing a vertical line that runs through the figure from the top of the head to the feet, passing between the eyes, down the nose, down the center of the neck, between the breasts, through the tummy and crotch and between the legs. This line is called the *axis* line, and divides the figure into two symmetrical halves. Place dots on the page to indicate the top of the head and the bottom of the legs (where the ankles will be) and join them. Drawing a straight line can be difficult, and a ruler can be used, but it is important to develop the skill of drawing free-hand, so practice joining the dots using hand and eye. Touch the uppermost dot with the sharp pencil point and move quickly to the lower dot. Do not watch the pencil move but focus on the point at the end of the line.

Draw the axis line, filling the page from top to bottom (small figures are like whispers and do not command attention). Divide the line into nine equally spaced sections using lightly drawn horizontal lines as seen at right. This will allow us to indicate the position of the different parts of the body. If so desired a 9 head scale can be drawn to the side of where the figure is to appear. This will make it easier, particularly when beginning, to place the parts of the figure accurately.

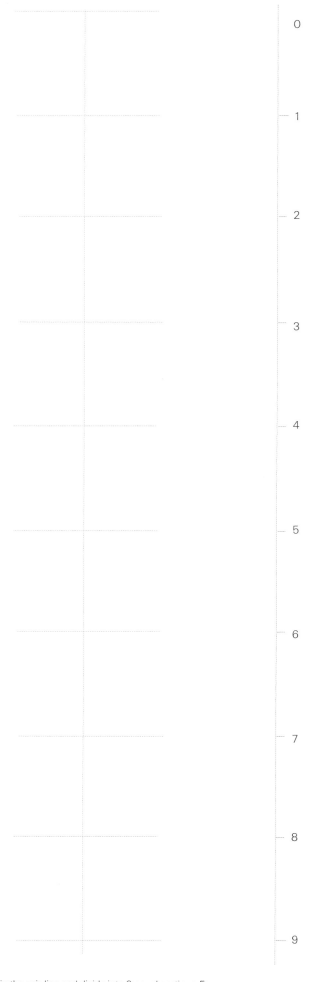

0

1

2

3

4

5

6

7

8

9

Lightly sketch in the axis line and divide into 9 equal sections. For a sheet of 14"x17" paper 1½" is the right size for the head—less if using smaller size paper. The 9 head scale is a usual reference to ensure accurate placement of the parts of the body.

drawing the croquis/
front view

DRAWING THE FRONT VIEW CROQUIS
We are now ready to draw the croquis. As
mentioned, the fashion croquis is based on a
scale equal in length to nine heads from the
top of the head to the ankles. Begin by drawing a vertical line—the axis line—and marking
the nine equally spaced points based on the
length of the head you are going to draw.

*1. Beginning with the head, place an oval
the shape of an egg in the first section
between 0 and 1. To draw this oval symmetrically (the two sides identical to each other)
place two dots on the axis line at 0 and 1, and
dots on either side of the axis line mid-way
between 0 and 1, approximately ⅔ of a head
apart. Practice making the shape in the air
before connecting the dots with the pencil.
This oval represents the head, and is slimmer
than the natural shape of the head. Think of it
as egg-shaped rather than as a hot-dog or
watermelon. Move from dot to dot to create a
symmetrical oval.*

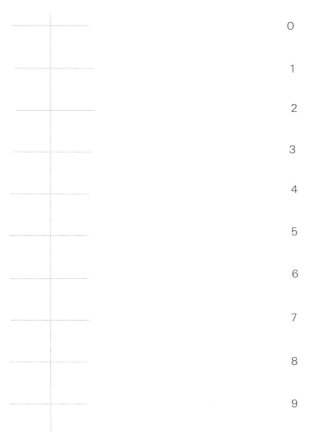

0

1

2

3

4

5

6

7

8

9

The fashion croquis is based on a scale equal in length
to nine heads from the top of the head to the ankles.
Begin by drawing a vertical line—the axis line—and marking the nine equally spaced points.

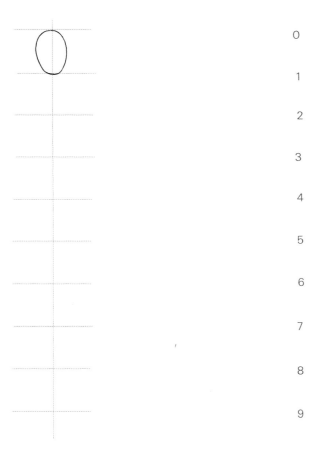

0

1

2

3

4

5

6

7

8

9

1. The head is drawn between 0 and 1.

croquis/
front view

2. Next draw the neck, moving half way down the axis line from 1 to 1½. The neck is slimmer than the head. It is a cylinder that connects the head from the jawline to inside the shoulders at the collarbone. It appears slightly wider at the base where it connects to the shoulders. The neck is often elongated to make the figure appear more graceful. Take the length of the head and the neck (1½ heads), and turn it sideways: this is the width of a woman's shoulders. Draw the shoulder line starting on each side slightly above the base of the neck and slanting down slightly to end slightly below the base of the neck, also where the collarbone is located. Draw a circle at each end of the shoulder line to represent the shape of the shoulder.

3. The top of the arm where it connects to the torso (where the armhole in a garment appears) is half a head in length, extending from 1½ to 2. The torso slants in slightly from the shoulders, as the body begins to taper towards the waistline, and bends inwards. We refer to this part of the figure in what follows as the armhole.

The shoulders are 1½ heads wide

0

1

2

2. The head is between 0 and 1, the neck from 1 to 1½
Shoulders are at 1½ and are 1½ heads wide.

0

1

2

3. The position of the shoulders is indicated with circles.
Armholes are drawn as ½ head long and slant inwards.
The collar bone extends from the base of the neck out
to the shoulders.

croquis/
front view

4. Place two dots at number 2 at equal distances from the axis (center line), midway between the axis and the sides of the body. These represent the highest parts—or the apex— of the bust (and will be used as guides for the placement of the princess lines, as discussed in the next chapter).

5. The waist is at number 3 and can be drawn with a width of ¾ of a head (the exact width of the waist is a matter of personal taste, but fashion figures look best drawn slim). Make sure the points marking the edge of the waist are equally spaced from the axis line so the waist appears symmetrical.

6. The next dot is just below the waist at 3¼. It is the point at the top of the pelvis and is called the ilium, the high point of the pelvis bone. It is important to establish this point precisely on the figure so the drawing is accurate overall. The ilium is the point at which a woman's hip begins to differ from a man's. At this point a man's hip becomes a vertical line whereas a woman's hip extends out at a diagonal. 7. The "hips" or "hip area" extends from the ilium at 3¼ to the base of the hip at 4. The hips are slightly narrower than the shoulders—about 1¼ heads wide.

8. Next, mark the crotch between the legs at 4¼.

9. Add the upper arms connecting the armhole to the elbow. The arms are drawn as two lines from the outer edge of the shoulder to a point at 3—the elbow. Tap your own elbow to your waist to feel exactly where the elbow fits—they are both at point 3 on the croquis.

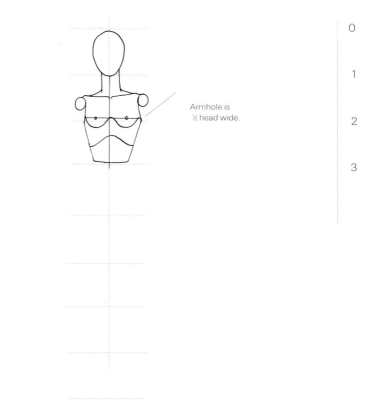

Armhole is ½ head wide.

0

1

2

3

4,5. The highest point of the bustline is at 2. The torso tapers to the waist at 3, which is ¾ to one head wide.

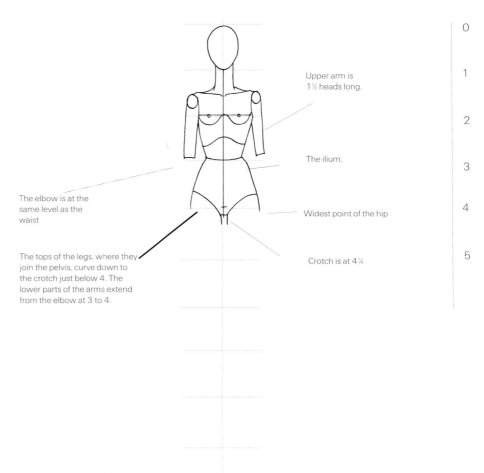

Upper arm is 1½ heads long.

The ilium.

The elbow is at the same level as the waist

Widest point of the hip

The tops of the legs, where they join the pelvis, curve down to the crotch just below 4. The lower parts of the arms extend from the elbow at 3 to 4.

Crotch is at 4¼

0

1

2

3

4

5

6, 7, 8, 9. The ilium is at 3¼ and is important as it is the point at which a woman's hips begin to extend out at a diagonal. The hips extend from 3 to 4 and are 1¼–1½ heads wide (usually slighter narrower than the shoulders). The upper arms extend from the shoulder to the elbows at 3. The position of the elbows is indicated with a circle.

10. Draw lines down from the crotch on either side to number 6, representing the inside edge of the thigh. Number 6 is where the knee is placed. Draw the other sides of the thighs from the outside of the hips at 4, tapering down to number 6. Draw these lines elegantly, each with a single movement and without lifting the pencil from the paper. Try not to make chicken scratches (lines made up of lots of smaller lines). The knee is about ¼ of a head wide. At this stage the position of the knees is indicated with little circles.

11. The lower arms are drawn in as slightly tapering cylinders extending from the elbows to the wrist at 4. Note there is an excellent fit of the wrist with the hip, just as there is of the elbow and the waist (tap the elbow to the waist and the wrist to the hip to see). A helpful proportion to remember is that the upper arm is one and a half heads long and the lower arm is one. The hands are indicated here but are complicated forms that will be discussed later. At this point use a simple triangle to represent the hands.

12. The next point is at 7. This point marks the widest point of the calf (a large muscle called the gastrocnemius*). Draw the line from the top of the knee to the calf, making the calf just a bit wider than the knee.*

13. Slide from the calf down to a very thin ankle at 9 (or, if preferred, just above 9 for a sporty, younger looking croquis).

14. The nine head figure measures nine heads in length to the ankle. The feet extend beyond that point. At this point, when beginning to learn to draw the figure, the feet can be drawn in as triangles or some other shape.

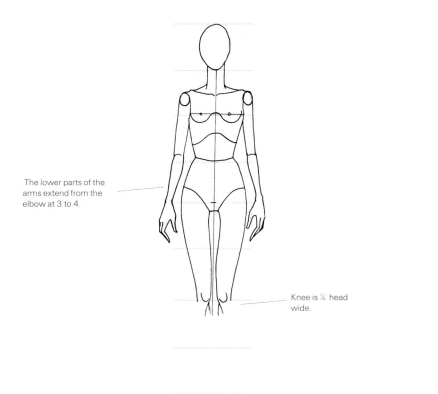

The lower parts of the arms extend from the elbow at 3 to 4.

Knee is ¼ head wide.

0	
1	
2	
3	
4	
5	
6	

10, 11. The thighs curve down to the knees at 6. Each knee is approximately one half of a head wide.

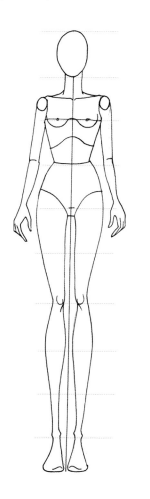

0	
1	
2	
3	
4	
5	
6	
7	
8	
9	

12, 13, 14. The lower legs begin at the knees at 6 and extend to the ankles at 9.

croquis/front view
fleshed-out/exercises

FLESHING OUT THE CROQUIS

To create a finished realistic look some muscles should be added to the croquis. Muscles give the rounded, fleshed-out look to the different parts of the croquis. How large the muscles are drawn is a matter of personal preference, but normally, for the fashion croquis, minimal musculature is indicated: in fashion drawing the "look" is long and lean. (For drawings of active sportswear larger muscles can be shown).

In fashion drawing it is not necessary to show much anatomical detailing (compared to medical drawing, for example) however it is appropriate and can be attractive to add some anatomical detail in the parts of the figure where it is most noticed, for example the contours of the collar bone (*scapula*), the roundness of the shoulder, the fullness of the bust, the shape of the ribcage, the softness of the tummy, the angularity of the knee. This anatomical detailing is indicated using shading with appropriate levels of light and dark in the relevant parts. It is described in detail in the section on shading later in this chapter, so eventually our croquis will look like the one shown here. Note that muscles of both the legs and the arms are longer on the outside edges of the body than the inside, as seen in the diagram.

EXERCISES

The croquis is the foundation for most fashion drawings and must be drawn well. Drawing it well requires practice. Try the following exercises to gain speed and to learn the croquis measurements:

1. Draw the figure five times with a light line. Use a mechanical pencil.
2. Draw the figure five times using a dark line. Use a soft pencil, 2B or 4B.
3 Draw the figure and fill in with a variety of patterns (a pattern is any image that is continuously repeated—stripes, dots, flowers, musical notes, etc.). Neatness is important.
4. Make a croquis out of cardboard or paper, make a croquis doily, a croquis cookie or simply repeat the earlier exercises until you are completely familiar with the proportions of the croquis.

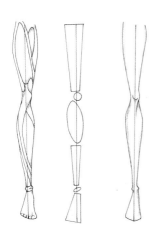

The muscles of the leg (as well as those of the arm) are longer on the outside, whether drawn in anatomical, diagrammatic or fleshed-out ways.

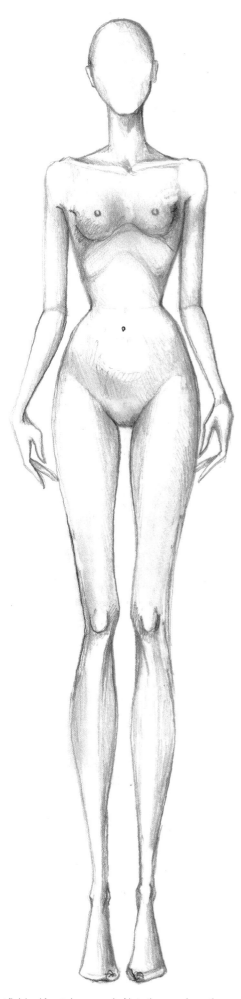

The fleshed-out finished front view croquis. Note the muscle on the outer side of the thigh is longer than the muscle on the inner side of the thigh, and the outer side of the calf muscle is also longer than the inner.

croquis/
back view

croquis/

DRAWING THE BACK VIEW CROQUIS

The back view is used in fashion drawing when it is necessary to show the details of the back of a garment, for example, the beautiful train of a wedding dress or where the detail of the back of a garment is important. Back views of garments often accompany front views in portfolio presentations so it is important to learn how to be able to draw garments on the back view figure. The overall proportions of the back view are, not surprisingly, the same as the front view, but different parts of the body appear in each view. As in the front view, the back view figure is symmetrical about the vertical axis line that runs from the center of the top of the head to the feet.

1. Begin by drawing the head as an oval, the same shape as in the front view. One small difference between the back view and the front view is that in the back view the neck is anchored inside the base of the skull (touch the back of the skull and feel the soft part where the skull begins). Draw in the neck as a cylinder starting just under ¼ up from the base of the oval and extending downwards ½ a head. The neck will appear shorter than in the front view, but is still half a head in length.
2. The shoulder blades are drawn as two lines about ¾ of a head long and lying about ½ a head apart on either side of the axis line that runs down the center of the back. They begin just below the line of the shoulder halfway between the end of the shoulder at the armhole and the end where it meets the neck. They are closest at number 2, bending out above and below that point.

	0
	1
	2
	3
	4
	5
	6
	7

1. In the back view the neck is turned up and fits inside the skull. The neck appears shorter but is still half a head long.

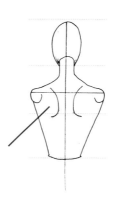

The shoulder blades are closest at 2 and bend out above and below that point. They are about ½ a head apart at the nearest point.

	0
	1
	2
	3
	4
	5
	6
	7

2. The shoulder blades are drawn as two lines about ¾ of a head long and lying about ½ a head apart on either side of the axis line that runs down the center of the back

croquis/
back view/exercise

3. The waist is at 3, as in the front view, and is the same width as in the front view. The hips are the same as the front view, ending at 4. The bottom is small and the cheeks rounded. Note that in the drawing the lower hip–the widest point of the hips– is located higher than in the actual human figure. Do not draw dark lines under the hip as this is a soft, full, rounded area of the body and black lines tend to make shapes look two-dimensional. The arms are the same shape as in the front view but the elbows are indicated by drawing a small curved line.

4. The legs in the back view are the same shape as in the front view except that the back of the knee is seen and the calves appear more rounded, indicated by shading, discussed later in the chapter. The tendons at the back of the knees can be indicated using two vertical lines or a horizontal line can be used to indicate a shadow.

EXERCISE
Draw 10 back views .

3. The waist is at 3, as in the front view. The hips are the same as the front view, ending at 4. The bottom is small and the cheeks are rounded. The hip is located higher than in the natural figure.

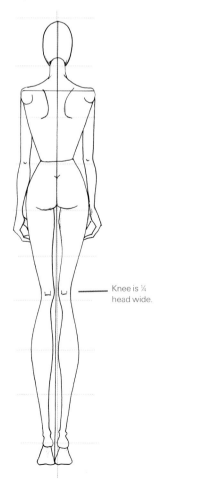

Knee is ¼ head wide.

4. The rest of the back view is the same as the front view except we see the backs of the elbows and knees. Think of arms and legs as cylinders when drawing.

croquis/
back view/fleshed-out

FLESHING OUT THE CROQUIS
As for the front view and all the other views, the finished back view croquis has muscles and is drawn with shading and detail. How to shade and how to draw the different parts of the body in more detail are topics covered later in the chapter.

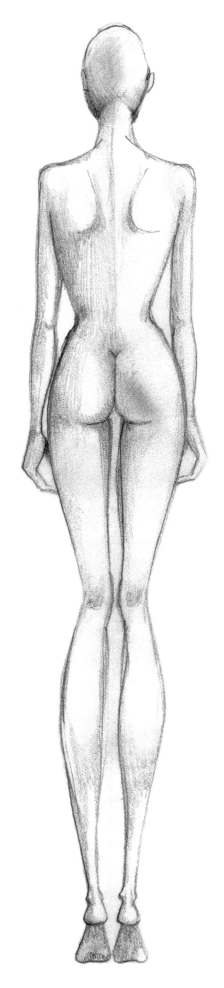

The finished fleshed-out back view figure.

croquis/side view/ balance line

DRAWING THE SIDE VIEW CROQUIS

The side view is used in fashion drawings where it is necessary to indicate features of a garment seen from the side, such as side seams or how a garment fits the hip and back (for example, jeans, pants and figure-hugging dresses). Contrary to what might be expected, when viewed from the side, the figure is *not* composed of vertical lines; almost every part involves lines that are placed at a diagonal to the vertical.

The vertical line passing through the top of the head, through the body and out through the foot just forward of the heel is in the same position that the axis line of the front view figure would be if the figure rotated through 90° to become a side view figure. The side view figure is not symmetrical, though, and axis lines are lines that divide symmetrical forms or shapes into identical halves. For the side view then, it is not possible to draw in an axis line to assist in drawing the figure. The vertical line here is, in fact, the *balance line*, an important concept in fashion drawing, showing how the weight of the body is supported. In upright figures (and most fashion figures are upright), the balance line will be a vertical line stretching down from the topmost part of the head, as though a plumb line had been dropped to the floor. For the upright figure with legs together it will pass between the feet; if the legs are apart it will pass between the legs; if, as will be seen further on, the weight of the body is on one leg, it will run through that leg.

The balance line is a useful aid when drawing fashion poses so they appear balanced and properly aligned and it is worth taking the time to work out where it is located and to sketch it in before starting to draw.

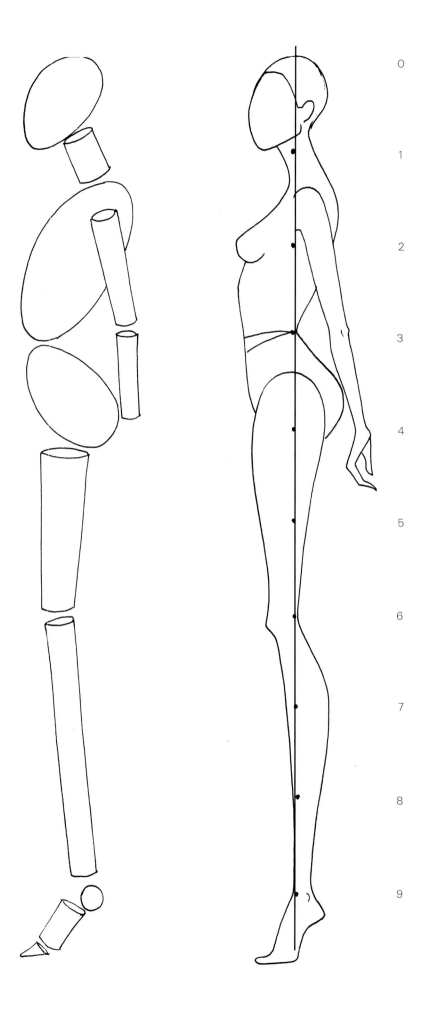

Contrary to what might be thought the side view figure is not composed of vertical lines but a collection of oval and cylindrical shapes positioned at different angles.

The side view figure is not symmetrical like the front view figure but it is helpful to draw in a vertical line running from the middle of the top of the head through the ankles as a guideline for correct positioning of the different parts of the body.

croquis/
side view

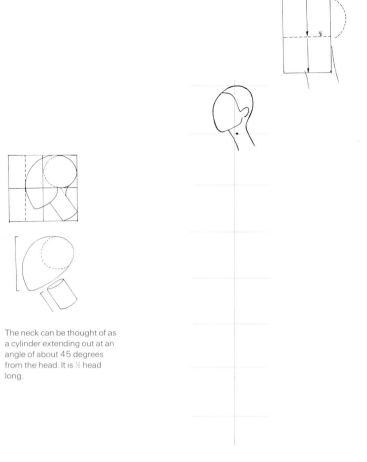

The head can be drawn as an oval or alternatively as a rectangle with a semi-circle attached where the back of the skull is.

0

1

2

3

4

5

6

7

1. Begin by drawing in the vertical balance line. This will allow us to place the parts of the body accurately. The head is drawn as an oval, set at a diagonal. (An alternative way to draw the side view head—shown in the diagram at top right— is to draw a rectangle about ⅔ of a head wide, and add a half circle to the top-right corner extending half way down the rectangle. This half circle represents the cranium—the back part of the skull—with the neck extending down from it.)

The back of the neck starts at the base of the cranium, approximately half way down the head. It can be thought of as a cylinder extending out at an angle of about 45 degrees. The front of the neck starts at a point approximately half way back from the front of the head. The neck is half a head long.

2. The upper torso is tipped forward—the balance line runs through (or just in front of) the shoulder, and the waist is positioned across the balance line, with most of the torso lying in front of it and a very small part behind. (It is quite acceptable to draw the waist lying completely in front of the balance line—the extra curvature in the back creates a fashionable figure.) Use an oval or a rectangle to plot the position of the torso. The line bends around the bust in an arc with the highest point at 2, angles over the rib cage and then extends straight down to the waist. At this point the upper torso meets the lower torso and begins to bend back. Take care not to tip the oval shape of the torso too far from the vertical or the croquis will appear pregnant!

We draw the arm here as pointing backwards slightly so that it is in a straight line with the neck. The usual position for the arm at rest is for the upper arm to be vertical, down the upper torso and the arm below the elbow to be bent up slightly. Drawing the arm in this pointed-back position allows the body (and garments) to be seen fully. (As a rule the body should be drawn so that all parts of the garments can be seen—they should not be obscured by arms or legs.) The hand here is fully drawn but at this stage it can be shown with a simple triangle or other shape. We learn how to draw the hand in detail later in the chapter.

The neck can be thought of as a cylinder extending out at an angle of about 45 degrees from the head. It is ½ head long.

1. Begin by drawing the head as an oval set at a diagonal. The back of the neck starts at the base of the cranium–the back part of the skull–approximately half way down the head. The front of the neck starts at a point approx half way back from the front of the head and slightly above the lowest point of the jaw.

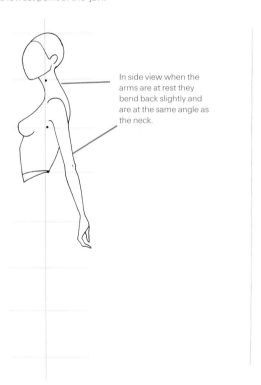

In side view when the arms are at rest they bend back slightly and are at the same angle as the neck.

0

1

2

3

4

5

6

7

2. The upper torso tips forward—the balance line runs through (or just in front of) the shoulder, and the waist is positioned in front of it.

croquis/
side view/exercise

3. The lower torso below the waist tilts backwards, following the curve of the bottom and creating a curve in the backbone, an area known as the lumbar region. The upper legs extend from the ilium to the ankle, with a straight bone in front and the full muscle in the back at 7½.

4. The knee is at 6 on the balance line, and the lower leg curves back behind it. The side view can be varied by thrusting the pelvis forward. This makes the upper body appear to lean backwards. The body must always appear balanced, though, and the vertical balance line must pass through the top of the head and the ankle.

EXERCISE

Draw 10 side view croquis.

Another useful exercise is to look at fashion photographs of side view figures and draw copies.

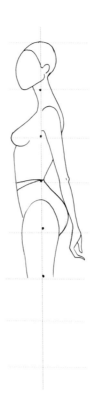

3. The lower torso tilts backwards, following the curve of the bottom and creating a curve in the backbone, an area known as the lumbar region. The upper legs extend from the ilium to the ankle, with a straight bone in front and the full muscle in the back at 7 ½.

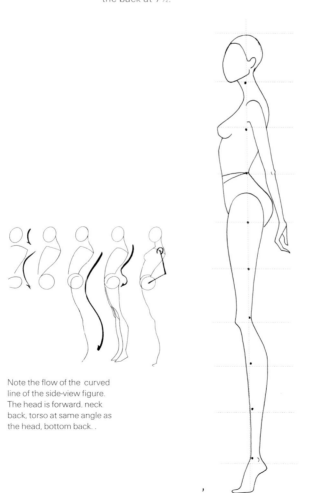

Note the flow of the curved line of the side-view figure. The head is forward. neck back, torso at same angle as the head, bottom back. .

4. The knee is at 6 and the balance line runs through it. The back of the lower leg curves back where the calf muscle is while the front is almost vertical. Note the feet are drawn as though wearing high-fashion high heels, with the heel raised.

33

croquis/
side view/fleshed-out

FLESHING OUT THE CROQUIS

As for the front view and all the other views, the finished side view croquis has muscles and is drawn with shading and detail. How to shade and how to draw the different parts of the body in more detail are covered later in the chapter.

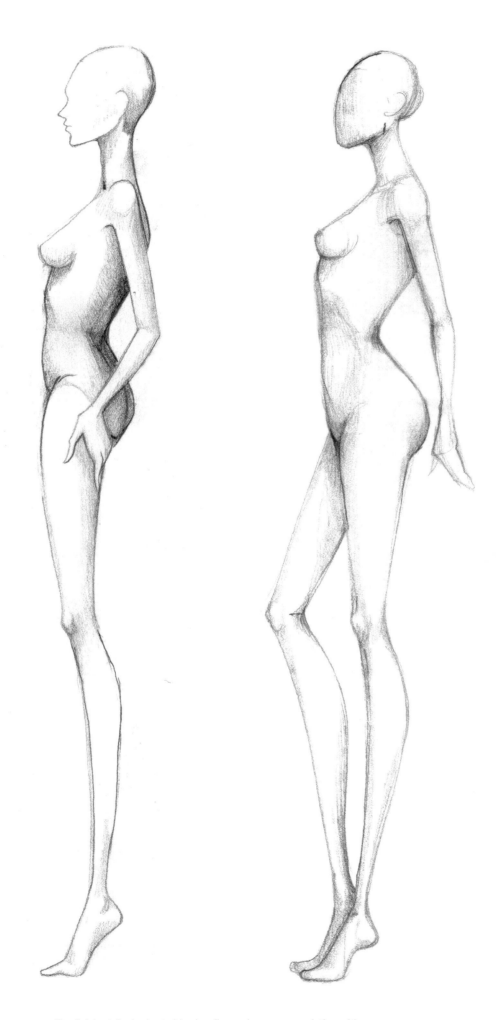

The finished fleshed-out side view figure. A common variation with one leg forward is seen on the right. When the legs move from the vertical the torso slopes forward.

croquis/
side view variations

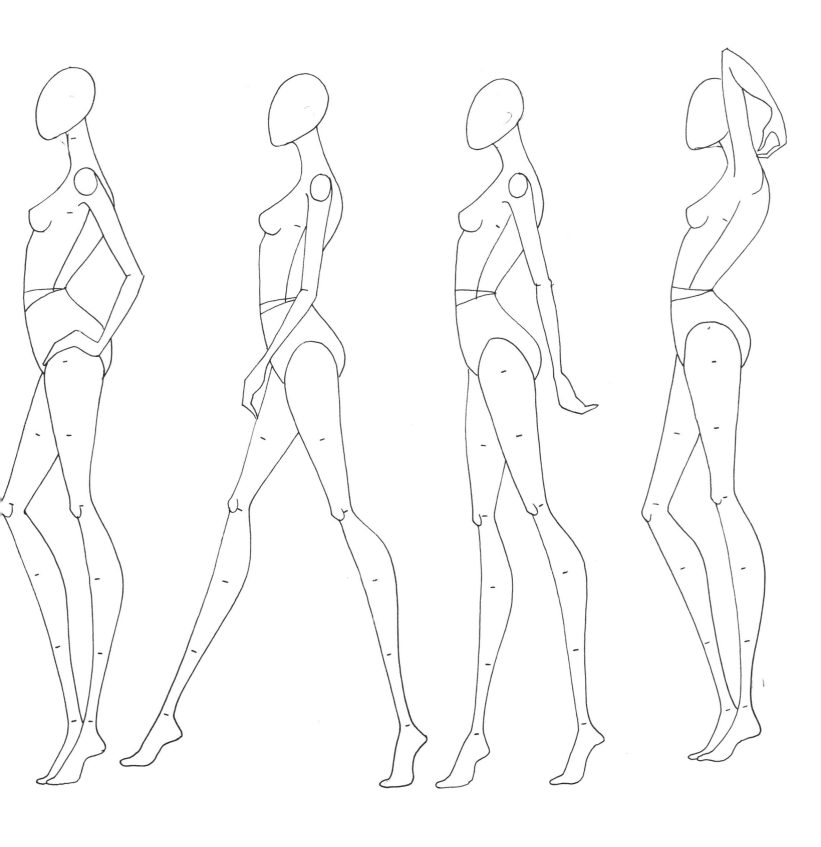

Side view variations. If the pelvis is pushed forward the upper torso bends back, seen in the drawing on the right. Note that once the legs move and are no longer vertical measurements should be made along the leg itself.

croquis/three-quarter view/foreshortening

DRAWING THE THREE-QUARTER VIEW CROQUIS

The next view of the figure to be learnt is the three-quarter view. The three-quarter view drawing is the drawing of the figure when turned and seen at an angle. When the figure is turned at an angle we see front and also some of the side of the figure. This makes it a useful view in fashion drawing because it allows a drawing to show the appearance of the front of an outfit and also one of the sides where we might wish to show interesting details.

The drawing of the three-quarter view figure is what is an example of what is known as a "perspective" drawing. Simply stated, perspective refers to the different way things appear from different points of view: Objects appear larger when they are viewed from a near point of view and smaller when they are viewed from further away. When an object is viewed from the front it appears different than when it is viewed from the side. For the purpose of this section on the three-quarter figure, however, we only need to be familiar with one aspect of perspective, the idea of *foreshortening*.

FORESHORTENING

Foreshortening is what happens to the appearance of objects in two types of visual situation: One, an object appears *smaller* the further away it is from the point of view. For example, as a train moves away from us down the railroad track it appears to become smaller. Two, when we view an object at an angle then the side of the object furthest from us appears smaller, or more compressed, than the side nearest to us. For example, if we hold a book in front of us and turn it through ninety degrees until we are looking at it from the side–at the spine of the book–then the side furthest away from us becomes gradually smaller or more compressed in relation to the side nearest to us–we say that that side appears *foreshortened*. In the three-quarter fashion figure, where the figure is drawn at an angle to the plane of the surface of the paper then the side that is turned away appears foreshortened. To express the three-quarter figure correctly we have to capture this effect of foreshortening in our drawings..

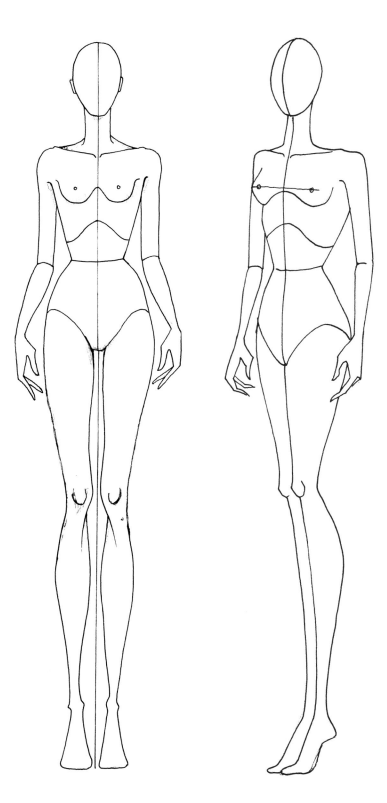

In the three-quarter view figure the side plane of the body is seen as well as the front.

Left, front-view figure; right three-quarter view figure. The front view figure is symmetrical on either side of the center-front line. The three-quarter view figure is the figure turned at an angle to the plane of the paper. The side turned away appears compressed, or "foreshortened" in the proportions 3:1 or ¾ to ¼ .

croquis/three-quarter view/guide lines

THREE-QUARTERS OR FIVE-EIGHTHS?

There are an endless number of views of the figure as it turns gradually from the front view to the side view. These views (except those very close to the full front or side view) are usually all referred to as three-quarter views, though sometimes, more accurately, the name indicates exactly how much the figure is turned—five-eighths or seven-eighths, for example. Here we refer to the three-quarter figure as the figure turned at exactly mid point between the front view and the side view—in other words, at an angle of 45 degrees to the plane of the paper. In this view the ratio of the size of the nearer side of the figure to the turned-away foreshortened side is 3 to 1, or ¾ to ¼.

CENTER-FRONT AND BALANCE LINES

The three-quarter figure is more difficult to draw than other views because of the fore-shortening on the side that is turned away. Two lines can serve as helpful guides when drawing it to ensure that the different parts of the figure are correctly positioned in relation to each other. These lines are the *center-front line* and the *balance line*.

The center-front line is a line indicating the center front surface of the figure running from the top of the head down through the center of the torso and between the feet. This line is located where the axis line would be in the front view figure, but because the figure is turned the line running down the center of the front of the figure has shifted to one side. As the figure turns and appears to compress (or foreshorten), the center-front line tracks where the center of the figure appears. This provides valuable guidance for correct placement of the parts of the body on the turned, foreshortened figure.

The other line is the *balance line*. The balance line is a vertical line that runs from the top of the head down through the ankles. It is the line the weight of the figure runs through—the ankles must always sit vertically below the head on this line. In the front view figure this line is in the same place as the axis line, but in three-quarter view the figure has turned and the balance line appears to one side.

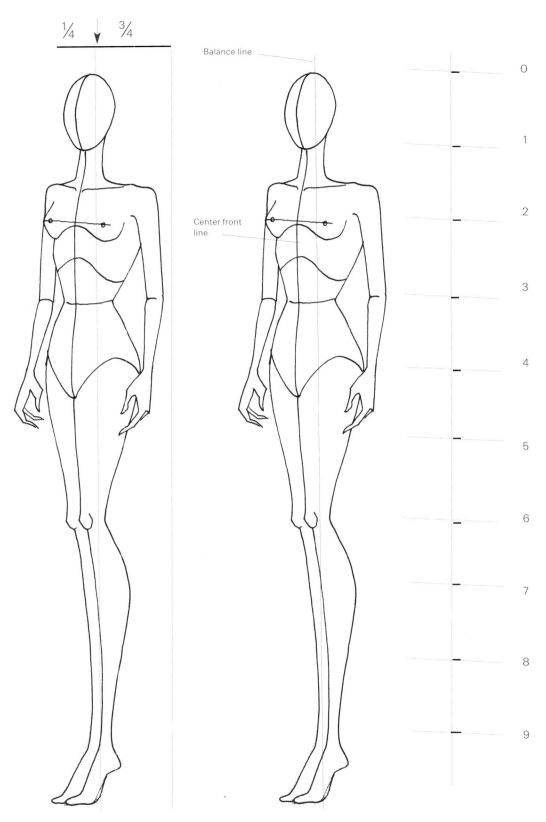

Left, In the three-quarter figure the side turned away appears compressed, or "foreshortened" in the proportions 3:1 or ¾ to ¼ . Right, the center-front line is a line running from the neck through the center of the torso to the center of the feet. As the figure turns and appears to compress (or foreshorten), the center-front line tracks where the center of the figure appears. The balance line is a vertical line that runs from the center of the top of the head down through the ankles.

Right, 9 head scale. The different parts of the body are in the same position on the nine head scale as the other views but they lie on a plane that is at an angle to the plane of the surface of the paper, so it is helpful to draw in a number of parallel lines to show the nine-head scale, but with the lines sloping slightly showing that the body is at an angle to the plane of the surface of the paper.

croquis/three-quarter view

DRAWING THE THREE-QUARTER VIEW FIGURE

As with the other views of the figure, it is helpful to draw in the nine-heads scale: The different parts of the body are in the same position as the other views but they lie on a plane that is at an angle to the plane of the surface of the paper, so it can also help to draw in a number of parallel lines to show the nine-head scale, but with the lines sloping slightly showing that the body is at an angle to the plane of the surface of the paper. The three-quarter view is more difficult to draw than the other views so draw slowly and check constantly to make sure proportions are correct.

1. Draw in the balance line running vertically through the top of the head. Draw the head as a simple oval. Because the head is almost cylindrical in shape, in contrast to the torso, which is flatter, in three-quarter view its outline does not change much in appearance from the front view (as opposed to a cube or pyramid, for example). Draw in the center-front line dividing the head and neck in the proportions 3 to 1. It is useful also to draw in the balance line as a vertical line starting at the middle of the top of the head, imagining it to extend down through the head and body and out at the feet. This ensures that the bottom of the legs end up in the right position–in a vertical line directly under the head.

2. The neck lies in the same 3 to 1 proportions on either side of the center-front line. Note that there is a break in the center-front line between the head and neck as in this view the neck is seen as behind the front of the head. The shoulders are 1½ heads wide, as in the front view, but are also drawn in the same 3 to 1 proportions as the head and neck on either side of the center-front line. Note that the shape of the shoulder on the non-foreshortened side of the figure is almost the same as in the front view figure, while the shoulder on the other side appears compressed and is a different shape.

3. Add the bust at 2, as in the other views. On the near side it is seen almost as in the front view; on the foreshortened side it is seen in profile extending over the arm. Make sure the breasts are at the same height. The center-front line passes down the middle of the chest between the bust, curving slightly as it follows the contours of the body. Start drawing the upper arms. On the near side the arm is almost the same as the front view arm. On the far side the arm disappears behind the profile of the breast.

1. Draw the head as a simple oval. Draw in the center-front line dividing the head in the proportions 3 to 1.

	0
	1

2. The neck is also in 3:1 proportions. The center line of the neck does not align with the CF of the head. Shoulders are 1/½ heads wide in 3:1 proportions.

	0
	1

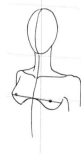

3. Add the bust at 2. Make sure the bust overlaps the arm on the side turning away–it is seen in profile.

	0
	1
	2

4. Draw in the upper torso tapering to the waist at 3. In the ¾ figure the edge of the breast on the side turned away is seen in profile, curving from the shoulder, and partly covers the arm on that side. On the near side the breast is located between the c-f line and the edge of the torso where the arm meets the torso. Make sure the breasts are at the same height (2) and at right angles to the c-f line. The top of the arm hidden by the breast on the side turned away is a convex curve.

	0
	1
	2
	3

croquis/three-quarter view

4. Draw in the rest of the upper arms. On the far side the outer edge of the arm is seen to emerge from about or just below the level of the breast . The inner edge is hidden behind the breast and torso until it emerges just above the waistline. The outer edge of the far side arm tapers at a steeper angle from the shoulder to the waistline. Draw in the upper torso tapering to the waist at 3. On the near side the edge of the torso emerges from behind the arm midway between the line of the bust and the waistline.

5. Draw in the hips and the line of the pelvis on both sides, extending to the crotch. Proportions for the hip/pelvis area are also in the ratio 3 to 1. Draw in the lower arms to the wrist at the same level as the crotch. Note that the hip on the near side has a fuller curve than the far hip as part of the buttock is seen. Draw in the upper legs from hip to knee. Because the near-side leg overlaps the far leg the legs also appear in the proportions 3 to 1. The knees at 6 are turned at the same angle as the body–they are not centered.

6. Draw in the lower legs. In three-quarter view more of the back of the leg is seen so the curve of the calf muscle is indicated.

5. Draw in the hips and the line of the pelvis on both sides, extending to the crotch. Proportions for the hip/pelvis area are also in the ratio 3 to 1. Draw in the lower arms to the wrist at the same level as the crotch.

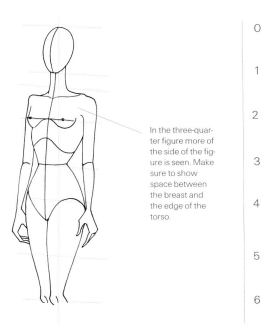

In the three-quarter figure more of the side of the figure is seen. Make sure to show space between the breast and the edge of the torso.

6. Draw in the legs. The leg turned away is slightly smaller than the nearer leg. The knees are indicated as ovals, pointing in the same direction as the figure.

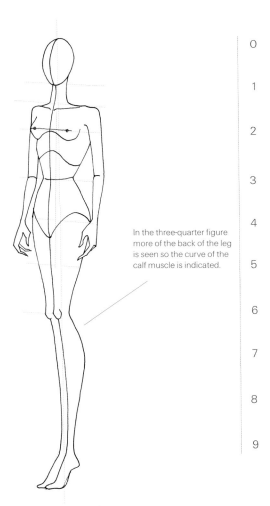

In the three-quarter figure more of the back of the leg is seen so the curve of the calf muscle is indicated.

croquis/three-quarter view/fleshed-out/exercise

FLESHING OUT THE CROQUIS

As for the front view and all the other views, the finished three-quarter view croquis has muscles and is drawn with shading and detail. How to shade and how to draw the different parts of the body in more detail are covered later in the chapter.

EXERCISE

Draw ten three-quarter figures. Look for these views in a magazine. Trace the edge of each figure.

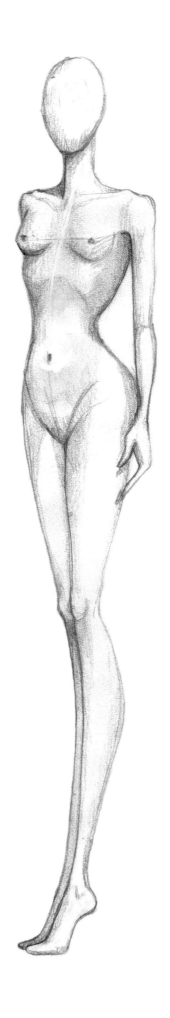

The finished fleshed-out three-quarter view figure.

croquis/three-quarter view variations

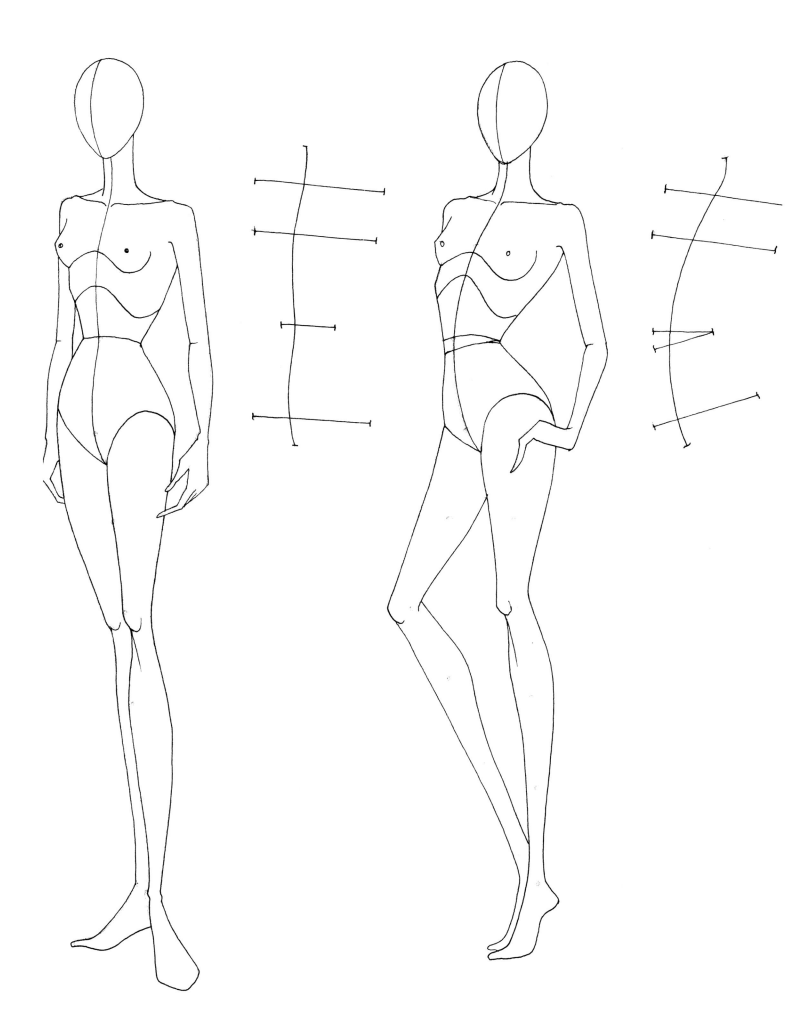

When one leg bends forward it causes the upper and lower torso areas to curve more than when the legs are together. This effect is seen in both the side and three-quarter views and can be used as a simple effective fashion pose.

croquis/back
three-quarter view

DRAWING THE BACK THREE-QUARTER VIEW
CROQUIS

The back three-quarter view croquis, like the front three-quarter view, allows two planes of the figure to be seen in the same drawing, in this case the back and the side. This view is useful when important detailing of the garments is present on both the back and side, for example in a swimsuit where the exact cut of the straps at the back and the side detailing has to be shown accurately. It is also the case for any garment that is backless, where not only the treatment at the back but also the cut of the fabric around the arm must be clearly seen. Any garment in fact where the silhouette of the back of the garment itself, the back of the sleeve and collar are essential aspects of the garment, is best shown in three-quarter back view, complementing the three-quarter front view.

As in the other views it is useful to draw in the nine-heads scale. The different parts of the body are in the same position as the other views but they lie on a plane that is at an angle to the plane of the surface of the paper, so it is helpful, as when drawing the front three-quarter view figure, to draw in a number of parallel lines to show the nine-head scale, but with the lines sloping slightly showing that the body is at an angle to the plane of the surface of the paper. It is useful also to draw in the balance line as a vertical line starting at the middle of the top of the head, imagining it to extend down through the head and body and out at the feet. This makes sure that the bottom of the legs end up in the right position–in a vertical line directly under the head, and the other parts of the body are correctly aligned.

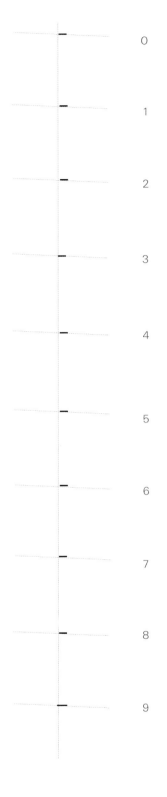

For the ¾ back view it is useful to draw in the nine head scale with sloping lines to indicate the plane of the back of the figure,

croquis/back three-quarter view

In the ¾ back view head the neck fits into the back of the head like a cylinder. The head is angled to one side of the vertical and the neck is angled the same amount to the other side.

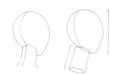

1. Begin by drawing in the balance line running vertically through the top of the head. Draw the head as an oval at a slight angle to the vertical. Draw a center-back line running from the center of the top of the head along the middle of the back of the head and down the back of the neck. In the turned head seen in the back three-quarter view this line, as with the front three-quarter view, divides the head in the proportions 3 to 1 (or ¾ to ¼). The rest of the figure is also divided in these proportions between the nearer side and the further-away foreshortened side. It is also useful to draw in a vertical balance line as the center-front line returns to this line at different points. Draw in the neck as a cylinder extending down at an angle (the same slope as the head) about one-half heads length.

2. First draw in the waist at 3 as a slightly upward-curving arc. The waist is seen as the same width in three-quarter view as in front view—about two-thirds of the length of a head. Plot in the position of the center-back line from the back of the head to the waist. This line will follow the position of the spine and curves back to meet the vertical balance line at the waist. Draw in the shoulders. As in the other views the shoulders are 1½ heads wide, sitting at the base of the neck. The shoulders overlap the neck on the near side so the neck appears slightly shorter in the front than on the other foreshortened side. Indicate the edge of the shoulder as an oval. Draw in the outline of the bust on the near side with the apex of the bust at number 2. Draw in the shoulder blades between 1½ and 2 as shallow half-moons.

3. Draw in the upper arms as cylinders beginning at the edge of the shoulders and extending to the waist at 3. When arms are relaxed they hang naturally behind the torso, and in the angled views of the figure this is noticeable.

4. Draw in the center-back line for the hip area. This line curves out in the opposite direction to the center-back line down the upper part of the body and ends at the bottom of the spine where it is hidden by the curve of the buttock. Draw in the outline of the hip on the near side. It extends out from the waist at a diagonal ending at 4, its widest point. Draw in the sphere of the right buttock as a hook shape looping from the base of the spine.

1. Draw the head as an oval at an angle. Draw in c-b line down middle of back of head. See text for detailed instructions.

0
1

2. Draw in waist at 3 as an upward curving arc. Plot in position of c-b line from head to waist. See text for detailed instructions.

0

1

2

3

3. Draw in upper arms as cylinders extending to waist at 3. See text for detailed instructions.

0

1

2

3

4. Draw in the center-back line for the hip area. See text for detailed instructions.

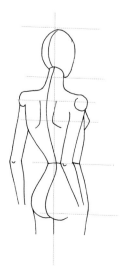

0

1

2

3

4

croquis/ back three-quarter view

DRAWING THE BACK THREE-QUARTER VIEW CROQUIS *(CONTINUED)*

4. Draw in the hip and buttock on the other side, also as a hook shape .parallel to the one on the near side. Draw in the lower arms from elbow to wrist and begin to outline the top of the legs.

5. Extend the legs down from the outer edges of the hips slimming to the knee at number 6. Note the nearer leg appears wider than far leg because of the overlap and foreshortening. Indicate the back of the knee with a half circle or vertical lines representing the tendon. Define the front of the knee by adding a bump to the line of the leg.

6. The back of the lower legs slope away from the knee around the calf and back in to the ankle. The front of the lower legs extend from the knee to the ankle, sloping slightly directly below the knee and then becoming almost vertical in the lower part to the ankle. At this point hands and feet can be drawn in as simple shapes; later in the chapter we discuss how to draw them in detail.

5. Draw in the upper part of the legs. The leg turned away is slightly smaller than the nearer leg. The knees are indicated as ovals, pointing in the same direction as the figure. See text for detailed instructions.

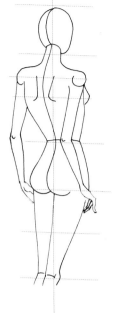

6. The back of the lower legs slope away from the knee around the calf and back in to the ankle. The front of the lower legs extend from the knee to the ankle , sloping slightly directly below the knee and then becoming almost vertical in the lower part to the ankle. See text for detailed instructions.

croquis/back three-quarter view/exercise

FLESHING OUT THE CROQUIS

As for the front view and all the other views, the finished back three-quarter view croquis has muscles and is drawn with shading and detail. How to shade and how to draw the different parts of the body in more detail are covered later in the chapter.

EXERCISE

Draw ten back three-quarter figures. Look for these views in a magazine. Trace the edge of each figure.

The finished fleshed-out back three-quarter view figure.

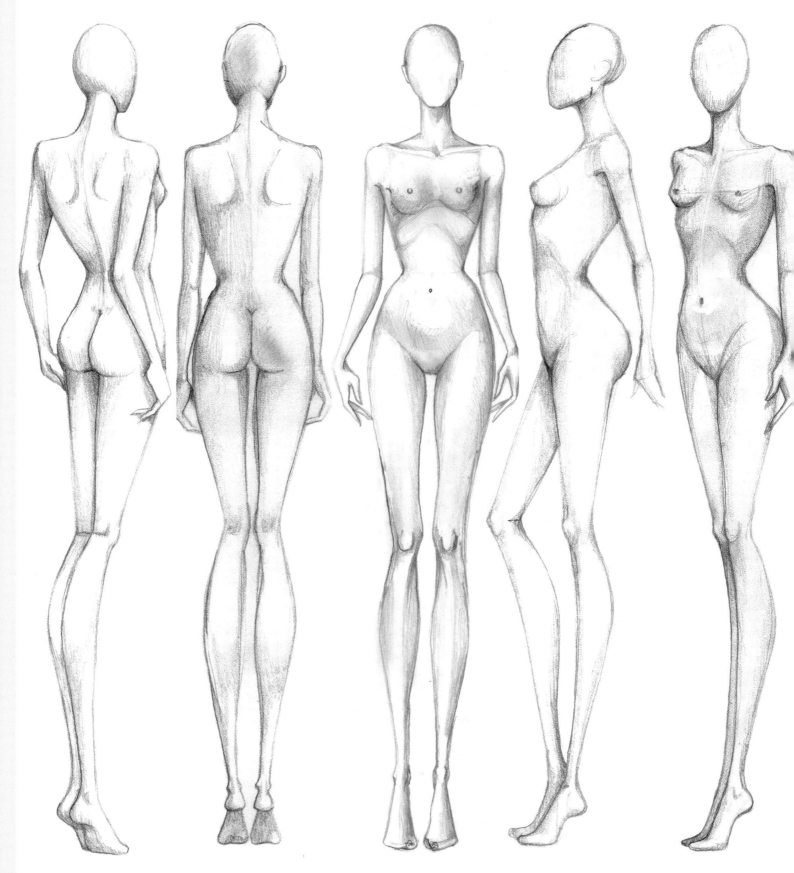

The finished fleshed-out back three-quarter,
back front, side and three-quarter view figures.

shading and value/ light and shadow

SHADING AND VALUE/LIGHT AND SHADOW

Real objects are three-dimensional: they have height, width and depth. As discussed in the introduction to the three-quarter view figure and the idea of *foreshortening* when objects are viewed at an angle, in three-quarter or another partial view, we can *see* they are three-dimensional, and not cardboard cut-outs as we are able to see part of the side of the object as well as the front. To draw these angled views so they appear realistic we use, as we have seen, the technique of *foreshortening*, imitating on the paper— a two-dimensional surface—how we actually see three-dimensional objects. In order for our drawings of objects to appear *fully* realistic, though, we have to reproduce not only the way that the two-dimensional sizes and shapes that represent a three-dimensional form have changed when they are seen at an angle, but also the way in which some parts of an object appear *light*, some parts appear *in shadow* and other parts appear in-between.

Seeing is the process in which the brain interprets *reflected light* that enters through the eyes. The objects we see appear in *color,* and this is because objects of "different colors" (as we rather inaccurately refer to them—color is a property of light, not objects) in fact absorb all the component parts of white light—the colors of the spectrum—with the exception of the color we see. For example, a blue object absorbs all the colors of the spectrum *except* blue, which is reflected to our eyes/brains and seen as blue. The colored light that is reflected and perceived by our eyes (in coordination with our brains) appears to be of different degrees of light and darkness. Where the surface of an object is *flat*, a lot of light is reflected from it, and that part of the object appears *light*; where the surface of the object is not flat, but bends away from the light, less light is reflected from it and it appears *partly in shadow*, darker; where the surface of an object is completely hidden from the light it appears *completely in shadow*. We see the extremes of darkness and light as *black* and *white*. This is true for objects with color as well as objects without color. For example, take a shiny, red silk dress: the lightest parts, where most light is reflected away from the surface, appear

Shading gives these fashion accessories a three-dimensional appearance.

shading and value
color/greyscale

white, as highlights; the darkest parts, in the depths of the folds, appear *black*. The rest of the dress appears as red, of differing degrees of light and dark. If we were to make an accurate drawing of this same red dress in *black and white*, we would see the same white and black at the extremes; the lighter and darker shades of red would be seen as different shades of grey.

VALUE/TONES, SHADES & TINTS

The lightness or darkness of a particular color is referred to as its *value*. LIghter colors are said to have *higher values*, the highest value being white; darker tones are said to have *lower values*, the lowest value being black. The range of greys—each different grey is called a *tone*— between black and white is known as a *greyscale*. Colors themselves have value, both *intrinsic value*, the value of a particular color (colors such as yellow are high value, and others such as blue, are low value, and the rest are in-between) and value that refers to whether they are a darker or lighter tones of the color—for example, a low value *navy blue* or a high value *sky blue*. Darker tones of colors are known as *shades* and lighter versions are known as *tints*. Every tone of a color has a corresponding value of grey in the greyscale, so a black and white drawing (or photograph) can reproduce the same range of values as the color drawing (or photograph).

This book is concerned with the principles involved in drawing fashion in so-called *black and white*, which means, in effect, that we are interested in how to represent the range of values in a drawing in *greyscale*, in the range of greys that lie between white at one extreme and black at the other. It is important to master drawing in grey-scale/ black and white before advancing to drawing fashion in color, where value differences must also be shown, but in a range of colors.

In drawing, the way light and shadows form in and around objects is represented by using *shading*. Shading means making an area darker by making a denser application of the drawing medium being used.

Color v. black and white/ greyscale. Every color has a corresponding greyscale tone of the same value. Some colors, such as yellow are light—high value—colors and others such as blue are low value.

shading/gradation of tone/ shading geometric forms

SHADING

Shading, also often known as *rendering,* is the key to making objects in a drawing appear three-dimensional. In order for the shading to give a realistic effect, though, it must show the full range of variations of light and dark displayed on the surface of an object, from the lightest highlights, which appear white, or almost white, to the darkest shadows, which appear black, or almost black. Not only must the full range of values be shown, but the order and way in which they appear must be realistic. The way different tones of light change across a surface is known as *tonal gradation,* or *gradation of tone.* If, for example, a surface moves gradually into shadow, gradually bending away from the light, a continuous gradation of tone can be observed. If, on the other hand (particularly in shiny objects) a raised part of the surface, seen as a white highlight, sits immediately adjacent to a hidden part, which appears black, then there will be no gradual gradation of tone, but the dark and light will stand in strong contrast to each other. This juxtaposition of the light and dark—known as *value contrast*—will heighten the light of the highlight and the dark of the shadow.

SHADING OF GEOMETRIC FORMS

Many of the three-dimensional forms of both the human figure and the clothes it wears (which mostly take the shape of the different parts of the figure) are similar to simple geometric forms, such as spheres, cubes or cylinders. To understand the principles of shading, then, it is helpful to examine how these forms are shaded when drawn on paper to appear three-dimensional. (It is also helpful to note that when drawing these three-dimensional forms they can be broken down into combinations of two-dimensional shapes: a cube is formed of a square and two parallelograms, a cylinder a rectangle with ellipses at each end and so on.) The methods for drawing three common three-dimensional forms that show up frequently in fashion drawing are described below. It is important first to decide on the location of the light source and where light will fall on the object, just as it would for the lighting of a real object. The further a part of the surface of the object is from the light, the more in shadow it will be; the closer it is

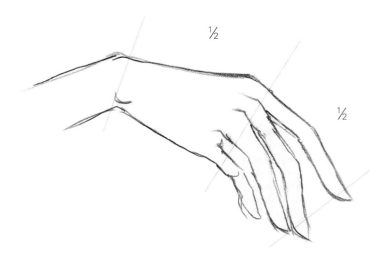

Top, hand without shading; bottom, shaded hand.
Shading is the key to making objects in a drawing appear three-dimensional. In order for the shading to give a realistic effect it must show the full range of variations of light and dark displayed on the surface of an object, from the lightest highlights, which appear white, or almost white, to the darkest shadows, which appear black, or almost black.

shading of geometric forms

to the light source the lighter it will be. In drawing, because light areas are made by leaving the page unmarked, and dark by applying shading, it is usual to work from light to dark, showing the transition from the areas which receive most light, and are brightest, to the areas which receive little or no light and are in the deepest shadows.

1. SPHERE. The outline of a 3-dimensional sphere is a circle, from which ever direction it is viewed–the same as its corresponding 2-dimensional shape. (Note that this is not the case with other 3D objects like cubes, pyramids or cylinders).
To draw a sphere, start by drawing a circle with a highlight at the top—a small area of light. This is the area that is facing the light source and receiving most light. Outside this small area the sphere bends away from the light and moves into shadow. At the bottom of the sphere its surface receives no light at all and is completely in shadow. The sphere is shaded by making it progressively darker as it bends away from the light. If the sphere rests on a table top it casts a round shadow known as a cast shadow. The point at which the sphere touches the table is very black and is known as the *tangency*. This area is drawn with a thick black line.
2. CUBE. A cube has six square faces set at right angles to each other. Start by drawing the face that is in front view and parallel to the plane of the paper with four equal sides. For the other two faces, create two parallelograms, drawing parallel lines that slant (in this case) to the right for the top of the cube and a third parallel line to indicate the side face. If the cube is lit from the front the front view face will appear light. The base of the cube is dark as it is tangent with the table top. Cast shadows appear to have the same shape as the cube and reflective light extends out in any direction
3. CYLINDER. The cylinder is shaped as a rectangle in one of its cross-sections and a circle in the other. When drawn at an angle to appear three-dimensional it is shown as a rectangle with ovals, or ellipses, at either end. It appears frequently in fashion drawing as a form used to express arms, legs, fingers, the neck, the nose, toes and lips, the drapes and folds of fabric.

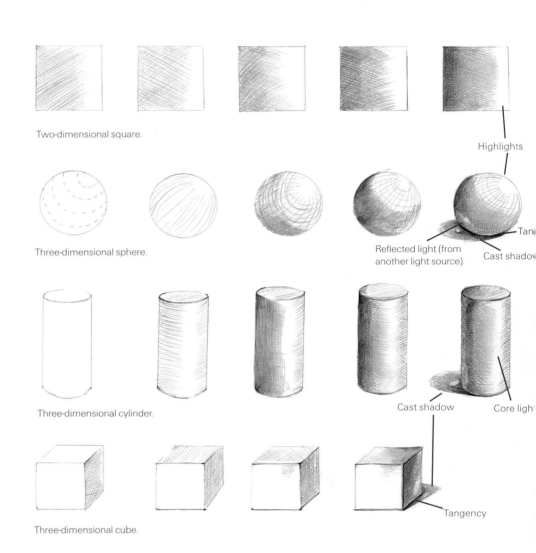

Two-dimensional square.

Highlights

Three-dimensional sphere.

Reflected light (from another light source).

Tan

Cast shadow

Three-dimensional cylinder.

Cast shadow

Core ligh

Three-dimensional cube.

Tangency

Building up shading on three-dimensional forms.
Each form can be viewed as made up of two-dimensional shapes which take on a three-dimensional appearance when shading is added. Shading is made with successive layered applications, with the parts in shadow receiving the densest applications and the highlights or corelights being shown by the unmarked white of the paper. Many parts of the body and the garments that cover them resemble these basic forms. When considering how to shade a part of a garment it is useful to decide which geometric form it resembles.

shading the body/ light source/

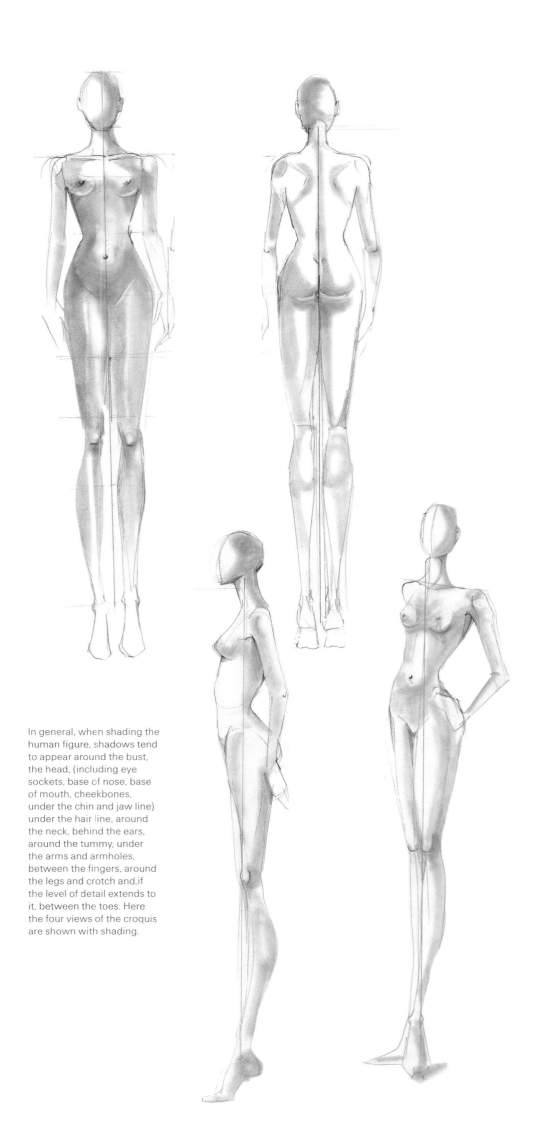

SHADING THE BODY/LIGHT SOURCE

Just as with geometric forms, to draw the *body* so it appears realistic it also must be shaded so that the patterns of light and dark in the drawing appear similar to the patterns of light and shadow that appear on it in real life, with the lightest and darkest parts as well as all the tones between clearly represented. Once the basic croquis is drawn the direction of the light source must be decided (in a drawing, unless we are making a drawing of an object that is in front of us, it is the artist who decides on the direction of the light source). If the light is from the *front* then the front of the figure will be lit and both sides will have shadows as they recede from the light; if lit from the *right* side the right side will be lit and the left in shadows; if lit from the *left*, the left will be lit and the right in shadows. It is also possible to have two or three separate light sources in a drawing and different parts in light and shadow—for example, the body might be lit and the head in shadow, or *vice-versa*— resulting in complex interplays of light and dark

Deciding on the position of the light source does not mean that all the parts of the body that are in light will be uniformly light and those in shadow will be uniformly dark: In the areas of the body that are turned towards the light, those parts that are most raised will be lightest and those that are hidden or receding from the light will be darker; there will be a gradation of tones from light to darker. In the areas that are in shadow there will be a similar range of values, but both the lightest and darkest values will be darker than those of the parts in light. *In general, when shading the human figure, shadows will tend to appear around the bust, the head, including eye sockets, base of nose, base of mouth, cheekbones, under the chin and jaw line, under the hair line, around the neck, behind the ears, around the tummy, under the arms and armholes, between the fingers, around the legs and crotch and, if the level of detail extends to it, between the toes.*

In general, when shading the human figure, shadows tend to appear around the bust, the head, (including eye sockets, base of nose, base of mouth, cheekbones, under the chin and jaw line) under the hair line, around the neck, behind the ears, around the tummy, under the arms and armholes, between the fingers, around the legs and crotch and, if the level of detail extends to it, between the toes. Here the four views of the croquis are shown with shading.

shading/ink v pencil
line weight and quality

INK v. PENCIL

Up to this point drawings have been made with pen and ink. Ink drawings have a clear, graphic line that is ideal for illustrating structure and shape. For shading, however, pen and ink is limited: very little variation of line thickness and weight is possible, and variations of darkness—light shadow through to heavy shadow—have to be indicated by varying densities of applications of lines, known as *cross-hatching*. *Pencil* is a much more versatile medium for shading, as it is easily possible to use leads of different degrees of hardness that apply more or less graphite to the paper that give different degrees of light and dark and also to vary the line thickness and weight with slight movements of the hand and wrist. For the remainder of this chapter, and in the next two chapters, where the emphasis will be on creating realistic, three-dimensional drawings with detailed shading, pencil will be used almost exclusively.

LINE WEIGHT AND QUALITY

When learning to draw it is important to be aware of the type of lines one is drawing right from the beginning so that good habits form early (bad habits are easy to acquire and difficult to change!). All drawings are made with lines, and the types of lines that are chosen and the way they are employed greatly affect the end result of the drawing. Lines have a variety of characteristics, including, besides location and direction, *weight* (the amount of pressure used to make the line and how light or heavy it appears in consequence), *thickness* and *texture*. The overall way that line is used in a drawing—the total of the individual choices made on use of line—is referred to as *line quality*.

A detailed description of the use of line in drawing *garments* is included in Chapter Six: Fabrics. At this stage, while still learning to master drawing the croquis, the following guidelines should be applied:

A THICK BOLD line will give the figure a strong, graphic presence and make it appear to have physical weight on the page.

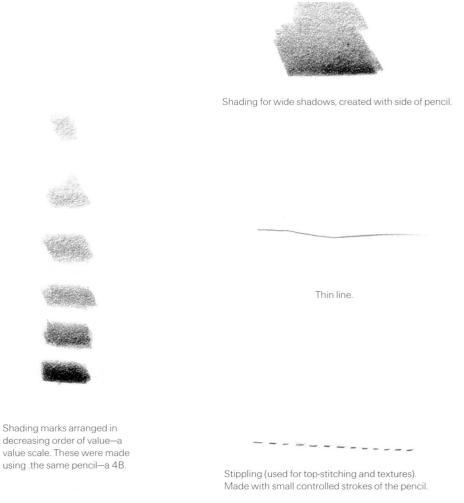

Shading for wide shadows, created with side of pencil.

Thin line.

Stippling (used for top-stitching and textures). Made with small controlled strokes of the pencil.

Shading marks arranged in decreasing order of value—a value scale. These were made using .the same pencil—a 4B.

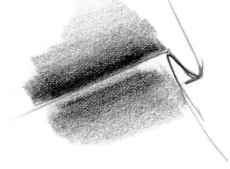

Shading for objects with highly contrasting values (for example, shiny fabrics). A dark value is used. next to a light value.

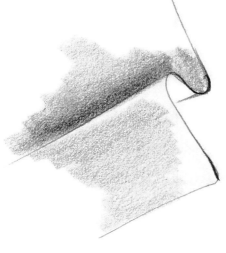

Shading for objects with values closer together (for example matt fabrics like linen or cotton). A medium-dark value is used and gradations appear betwen it and the lightest value.

shading/line weight and quality/exercises

A THIN line will do the opposite, making the figure appear light and ethereal. A line that is important in fashion drawing is called a *nuanced line*. A nuance is a slight or subtle change of meaning, and a *nuanced* line is one that changes subtly from thick to thin or from dark to light.

NUANCED LINES

Nuanced lines are used to express the quality of light. Light, as already mentioned, reflects off flat surfaces but does not bend, so when a surface bends away from the light it moves into shadow. A nuanced line, as described below, is able both to express areas of the body that are flat, and therefore well lit, and also areas that bend away from, and therefore do not receive, light. Areas in light are indicated by making the line outlining the edge of the area *thin*, and areas away from the light by making the line *thick*, indicating shadow. A nuanced line is thicker round the chin, armhole, waistline, crotch, elbow, knee and ankle, areas where the body bends into shadow, and thinner along the flat planes—the length of the arm and leg, the outside curve of the hip, the side of the neck.

A nuanced line is made by pressing down on and lifting up on the pencil with one fluid movement. The line should be made in one continuous movement to appear smooth and elegant. (When making lines, a common mistake is to move the pencil slowly down the page with little strokes, called chicken scratches. This is a definite "do not do" as it gives the illusion of texture as opposed to the outline of the figure.)

EXERCISES

1. Practice drawing and shading spheres, cubes and cylinders. Use the full range of values of dark and light and show highlights, cast shadows and corelights.
2. Fill a page with lines of different weight and thicknesses.

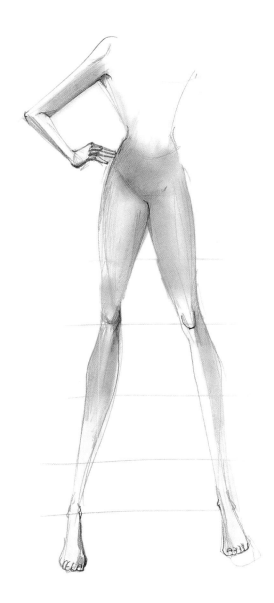

Shading techniques: Using the same pencil, varying the pressure of application. The range of darks and lights can be achieved using a single pencil—here a 2B— and varying the pressure with which it is applied. The continuous, even gradation of tone in the shading is achieved by smudging the pencil immediately after application using a stump or cotton swab.

Nuanced line.

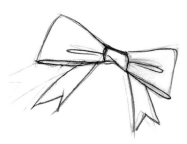

A bow drawn with a thick bold line has a strong graphic presence.

Thicker and darker nuanced line.

A bow drawn with a thin light line has a delicate, ethereal presence.

lineweight and quality/ shading/exercises

Skilled line use will develop with experience.
When starting to draw, beginners should try
to be aware of the appearance of the mark
being made on the paper as well as on creating accurate shapes and proportions .

TECHNIQUES FOR SHADING WITH PENCIL
Shading with pencil is made easier if different
pencils of different degrees of hardness are
used, though in fact, as seen in the drawings
on the preceding page, all effects can be
achieved using only one pencil with differing
amounts of pressure and more or fewer applications. It is best to use a 4B or 6B pencil for
the darkest areas and an HB for the lightest
areas.

In shading, the aim is to achieve an even and
continuous application of tone that appears
like a mist or smoke, either of the same even
value or of values shifting from light to dark.
The individual pencil marks are not usually
seen (unless a particular special effect is
desired). Apply pencil in a motion that is similar to the shape of the object being shaded— a
circular motion for a sphere, long strokes for
cylinders such as arms and legs and so on—
and then *smudge the pencil almost immediately*. Smudging can be done with a stump (a
pencil without lead) or a cotton swab.
Smudging with the finger is not advised as
there are oils in the skin that mark the paper.

EXERCISES
1. Draw the four views of the figure and shade.
Show shadows in the arms, legs, tummy, bust
and face.
2. Practice drawing nuanced lines. Draw the
four views of the croquis using nuanced lines.

| 2H | HB | 2B | 4B |

Shading techniques: Using pencils of differing degrees of hardness.
These drawings were made using successively darker pencils—2H, HB, 2B and
4B, as shown above right. The areas where the different pencils are used are
indicated by dotted lines. The lighter pencils are used in the parts where the
body is lightest and reflects light. and progressively darker pencil is used for the
parts that bend away from the light. The underside of the arm and the inside of
the leg are darkest and are shaded with the 4B pencil.

face/
front view

The face is an oval: as mentioned, it is an egg shape rather than a hot-dog or watermelon. In fashion drawing the face is not as important as in real life, where it conveys much information. In fashion drawing the face is mainly a complement to the clothing (and indeed is often treated like an accesory). If the face is intended to convey additional information in drawing, such as mood, attitude or a particular expression then that information should be simple and direct.

Although we return to learning how to draw the individual features of the face in greater detail later in the chapter we begin by showing how to draw the complete face. This is because it is essential to understand the proportions and positions of the features relative to each other on the face in order to be able to draw a face that looks life-like. If the sizes and relative positions of the face are not drawn accurately the face will look distinctly odd.

The fashion face is beautiful, but slimmer and smaller in proportion to the rest of the body than the natural face (in the nine head figure it is ⅑ of the length of the figure as opposed to ⅛ in the natural figure). Like the real face, however, it is perfectly symmetrical (more in fact than most real faces) and it is important to measure carefully, for the smallest shift in the eye or mouth can make the face appear to look insane or like a cartoon. A great amount of practice is required in order to become proficient.

The features of the face are all approximately the same size. The nose is the least important feature and should be drawn with a minimum amount of lines and shading: often the base is all that is needed. The eyes are very expressive and provide information on mood, often giving useful indications as to the style of the clothes in the drawing. Eyes are slimmer than is often thought and the iris—the colored part of the eye— is only about one-third of the total space of the eye. The fullest part of the face is the mouth: the bottom lip a full upward curve and the upper lip a full curve with a small indentation.

When drawing the face either work down from the eyes or start from the nose or mouth. Draw the face after drawing the other parts of the body and garments; as the face is so seductive it is easy to spend too much time on it. It is, after all, really only an accent to the clothes! Always keep the pencil sharp so the line can be made as precisely as possible.

The starting point for the face. Begin by drawing an oval and divide in half vertically and horizontally. The face is curved, not flat, and the lines bend round the surface.

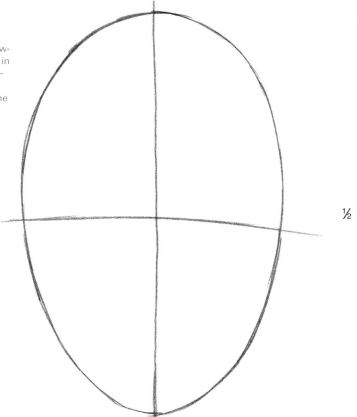

½

The fashion face with all features added before final fleshing out and shading.

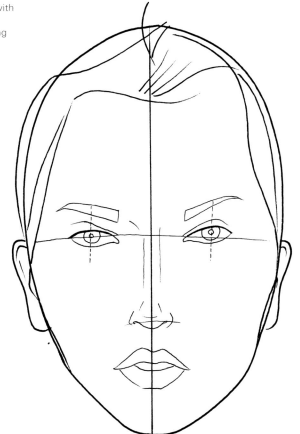

face/front view/ exercise

DRAWING THE FRONT VIEW FACE

Let's begin by drawing the front view of the face.

1. Draw the oval shape of the face and draw in the vertical axis line, dividing the face into two equal parts. Add another line cutting the face exactly in half horizontally, so the face is divided into four parts. The horizontal line marks the the eye level. The eyes should never be placed above this line as the face will then appear extremely old. (As babies, our eye level is only one third up from the bottom of the head; it gradually moves up as we mature, ending up almost exactly in the middle of the head. This is true for both men and women.)

2. Having divided the head in half for the eye level, divide the distance between the eyes and the bottom of the head in half again. This point is the bottom of the nose.

3. Divide the distance between the bottom of the nose and the bottom of the head in half again. This point is the bottom of the mouth. It is important to place the mouth close to the nose. The jaw begins below the ears, level with the center of the mouth and the chin is directly under the mouth, no wider or smaller than the mouth. It is important the chin and mouth are the same size. The jaw tapers in on both sides of the face until it meets the chin (above the jaw—between the ears and the beginning of the jaw—the outline of the head also tapers, but less so).

4. The top of the ear is aligned with the top of the eye, and the bottom with the bottom of the nose.

5. The hair line is approximately ⅛ to of a head length from the top of the head and extends across the eyes—like an umbrella for the eyes—and then moves down from the eyes to the ears. The outside edge (or silhouette) of the hair cascades from the top of the head (the crown), moves close to the skull to the eye level and then falls softly to the shoulders. Slim down the hair and head so that the eyes float down to the clothes.

EXERCISES

1. Select 10 front view faces from a magazine and copy, bringing out shading and line quality. Avoid smiles.

2. Practice drawing the features separately. Refer to the sections below if needed.

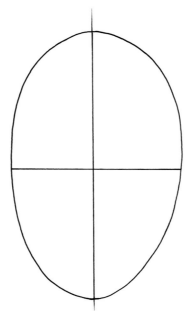

Eye level

1. Draw an oval and divide it vertically and horizontally into four equal segments. The horizontal lne is the level of the eyes.

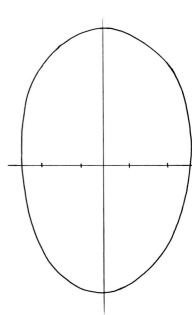

2. Mark out the position of the eyes. All the features on the face are the same size. The eyes are placed one eye-width apart and one eye width in from the side of the head.

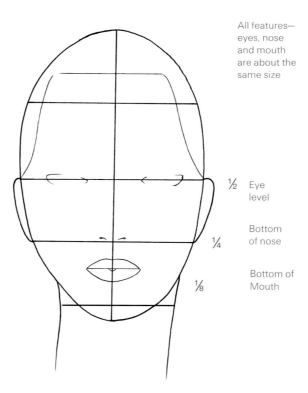

All features— eyes, nose and mouth are about the same size

½ Eye level

¼ Bottom of nose

⅛ Bottom of Mouth

3. The bottom of the nose is indicated at ¼ Divide the space between the bottom of the nose and the chin in half and this indicated the position of the center of the mouth. Ears fit between eye level and the top of the nose.

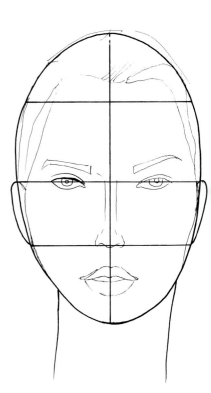

4. The hairline is approximately ⅛ to ¼ of a head length from the top of the head and extends across the eyes, like an umbrella for the eyes. Fill in the details. Keep the head slim.

The finished face is eye-catching and a little provocative.

Front view face. Artifice and high style combine in this rendering of a wedding veil inspired by a design of *Comme des Garcons*. Note the flower petal motif of the veil continuing to the false eyelashes.

face/
side view

SIDE VIEW FACE

The features of the side view face are in the
same positions on the vertical axis as in the
front view face but they appear as quite different shapes and sizes from their appearances
on the front view face and are aligned differently. As with the front view face, these
shapes that represent the features have to be
drawn in the correct proportions and locations.

DRAWING THE SIDE VIEW FACE

*The basic shape of the side view head is an
oval , most of which is contained in a rectangle. When beginning to draw it it is easiest
first to draw such a rectangle, extending it by
adding an arc where the upper back part of
the head will be, and then plotting the rest of
the shape of the head. Divide the rectangle in
half horizontally and the bottom half in half
again, and also divide the original retangle in
half vertically.*

*1. Begin by drawing the nose. The slope of the
nose starts halfway down the head. The nose
is triangular in shape with the bridge twice as
long as the base. The angle of the nose can be
varied according to personal taste. The tip of
the nose is rounded and the base curves
round into the upper lip.*

*2. In profile the mouth is shaped like a heart
sitting on its side, with the lower lip slightly
further back on the head than the upper. On
the head the mouth is close to the nose and
must be kept close in a drawing. It lies on the
same vertical axis as the nose, directly
beneath. The corner of the mouth aligns with
the front of the eye. In profile, the jawline is
seen in outline. It is curved, and starts in alignment with the center of the mouth.*

*3. The eye is a wedge shape that sits halfway
down the head; the top of the wedge shape
represents the bottom of the eyelid. The iris is
in the front of the eye, just behind the front of
the eyelid, and the lash extends out from the
eyelid. The eyelash starts at the front of the
head just above the eye and extends up
around the eye. (If drawn downwards it gives
the eye and face a sad look.) The ear is behind
the center of the rectangle and its mid point
aligns with the center of the eye. It is about
one quarter of a head in length and can be
drawn with one or two lines. The hairline*

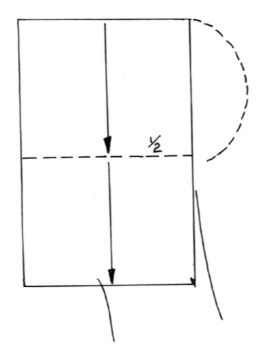

1. The basic shape of
the head in side view
can be seen as a rec-
tangle plus an arc. Eye
level is at ½

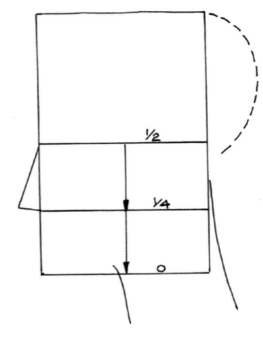

2. The nose is
between ½ and ¼.
The bridge is twice
the length of the
base.

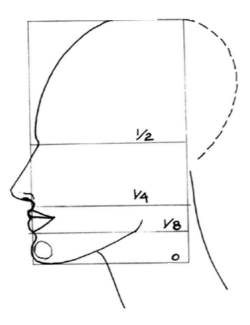

3. The mouth sits directly
under the nose. The chin is
directly under mouth. The
jawline slopes up to mouth
level.

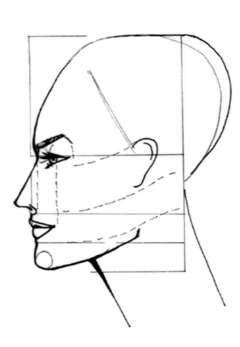

4. The eye is at ½. The ear is
at the level of the eye and
top of nose. The hairline
slopes from forehead to ear.

face/side view/ exercise

begins near the top of the head, falls in a close to straight line to the middle of the front of the ear and continues from the lower back of the ear to the back of the head above the jawline.

Because the head is oriented diagonally it is more difficult to align the features than in the front view. This series of diagrams on the right show how to align the features correctly.

EXERCISE
Select 10 side view faces from a magazine and copy, bringing out shading and line quality. Avoid smiles. Pay attention to the location of the hairline. Keep the face and neck slim.

Note that the side view head slants diagonally forward. The back of the head—the cranium—is rounded. Because the head is oriented diagonally it is more difficult to align the features than in the front view. This series of diagrams show how to align the features correctly.

The forehead extends to ½—the eye level—where the nose begins. The nose extends down to just above ¼ and then turns back to the base, directly under the mouth. There is a small semicircular indentation between the base of the nose and the mouth. The mouth is directly beneath the nose.

The chin is the same size as the mouth, is directly beneath the mouth and curves back to form the jawline. The jawline extends to the level of the top of the mouth, directly below the ear.

The eye is the shape of a triangle positioned with the top side placed horizontally as shown in the diagram.. The iris—the colored part of the eye— sits in the front of the eye and is drawn as a slim ellipse. The eyelash curves out beyond the eye; the eyebrow begins above and in front of the eye and extends back behind the eye. Add a darker, more detailed line to the eyelashes. Fill in the silhouette of the hair noting that the hairline extends ¼ way down from the top of the head, extends out to the same level as the eye and then slants down to the ear.

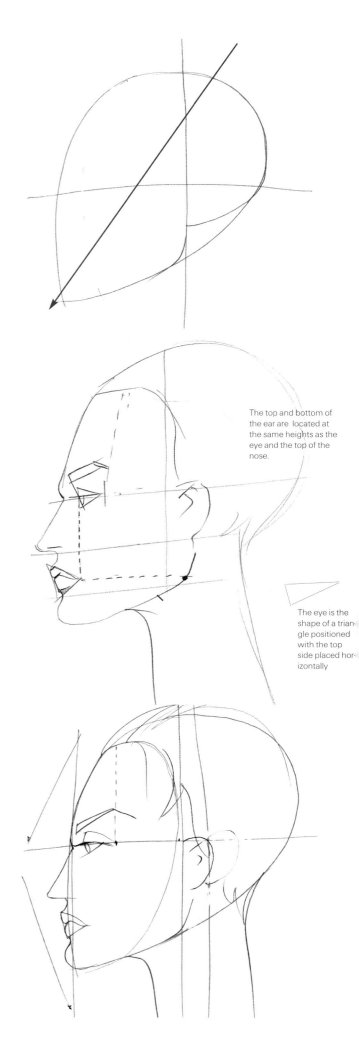

The top and bottom of the ear are located at the same heights as the eye and the top of the nose.

The eye is the shape of a triangle positioned with the top side placed horizontally

Drawing the side view face.

60

face/
side view

The finished side view face. Shading is applied around the cheek and under the jawline. Note that the features are full but when seen in profile in the side view are only half the width they appear in front view. Note also that the plane of the forehead ends in a line from the corner of the eye and the hairline slopes to the front of the ear.

face/
three-quarter view

THREE-QUARTER VIEW FACE

The three-quarter face is the face drawn at an angle so that one side appears compressed– foreshortened– and the features on this side appear smaller than on the nearer non-foreshortened side (though the features on each side of the face are the same size as the others on the same side). Begin drawing three-quarter faces seen straight-on, from eye level, not from above or below; this makes it easier to draw them in correct perspective, as foreshortening only takes place in one plane. It also means that the vertical positioning of the features on the head is the same as on the side or front view face.

DRAWING THE THREE-QUARTER VIEW FACE

1. First draw an oval, curving more on the near non-foreshortened side than on the far foreshortened side. Draw in the center front line curving slightly from the vertical down the front of the face. In the three-quarter face the center-front line is drawn. as when drawing the three-quarter figure, so that the foreshortened side of the face is about one quarter of the total area of the oval and the near, non-foreshortened side is three-quarters, i.e in the proportions 3:1. Draw in a line to divide the head in two horizontally. This line is the eye level line and also curves around the head from the top of the ear on the near side through the eyes. Make a mark on the center-front line halfway between the eye-level line and the bottom of the head. This gives the position of the bottom of the nose.

2. It is possible to start drawing the features in any order, but it is usually easiest to start at the nose and then the mouth. First draw in a short line to represent the base of the nose. This line falls either side of the c-f line, about three-quarters on the near side and one quarter on the far side. It is parallel to the eye-level line and curves up slightly as it bends around the foreshortened side of the face. Lightly draw in the outline of the bridge of the nose starting with the indentation at eye level ending at the end of the line showing the base of the nose on the foreshortened side. Draw in the shape of the nostrils. Indicate the neck joining the head at an angle to the vertical almost the same as that of the head but in the other direction.

3. Draw in the mouth, first drawing in the line where the lips meet, again in the ratio ¾ to ¼ across the c-f line, then the lines for the bottom and top of the lips in the same ratio. Add definition to the nose.

1. Begin by drawing the head as an egg shape with greater curvature on the nearer side. Draw in the center-front line dividing the head approximately in the ratio ¾ to ¼, and divide it in two horizontally to indicate the level of the eyes. Mark the position of the bottom of the nose halfway between the eye-level line and the bottom of the head on the c-f line.

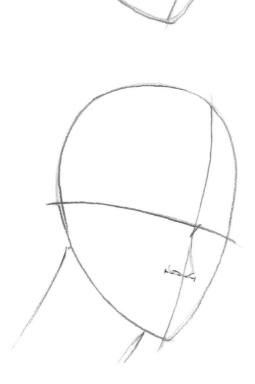

2. Draw in a short line to show the base of the nose, sitting in the ratio ¾ to ¼ across the c-f line and start to shape the nostrils. The bridge of the nose starts as an indentation at eye level and then slopes down in profile ending at the end of the nose base line on the foreshortened side of the c-f line.

3. Draw in the mouth, first drawing in the line where the lips meet, again in the ratio ¾ to ¼ across the c-f line, then the lines for the bottom and top of the lips in the same ratio. Add definition to the nose.

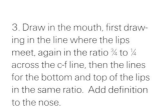
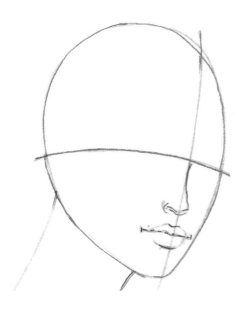

face/
three-quarter view

4. Draw in the chin as a flat oval lying directly under the mouth and the same size as the mouth, also lying in the ratio ¾ to ¼ across the c-f line and extending to the line of the jaw.

5. The eye nearer to the point of view sits approximately one eye's width in from the ear and a slightly lesser distance from the c-f line running through the nose. The inner edge of the eye aligns with the corner of the mouth. On the foreshortened side of the face the eye is drawn immediately next to the bridge of the nose and fills the gap between the nose and the edge of the face. The top of the ear sits on the eye-level line where it meets the side of the head. The ear sits within the curve of the outline of the head in the three-quarter view. On the near side the eyebrow arches over the eye following its shape but flattening on the inside edge. On the foreshortened side only the upward arch of the brow is seen, ending at the side of the head.

On the foreshortened side of the face the line of the forehead extends to the top of the eyebrow. Below the eyebrow the eye socket is seen in profile. The amount of indentation of the eye socket varies among different races—for Africans the eye socket is well set-in whereas for Asians the contour is almost flat.

6. Refine the profile of the cheekbone on the far side—the profile extends out at the cheekbone and then slopes back to the c-f line in the middle of the jaw. Draw in the hairline, flat across the forehead to the outside of the eye and then sloping down to the inside of the ear.. The hair curves from the center-front line and is shaded at the edges. Add shading inside the ear, around the eye sockets and to the side planes of the face as well as the lips and chin.

4. Draw in the chin as a flat oval lying directly under the mouth and the same size as the mouth, also lying in the ratio ¾ to ¼ across the c-f line.

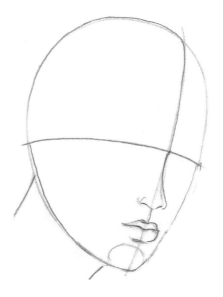

The most difficult features to draw in the three-quarter face are those on the side that is turned away. The eye on that side appears foreshortened and is partly obscured by the nose; it must be drawn directly from the line of the nose. The eyebrow is foreshortened and extends from the corner of the eye to the side of the head.

5. The near eye sits approximately one eye's width in from the ear. The inner edge of the eye aligns with the corner of the mouth. On the foreshortened side the eye is drawn immediately next to the bridge of the nose and fills the gap between the nose and the edge of the face. The top of the ear sits on the eye-level line where it meets the side of the head. On the near side the eyebrow arches over the eye following its shape but flattening on the inside edge. On the foreshortened side only the upward arch of the brow is seen,

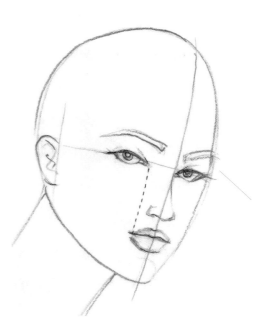

In Asian faces the outline of the eyesocket on the foreshortened side is almost flat. For Cauc-asians, Africans and others the eye is more set-in and there is an indentation beneath the eyebrow.

6. Refine the profile of the cheekbone on the far side. Draw in the hairline, flat across the forehead to the outside of the eye and then sloping down to the inside of the ear. The hair curves from the c-f line and is shaded at the edges. Add shading inside the ear, around the eye sockets and to the side planes of the face as well as the lips and chin.

The complete shaded three-quarter face.

face/ front/side/three-quarter view/different viewpoints

Tilting the head introduces diagonals into the vertical lines of the figure giving it a sense of movement and dynamism. Practice drawing tilted heads by tracing these drawings.

face/ front/side/three-quarter view/different viewpoints

face/ front/side/three-quarter view/different viewpoints

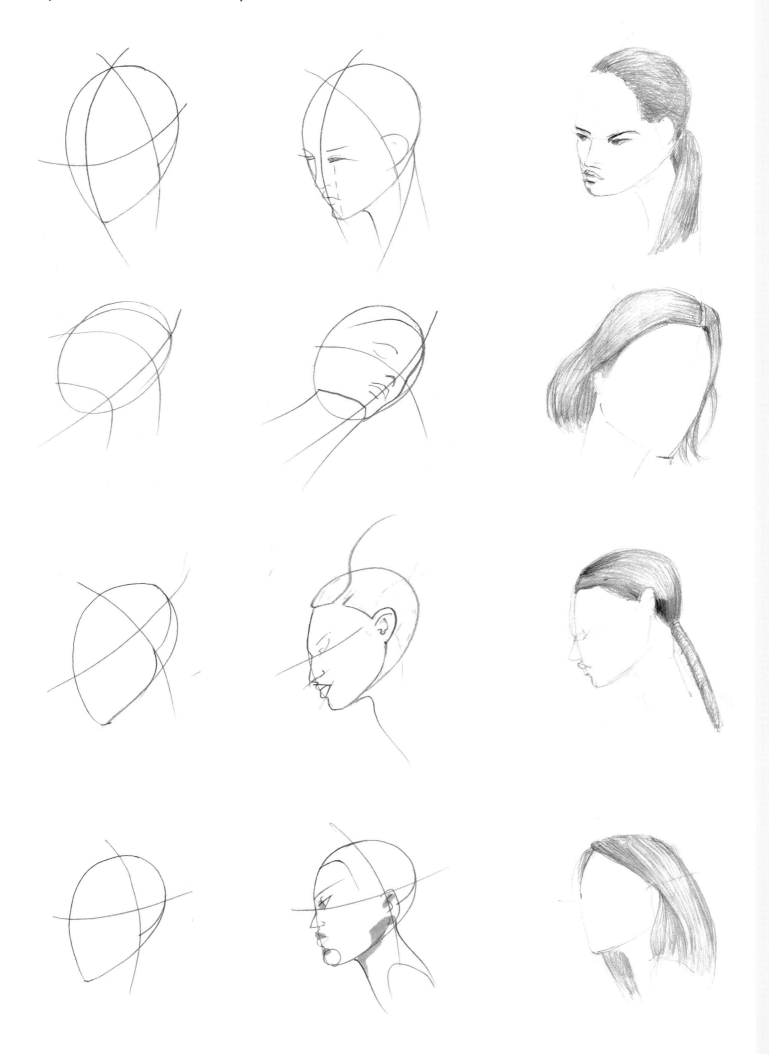

face/ front/side/three-quarter view/different viewpoints

eyes

The eyes express much of the emotion of the face so must be drawn carefully: slanting the eye down makes the face appear sad, drawing a straight eye makes it look bored, drawing the eye up at the outer edge makes it look happy. The eye is drawn slanting upwards, beginning at eye-level (half-way down the head). At eye level the face is five eye widths across; the eyes are positioned one eye length from each edge of the face and there is one eye length between them—the "third eye". See page 46 for accurate sizing and positioning of the eye on the face.

DRAWING THE EYE

1 The eye is slim, shaped like an almond or goldfish. The upper line can be drawn with three movements: Starting with the inner edge of the eye—here shown on the right— closest to the nose, draw the line of the eye up for ⅓.of the distance, flatten it out as it stretches over the iris for one third and down for the final ⅓.

2.The lower line of the eye curves up slightly, parallel to the upper line for a short distance, then down slightly then slopes up to meet the upper line at the outer point of the eye.

3. The iris itself is one third of the width of the eye and sits slightly under the eyelid. About ⅔ of the sphere of the eye is visible, the rest covered by the eyelid. The pupil is drawn in the center of the eye as a small crescent.

4. The upper part of the iris is slightly darker because a shadow is cast from the eyelid onto the iris. The pupil is the darkest point of the eye with often a pinpoint of light on it. The outer edge of the iris is also dark. A second line can be drawn parallel to the lower lid to show depth if so preferred.

5. Lashes can be drawn with curved lines that sweep outwards from the upper and lower edges of the eye. Eyelids are parallel to the upper line of the eye. Eyebrows are wider than the eye, and arch up at the edge of the eye. Do not make the eyebrow into an alpine mountain or Indian tepee by drawing a point in the middle.

6. The eyelid is the same shape as the eye and can be made higher to show a more deep set eye.

7. Draw in eyelashes subtly, using a simple, dark tone. Eyelashes grow from the edge of the eye upwards and outwards with the last eyelashes dipping down for a flirtatious look.

8. Do not make the eyelashes straight or they will appear to injure the eyelid. Do not make the iris a full circle as it will make the eye look as though it is in shock.

1. The upper line of the eye can be drawn with three movements starting from the inner edge—here on the right.

2. The lower line of the eye arcs up to the outer point of the eye. Note the eye turns up at the outer corner.

3. The iris is ⅓ the width of the eye and sits under the eyelid–about ⅔ of the sphere is visible. The whites of the eyes are slim. There is a second line that can be drawn at the lower edge of the eye to indicate that the eye is recessed in the eye socket if so preferred.

4. The upper part of the iris is slightly darker because a shadow is cast from the eyelid onto the iris. The pupil is the darkest point of the eye with often a pinpoint of light on it. The outer edge of the iris is also dark.

5-8. Lashes can be drawn with curved lines that sweep outwards from the upper and lower edges of the eye. The line of the top of the eyelid where it meets the eye socket is parallel to the upper line of the eye. Eyebrows are wider than the eye and arch up from the edge of the eye. See text for more detail.

Fully shaded eye. Note upper lid is darker than lower lid and iris is partially covered by lid.

Fully shaded side view eye. Note the position of the iris in relation to the lashes.

eyes/eyebrows/
do not do's

Slimmer eye used to denote a sophisticated expression.

A deeper set eye achieved by widening the lid and shading. African or Latin eyes are often more deep set like this.

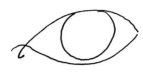

DO NOT DO:
Eyeballs in shock!

Side view eye with eyebrow.

A more shallow eye socket. Asian eyes are often like this.

DO NOT DO:
Steel eyelashes

Variation of side view eye with head tilted down.

Positioning of three-quarter eyes

DO NOT DO:
Alpine eyebrows

Position of eyes in relation to nose in three-quarter view.

Note that in the side view eye the eyebrow tilts upwards

Lovely eyebrows

mouth

The mouth is sensuous and expressive. In fashion drawings we use it as an accessory to the garments, indicating mood and attitude. The corners of the mouth tell all!

DRAWING THE MOUTH

1. Begin by drawing an oval as wide as the eye socket.
2. Draw a line through the center of the oval.
3. Make an indentation in the top of the lip to match the V at the bottom of the nose (see the next section for how to draw the nose).
4. Because the mouth is lush and round and full, make the center and the bottom parts of the mouth darkest.
5. Leave a spot of light at the center of the bottom lip to express light and shine—a little dew drop.
6. Curve the edges of the mouth up to express happiness and down to express sadness.

1. Begin by drawing an oval the same width as the eye socket.

3. Make an indent in the top of the lip to match the V at the bottom of the nose

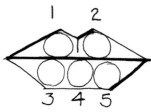

5. Leave a spot of light at the center of the bottom lip to express light and shine

2. Draw a line through the center of the oval.

4. The darkest areas of the mouth are where the lips meet and under the lower lip.

6. Curve the edges of the mouth up to express happiness and down to express sadness

A mouth can be broken into five circles

Soften lines

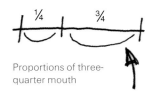

Proportions of three-quarter mouth

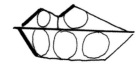

Setting three-quarter mouth with circles

Shaded

Shaded three-quarter

Shaded three-quarter

Shaded open up

75

mouth/side view/three-quarter view/do not do

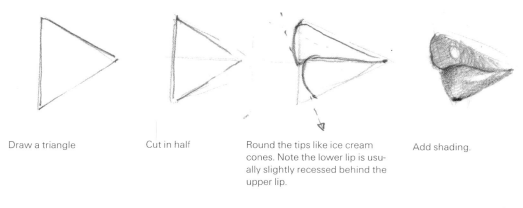

Draw a triangle

Cut in half

Round the tips like ice cream cones. Note the lower lip is usually slightly recessed behind the upper lip.

Add shading.

Drawing the side view mouth.

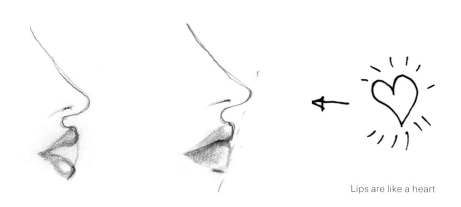

Lips are like a heart

DO NOT outline the nose— it looks like an elephant foot

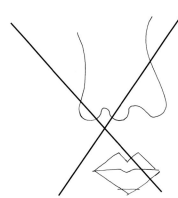

When the face is drawn in ¾ view the nose and mouth must also be in ¾ view and correctly aligned.

In the side view, when the mouth and nose are seen in profile the base of the nose and the center of the mouth are parallel.

When the head is tilted back we see the underside of the nose and the other features lie along an arc.

DO NOT make the mouth pointed

nose

1. The nose is a delicate arrow. On a woman's nose the nostrils angle at a slight V.

2. When beginning to draw it is best to ignore the bridge of the nose—the edge of the nose running from between the eyebrows to the tip—as the tendency is to draw it with too hard a line, which makes the nose the focal point of the face, as opposed to the eyes or mouth. Do not outline the nose—it makes it look like an elephant's foot!

3. The nose is as long as the eye socket is wide. Be careful not to exaggerate the length. (We expect the nose to be longer than it is because it pokes out at us.)

4. The nose begins halfway down the head and ends three-quarters way down (or one quarter up) the head.

5. Add shadow at the base to give the nose an upward tilt.

The base of the nose turns up.

The bridge of the nose is twice the length of the base of the nose.

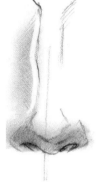

The bridge of the nose should be drawn with subtle lines and shading rather than big black outlines. This is the anatomically correct version of the nose.

The tip of the nose—the part that sticks out the most— is shaped like an arrow. Shading can be applied under the tip of the nose to make the tip appear to protrude. This is the typical fashion nose with no indication of the bridge.

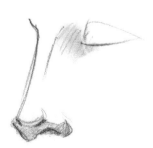

The nose in three-quarter view. The silhouette of the bridge of the nose is at an angle between that of the side view and the vertical of the front view. The nearer nostril becomes a slightly fuller curve and the further nostril is almost completely hidden.

ear

The ear is postioned at between ½ and ¼—
between the level of the eye and the bottom of
the nose. The ear is shaped like a hook or question mark. To indicate more detail in the ear,
add a second line in the shape of an S inside
the top edge. (Note that detail of the ear is not
necessary in most fashion drawings.) It is
essential that the position of the ears is drawn
correctly, corresponding to different positions
of the head: when the head bends back the
ears appear lower on the head, and when the
head bends forward the ears appear higher.

Shading can be applied to the interior of the ear
if the rest of the face also has detailed shading.

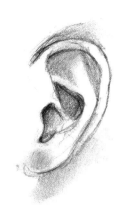

The natural (anatomi-
cally correct) ear

Complex fashion ear

Simplified fashion ear

Front view–natural ear

Front view–fashion ear

Back view–natural ear

Back view–fashion ea

hair/straight/curls/ do not do's

HAIR

Hair is drawn by first sketching the outline with simple shapes, adding the texture and shading, and finally drawing in the details of the different parts of the hair (a process that is quite similar to drawing a fashion garment, as will be seen in the next chapter). The outline of the shape of the hair follows the inside hairline (where the hair meets the forehead and sides of the head) and then traces the basic shape of the hair on top. The hairline is one quarter of the distance down from the top of the head, extends across the breadth of the eyes (an umbrella for the eyes) and falls to the ear.

1. Draw the shape of the hair starting from the inside line of the hair or from the top of the head, called the crown. Draw the shape close to the face until the eye level is reached.
2. Straight hair can be drawn easily by breaking up the edge of the hair shape using straight lines. A technique for making straight hair is the following: choose a small piece of paper with a straight edge and place on top of the piece you are drawing on. Line up the straight edge of the small piece of paper with the edge of the hair and draw parallel lines from the small piece to the drawing paper, so creating a nice even edge for the hair.
3. When drawing curls, fill in the basic shape of the hair. Do not draw lots of lines inside the basic silhouette of the hair, especially lines which overlap, as this makes the hair look like a bird's nest. Break up the outer edge of the shape with half circles of different sizes.
6. Do not let hair get too wide above the eye level: it does not normally grow out horizontally!
7. Do not make parts (partings) larger than the head itself.

1. Draw the shape of the hair starting from the inside line of the hair or from the top of the head. Draw the shape close to the face until the eye level is reached.

2.Draw in the shapes in the interior of the hair and break up the edge of the hair using thicker lines

3. Add detail to the edges of the hair and add shading at the edges and in the parts (partings).

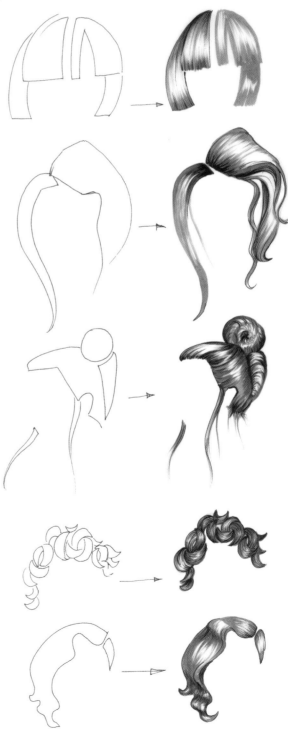

hair/exercises

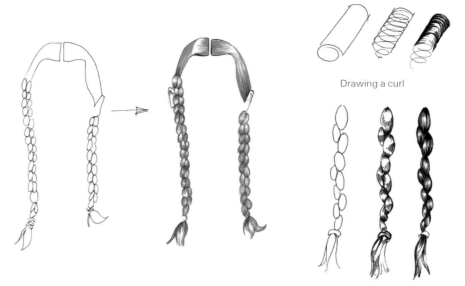

Drawing a curl

Drawing a braid

8. Draw braids as intersecting chains which are dark where the chains overlap.

9. Draw long hair by shading the skin and adding tone behind the silhouette of the hair. All hair, including blonde, has very dark and very light areas. The dark areas tend to be closer to the face. Looking at photographs of hair styles is extremely helpful when drawing hair.

10. Using the sharp edge of an eraser, make quick strokes to add highlights where you decide.

EXERCISES

1. Look at fashion magazines to find hairstyles that you like and trace them. Fill in the silhouette with pencil as if it were flat.

2. Copy hairstyles, beginning with simple shapes, remembering that hair has to grow from the skull. Draw a part (a parting) in the hair, remembering that the part is on the head and cannot be drawn beyond the head. Now draw a few lines for the hair from the part to indicate the direction of the hairstyle.

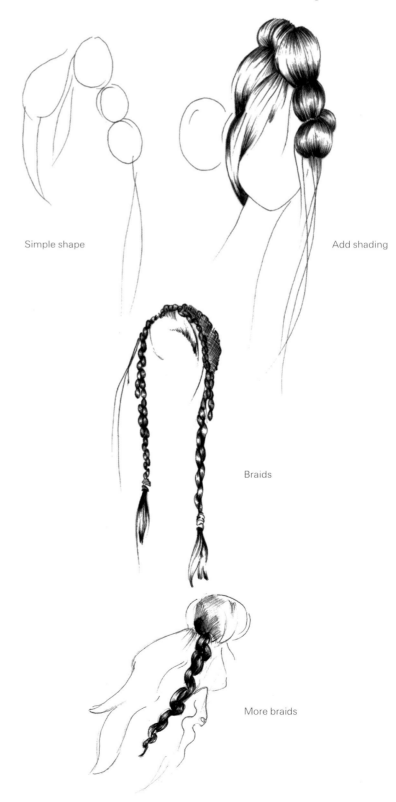

Simple shape

Add shading

Braids

More braids

hair

Twists and turns of the hair.
Look for simple shapes and highlights.

hair

It is easiest to draw complex hair by breaking it down into the simpler shapes of the different parts of the hair, as can be seen in the diagrams that accompany these drawings. Note that hair is darker closer to the face, in the areas around the back of the neck and at its outer edges. Keep in mind that where hair bends towards the viewer it is light and where it bends away–into valleys and folds, it is dark.

hair

Variations of hair and face with the emphasis on contemporary.
fashion. Copying these complex faces helps develop skill levels.

hair

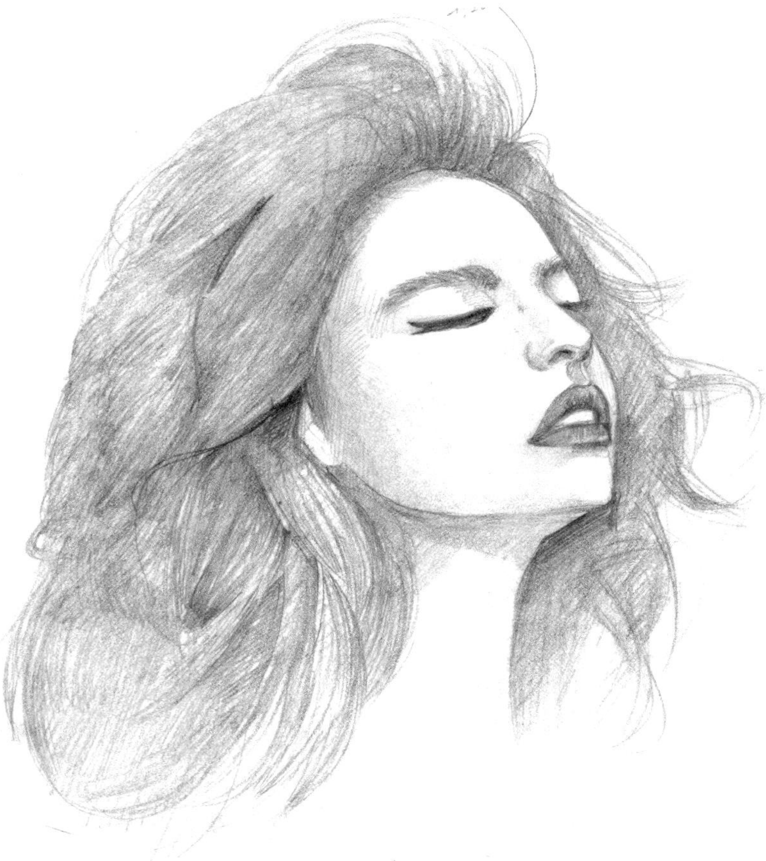

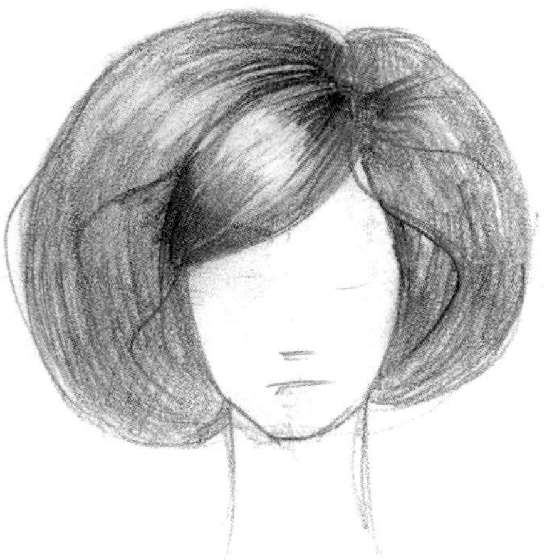

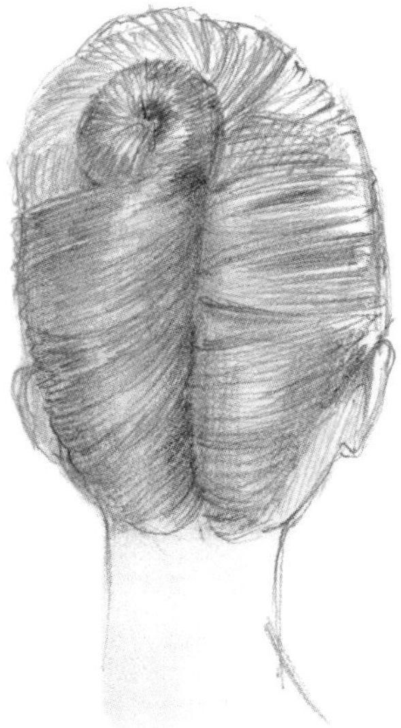

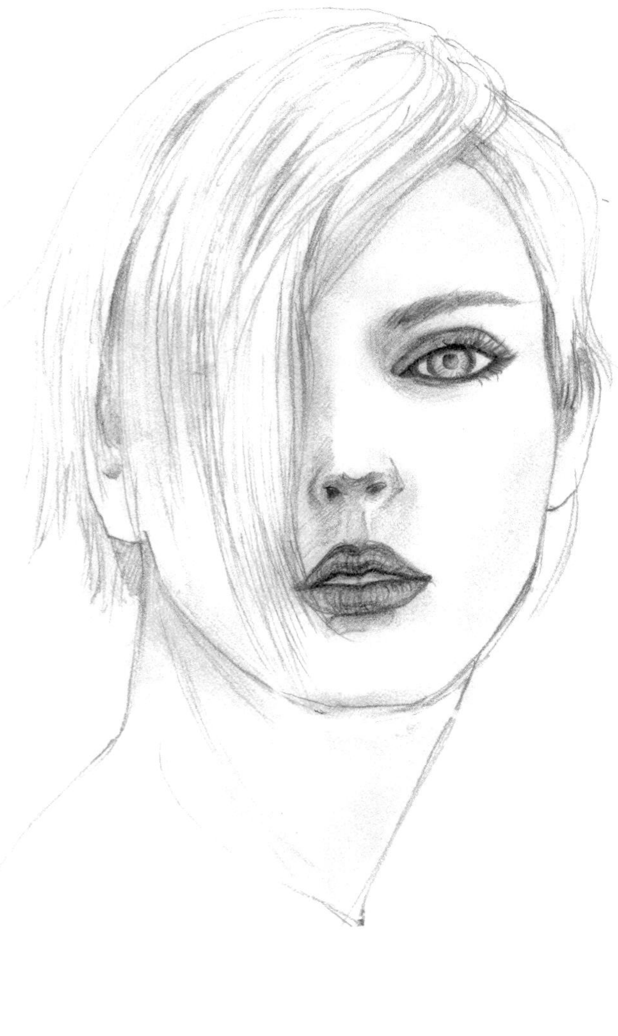

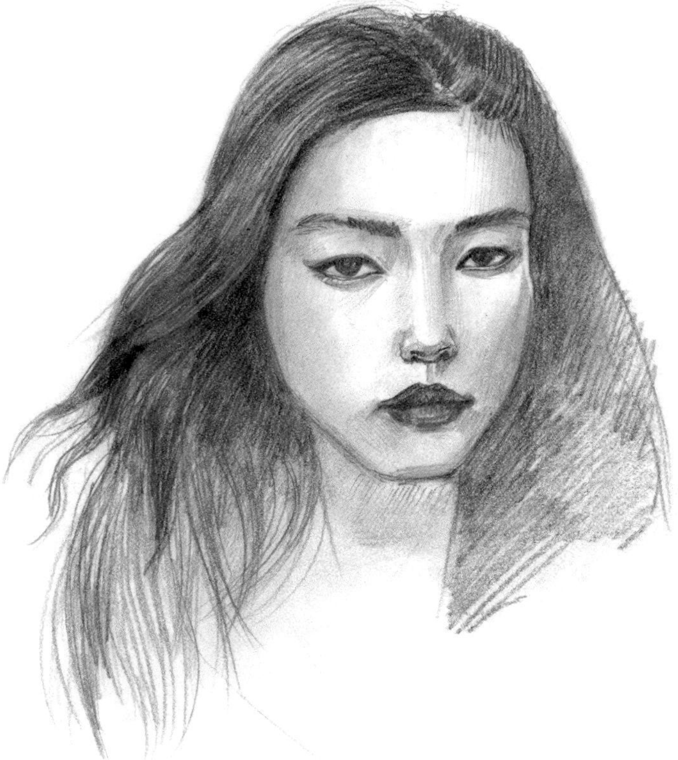

hair

hands

HANDS

The hand is much larger than we expect: it is approximately equal in size to one head (Do you recall being frightened as a child and covering your face with your hands?) In fashion drawing it can be varied in size: when drawing high fashion we make it long and elegant; when drawing street fashion it can be made shorter–about three-quarters of a head's length.

The hand is a wonderful tool in fashion drawing, so should not be hidden. It is very effective for drawing attention to an important feature—for example the collar, waist, or an important pocket—simply by pointing it. The hand should not point away from the figure, however, as it will lead the eye out of the drawing—to a neighbor's work or to a blank space! And do not point the hand to the ground as there is nothing there! The hand and fingers are long, tapered and elegant.

The hand can be used also to express moods and attitudes in a drawing. If the fingers are spread the figure will appear to have energy; if the hands are dropped to the sides of the body the figure will appear to be at rest. A good way to begin learning to draw the hand is to place your own hand on the page and trace around it. Do so three times—it is nice having a perfect model for this part of the body so conveniently on hand (pun intentional!). Note that the wrist is much slimmer than the hand; by tapering the arms down to slim wrists in our drawings elegant forms can be created regardless of whether a full-bodied or a slimmer croquis is being drawn.

DRAWING THE HAND

1. Start by drawing a palm as a rectangle measuring half a head. The finger area is also a rectangle, and also half a head.
2. Divide the edge of the palm into four equal sections. It is easy to begin by dividing the line in half and then each half in half again.
3. Start to shape the fingers. Each finger is very thin, and they are all the same width. Finger number one is almost half a head. Finger number two is the longest finger—half a head long. Finger number three, the ring finger, is the same as number one, comparatively long. Finger number four—the pinkie—is the baby, approximately two-thirds the length of finger number three.

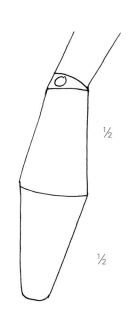
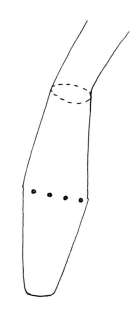
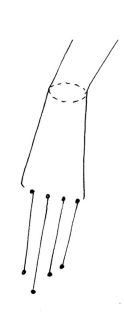

1. Both the palm and the fingers are half a head long.

2. Divide the palm into four sections for the four fingers.

3. Plot the positions and lengths of the four fingers

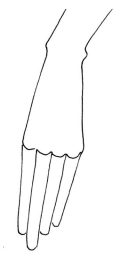

4. Shape the fingers.

The thumb is joined to the palm with a wedge—section number 1. The two joints of the thumb are always indicated.

5. Add the thumb.

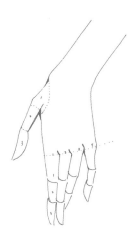

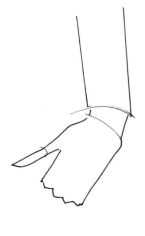

6. Define the joints in the fingers and relative angles the fingers point out.

The completed hand.

Appearance of the hand on the hip, or when made into a fist.

3. First draw in each finger as a single line then stop to check the measurements. Flesh out the finger by adding a second line, making sure that the finger remains the same width from top to bottom. If we wish to add a fingernail, be careful to place it directly on the finger, not crooked and not protruding from the tip. It is best not to draw nine-inch nails.

4. Lightly sketch in the shape of each finger.

5. The thumb is made of two equal-sized bones. It can be tricky to draw as it is so different from the rest of the hand. The thumb fits into the hand halfway up the palm. It is important to include a wedge between the wrist and the thumb so that all these areas fit together.

6. Each finger has three joints. Look at your relaxed hand. You will see that when the fingers are not squeezed together they point at slightly different angeles. This is how a natural hand looks, so if you wish you can alter the angles the fingers point out at in the drawing.

The side view of the hand is made from a triangular shape about half a head high, and with one side thinner than the other. The first finger is drawn out from the thin point of the triangle, almost one half a head in length. Finger number two extends out from the same point, a little longer. Finger number three extends from the same point and is a little shorter. Think of the open blades of a Swiss Army knife when drawing the fingers of the side view hand. To finish the drawing, add the thumb by placing a wedge from the wrist to halfway up the palm and fit the thumb onto the wedge. DO NOT attach the thumb to the wrist—a common mistake.

EXERCISES

Draw your own hand. Draw your friends' hands. Fill three pages with as many hands as you can draw.

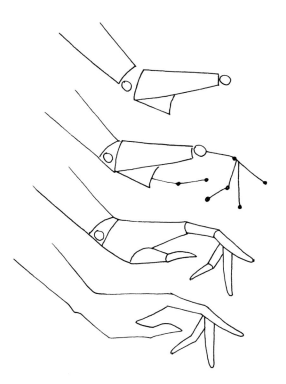

Drawing the side view hand. First draw the main part of the hand as a triangular shape with a smaller triangle underneath for the thumb. Plot the positions of the fingers and thumb and then flesh out.

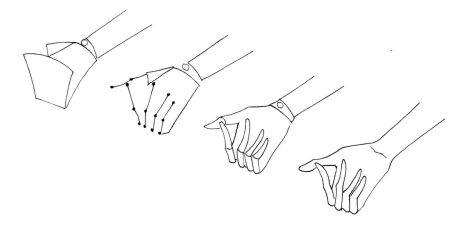

Drawing the outstretched hand, fingers beckoning the viewer into the drawing. The fingers together form a fan shape in front of the wedge shape of the palm behind. Again, plot out position of fingers and thumb and then flesh out.

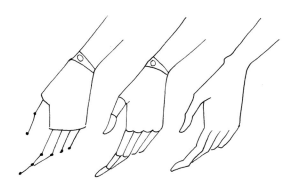

Typical pose for hands at rest by side of figure.

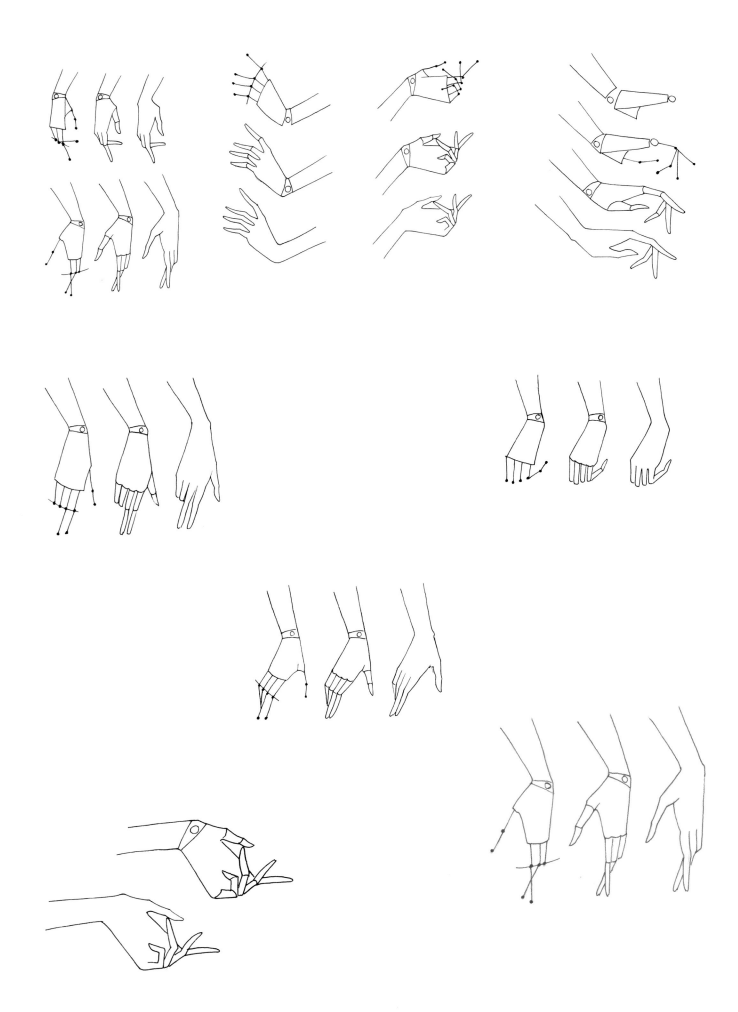

Variety of poses of left and right hands.

hands

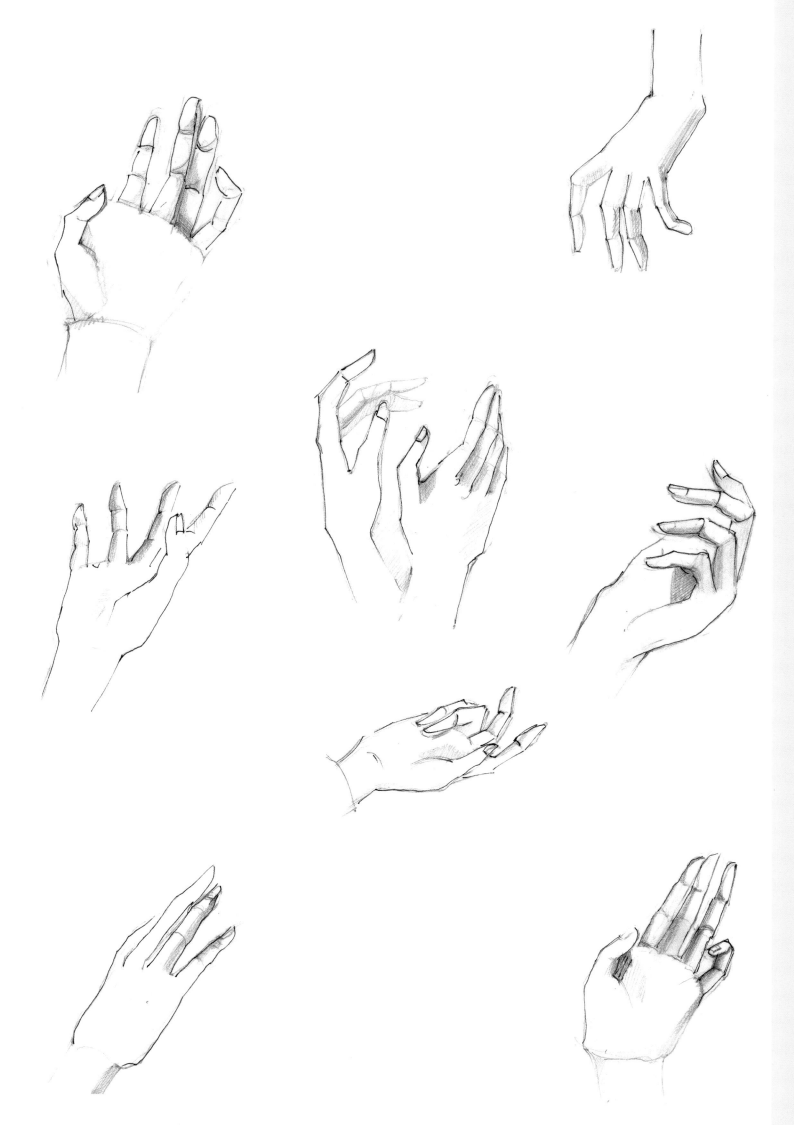

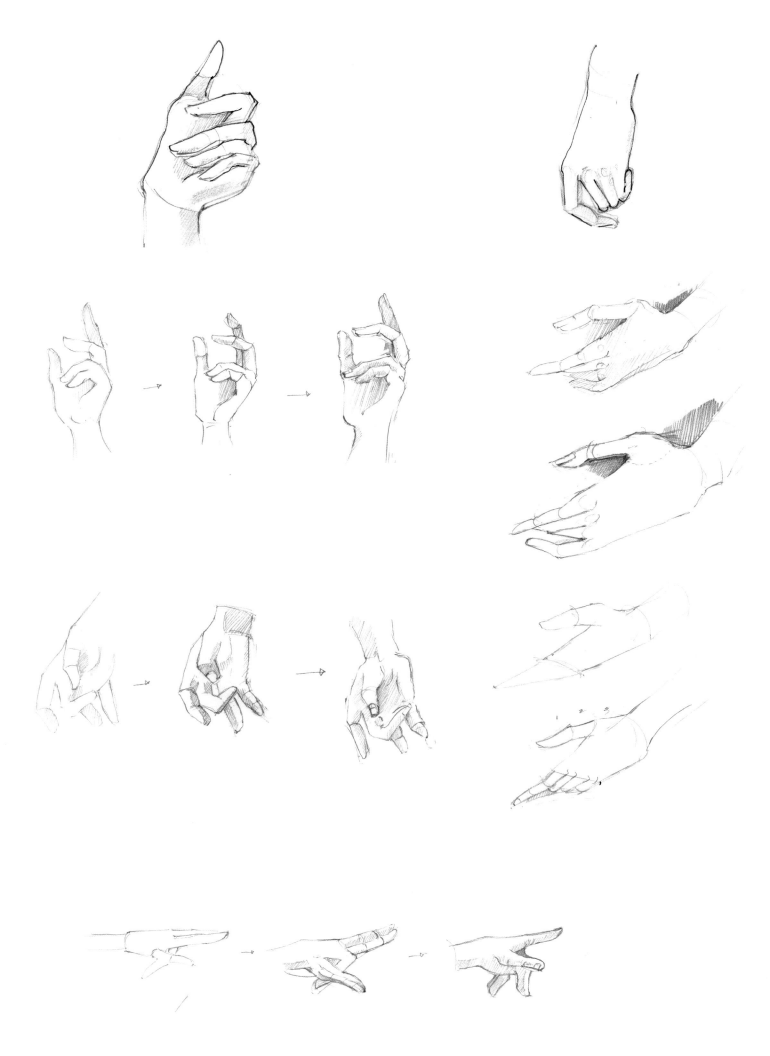

Advanced variations of the hand

hands/position of hands and arms

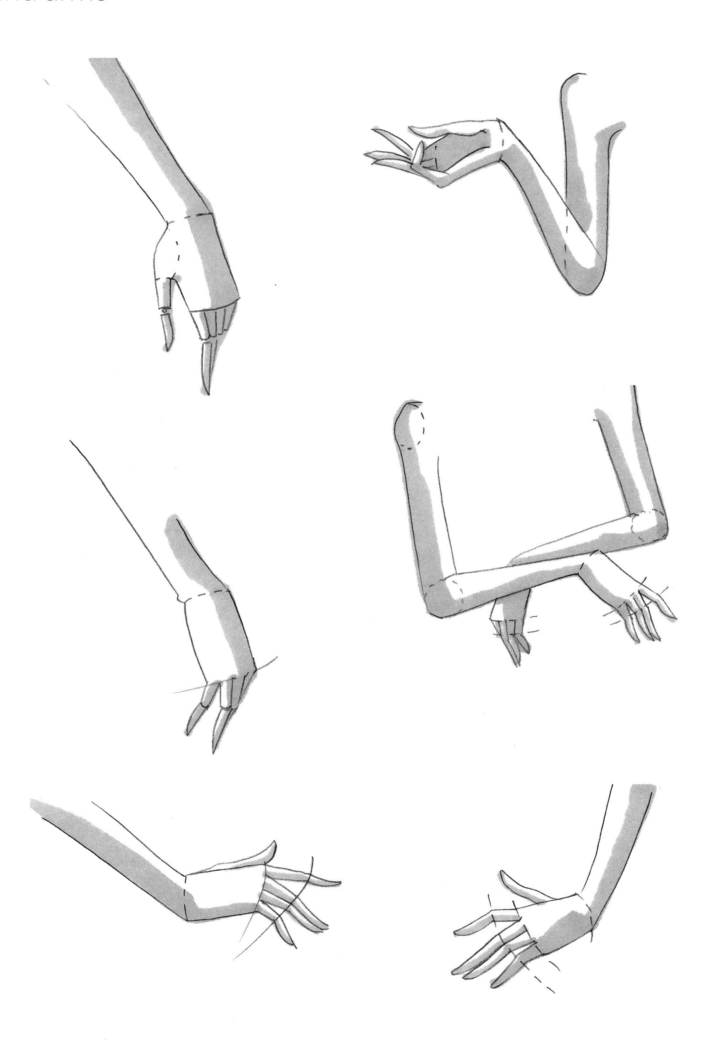

feet/exercise

FEET

The foot is equal to one head in length and is long and slim, just like the hand. It is made up of the ankle bone, which is higher on the inside and lower on the outside, engineered to support the weight of our body (think of the construction of the arch of a bridge).The foot only appears its full length in side view, however, and in the fashion side view it is usually angled up, the shape it forms when wearing high heels. In front view it if foreshortened, but again, as the foot is usually angled up to the ankle it is seen as about one half a head in vertical height.

DRAWING THE FOOT

1. The foot is often drawn at an angle, to express grace. It is slim, as mentioned, and is made of a rectangle for two thirds of its length and a triangle for the remaining third. The ball of the foot is the widest point and tapers into the large toe. The toe-nail appears to rest on the top of the toe like a crescent moon. The remaining four toes are shorter and are drawn at an angle up from the inside of the foot.

2. The arch of the foot can be expressed by drawing a curve from the ankle to the ball of the foot.

3. When drawing a shoe on the foot, remember that all lines bend around the form of the foot.

4. The foot from the side is also one head and can be drawn as a triangle. Divide the foot into three equal parts placing a circle at the heel, a square at the arch and a triangle at the toe.

5. To draw the foot in the shape it takes when wearing a high heel, slant the middle—the arch—at an angle and draw the toe as a triangle which rests flat on the ground.

6. A three-quarter foot is also usually drawn as viewed from above so it appears as a triangle slanting at a 45° slope. The foot can also be regarded as composed of different shapes—the heel a circle, the arch a square and the toes a triangle.

7. The back of the foot can be drawn by tapering down the leg from below the back of the knee to the ankle bone, which is longer on the inside than the outside indicating the Achilles tendon running down the back and then widening out at the heel. From the tendon the heel can be drawn as a circle measuring one third of the foot. The underneath of the arch tapers in on each side and widens out at the toes, which are not seen.

EXERCISE

Draw three pages of feet, with or without shoes.

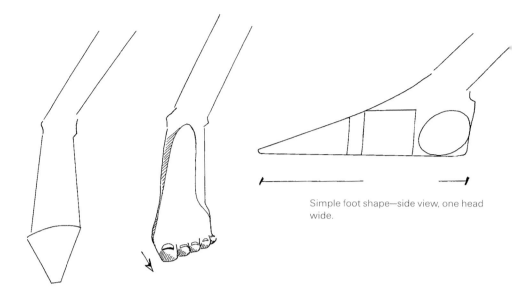

. Simple foot shape—front.   Add the toes.

Simple foot shape—side view, one head wide.

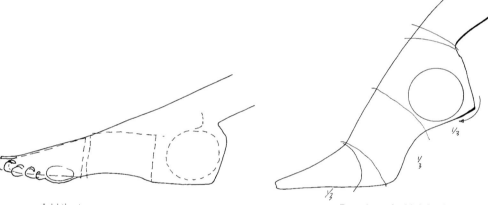

Add the toes.   Foot shape for high heels.

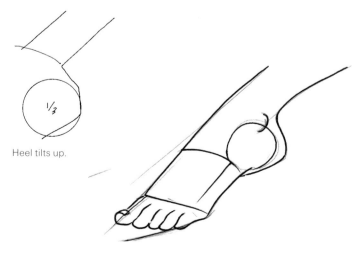

Heel tilts up.

Three-quarter foot

feet

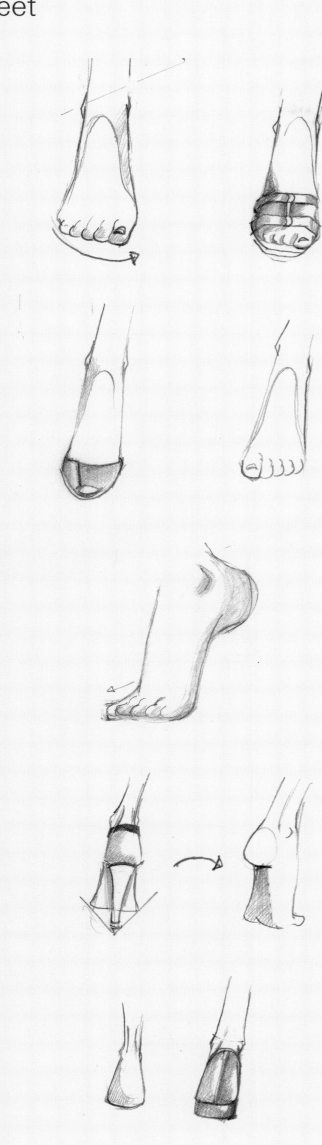

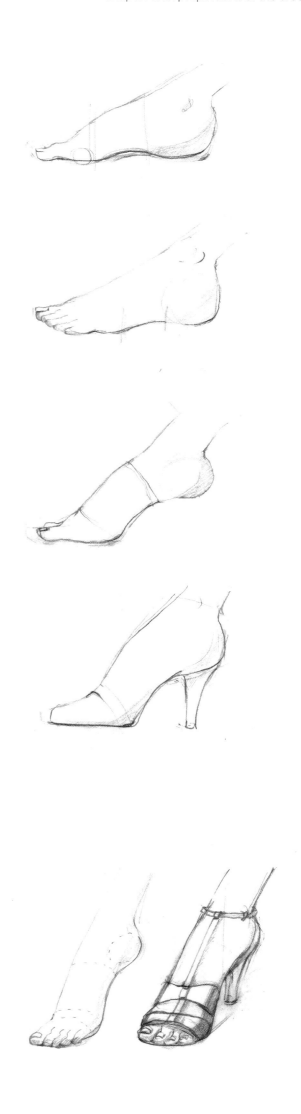

Back, back three-quarter and side views of feet in high heels. In fashion in general, as in most of the drawings on this page, feet are usually shown wearing high heels, and the foot is steeply inclined. Note the tendon prominently seen in the back and back three-quarter views stretching down the back of the leg.

fashion poses/
S curve

FASHION POSES/THE S CURVE

Fashion garments usually look their best when seen in poses that show off the drape and flow of the fabric as well as the design features, and also emphasize the silhouette. The poses best suited to achieve these ends, both on the runway and in drawing, are those that introduce angles into the figure. The vertical and horizontal lines and axes of simple, "feet-together and arms-by-the side" poses seem to suggest stability and an absence of movement, whereas angles—which create diagonals in the figure—suggest the opposite—energy, dynamism and movement. Angles can be introduced into a pose simply by bending an arm or even just tilting a hand, leaving the rest of the body static. In the S curve— a classic fashion pose—the figure itself forms a long, elegant diagonal.

In the S curve pose the weight of the figure is shifted onto one leg, tilting the hip up on that side of the figure.

The S curve pose can sometimes be difficult to understand. To understand it more easily let's think about walking: When walking, the weight of the body shifts from one leg to the other and the hip swings up on the side where the weight is placed: When the right foot is on the ground supporting the weight of the body the right hip is up; when the left foot is on the ground supporting the weight of the body the left hip is up. In each of these moments when one of the feet is on the ground supporting the weight of the body the body is in the S curve pose. In other words, when walking the body assumes a series of S curve poses.

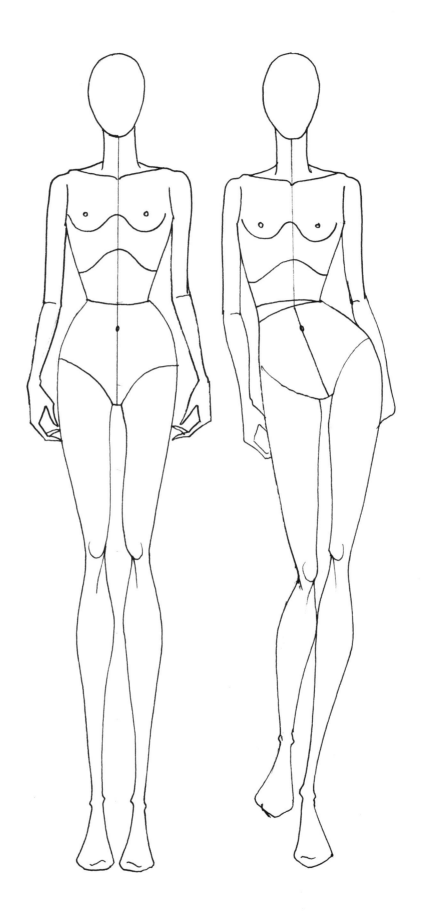

Front view pose, S-curve pose. In the S curve pose the weight of the figure is shifted onto one leg, tilting the hip up on that side of the figure. The waist shifts from the horizontal to angle down from the raised hip.

fashion poses/
S curve

To understand the S curve pose in order to draw it, it is best first to experience what it feels like: Stand up and place all the weight on one leg—let's say the right leg. Notice that the right hip tilts up. The hip is one large bone and the center and the sides of the hip all shift to the right. The left leg, that is not bearing the weight, is free to move to any angle. Look in a mirror: the body is forming the shape of an 'S'. Note that when the weight shifts onto one leg, the body's vertical balance line runs from the neck through the weight-bearing foot. The leg has shifted from the vertical in the front view to a diagonal running from the hip to the foot which lies on a vertical line—the original balance line—drawn down from the neck.

DRAWING THE S-CURVE FIGURE—DIAGRAM FORM
Before drawing the full fleshed-out S curve figure we will learn to draw it as a diagram which will teach us how to make sure the angles of the waist, hips and weight-bearing leg are correct. This will make it much easier when we go on to draw the full fleshed-out figure.

1. Draw the top half of the front view croquis to the waist at 3. The torso can be drawn as a simple bucket shape (known in geometry as a trapezoid—a shape with at least one pair of parallel lines). Decide which leg will be the weight-bearing leg—here we make it the right leg. In the S curve the hip is raised on the side of the weight-bearing leg and the waist angles down from that side. Draw in the new position of the waist angling at 25 to 35 degrees from the outside of the waistline on the raised hip side. Draw in the center-front line extending at right angles from the middle of the newly positioned waist to the new position of the crotch at 4¼.
2. Draw in a line crossing the center-front line at right-angles at 4, one and a half heads wide, the same length on either side of the c-f line. This is the new line of the hips; we call it here the "S curve hip line". The ends of this line indicate the high points of the hips on both sides.

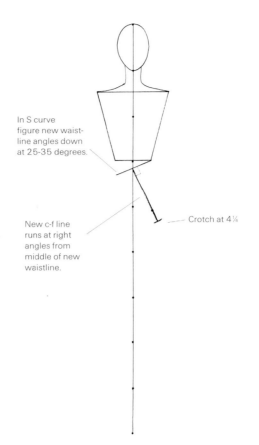

In S curve figure new waist-line angles down at 25-35 degrees.

New c-f line runs at right angles from middle of new waistline.

Crotch at 4¼

1. Draw a simplified top half of front view croquis to the waist at 3. Draw in the new position of the waist-line angling down from side of raised hip. Draw in the new c-f line for the lower part of the figure from the middle of the new waistline to the crotch at 4¼.

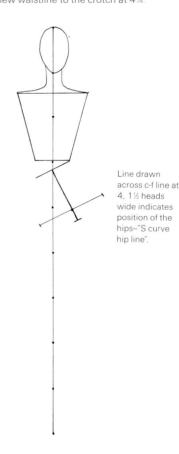

Line drawn across c-f line at 4, 1½ heads wide indicates position of the hips—"S curve hip line".

2. Draw in the new line of the hips cutting c-f line at a right angle at 4. The hips are 1½ heads wide. The ends of this line are the high points of the hips on each side.

fashion poses/
S curve

The S curve figure is
more advanced. Work
slowly and carefully.

*3. Indicate the edge of the hips on each side
with lines joining the ends of the new waistline
to the high point of the hip on each side.*

*4. Draw in the position of the weight-bearing
leg by joining the high point of the hip on that
side to the ankle at 9. In the S curve the ankle of
the weight-bearing leg is always on the vertical
balance line.*

*5. Draw in the position of the leg on the other
side. As this leg does not bear weight it can be
placed in virtually any position. See the other
variations in this section of the book. This completes the diagram of the S curve figure. Once
we are able to draw this diagram it becomes
much easier to draw the fully fleshed-out figure,
which we do on the next page.*

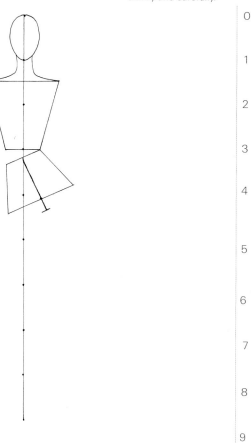

0
1
2
3
4
5
6
7
8
9

3. Indicate the edge of the hips on each side with
lines joining the ends of the new waistline to the high
point of the hip on each side.

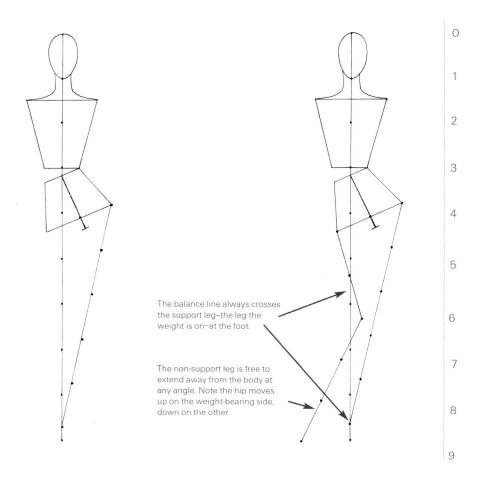

The balance line always crosses
the support leg–the leg the
weight is on–at the foot.

The non-support leg is free to
extend away from the body at
any angle. Note the hip moves
up on the weight-bearing side,
down on the other.

0
1
2
3
4
5
6
7
8
9

4. Draw in the position of the weight-bearing leg by joining the high point of the hip
on that side to the ankle at 9. In the S
curve the ankle of the weight-bearing leg is
always on the vertical balance line.

5. Draw in the position of the leg on the
other side. As this leg does not bear
weight it can be placed in virtually any
position. See the other variations in this
section of the book.

fashion poses/
S curve

DRAWING THE FULL S CURVE FIGURE

Turning to the full S curve figure, we will learn to draw the most common, and simplest, form of the figure, where the top part of the figure remains upright. There are many variations of the figure as will be seen later in the chapter.

1. Draw in the head, neck and upper torso, including the bust, ribcage and upper arms extending to waist level at 3. Lightly draw in the balance line-a vertical line starting at the top of the head and running through the front center of the figure. Continue this line vertically to its full nine head length where the ankle will be drawn. (Note that the S curve figure is the same length as the front view figure; although the line of the weight-bearing leg shifts from vertical to diagonal the overall length of the figure remains the same.)

2. Decide which leg will be the weight–bearing leg–here we make it the right leg. In the S curve the hip is raised on the side of the weight-bearing leg and the waist angles down from that side. Draw in the new position of the waist angling at 25 to 35 degrees from the outside of the waistline on the raised hip side. Draw in the continuation of the center-front line at right angles from the middle of the new waistline to the position of the crotch at 4¼. To plot the position of the hips accurately we draw in a new guide line–the S curve hip line–running from the widest part of the hip on one side to the widest part on the other side of the body, as we saw in drawing the diagrammatic S curve figure in the last section. This line is 1½ heads wide–the width of the hips–and lies equally on either side of the center-front line.

3. Draw in the line of the hips on each side by joining the edges of the new waistline to the widest points of the hips on each side, on the ends of the S curve hip line. Indicate the position of the tops of the legs.

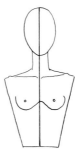

1. Draw in upper part of body to waist at 3. Draw in the vertical balance line

0

1

2

3

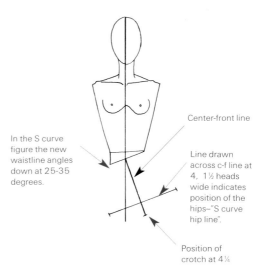

In the S curve figure the new waistline angles down at 25-35 degrees.

Center-front line

Line drawn across c-f line at 4, 1½ heads wide indicates position of the hips–"S curve hip line".

Position of crotch at 4¼

0

1

2

3

4

5

2. Draw in the new waistline at an angle of 25 to 35 degrees sloping from the outside of the waist on the raised hip side. Draw in the c-f line at right-angles from middle of new waistline. Continue to crotch level at 4¼. Draw in S curve hip line crossing lower c-f line at 4, 1½ heads wide.

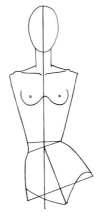

0

1

2

3

4

5

3. Draw in the line of the hips by joining the edges of the new waistline to the widest points of the hips on each side, on the ends of the S curve hip line. Indicate the position of the tops of the legs.

fashion poses/
S curve

4. Draw in the position of the weight-bearing leg by joining the high point of the hip on that side to the ankle at 9. In the S curve the ankle of the weight-bearing leg is always on the vertical balance line.

5. Draw in the position of the leg on the other side. As this leg does not bear weight it can be placed in virtually any position. See the other variations in this section of the book.

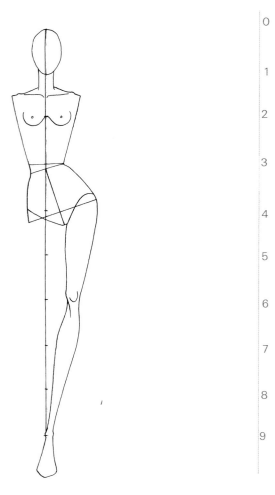

4. Draw in the position of the weight-bearing leg by joining the high point of the hip on that side to the ankle at 9. In the S curve the ankle of the weight-bearing leg is always on the vertical balance line.

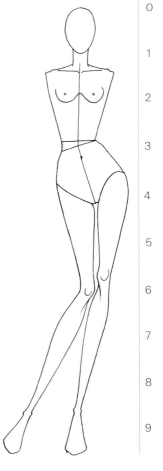

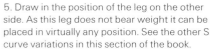

5. Draw in the position of the leg on the other side. As this leg does not bear weight it can be placed in virtually any position. See the other S curve variations in this section of the book.

S curve/3/4 view/ fashion poses/exercise

THREE-QUARTER VIEW S CURVE

When drawing S curve poses in three-quarter view, as for straight poses in three-quarter view, draw in the center-front line and make sure the two sides of the body are in the ¾ /¼ proportion, with the side turned away being foreshortened. It is important to keep these proportions all the way down the figure: a common mistake is to draw the hips on the three-quarter figure symmetrically, without foreshortening on one side, giving the figure a distorted look. Remember also that in three-quarter view we see the *side* of the body as well as the front. Leave space to show this side plane all the way down. Also, pay attention to the positioning of the knees and feet in the three-quarter figure: they must correspond with the alignment of the figure.

Three-quarter S curves are not the easiest of poses to draw but are a common and important pose in fashion drawing. It is helpful to study three-quarter S curve poses in fashion magazines to become familiar with how the proportions of the figure appear when it forms this pose.

FASHION POSES AND THE S CURVE

The S curve introduces interesting diagonals into the fashion figure, creating a dramatic feel ideal for displaying garments to best effect. Numerous variations of the figure are possible, as is seen in the drawings in this section. Changing the position of the arms can also enhance the pose; note that when the arm moves, the line of the shoulder remains horizontal as long as the arm is parallel to or below the shoulder. When the arm moves above the shoulder, the horizontal line of the shoulder moves up with the arm, so that the shoulder becomes an extension of the arm and fits close to the neck. See the drawing later in this section to see this effect.

EXERCISE

Pick favorite pictures and poses from your scrap file. Draw a line through the center of the bust, waist and hip. If the line moves to the right the weight is on the right hip, if it moves to the left the weight is on the left hip. Create a croquis using the above rules that expresses this shift in weight. After drawing this croquis, add eyes, nose, mouth, hair, hands and feet.

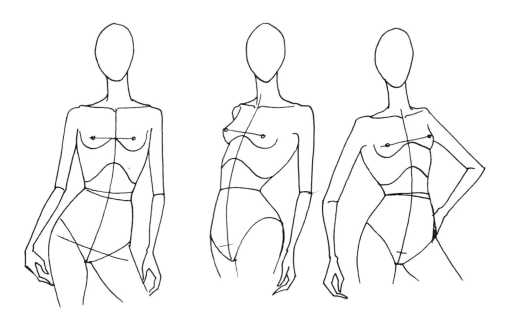

Numerous variations of the S curve figure are possible. Here the figure on the left has the hip up but the shoulders are still horizontal. The shoulders of the middle and right figures, which are also seen in three-quarter view, have dropped, so the mid-section of the torso is compressed.

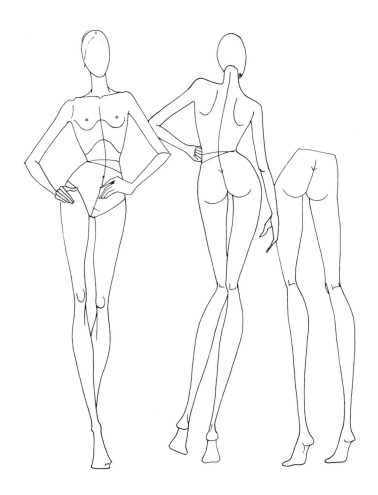

The pose on the left is a walking pose. When walking the body forms a succession of S curves as the weight shifts from one leg to the other. Here the weight is on the left leg and the right is about to swing through. In back view note the buttocks slope in the direction of the raised hip.

fashion poses/
S curve/variations

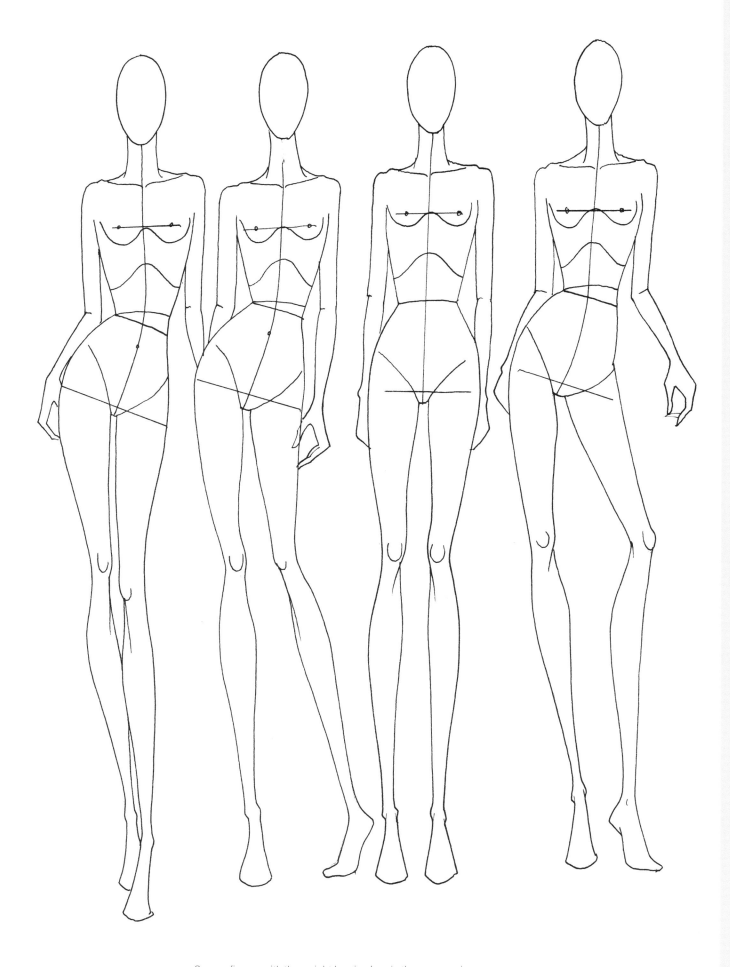

S curve figures with the weight-bearing legs in the same position— on the left (except for the non-S curve front view figure
third from left for reference). The right leg can shift to different
positions without affecting the other shapes in the body.

fashion poses/
S curve/variations

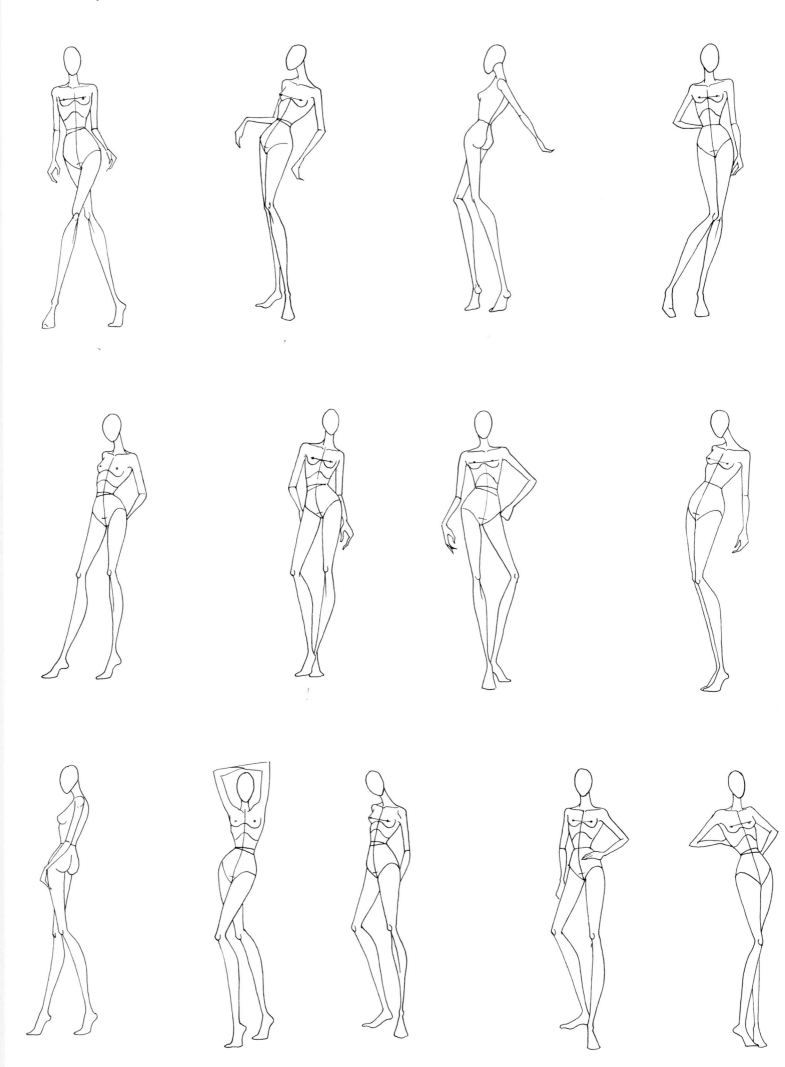

fashion poses/
S curve

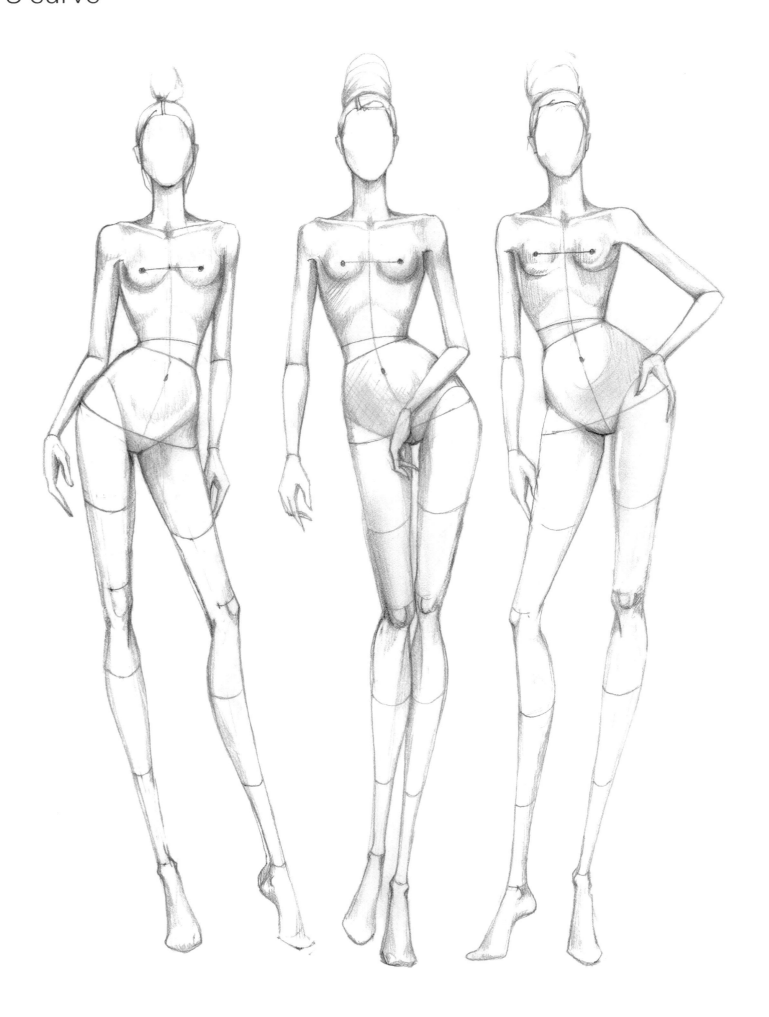

S curve poses, shaded figures. Left, weight on left leg; middle, weight on the front leg; right, weight on the right leg.

fashion poses/
S curve

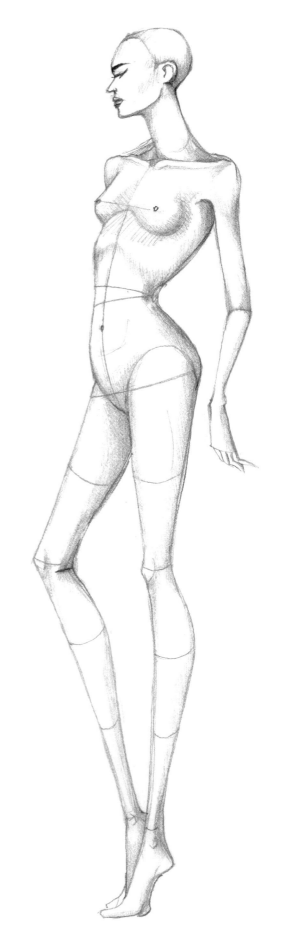

S curve pose, front view with arms over head, weight on the leg on
the right. S curve three-quarter view, weight on the leg on the right.

fashion poses/
S curve

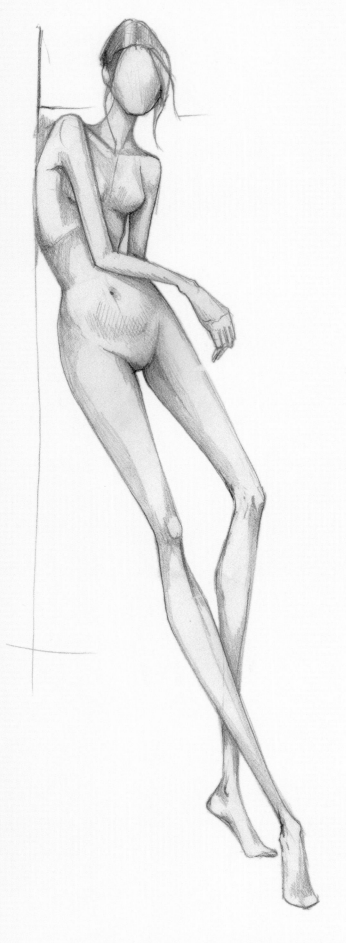

Left, S curve reclining three-quarter view, weight on the front left leg
(also partly supported by the wall). Right, back view S curve walking
pose. This pose is caught in mid-stride with the weight on the left leg.
Note the exaggerated drop in the left shoulder.

fashion poses/
S curve

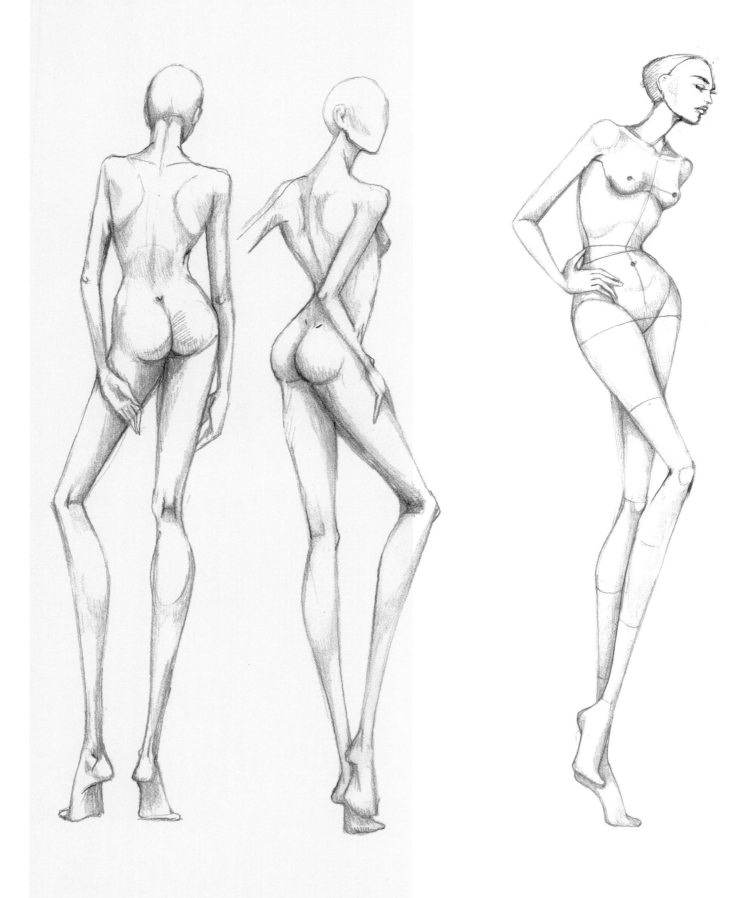

Left, S curve pose, back view, weight on right leg. MIddle,
Three-quarter back S curve pose, weight on leg on left.
Right, weight on the back leg.

fashion poses/
S curve

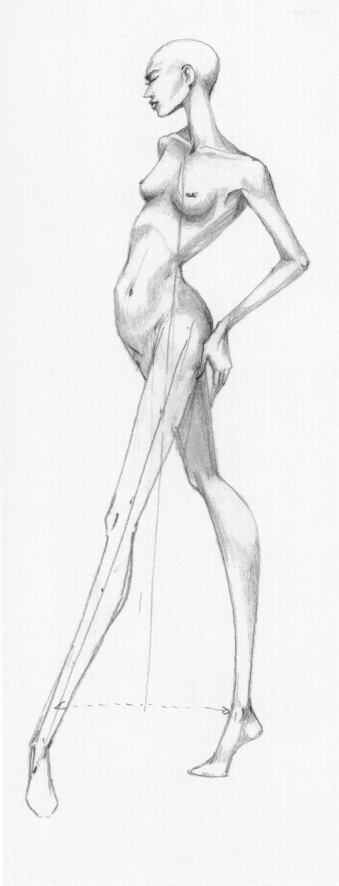

Left, S curve walking pose, weight on left leg. Right, three-quarter S curve with weight on right.

fashion poses/
S curve

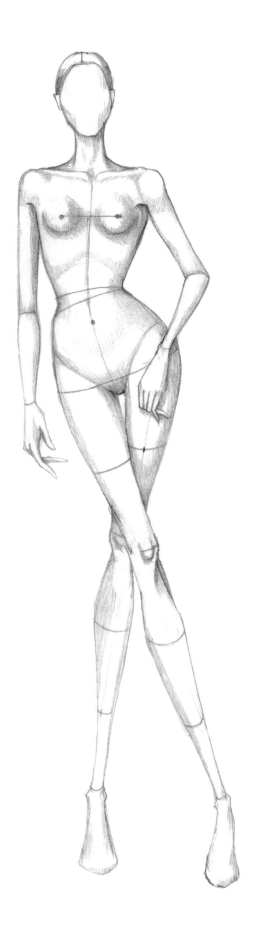

S curve pose, three-quarter view, weight on the right–back– leg.

Three-quarter S curve pose, weight on left–back–leg.

fashion poses/ S curve

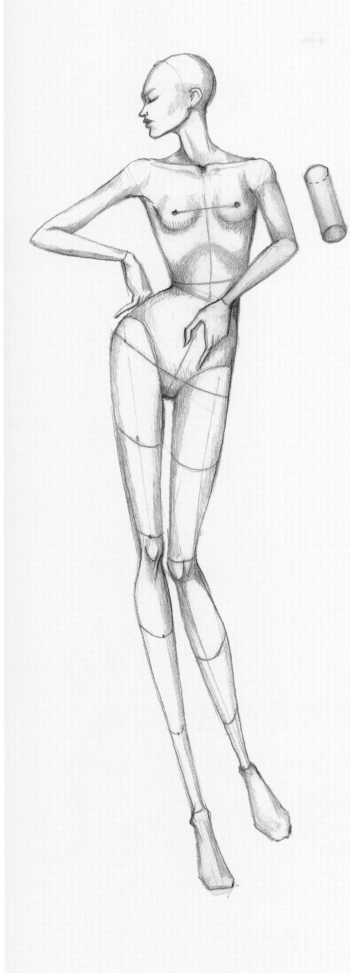

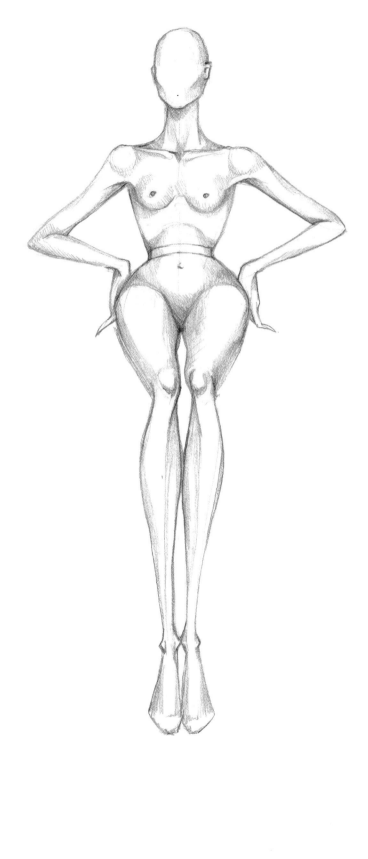

S curve pose, front view, weight on the left leg. The arms extend out from the body; the right upper arm is foreshortened and, to a lesser extent, the left lower arm. The back leg is also slightly foreshortened.

Sitting pose. The plane of the lower part of the legs is in front of that of the torso, closest to the point of view, so these parts of the body appear proportionately larger. Because of the angle they are viewed at, the upper legs appear much foreshortened.

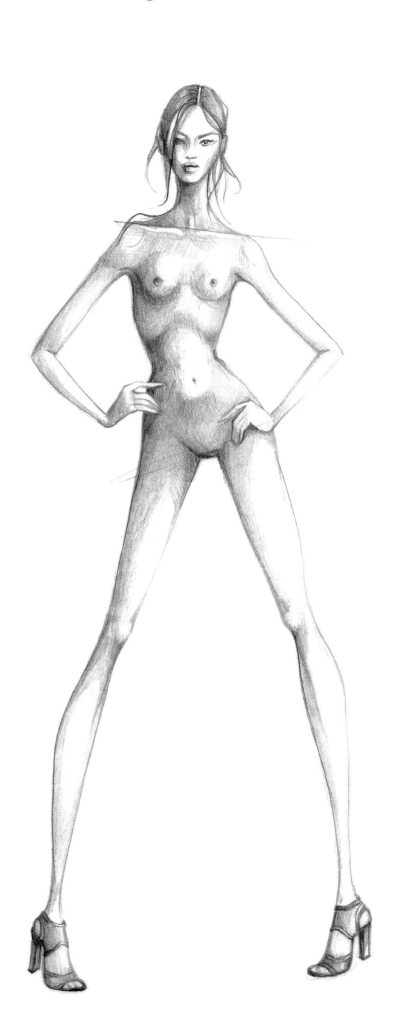

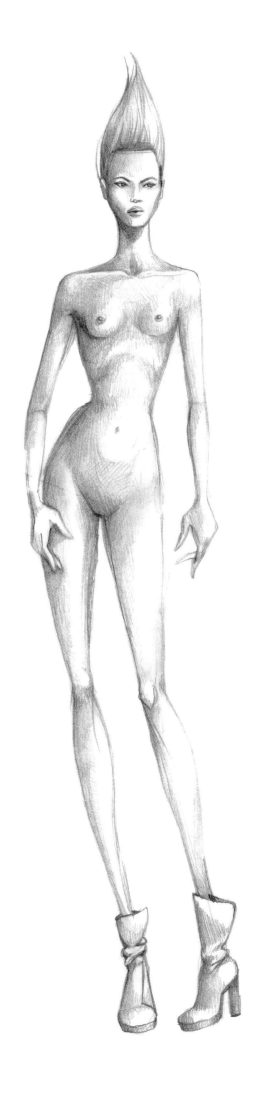

The finished woman— flesh her out!

the complete figure/
with clothing

The croquis with clothing

different racial/ ethnic characteristics

Every fashion figure tries to create expressions of beauty, health, energy, seduction, humor and the ideas of what is fashionable at the moment. Fortunately there are enormous variations from one race to another and each may be a wonderful variation on the theme of beauty. The Asian face is drawn with a higher eyebrow, slimmer eyes and less eyelid. Hair is dark and straight and the mouth is round and full. The Japanese face has pale skin and slim, delicate bones. The Korean face has fuller eyebrows, stronger bones and a stronger chin. The Chinese face is round with round dark eyes with limited shading at the eyelids, noses with straight bridges but full bases and a soft, round mouth. Hair is very black and very straight.

The black, or African, woman has dramatic deep-set eyes and stronger eyelids which require more shading. Eyebrows are stronger and can be drawn with a full arch. The nose is drawn with a broader base, the mouth is round and wide and the lips are full; the cheek bones are high, the hairline is high and the forehead is rounded. There are many variations on skin tone depending on specific nationality and genes. Skin tone can range from aubergine to cinnamon.

different racial/ ethnic characteristics

Northern Europeans have strong bones, thin, strong noses and wide mouths and eyes. The eyes are set wide apart but do not require a great deal of shadow at the lid. The mouth is wide but can be drawn with a thinner lip or full. Skin tone is usually light. Hair is usually fair but there are many exceptions.

Southern Europeans are principally the Latin races. They have round deep set eyes and wide arched brows, full wide mouths, high cheek bones and strong chins. Hair is often blue-black, full and lush. The Latin eye tends to have a flirtatious down-curve at the end of the lash.

different racial/
ethnic characteristics

chapter two:
drawing clothes on
the figure

beginning to draw/
learning about fashion

BEGINNING TO DRAW

This book teaches how to draw fashion realistically and accurately so that it can be used as a powerful tool for fashion design. When learning to draw with the intention of using drawing to *design* fashion though, it is important to focus first on *developing the drawing skills themselves*. In fashion, as in other areas of design, presentation is an important part of the overall design and production process (after all, fashion itself is an important part of how we humans present ourselves visually). Unless the drawings are accurate and attractive they will not hold the viewer's attention. It is therefore best to focus one's efforts first on learning to draw and aiming to achieve a certain level of proficiency. When one can draw at an adequate level of proficiency then the designs will always look better.

LEARNING ABOUT FASHION

Fashion drawing is a type of technical drawing; its primary purpose is to convey information about garments. The information included in the drawings has to be clear and meaningful. This means that (unless one has spent many years following fashion and has made a recent decision to learn how to draw it) when learning to draw it is important at the same time to learn as much as possible about fashion itself in all its aspects—the appearance of different types of garments, their construction, contemporary designers' work, fashion poses, hair and make-up styling, the differences among fashion in different markets, along with the many other components of contemporary fashion. This book contains a large quantity of technical information about modern fashion garments, in both visual and textual form. The reader should become familiar with and use this technical information as constant reference when drawing and designing. This information should be supplemented as much as possible, though, by taking every opportunity to look at and read about fashion with a view to acquiring deeper knowledge of the subject and developing an "eye" for, as well as a sensitivity to fashion trends.

Fashion design ideas are more effective if the drawings that present them are attractive, clear and show a knowledge of the technical aspects of fashion. This long tailored silk satin coat over a silk satin pant is drawn precisely so the drape and fit are clearly seen, the shading of the drape indicating the type of the fabric. The pose is a mid-stride one so that the coat is open in the front, showing the silhouette of the pants. The face is interesting and attractive but simple enough not to draw the attention away from the garments.

beginning to draw/ learning about fashion

THE FASHION DESIGN PROCESS

The fashion design process itself is one of developing, refining, adapting, and combining, in new ways, elements of fashion that have in many cases existed for a long time, in some cases for hundreds or even thousands of years. Just as with a written and spoken language, though, new design creations have to "make sense": they have to be made up of real elements that are put together, from a construction and style point of view, in meaningful combinations, like words in a sentence. The larger the "vocabulary" of fashion elements you have acquired, then the larger the number of design possibilities—new combinations of existing elements—that you can create.

When beginning to study fashion it is important to make an effort to see and touch *real* garments, not just to look at pictures. This can be done by visiting stores (across a range of markets, so the very best designer clothes can be experienced as well as cheaper versions of similar garments, along with more popular everyday wear), attending fashion shows and costume exhibits and viewing videos and fashion shows on TV. A variety of the best fashion magazines should be read regularly and there are scores of internet sites and blogs dedicated to fashion. These will often (though not always) show examples of the work of the best designers, the best models, the best photography and the most modern poses and styling. It is important not to restrict oneself to existing preferences and tastes in fashion, and to look at a wide range of garments: not only do tastes changes, but in the modern world trends are picked up from a very broad base of influences and cut across markets and different areas of design.

Collect images from magazines and other sources, study them and then catalogue them, according to interests and priorities, in a scrapbook or separate files as source material for different types of clothing (skirts, desses, jackets, tops, active sportswear, lingerie/ swimwear, coats, and so on), different poses and body types, different styles of hair and makeup, accessories and other categories. The more information that is collected, the better, as it is quite common to refer to dozens of images of existing garments when making a fashion drawing for a new design.

Striving continually to learn more about fashion and improve drawing skills will improve design skills. This outfit is designed for the junior market. Note the youthful pose, chosen to show the mood of the garments and the type of person they are designed for.

planning the drawing

PLANNING THE DRAWING

When beginning to draw, the emphasis is on developing basic drawing skills as quickly as possible more than thinking about design. Rather than making drawings of new garments, it is best to practice copying existing garments. Copying professional photographs of existing garments is excellent practice for learning to draw the fashion croquis and clothes on the figure, and much can be learnt from the way the clothes and model have been styled and posed for the shot. When beginning, trace the silhouette, drape and folds and details of the garment using tracing paper and then transfer to drawing paper. This is a great help in understanding how to form the basic shapes of garments and how they are constructed. Once basic drawing skills have been acquired, it is then possible to move on to making drawings of new garments.

When drawing new garments, time invested in planning out the various elements of the drawing beforehand will be amply rewarded, resulting in a superior end product and making for a quicker and smoother execution of the design drawing. Most good design is a result of painstaking crafting of ideas, and professional designers spend many months preparing a new collection. Do not spend *too* much time planning, though, or the spontaneity will begin to disappear. Have a clear idea of the principal elements of the drawing and refine them as the garment begins to take shape on the page.

It is common to have fabric swatches to hand when making a drawing, so that the design is made with a particular fabric in mind. This can inject a good dose of realism into the drawing: the visual and textural qualities of the fabric, how it folds and falls, its character and mood are all experienced directly and conveyed in the drawing. The cost of the fabric is also known, which is an important consideration when designing for a particular market. The fashion industry categorizes clothing into various classes corresponding to a view of the type of person who will wear them—the different "markets" for the clothes. These classes of clothing include junior, missy, designer, young designer, career, active sportswear, budget, contemporary and other specialized markets. If designing a garment for a particular market then research will have shown that the garment must meet a number of specific design

Time invested in planning the drawing makes for a better end product and smoother execution of the design drawing. Before beginning to draw it is best to have a clear idea of the garment that is to be drawn: what type of garment it is, who is going to wear it and what occasion it is intended for. This outfit is designed for the "missy" market; the pose is youthful but serious and self-assured.

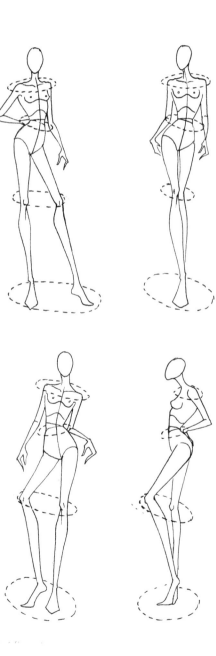

The angles of the body in the pose affect the angles at which garments drape, particularly at the neckline, waist and hems.

planning the drawing

criteria appropriate for that market, and the economics of making a garment for that particular market segment will define within narrow limits the fabric and method of fabrication to be used. For those learning to draw fashion who are planning to work in the fashion industry, a rapid familiarization of the markets the company manufactures for will take place once in the workplace, but it is useful to develop awareness of the different categories of clothing so that designs and drawings have a relation to the realities of the marketplace from an early stage. For those *not* contemplating a career in fashion, these categories will be of interest but it is more important to direct efforts to learning to draw a wide range of different garments.

Before beginning to draw it is best to have a clear idea of the garment that is to be drawn: what type of garment it is, who is going to wear it, what occasion it is intended for. Visualize the garment as clearly as possible, not just the appearance, but also how it will fit, how the fabric will feel and how it will drape on the body. If only one, or a small number of features of the garment is going to be dominant—such as the silhouette, for instance— this has to be thought out first, and the other elements of the garments elaborated in subsequent steps. Rough sketches can be made of the different features of the garment to help work towards the final versions. Ideas for details and accessories can be jotted down, but these (unless, of course, it is an accessory that is the subject of the drawing) can be worked out and included as the drawing progresses.

It is helpful to have on hand the clippings made from magazines on different garments, poses and styles. These will provide inspiration and help clarify ideas.

The power of drawing in fashion design: This dress, for the "designer" market, contains so much fabric it would be very difficult to design by draping the fabric. Drawing allows a clear realistic version of the final design to be seen quickly and easily.

choosing the pose

CHOOSING THE POSE

The first decision when planning a fashion drawing is the pose. In choosing the pose of the croquis, the first question to ask is always "what pose will show off the garments the best?" If important design details are located in the side or back of the garment it will be necessary to choose a pose that will show them off effectively: a three-quarter view pose will be most appropriate. If a garment has plentiful and elaborate drape an S curve pose will raise the hip on one side of the figure causing the fabric to drape at an angle, showing it to best effect.

Besides the practical considerations of presenting the garment, the pose should also suit the type of garment and occasion. For example, a dramatic designer evening gown should be set off with an equally dramatic pose, as well as dramatic hair and makeup styling; an active sportswear outfit is usually best shown on a pose that relates to the sport in question. More everyday garments can be paired with more naturalistic poses. Observe women's body language (which is quite different from men's) and note the type of gestures made with the hands and arms and face; except for the cases mentioned of showing off dramatic designer wear and active sportswear, and also for energetic teenagers, the limbs are mostly kept close to the body and gestures are not as expansive as those used by men, though poses are often struck that show off the curves of the body. Bear in mind also the effect of the pose on the overall composition of the drawing: for example, use the hand as a pointer to draw attention to the important parts of the garment; do not point it outside the drawing or it will suggest there is something more interesting out there.

It has become popular in the styling of contemporary fashion photography—responding to trends in fashion merchandising— to present the model in a more complex setting, and to show glimpses of her inner life; the fashion becomes part of a bigger story and is identified with a lifestyle or particular activity. If taking a similar approach in fashion *drawing*, poses should also be suited to the story being created.

The poses on this and the following two pages are young, energetic, sexy, fun and sassy. They show a different attitude to how we see ourselves in our clothes: now, clothes are chosen to express our personalities rather than our bodies showing off the clothes.

modern fashion
poses

Center-bottom—Bad Pose. This is a poorly conceived pose: the silhouette of the pant legs is unclear because the legs are too close together, the arms hide the details of the belt and the hair covers the face. When deciding on a pose it is important that all the essential information on the garments can be clearly seen.

defining the garment/
the fashion silhouette

DEFINING THE GARMENT

Moving on to the garments themselves, what are the features that define a garment, those that make it unique and different from other garments? The principal defining features are SILHOUETTE, DRAPE AND FIT, DETAILS, FABRIC. These elements are introduced below, and discussed and illustrated in detail in each of the sections on different types of garments. There are numerous interrelations among these features, each providing some information about the others, and it is important that the information each provides is consistent with the information from the others. These interrelations are commented on in the introductory sections below on each of the defining features and then in the sections on different garment types.

THE FASHION SILHOUETTE

The silhouette is the contour, or outside edge, of a garment—its basic shape. The silhouette is the single most defining feature of a garment, providing detailed information on the type of garment and indicating drape and fit, often also indicating fabric type and details. The silhouette is the key to understanding the garment and must be drawn accurately or the garment will be misunderstood. Garments are three-dimensional, and the silhouette of the garment is also three-dimensional, although in a drawing it has to be represented on a two-dimensional surface. If a garment has interesting silhouette features at the side and back as well as the front a pose has to be chosen that will allow these to be seen: typically a three-quarter view pose.

When drawing the silhouette of garments it is important, no matter what level of proficiency one has attained, always to bear in mind that garments *bend around the body*. Special attention must always be paid to make sure the collar bends around the neck; sleeves end in cuffs or hems that bend around the arm (unless there is a crease or pleat); in a skirt or the skirt of a dress the body of the skirt and the hem bend around the body.

Silhouette. The silhouette is the single most defining feature of a garment. As well as the basic shape of the garment the silhouette provides information on fit and drape and also often fabric type and details. For a complex garment like this dress, besides the silhouette—here indicated by the thick black line—it is helpful to sketch in the outlines of the constructional details inside the silhouette, here drawn with a lighter line.

defining the garment/
details/fabric

DETAILS

Details are the smaller parts of a garment that
either form part of the garment's construction,
and are then known as "constructional details"
or are included for decoration; sometimes they
are a combination of the two. Examples of
details are seams, pleats, buttonholes, gathers,
darts, ease, shirring and topstitching.
Decorative details include trim, pockets, zippers.

Details are often important features of a garment, particularly in those that are tailored and
of better quality. If a drawing is going to serve
as the basis for technical construction drawings
(flats) then it is important that constructional
and other details are clearly and accurately
shown.

FABRIC

Fabric is at the core of fashion design, and the
greatest fashion is almost invariably an inspired
combination of beautiful fabric and exquisite
design. Even when clothing is not high-fashion,
the fabric of the garment is often its most important aspect, either for reasons of appearance or function, or both (for example, a leather
miniskirt or an active sportswear garment fea-
turing a new high-tech fabric to wick perspira-
tion from the body).

If the silhouette and drape of a garment are
drawn accurately then these features alone will
give an indication of the type of fabric used in
the construction. For the most effective presentation of new garments though, it it best to
draw them so they appear realistic and accurate in as many ways as possible. If fabric of the
garment can be immediately recognized, with a
high degree of certainty, then this makes a significant contribution to achieving a realistic
and accurate depiction of how a finished garment will look.

Because of the importance of fabrics in fashion
and fashion drawing and because the techniques for rendering different fabrics accurately
are relatively advanced, a separate chapter of
the book is devoted to them. It is best to focus
first on mastering how to draw the different
fashion garments—the subject of this chapter—
before perfecting techniques for drawing fabrics. In this chapter, which covers how the

The finished, detailed fashion drawing. This drawing contains a large amount
of information about the garments: the complex silhouette is clearly perceived;
the different types of fabric used in the construction are indicated by the variations in drape—both crisp and softly draping folds and a stiff underskirt. The
detailing is very important in this garment, and this is skillfully rendered at the
shoulder, down the left side of the figure and at the wrist and feet/ankles. Note
that all the elements of the drawing—the hair, the shoes—accentuate the flow
and drape of the dress.

defining the garment/fabric

principal fashion garments are drawn, the fabrics of the garments are identified by no more than simple classifications into heavy or lightweight, shiny or matt, or soft or crisp. The different fabric types that are used in this chapter are drawn in the following ways:

SOFT FABRIC is depicted with a soft pencil—a 2B or 4B.

LIGHT AREAS of a fabric tend to be thin and shadowy areas wide.

SHINY FABRIC requires a contrast of very dark shading in the interiors of the folds—the valleys— and crisp white lines along the tops of the folds. The darkest part of the shadow appears next to the lightest area at the crest of the fold. The same rule applies for MATT FABRICS, but there is much less variation between the dark values in the interiors and the lighter values on the tops of the folds.

HEAVYWEIGHT fabrics such as four-ply cashmere, silk brocade, heavy leather, corduroy, cable knit sweaters and others are drawn with wide folds and wide shadows.

1.

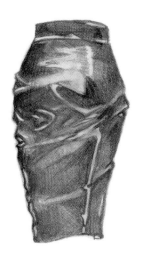

Top, a skirt made from a light fabric, indicated by the flowing pleats drawn with a curved fine line. Center, a skirt made from a heavy matte fabric indicated by the heavier line weight and wide straight pleats. Bottom, a skirt made from a shiny fabric such as leather, with wide folds and contrasting highlights and dark areas.

garments/
general points

GENERAL POINTS TO KEEP IN MIND WHEN DRAWING GARMENTS.

A number of points are common to drawing all types of clothes and should be constantly kept in mind:

1. The figure, particularly the female figure, is formed of curves, and has very few straight lines. Clothes tend to follow the form of the figure, bending around the figure in curves, and this is how they should be drawn.

2. In general, lines bend up above the waist and down below it.

3. Clothing bends around the figure and moves as the body moves. When the body moves the center-front line of the body moves. It is important to know where the center-front line of the body is in every position and to check that the center-front of the body and the clothes

4. Princess lines—the style lines seen on the dress form—line up half way between the side seams and the center-front line of a garment, and fall from mid-way between the center-front and the sides of the shoulders over the bustline, and at the waist mid way between the center-front and the side of the hips. The princess line is an important indicator of where to place pockets, belt loops and seams in tailored garments.

5. When garments are symmetrical (and the majority are) then it is important to show the symmetry clearly in the garment. The figure itself is always symmetrical.

6. The bust and shoulder lines are parallel and should not be drawn at different angles.

7. Important details should not be obscured with a body appendage. Adapt the pose to the garment.

8. Do not outline everything with a heavy black line—it makes garments appear two-dimensional.

The bust and shoulder lines are parallel and should not be drawn at different angles.

Lines above the waist generally bend up, and below the waist, down. Compare the bracelet on the right arm and the belt at the waist.

Do not obscure important details with a body appendage. Adapt the pose to the garment. The bag is cleverly positioned so it will not obscure the intricate embroidery on the right leg.

The center-front of the clothing and figure must be in alignment. Note the zipper.

The figure, particularly the female figure, is formed of curves, and has very few straight lines .

Garments —and the figure underneath-are symmetrical. Note the thighs and the legs of the pants.

Do not outline everything with a heavy black line—it makes garments appear two-dimensional. There is no black line around this silhouette.

Note the cuffs of the pants *curve* around the body.

Points to keep in mind when drawing garments.

skirts

SKIRTS

The first garments we will look at are skirts. Skirts are the simplest of garments to draw but display all the features that have to be clearly shown in good fashion drawing: the type of fabric used, how it is sewn together, how it folds and drapes (the direction in which it falls) and how it fits the figure.

A skirt can be thought of as a single tube, or cylinder, enveloping the body, circling around the waist, flowing over the hip and covering the lower part of the body. Because a woman's hips are wider than the waist various constructional devices are used to eliminate the excess fullness of the fabric and make the garment fit the waist. These devices include seams, tucks, ease, gathers and pleats, all described and explained in detail a few pages on. If the design of the skirt requires that gathers, pleats or shirring (several rows of gathers) are included, then these details require more fabric and they will result in a skirt with a wider hemline. Straight skirts, where a relatively small amount of fullness has to be eliminated at the waist, are usually constructed with darts (v-shaped tucks) or shaped pieces of fabric joined by seams.

Numerous types of skirts exist, differentiated from each other by variations in silhouette and drape—length, fullness, position of the waist, tiering, finishing of the hem and differing construction in the body of the skirt. Included below are descriptions of how to draw three basic types of skirts: straight skirts, full skirts (without pleats) and pleated skirts.

In front view, with the figure posed symmetrically, skirts have little drape. It is usual, then, to draw them on a variation of the S curve pose so the drape of the fabric can be seen. The explanations below are all based on that pose.

Skirts are drawn on the lower part of the figure; and the top half omitted, but a simple version of the rest of the figure can be included if so preferred.

Silhouette   Drape and fit   Details

Skirt lengths. From left, mini; above-the-knee; knee; mid-calf; ankle-length; floor-length.

skirts/
straight skirts

STRAIGHT SKIRTS

Straight skirts have no fullness—the silhouette drops vertically down from the widest point of the hips, or in some cases even tapers back into towards the knees for a sheath-like fit. Straight skirts are drawn with the following steps:

1. Draw in the lower half of a simple S curve silhouette with the weight-bearing leg on the left side. Draw in the waistband as two elliptical lines curving around the figure at the waist.

2. Here we work from top to bottom, but it is also possible to draw the silhouette of the whole skirt and then return to fill in the details. First we fill in the detailing at the top of the skirt—the belt loops and button closure on the waistband and the slash pockets, side seam, princess seams and beginning of the center seam, located on the center-front line of the garment.

3. Continue by drawing the rest of the silhouette of the garment to the hem, which curves around the legs below the knee. Note the skirt drapes below the knee on the non- weight-bearing leg side, indicated by bumps in the silhouette. Draw in the detailing of the covered zipper to the left of the center seam.

4. Plot the position of the main folds—at the crotch and from the hip to the knee– and start to shade the garment. Where the legs touch the fabric the fabric is stretched towards the light and is left unshaded.

5. To finish off, fill in the folds using the side of the pencil. Note the shadows under the belt loops. The dots above the hem represent a hand- or blind-stitched hem. Draw in any other detailing in the waist area such as shirring, pockets and belts. Darts and seams should be drawn at equal distances from the centerfront line of the garment and curve to reflect the position of the figure underneath. Darts and belt loops are usually (though not always) placed on the princess lines. Note that neither hems nor waistlines are drawn as horizontal lines—they are always curves that bend around the figure.

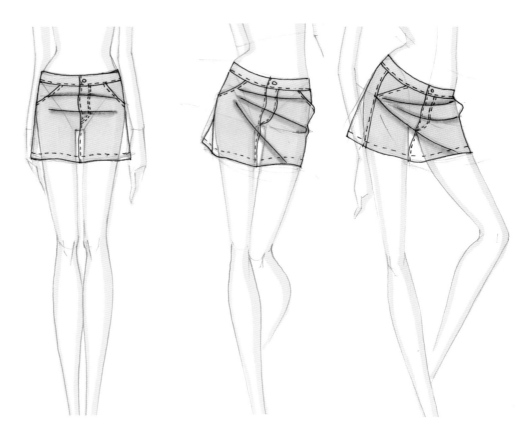

Straight skirt (short): Points of tension/where drape forms. Left, weight equally distributed, front view; center, S curve, front view, weight on left/front leg; right, S curve, three-quarter view, weight on left/front leg. Note in the S curve pose the fabric pulls from the raised hip. Note also that the waistband is not straight but bends around the body.

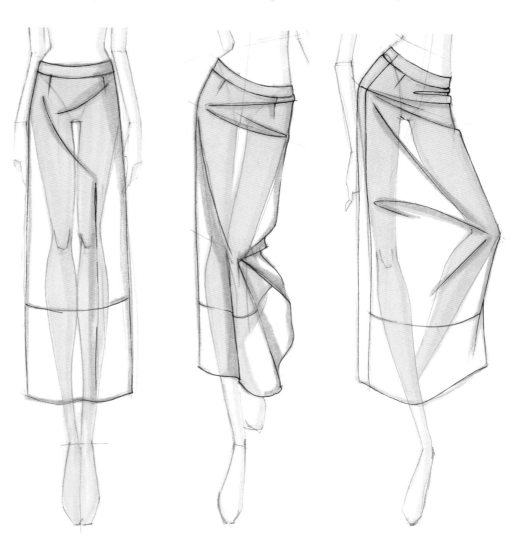

Straight skirt (long): Points of tension/where drape forms. Positions same as short skirt. The weight of the extra fabric creates more drape than a short skirt. Where the knee is against it, the fabric also pulls away from it.

skirts/
straight skirts

  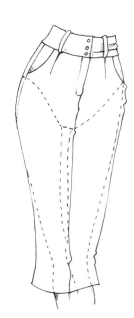  

Drawing straight skirts. 1. Draw a simple below-the-waist S curve silhouette with the weight-bearing leg on the left side. Draw in the waistband as two elliptical lines curving around the figure above the waist .

2. If you prefer to work from top to bottom, fill in the detailing at the waist—the belt loops, button closure, drape in waistband, princess seams and beginning of the center seam. These can also be drawn in last if so preferred.

3. Draw in the hem, which curves around the legs below the knee and the rest of the silhouette. Note the skirt drapes below the knee on the non-weight bearing side. Draw in detailing of the covered zipper.

4. Plot the position of the main folds—at the crotch and from the hip to the knee— and start to shade the garment. Where the legs touch the fabric the fabric is stretched towards the light and is left unshaded.

5. Fill in the folds using the side of the pencil. Note the shadows under the belt loops. The dots above the hem represent a hand- or blind-stitched hem. Draw in any other detailing in the waist area such as shirring, pockets and belts

1. Dart on left; on right, modified sarong-wrap effect with gathers to a diagonal seam and button-over flap.

2. Waistband with belt loops.

3. Pleated skirt with decorative belts and buckles.

4. Waistband and tucks.

Ways the skirt is fitted to the waist.

Shading straight skirts. 1. Draw the silhouette of the skirt keeping in mind that the body is cylindrical and the skirt wraps around it. .

2. Draw in waist details. Belt loops and darts usually sit on princess lines. Tension line falls from hip across front of the body. Areas of excess fabric drape away from the body and are shaded.

3. Shade interior areas of each fold with a smooth tone. Make sure shading is smudged and even. Add darker shadow at far left if light source is on right.

skirts/ full skirts

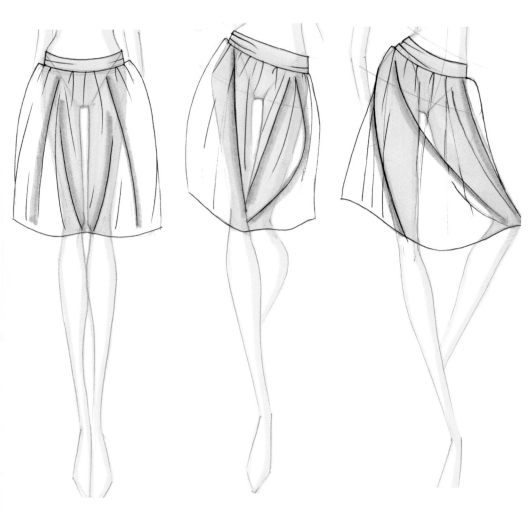

FULL SKIRTS

Full skirts are made with several widths of fabric, either by (i) cutting in a circle with a circular hole for the waist, (ii) gathering or shirring the sewn fabric at the waist, or (iii) sewing together gores—tapered sections of fabric. Gored skirts can contain up to twenty or more gores. The description below is for full skirts that are gathered. Gored skirts are commented on in the next section along with other types of skirts.

1. Lightly draw in the bottom half of the figure and add a simple outline of the outer edge of the silhouette of the garment. The shape of the skirt is an important feature and must be drawn correctly before adding further details of the silhouette and the constructional and design details. Remember to visualize the hem as the front part of an ellipse, curving around the figure.

2. Begin to indicate the positions of the gathers in the body of the skirt. (Gathers are where a wide area of fabric is compressed into a narrower area, described in detail later in the chapter). They all begin at, and not below, the waistband, where the fabric is "gathered" together. Do not make the gathers all the same length, and make the line lighter lower in the garment where the folds become less tight than nearer the waistband.

3. The gathers form folds at the hem of the skirt that have the appearance of cylinders, or cones, alternately facing out and then in. These cylindrical shapes will be of similar size, depending on the weight and stiffness of the fabric (or, sometimes, its motion—for example if a drawing is made of a skirt on a dancing figure). To plot the position of the folds at the hem it is useful to draw in a second line parallel to and above the hem and to draw the folds of the hem—the bottom parts of the cylinders—undulating between this line and the hemline.

4. Because a full skirt contains more fabric the figure is barely discernible under the garment (unless it is made of a transparent or semi-transparent fabric). As with straight skirts, with full skirts in the S curve pose there will be some drape on the side of the raised hip, and a subtle breaking of the fabric at the knee on that side if the skirt falls below the knee, but most of the drape in the skirt comes from the fall of the gathered fabric.

5. Lightweight fabric will form large numbers of shallow folds at the hem; heavier and stiffer fabric will form smaller number of deep folds.

Full skirt: Points of tension/where drape forms. Full skirts flare out from the waist and then form vertical drape. The body defines the drape: drape forms from the knee when it touches the fabric, as seen in the S curve pose at the right.

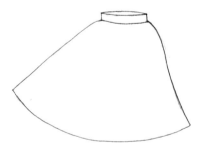

Drawing full skirts.
1. Draw a simple silhouette .

2. Define the gathers at the waist and the folds at the hem (draw a line parallel to the hem to plot the upper boundary of the folds.

3. Fill in the shadows along and under the folds of the drape.

skirts/
pleated skirts

PLEATED SKIRTS

Pleats are another way to control the fullness in full skirts as well as being an attractive and varied design feature in their own right. Pleats are folds inserted into the fabric at regular intervals. They are usually made flat by pressing or, in modern synthetic fabrics they can be permanently applied with a heat-setting process. Often the top part of the pleats are stitched down to give a a sleeker fit at the top of the skirt and enhance the way the pleats fall below (particularly with unpressed pleats that otherwise would not retain their shape). These are called *stitched-down* or *stitch-down pleats*.

There are numerous types of pleats. The techniques for drawing pleated skirts are the same as for all full skirts, but the pleats must be drawn carefully so they are clearly identifiable.

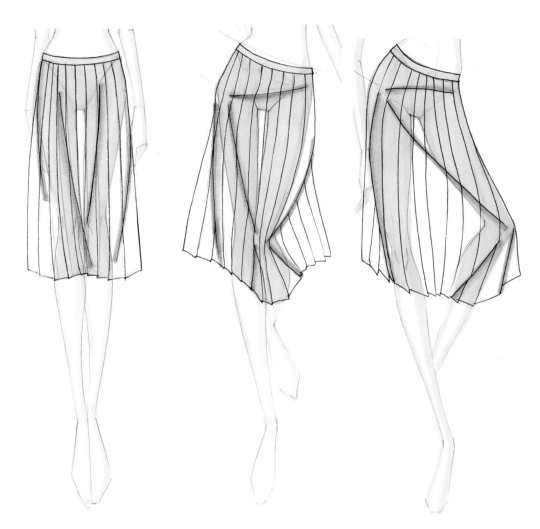

Pleated skirt. Points of tension/where drape forms. Pleated skirts are full skirts and the points of tension and drape lines are as shown in those diagrams.

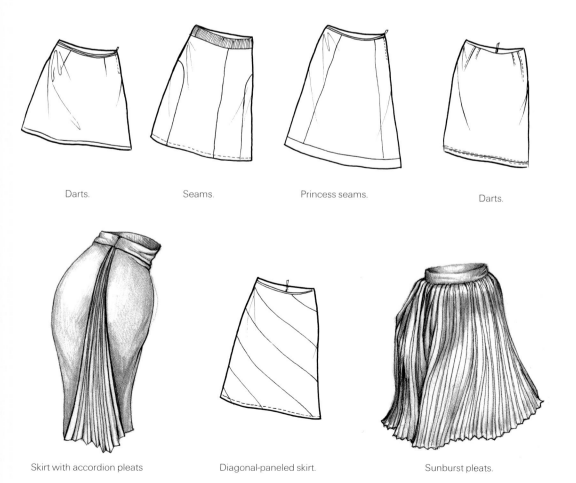

Darts.   Seams.   Princess seams.   Darts.

Skirt with accordion pleats   Diagonal-paneled skirt.   Sunburst pleats.

pleated skirts

Knife pleats, shaded.

Inverted pleats, shaded.

Unpressed pleats, shaded.

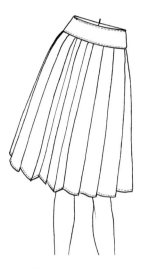

Wide knife (or side) pleats

Inverted pleat
(stitched down)

Kick pleat

Box pleats

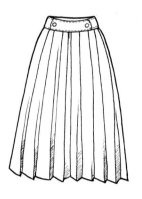

Knife (or side) pleats

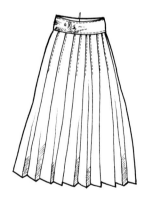

Stitched-down pleats

Mushroom pleats

Skirt with two tiers of
mushroom pleats.

Unpressed pleats

Broomstick skirt. Not strictly a pleated skirt, a
broomstick skirt is made by tying the wet
skirt around a broomstick, producing a vertically wrinkled effect when dry.

Unpressed pleats

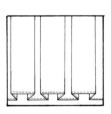

Box pleats

Pleated godet

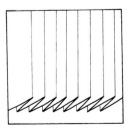

Tight knife pleats

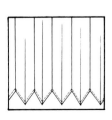

Accordion pleats

Unpressed pleats

skirts/gores/
godets/slits/waists

GORED SKIRTS, GODETS

Gores are shaped sections of fabric that allow the waist of a skirt to be shaped without the use of tucks or gathers. The number of gores used to make up the skirt can range from four to over twenty. The shape of the gores at the hem can be varied to create different hemline silhouettes Godets are pieces of fabric, usually triangular or semi-circular, inserted into the hem of gored skirts at the seams to give a flounced effect.

SLITS are of different lengths and can be located in different parts of skirts, usually along the seams. Except with wraps, where the slit is hidden by the overlapping fabric, slits are shown with a diagonal slash at the top of the slit and shading is used to show the opening.

WAISTS. A reminder shown here in the illustrations: waists can bend both upwards and down, depending on slightly different points of view, but they always bend!

SEAMS, GORES AND YOKES

A seam can run through any section of the garment, helping to create its shape and architecture. A seam is drawn with a thin line. Remember to put seams at the armhole and waist if they are required.

A yoke is a horizontal pattern piece. It is used to control ease or fullness. Yokes are used at the shoulder and at the hip line and now in many different areas of garments.

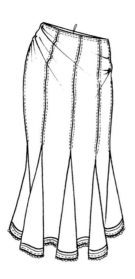

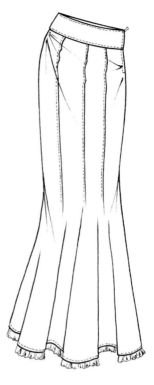

Gored skirt with asymmetrical yok

Gored skirt with set-in godets.

Trumpet skirt. This gored skirt
is cut to flare out at the hem.

Gored skirt with set-in godets.

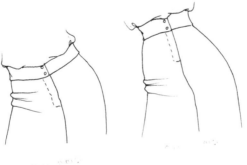

Waists can bend upwards or
downwards, but they do
always bend–if seen straight
on they bend at the edges.

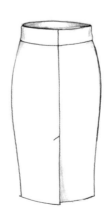

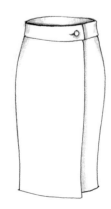

Open slit   Overlapped (kick pleat)   Side slit   Wrap

skirts/flounces/
tiers/exercises

FLOUNCES

Flounces are ruffles—strips of fabric gathered along one edge to form folds—that are attached to the hem of skirts. Flounces can be aplied to both straight and full skirts; they are wider and often of a lighter fabric than the main body of the skirt, so add even more folds.

TIERED SKIRTS

Tiered skirts consist of tiers of fabric—often flounces—on a straight or flared skirt. Tiers are usually attached to an underskirt (though can be attached to each other) and usually overlap.

GATHERS

Gathers—or "gathering"—is where a large area of fabric is compressed into a smaller area, usually at the waist or some other seam.

EXERCISES

1. Choose ten skirts of different types from photos in magazines. Trace the silhouettes practicing varying the line weight and nuancing the line in the silhouette.
2. Copy the same skirts but focus on reproducing the drape and folds accurately.
3. Draw (i) a straight skirt with an inverted pleat; (ii) an accordion-pleated skirt with a gathered waistline; (iii) a straight skirt with a flounce and (iv) a tiered skirt.

Jean-style skirt with flounce. Note the double top stitching typical of jeans and jean-style garments..

Flounce.

Skirt gathered at waist.

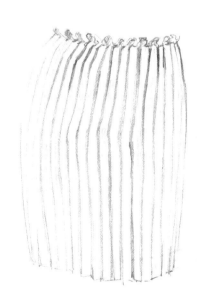

Skirt with knife pleats. Each pleat must be shaded separately.

Tiered skirt. Note that each tier is sewn onto an underskirt, so fits *under* the tier above. Each tier requires a hem; note the hem stitching.

Mini skirt with embroidered yoke and fur mid-section. Silhouette has to be drawn with a broken line to indicate texture of fur.

Ankle-length full skirt. Fabric gathered at waist line and curved at the hem. Use dark values to indicate interiors of deep folds

Stitched-down pleats. Darker shadows form in the center where the body is not close to the fabric.

Complex, tiered, pleated skirt.

Short skirt with darts at waist and asymmetrically tiered accordion pleats. Note the top stitching on the darts.

Start by drawing simplified diagrams of the tiers before adding detail.

skirts/various

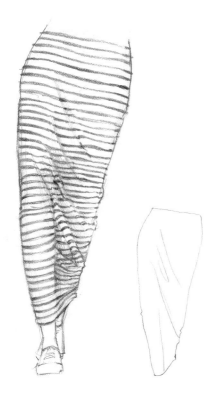

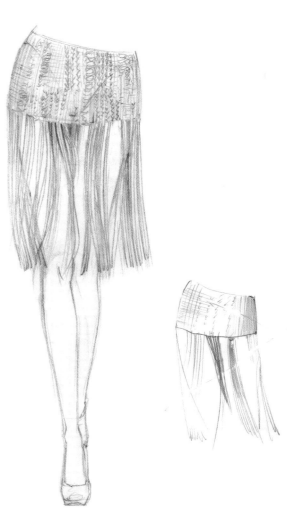

Carefully plot the point where each pleat origi-nates at the waistband and where it ends at the hem.

Ankle-length straight knit skirt with horizontal stripes. Note the bend in the stripes as they are drawn over a drape or around the leg. Using the curve of the hem can help to plan the direction of the stripes higher up the skirt. .

Full skirt with crystal pleating. Note that this complex skirt needs to be carefully shaded to show where areas of pleat fall forward or recede.

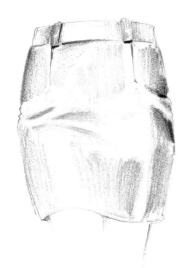

Short leather skirt with belt loops and darts. Note that with leather there is a contrast of values to indi-cate shine. The belt loops are wider than the waistband and have a cast shadow.

Knee-length skirt with long fringe. Note that the fringe falls in a variety of directions creating a sensation of movement.

skirts/various

Short skirt with complex asymmetrical drapes. Shadows are used under the drape to accentuate the depth of the folds of the fabric.

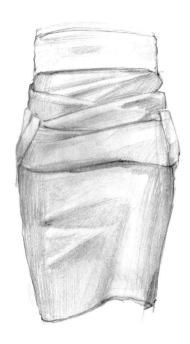

Knee-length skirt with asymmetrically wrapped yoke. Note that shadows on the right side define the shape of the leg underneath.

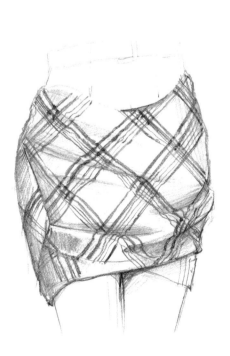

Mini skirt with diagonal plaid pattern. The plaids have to follow carefully the curve of the drape.

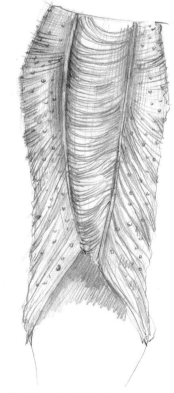

Beaded, ruched skirt with two seams. Lots of shading is used to create dimension in the complex drape and underneath each bead.

Handkerchief hemmed skirt.

Skirt with scalloped hem.

Skirt with lace-trimmed hem.

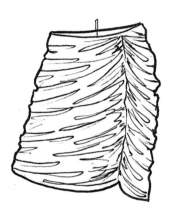

Ruched skirt.

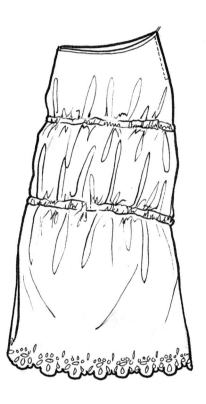

Three-section ruched skirt with lace-trimmed hem.

Short skirt with fringed hem.

Short skirt with tucked seams at hem.

Knee-length skirt with trapunto stitching.

Skirt with transparent lower section.

Skirt and blouse combination.

Skirts in combinations with blouse
and scarf and blouse and sweater.

pants/general points

PANTS

Since women now engage in most activties that were previously restricted to men, they have, quite naturally, increasingly adopted the garment most suited to a large number of those activities: pants. Pants (or slacks) are practical, comfortable and stylish and are now worn on a wide variety of occasions ranging from formal evening and career wear to all manner of sports and casual wear.

Pants can be difficult to draw and care must be taken to make sure they look right. They can be thought of as being made up of six sections—the waist area, the hip/pelvis area, each of the top part of the legs from hip to knee and each of the bottom part of the legs from knee to ankle (or wherever the legs end). Care should be taken to ensure each section is correctly drawn. Note that the left and right leg are thought of separately as they are usually posed differently, so are of different shapes and the drape of the fabric will be different.

GENERAL POINTS TO KEEP IN MIND WHEN DRAWING PANTS

There are a number of other key points to be kept in mind when drawing pants:
(i) It is important to make sure that the center-front of the garment and the center-front of the body are aligned at all times so the pants are seen as properly fitting the figure.
(ii) If a zipper is included, then the flap covering the zipper must be drawn and positioned correctly: the zipper is always indepedent of the waistband; it ends at the bottom of the waistband and there is a snap or button at the waistband to allow access to the zipper. Zippers are almost always placed on seams, whether front, back or side, and it is important to show this seam continuing below the zipper.
(iii) Hems must be drawn in the correct position, according to the style of pant being drawn. They must also be seen to bend around the leg.
(iv) Details—and these have become increasingly varied and important styling elements—items such as pockets, pleats, belt loops, fly labels and bar tacks must be drawn correctly and in the correct position; they are often accompanied with top-stitching.

Silhouette

Drape and fit

Details

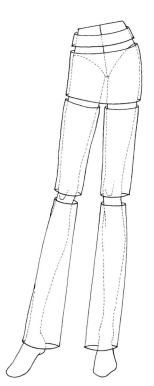

For drawing purposes pants can be thought of as comprised of six sections.

It is important to make sure that the center-front of the garment and the center-front of the body are aligned at all times so the pants are seen as properly fitting the figure.

When the leg bends, the pant breaks at the knee. Drape in pants appears in each leg and the waist/thigh section.

points of tension/ drawing pants

(v) The lines that define pants are mainly vertical. When drawing, it is easier to work from the top of the page downwards so one is always drawing on clean paper and the drawing is less likely to be smudged. It also seems intuitively easier and more natural to show the length of a pant leg that falls downwards by making downwards strokes.

(vi) In pant legs most of the drape appears at the knee where the garment is not as closely fitted to allow for movement of the joint. See Chapter Six: Fabrics for how to show drape in different fabrics.

DRAWING PANTS

To draw pants, begin by drawing the bottom half of the croquis—from the waist to the feet. (For both pants and skirts the garments can, if so desired, also be drawn on the full croquis and paired with a simple t-shirt or top.) It is best to use a variation of an S curve pose when drawing pants, so that the drape can be clearly seen in the supporting leg, along with the fit and construction details. Choose a pose with the legs apart so the silhouette can be clearly seen.

1. Draw in the waistband as two parallel curves. Think of the waist as an elliptical shape extending round the back of the figure, with the part that is seen as the front part of that ellipse. It is usual to draw the waistband as upwardly sloping, as though the point of view was slightly below; if the pants are low-cut then the waistband can be drawn sloping down. If there is no waistband only one line is drawn. Note that there are folds and drape in almost all waistbands—only a small number contain internal construction that eliminates it.
2. Draw the silhouette of the hips and pelvis area of the pants. All pants have a center-front seam, and this should be drawn in lightly. Draw in the princess lines (as guidelines) midway between the center-front and the edge of the pants.
l

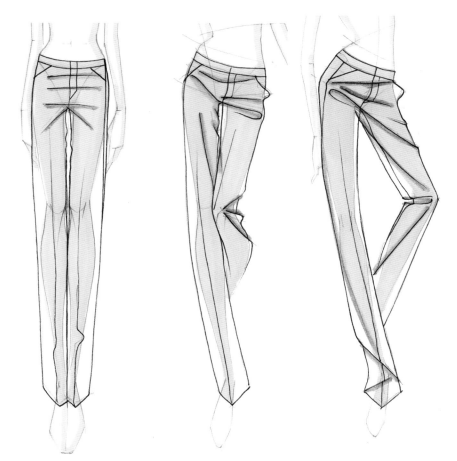

Straight-legged pants. Points of tension/where drape forms. Left, weight equally distributed, front view; center, S curve, front view, weight on left/front leg; right, S curve, three-quarter view, weight on left/front leg. Note in the S curve pose the fabric pulls from the raised hip.

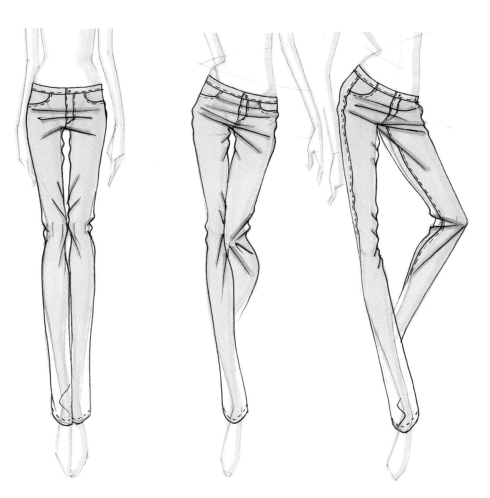

Jeans. Points of tension/where drape forms. Positions same as straight-legged pants above. Denim is a heavier fabric than that used in the pants above and forms wider folds.

drawing pants/
various styles/exercise

3. Draw in the inside edge of the support leg from the crotch to the ankle. This can be drawn either as one line, stopping at the knee to indicate folds, (particularly for fabrics like denim which is a thicker fabric and will have wider folds) and continuing to the ankle, or as two, with a small area of overlap at the knee to indicate the subtle break of a more classic cut and fabric with slightly more body.

4. Draw in the hemline of the support leg. For both legs, the hemline is a shallow curve that bends out from the ankle. As when drawing the waistline, the shape is basically that of half an ellipse, varying according to the position of the leg and width of the pant leg. For wide-legged pants the hem can extend beyond the line of the hip; for average width pants the edge of the hem will fall almost directly beneath the hip line.

5. Draw in the other side of the support leg. If the hem is wide a fold of drape forms at the hip and falls diagonally across the leg to the outer edge of the ankle (in slimmer pants this drape line is less obvious). When drawing pants in three-quarter view, as we are doing here, the side seam is visible, so first draw in the outside silhouette of the pant, following the line of the leg and then a second line to show the side seam. The line of the side seam is close to and almost parallel to the outside silhouette of the pant; its exact location depends on the width of the pant leg.

6. Draw in the outside edge of the other leg from waist to ankle, If the leg is straight it can be drawn as one straight line from waist to ankle. If the leg is bent, as in the drawing here it angles at the knee. Draw in the hem as with the support leg. The hem fits against the front of the leg and forms drape behind the leg. Draw in the inside edge of the leg from the crotch to the hem again using two lines representing the inside silhouette of the pant leg and the inseam of the pant leg.

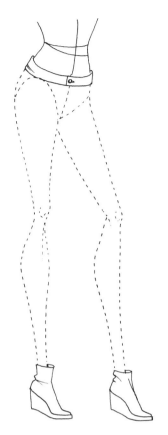

1. Draw in the waistband as two parallel lines. Think of it as two ellipses usually sloping–up or down. Drawing pants is complicated so study detailed instructions in text.

2. Draw the silhouette of the hips and pelvis area. Lightly draw in c-f seam and princess lines.

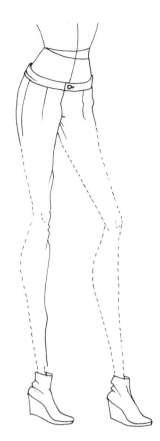

3. Draw in the inside edge of the support leg as one or two lines indicating folds at knee. Study detailed instructions in text.

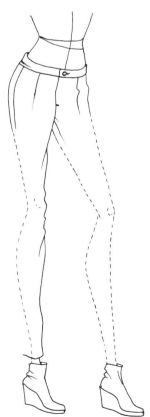

4. Draw in the hemline of the support leg–a shallow curve bending from ankle in shape of an ellipse.

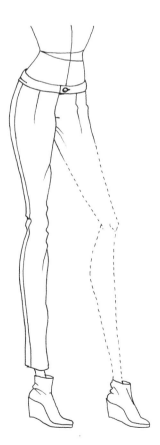

5. Draw in other side of support leg. Study detailed instructions in text. .

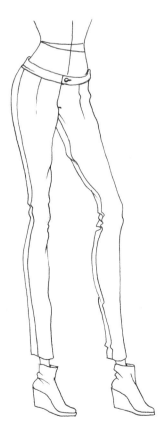

6. Draw in outside edge of other leg from waist to ankle. Study detailed instructions in text.

drawing pants/ various styles

DRAWING PANTS (CONTINUED)

7. Up to this point the instructions can apply to drawing almost any type of slim-legged pant. From this point we finish off our drawing as a pair of denim jeans and the instructions refer to jeans only.

Draw in the pockets– classic jeans j pockets. The pockets are each indicated using two thin lines of stitches–they look like a column of ants–called double- needle cover stitches, a stitch used to sew down thick fabric. Draw in the belt loops placed on the princess lines and usually wider than the waistband.

8. Draw in the cuffs. Notice that they are wider than the pant leg and are drawn parallel to the hem.

9. Add the zipper on the right side of the center-front seam. Note that women's jeans have the zipper on the same side as in a men's pant–the right. The zipper is indicated by a broken line of double-needle cover stitch from the center-front seam curving to the right and then going paralle to the center-front seam up to the waistband. Double needle stitching is also indicated on the waistband. The inseam has a line of single-needle stitching stretching from the bottom of the cuff to the crotch.

10. Add drape at the crotch, down the upper leg and at the knee. Look for the areas where the body bends to indicate drape. Examine the diagrams on the previous page showing points of tension and drape.

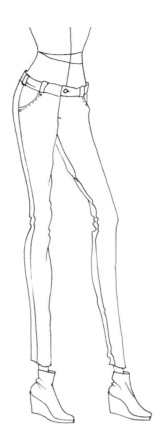

7. From this point detailing is added that identifies the type of pant– in this case a denim jean. Draw in pockets and belt loops. Study detailed instructions in text.

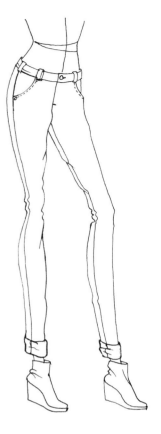

8. Draw in cuffs. Note they are wider than the pant leg and are drawn parallel to the hem.

9. Add zipper on right–in jeans the same side as in men's pants. The zipper is shown by broken line of d-n stitching, also seen at waistband and inseam.

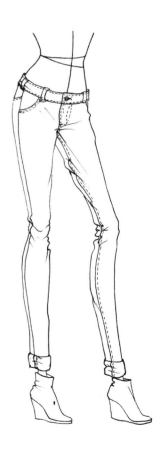

10. Add drape at the crotch, down the upper leg and at the knee. Look for the areas where the body bends to indicate drape.

drawing pants/
various styles

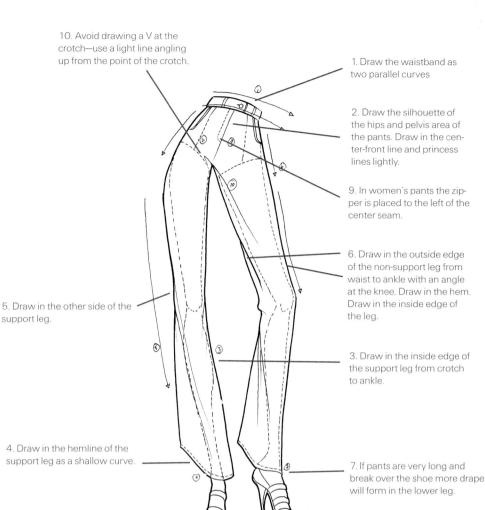

10. Avoid drawing a V at the crotch—use a light line angling up from the point of the crotch.

1. Draw the waistband as two parallel curves

2. Draw the silhouette of the hips and pelvis area of the pants. Draw in the center-front line and princess lines lightly.

9. In women's pants the zipper is placed to the left of the center seam.

6. Draw in the outside edge of the non-support leg from waist to ankle with an angle at the knee. Draw in the hem. Draw in the inside edge of the leg.

5. Draw in the other side of the support leg.

3. Draw in the inside edge of the support leg from crotch to ankle.

4. Draw in the hemline of the support leg as a shallow curve.

7. If pants are very long and break over the shoe more drape will form in the lower leg.

Steps for drawing pants. See main text for detailed explanations..

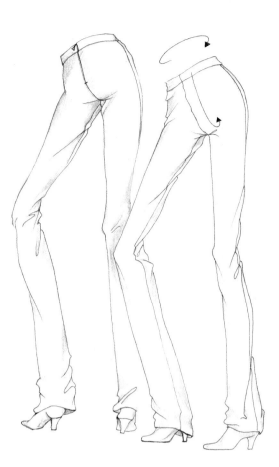

A common pose when drawing pants is to show one leg bent. The fabric of the pant must be shown draping from crotch to knee. Note that the c-f seam/zipper bends all the way under the crotch.

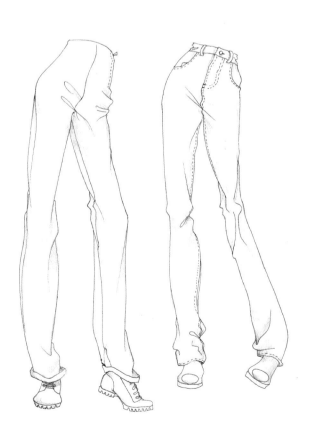

Left, pant with crease. Note the hem ends at a point and drapes as it falls over the shoe. Center, a cuffed-hem pant. The hem bends around the pant and is wider than the pant leg. Right, note that the hem of the pant curves in the same direction as the foot and shoe.

drawing wider pants/exercise

DRAWING PANTS WITH A WIDER CUT

Where pants are cut more fully, with more fabric, more drape is seen.

1. Draw the bottom half of the croquis in three-quarter view. These pants are low-waisted so indicate the waistband using two parallel lines bending down as ellipses below the waist.

2. Draw in the center-front seam of the pant paying close attention to the curve of the seam below the crotch. Draw the silhouette of the pant around the hips, with appropriate bumps in the line at the hip on the right leg where it is bending. On the support leg, on the left, a little drape is shown but it is not as pronounced as on the other leg. With long, full pants the fabric falls over the shoe. Note that the pant is drawn closer to the right sides of the legs following the position of the body underneath.

3. For wider cut pants the areas where most drape is seen are (i) from the crotch to the knee, (ii) from the knee to the ankle and (iii) from the hip to the ankle. In this drawing the drape originates at the crotch and extends to the knee on the right hand side and then from the knee to the ankle, and on the left, from the hip to the mid-calf and ankle areas.

4. Add stitching for the zipper, waistband, pockets and belt loops. Note that for this formal women's pant the zipper lies on the left side of the center-front seam. Dots are drawn at the hemline to indicate a blind-stitched hem (a hand-stitched hem). Shade appropriately in the interiors of each fold.

EXERCISE

Draw 10 styles of pants clearly showing fit and drape.

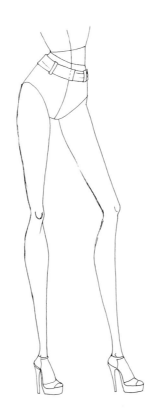

1. Draw the bottom half of the croquis in ¾ view. These pants are low-waisted so indicate with two parallel elliptical lines below waist.

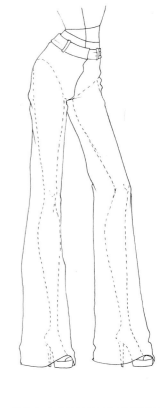

2. Draw in c-f seam of pant, paying attention to curve of seam below crotch. Draw silhouette around hips indicating drape on right. Pant falls over show. Note pant drawn closer to right leg, following position of body underneath.

3. For wider pants drape is seen from crotch to knee, knee to ankle and hip to ankle. See detailed instructions in text.

4. Add stitching for the zipper, waistband, pockets and belt loops. Note here the zipper lies on the left side of the center-front seam. Dots are drawn at the hemline to indicate a blind-stitched hem. Shade in the interiors of each fold.

pant lengths/hem treatments/details

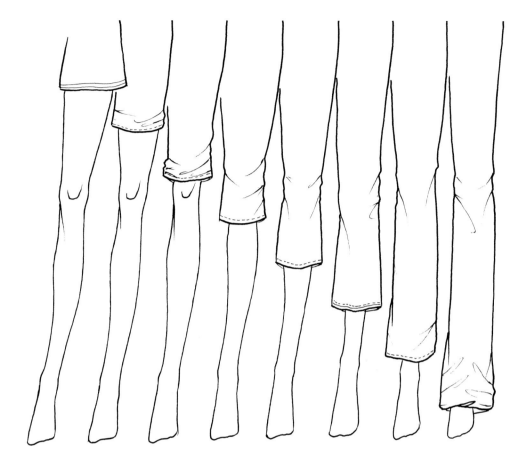

Pant lengths, from left: short shorts; mid-thigh; above-the-knee; knee; below-the-knee; mid-calf; above-the-ankle; floor.

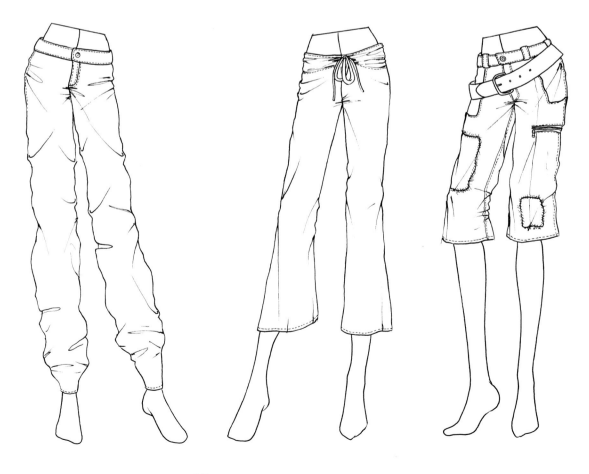

Different lengths and hem treatments, detailing.

pants/jeans

Drawing classic five-pocket denim jeans.
1. Draw the silhouette and croquis. Note the double row of top-stitching is included right from the start. Without this important feature the garment will not look like jeans.

2. Indicate the drape at the thigh and knee using the side of the pencil.

3. Finish off the shading using a 2B pencil.

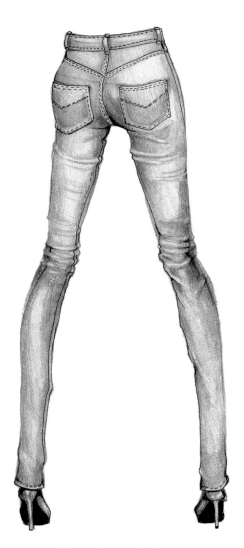

Skinny leg jeans back view.

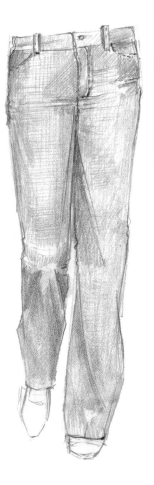

Denim jeans, three-quarter, back and front views. Denim is a thick,
heavyweight fabric that drapes in wide folds. Note in these drawings
that everything—the cuffs, belts and legs—*bends* around the body.
The zipper is placed to the right of the center-front seam.

pants/jeans/
shorts

Stretch-denim skinnyleg pants. Made with diagonal seams and two types of denim. Note that for this pant, as for all denim pants, the stitching at the zipper seam, pockets and inseams is double needle.

Slim-fit denim jeans with cutouts at knees.

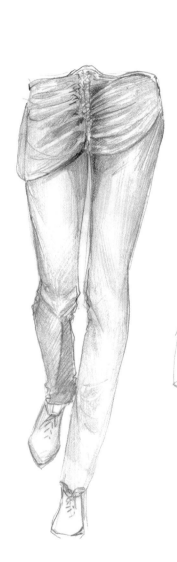

Designer pant with ruched fabric sewn from center seam below waist. Note that the folds of the ruching are shaded with a dark value and shadows are also added under the draped section of fabric to indicate depth.

Cutoff cuffed denim pants.

Cutoff denim shorts.

pants/jeans/
shorts

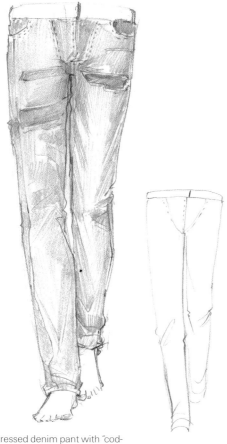

Stressed denim pant with "cod-
piece" stitching at crotch.

Cuffed shorts with pleated yoke
belted at waist.

Cuffed capri with lapped zipper.

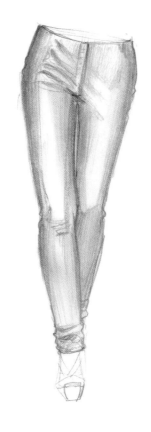

Tight-fitting pants with c-f zipper.

Designer jodhpur–inspired pant.

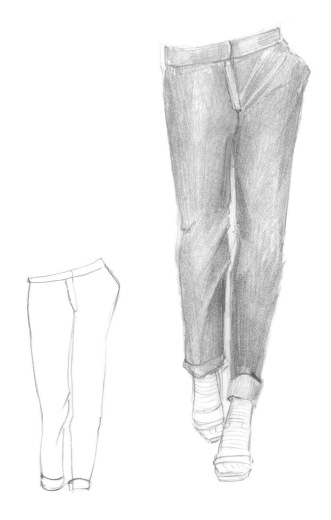

Harem pant. The soft fabric is cut wide and falls in full, wide folds. These are indicated by light shading in the interior of each fold. Note the left leg is bent and the foreshortening is indicated by shading from knee to ankle. Where the legs touch the fabric of the pant it is stretched and does not fold, so appears lighter than the draped fabric in the other parts of the pant.

Straight-legged pant with low-cut waistline, cuffed hem. Note that cuffs bend in a convex or concave curve—in this case, the front cuff bends up as the leg is angled forward, and the back cuff bends down as the leg is angled back.

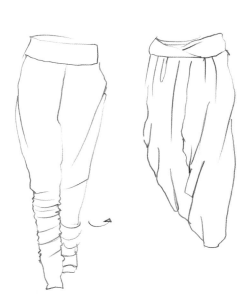

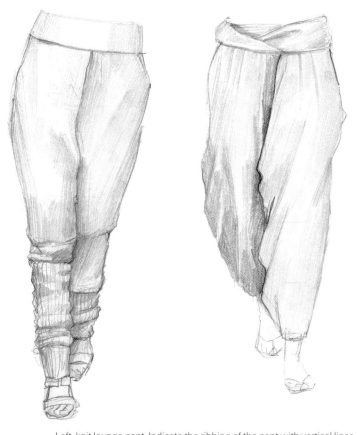

Left, knit lounge pant. Indicate the ribbing of the pant with vertical lines that bend around each fold. Right, harem pant with asymmetrical waist.

Typical combination of denim jean and jacket. Jeans have patched knees. Show the seams that give the shape of the patches and add shading at the edges to show the patches have thickness and sit on top of the jeans.

Jacket and pant by Rick Owens.

pants/jodhpurs

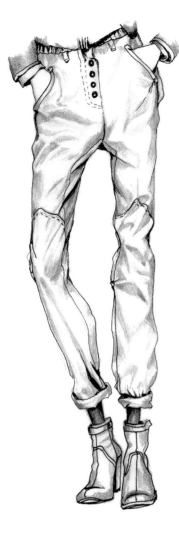

Designer jodhpur made of fabric that drapes easily. Notice the cowl draping at the hips and above the knees.

Designer chino with rolled cuffs, exposed fly-front buttoned closure. Note the hands in the pockets create drape under the pockets. Note the clearly defined seaming at crotch and above knees bends around the shape of the body in those areas.

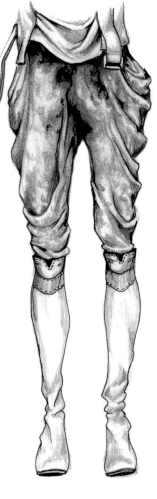

High waist dress slacks with center-front crease and bootleg silhouette at hem.

High-waist slim-leg flared pant. Note how the pattern of the pants bends around the body underneath and around the folds of the drape.

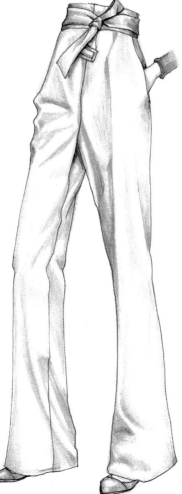

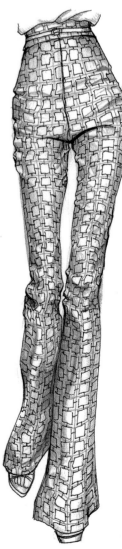

blouses/shirts/tops/

BLOUSES, SHIRTS, TOPS, KNITTED
SWEATERS/TOPS
BLOUSES are feminine garments constructed
either with or without a collar and with or without
buttoned fronts, They are usually lighter and of
softer fabric than shirts (which are primarily
mens-wear but have also been adopted by
women). Blouses are generally drawn using more
soft drape than shirts.

SHIRTS usually have more tailoring than blouses,
often with long sleeves, sleeve plackets, cuffs, collar stands and collars, buttons and button
bands/extensions. Because of the construction
they contain shirts also generally have more
straight lines than blouses. Illustrations of a number of different shirts for women are included in
this section.

TOPS is the generic name for all garments worn
on the upper body, so includes blouses and shirts,
but usually refers to a less formal and less constructed garment—for example, camis and t's.
Tops are often used in active sports (or adapted
as casualwear from active sportswear), but are
also worn as eveningwear, usually revealing a
combination of arms, neck and chest and back.

Silhouette   Drape and fit   Details

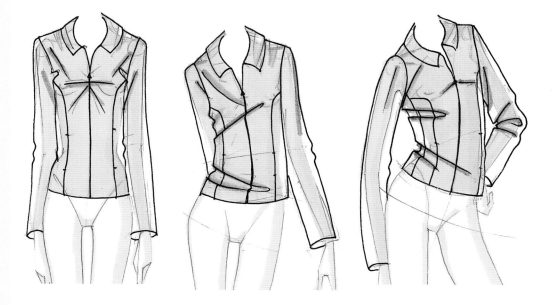

Blouses. Points of tension/where drape forms. Left, torso straight—note the tension line at the bust; center, left shoulder down in typical S curve pose—note the
tension points at the waist and diagonally from the bust as the bust slopes down;
right, left shoulder down in S curve pose, three-quarter view with right arm bent
and left away from body—tension points seen under armholes, at bend of right
arm , at bust and at the waist on the left side where the body is compressed.

157

blouses/shirts/tops

DRAWING A SHIRT OR BLOUSE

Blouses and shirts are usually made of woven fabrics that do not stretch and drape away from the body. It is important to show this fullness when drawing them. (A DO NOT DO is to draw the garment as though it appears to be tattooed on the skin.)

1. Draw the upper part of the body in three-quarter view. Define the center-front line carefully.

2. Working from top to bottom, define the collar band as an elliptical form around the neck. The shoulder seam rests on the shoulders. The armhole bends elliptically around the arm and is wider than the arm. A side seam is drawn from the armhole to the waist in this design; the outer line is the silhouette of the blouse. Note that the blouse is fuller above the waistline, where it is gathered in. A placket is drawn from the center of the collar, on each side of the center-front of the garment, reaching down to the gathered waist and from there to the shirt tail front of the blouse. Indicate the gathers forming at the waist and the spread of the blouse below the waist.

3. The long set-in sleeve is drawn with drape at the lower armhole and elbow and is gathered to a cuff above the wrist. Note that the upper arm and forearm are cylindrical forms and to appear correct the drape has to look as though it is curving round the cylinders at the elbow and cuff. Do not draw straight lines when drawing a cuff! Make them bend!

4. The upper part of the collar starts at the top of the collar band and slopes down to the shoulder line. As this is three-quarter view, the line of the collar is shorter and closer to the vertical on the side furthest away, longer and less steeply sloped on the nearer side. The collar bends around the neck and ends at a point on each side. The spread of the collar—the edge that runs from the top button to the point—is drawn as a slightly upward-curving line down to the points. More details are added, including a second line at the shoulder to indicate a yoke, a button with a horizontal button hole at the center-front of the collar band and buttons drawn evenly spaced down the front of the placket with vertical buttonholes.

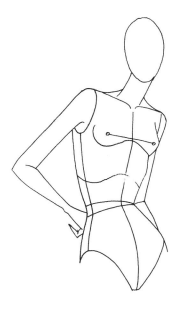

1. Draw the upper part of the body in three-quarter view. Define the center-front line carefully.

2. Work from top to bottom defining collar band as elliptical form. The armhole is also elliptical. See detailed instructions in text.

3. Long set-in sleeve is drawn with drape at the lower armhole and elbow and is gathered to cuff above wrist. Drape in sleeves looks like it is curving around cylinders. Cuffs always bend.

4. The upper part of the collar starts at top of collar band and slopes to shoulder. Collar bends around neck and ends at points on each side. More details are added including yoke, button and hole c-f collar and buttons down placket with veritcal buttonholes.

tops/blouses

Three-quarter length sleeve blouse with hidden placket and basic collar. Note that the shading subtly defines the shape of the bust underneath and that the placket as well as the stripes also curve to suggest the shape underneath.

Camisole top with cowl neckline and embroidered shawl. Note the soft wide shading that defines the wide folds of the cowl. The shawl is made of a shinier fabric so is drawn using two values of shading.

Shirt with basic collar, hidden placket and cuffs on the figure. Note the shading under the collar to indicate that the collars "stands up" above the front of the shirt, shading under the placket, around the cuffs and sleeves. When shading sleeves always think of shading a cylinder.

Shirt with basic collar, hidden placket and cuffs.

Shirt with basic collar, hidden placket and cuffs, opened at front to show garment underneath and positioning of buttons.

tops/blouses

Peasant blouse with wide gathered neckline, drawstring tie, ruffle cuffs, tucked into belt creating blouson effect—a wide drape.

Self-tie long-sleeved blouse. The collar stand, which curves around the neck above the shoulders, extends into the tie. The "set in" sleeves are attached to the body of the blouse with seams at the shoulder.

Drop shoulder blouse with wide bateau (boat) neckline and asymmetrical hem.

Scoop neck wide armhole top with bias trim. Note the soft folds of this garment could indicate a knit or lightweight fabric.

Empire waisted camisole with spaghetti straps and embroidered brassiere. This garment is made of a very lightweight fabric gathered into the bustline, forming many folds that appear as slim cylinders, indicated by shading lightly between each fold.

Spiral-strapped sleeves sewn into bias trim. The diagonal slope of the armholes echoes the shape of a raglan sleeve.

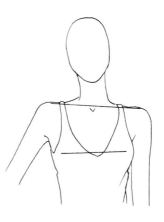

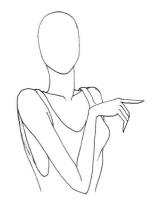

Scoop neckline tiered ruffle sleeveless blouse. Ruffles are drawn with shadows in the interior—the valleys—of the folds.

When drawing tops make sure the shoulder line and bustline line point the same way.

DO NOT DO. Do not hide important style lines and details with the position of the arm and hand.

Wide spread Windsor collar blouse with asymmetrical button closure and button-down yoke, three-quarter length sleeves with cuffs, multiple-tiered knife pleats gathered into empire waist. All the parts of the blouse and each of the pleats have to be shaded individually in order to make the construction clear.

Long blouse with self-tie wrap and raglan sleeves, rolled collar with high stand, standing above the shoulder. Tie must be carefully shaded so the knot appears to curve around the edges of the tie.

Dress blouse with hidden placket and short set-in sleeves gathered at arm-holes, decorative seams. Indicate gathers with wide shading inside the folds. The gathers cause the outline of the blouse to curve up from the shoulder.

Convertible collar long-sleeved shirt

Plackets and buttons must be drawn to follow the shape of the body underneath—especially noticeable when drawn in three-quarter view.

blouses/shirt/
corsets

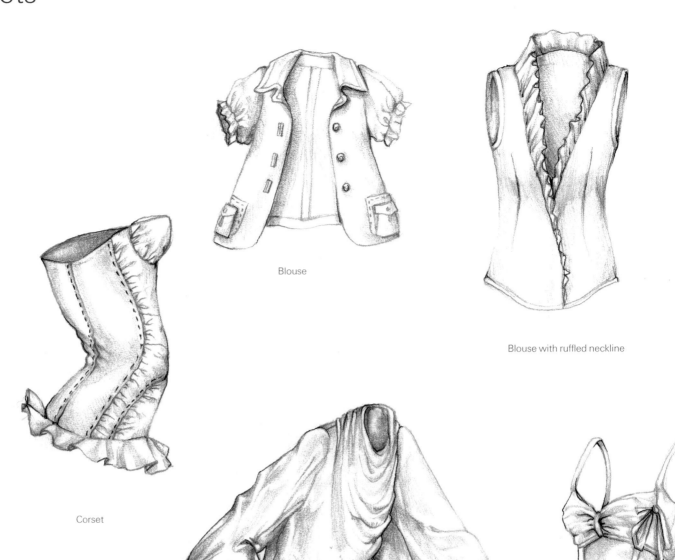

Blouse

Blouse with ruffled neckline

Corset

Blouse with cowl neckline

Corset with ruched brassiere.

Blouse with Bertha collar.

Short-sleeved shirt.

Asymmetrical top.

Double-breasted blouse.

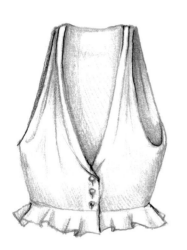

Ruffle hemmed top.

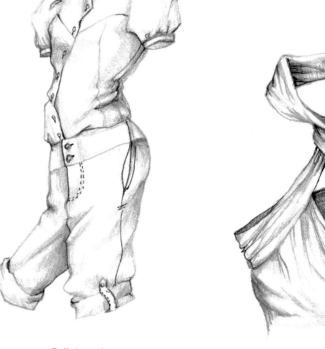

Puff-sleeved top.

Twisted halter-neck top.

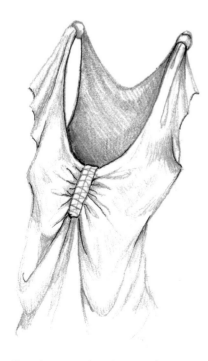

Sleeveless top gathered to center inset.

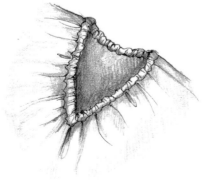

Gathering at neckline.

T-shirt.

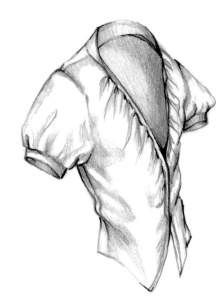

Blouse with short sleeves gathered at cuff.

Spaghetti-tie top with floral appliqué.

Slip-style top

Sleeveless top gathered into empire waist below bust.

Blouse with smocking on yoke and armband.

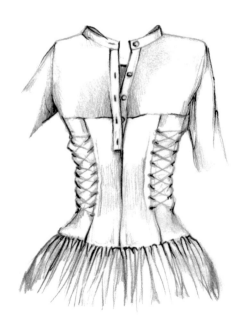

Blouse with fagoting and buttoned placket.

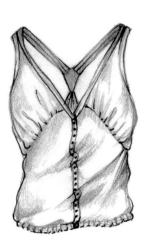

Sleeveless top with diagonal gathers below bust. .

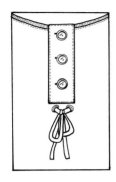

Flap front with tie.

Lace trim

Shirring

Embroidered cuff with tie.

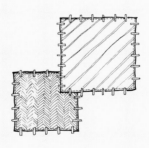

Patch pocket with ruffles and tie.

Square pocket with inverted pleat and ruffles.

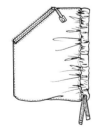

Zip pocket with gathers and tie.

Appliqués with whip stitching.

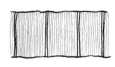

Trim.

Eyelet trim.

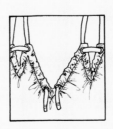

String ties.

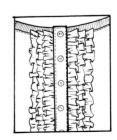

Ruffles

Padded zip pocket.

Ribbon trim with tie.

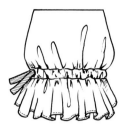

Cuff with casing.

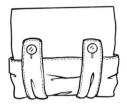

Button tab with cuff.

Scalloped lace trim.

Puff sleeve.

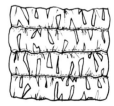

Ruching.

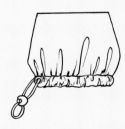

Cuff with button tab stop.

Herringbone trim.

Zip pocket with lacing and gathers.

Cuff with string tie.

Floral appliqué.

sleeves/set-in/ raglan/kimono

Although there is a wide variety of sleeve styles, most consist of one of three types:
1. SET-IN SLEEVES, cut in one or two pieces (in tailored jackets and coats two pieces is more common) and attached to the armhole with a seam around the upper arm where it joins the shoulder.
2. RAGLAN SLEEVES, attached to the bodice of the garment with a diagonal seam or seams (up to three) that ext- ends up to the collar.
3. KIMONO SLEEVES, which are cut in one piece with the bodice of the garment and seamed above and below the arm.

Sleeves can be straight and formal, as in tailored garments, sometimes combined with shoulder padding to give an exaggeratedly geometric silhouette, or soft and magnificent, with fullness and drape both above and below the elbow.

The arm is one of the parts of the body shaped like a cylinder, and sleeves, which cover the arms, take a similar form. It is important to keep this in mind when drawing sleeves and to draw them to appear three-dimensional, bending around the arm. With eye level at the middle of the sleeve-on-the-arm, close to the elbow, sleeve hems appear to bend upwards above the elbow and downwards below the elbow. Above the elbow the sleeve rests along the upper arm and excess fabric hangs below; below the elbow the sleeve rests on the inside edge of the arm from the elbow to the wrist and excess fabric drapes beneath.

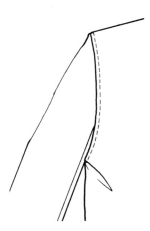

Set-in sleeve.

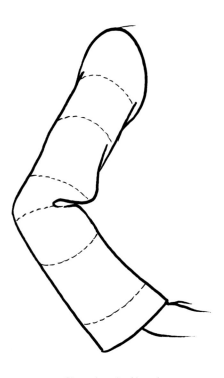

Sleeve lengths. Note the upward curve of the sleeve hems above the elbow and the downward cuve below the elbow.

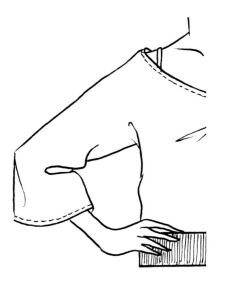

Kimono sleeve.

Raglan sleeve.

sleeves/narrow

NARROW SLEEVES

The main differences in sleeves when drawing them are between narrow and full sleeves rather than the three types of sleeves.

1. First draw the arm with elbow bent so that the detailing at the hem of the sleeve will be closest to the point of view.

2.With narrow fitted sleeves where the cap (the area of the sleeve where it fits into the armhole) sits at the point where the upper arm meets the shoulder (the usual position for tailored or more formal sleeves), first draw the cap, starting at the back of the shoulder, and then continue with a smooth, quick line to the elbow. The cap bends around the shoulder.

3. At the elbow the silhouette bulges out where the excess fabric that allows for ease of movement at this joint breaks. Draw this area nuancing the line to show where the fabric bends in and is in shadow (thicker line) and where it is straight and reflects the light (thinner line). The sleeve may be constructed from a drop shoulder and appear more relaxed, or a pad may be used that gives a sleeve a more architectural appearance. If the cap sits off the shoulder (a dropped shoulder sleeve), the cap is drawn as an upward curve around the upper arm below the shoulder.

4. Draw the other side of the arm starting just inside the first line showing the cap of the sleeve at the back of the shoulder, and continuing with a quick, smooth line to the wrist. The overlapping lines indicate the slight break in the fabric at the shoulder line where the body is present under the garment. WIth a dropped shoulder sleeve the line continues down from the lower-placed cap and there is no break in the fabric.

5. Add detailing. Sleeves end in hems or cuffs. Make sure to show hems and cuffs resting on the wrist—again, fabric is subject to the laws of gravity even when it bends. When seen front view with the arm hanging by the side cuffs slope up from the outer arm to the inner arm. The details of hems or cuffs should be drawn in last. Gathers, as with gathers at the cap at the other end of the sleeve should be drawn straight out from the seam and hooked over at the end.

6.Add shading.

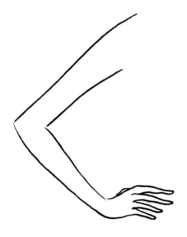

Drawing narrow sleeves. 1. Draw the arm with the elbow bent.

2. Draw the cap, starting at the back of the shoulder, continuing with a smooth, quick line to the elbow.

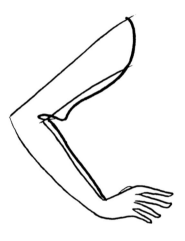

3. At the elbow the silhouette bulges to indicate the excess fabric required for ease of movement. Use a nuanced line here. Continue the line to the wrist.

4. Draw the other side of the arm starting just inside the first line, and continuing with a quick, smooth line to the wrist. The overlapping lines indicate the slight break in the fabric at the shoulder line.

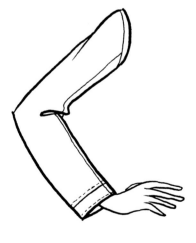

5. Add detailing.

6. Add shading.

sleeves/full/
exercises

FULL SLEEVES

1. Draw the arm with elbow bent so that the detailing at the hem of the sleeve will be clearly displayed.

2. For sleeves with fullness, start drawing the cap and the line of the inner side of the sleeve but stop the line where the drape of the fullness of the sleeve appears in front of it. Indicate this with a line that starts around the mid-upper arm, forms a wide fold and creases at the elbow. All these lines are curved, without angles, and are continuous and unbroken, showing the fabric's drape.

3., 4.Below the elbow, if there is fullness in the fabric the silhouette is fuller. If the garment is made of a stiff fabric the fullness will stand out from the arm underneath on both sides; if made of lightweight fabric the excess fabric falls only on the outer (lower) edge of the sleeve. Draw in the sihouette of the other side of the sleeve and indicate the position of the gathering at the cuff.

5. Make sure to show hems and cuffs resting on the wrist—fabric is subject to the laws of gravity even when it bends. When seen front view, with the arm hanging by the side, cuffs slope up from the outer arm to the inner arm.

6. The details of hems or cuffs should be drawn in last. Draw the gathers like petals, extending straight out from the seam and bending over at the end. They do not intersect.

Full sleeves can be gathered at the cap as well as the cuffs (puff and balloon sleeves are examples of this).

EXERCISES

1. Draw a blouse with six different types of sleeve.

2. Draw a full gathered sleeve (i) with a light fabric and (ii) with a heavier fabric. Show clearly the differences in the drape of the fabric when arm is bent.

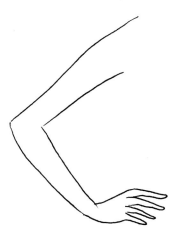

Drawing full sleeves. 1. Draw the arm with the elbow bent.

2. Start drawing the cap and the line of inner side of the sleeve but stop the line as the drape of the fullness of the sleeve appears in front of it, and indicate this with a line that starts around the mid-upper arm, forms a wide fold and creases at the elbow.

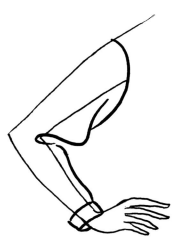

3. Continue below the elbow matching the silhouette to the amount of fullness in this area. Stiff fabrics stand out on either side of the arm; lighter fabrics will fall on the lower edge only.

4. Draw in the sihouette of the other side of the sleeve and indicate the position of the gathering at the cuff. Make sure to show the cuff resting on the wrist.

5. Add more detailing in the cuff area.

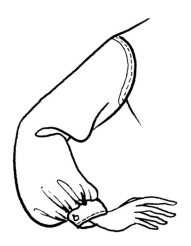

6. Finish off detailing and add shading.

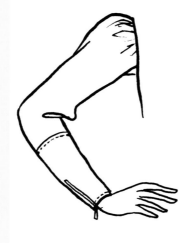

Gathers in sleeves, at caps and cuffs. 1.

Gathers in sleeves, at caps and cuffs. 2.

Gathers in sleeves, at caps and cuffs. 3.

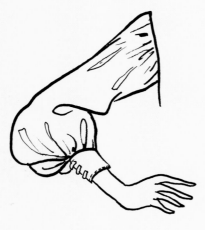

Gathers in sleeves, at caps and cuffs. 4.

Juliet sleeve.

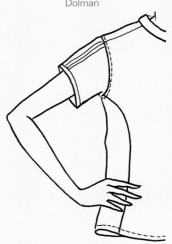

Dolman

Set-in sleeve.

Very short set-in sleeve..

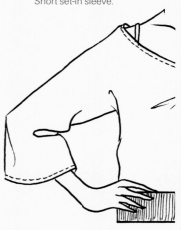

Short set-in sleeve.

Set-in, flared sleeve with ruffle at cuff.

Short sleeve raglan

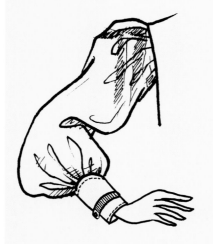

Wide-hemmed Dolman

Set-in

Circular

Puffed sleeve

Set-in bell

Balloon

Tulip

Raglan

Set-in bell

Saddle shoulder sleeve

Lantern

Petal

Cap

This page and page opposite: Complex shading of sleeves made from
Spring, Summer, Fall and Winter fabrics of different weights, types and textures. Study and copy these to develop advanced skills.

sleeves/shaded,
on-the-arm/detailing

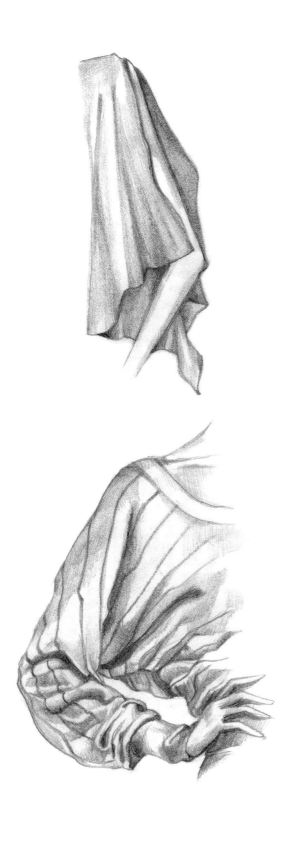

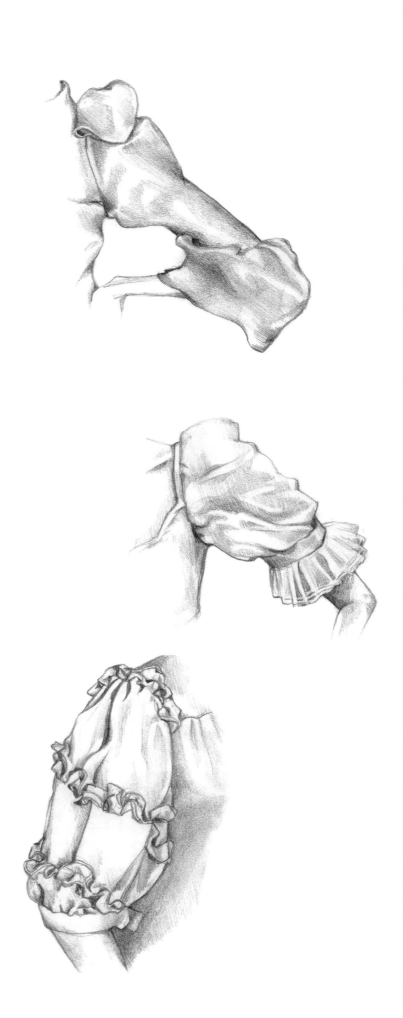

armhole treatments

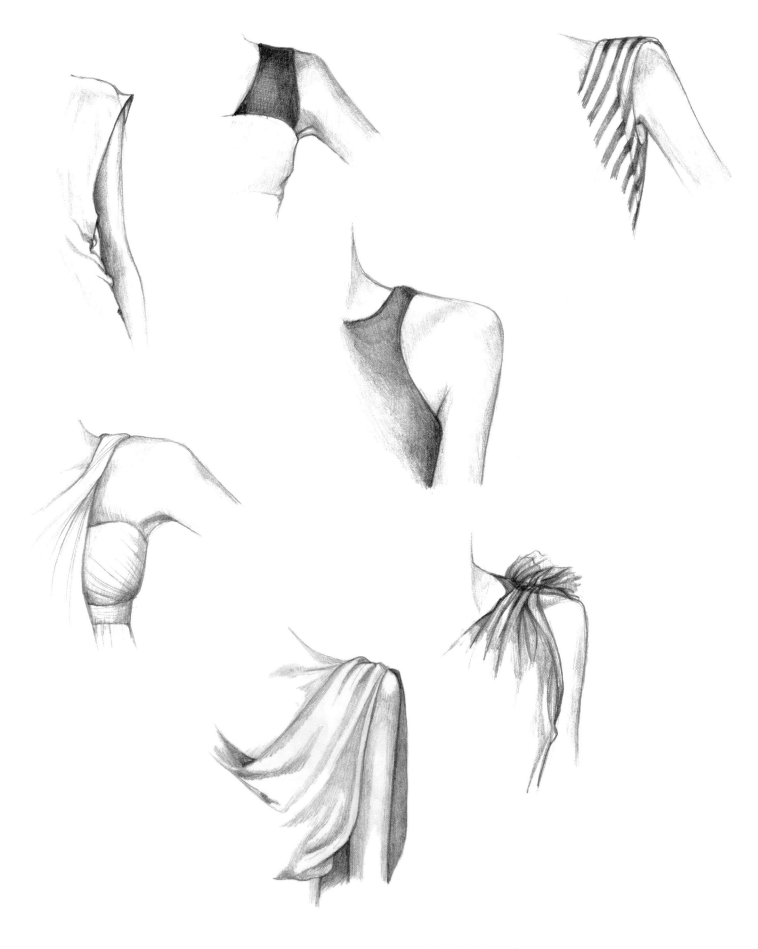

Armhole treatments. Note that under the arm the fabric bends down so it
sits beneath the tendons of the arm at the top of the ribcage.

necklines and collars

NECKLINES AND COLLARS

Necklines and collars are common to a range of garments—dresses, blouses, shirts, tops, jackets, robes, capes and coats. Although not always the largest part of a garment, they are almost always prominent and are often tricky to draw, sitting as they do in close relation to the head and neck and often seen in three-quarter and other angled views.

The area around the neck of a garment can be finished either by attaching a collar—a separate detail with varying degrees of construction and complexity—or finishing off the garment into a simpler opening for the neck, often combined with the garment's principal closure at the front or the back, and referred to simply as its NECK-LINE. Necklines are finished using facing, top-stitching or a variety of types of binding that follow the edge of the neck of the garment itself. A selection of necklines can be found in Chapter Five: Encyclopaedia of Details.

Necklines are symmetrical (with the exception, of course, of the small proportion of necklines that have asymmetrical construction) and encircle the neck. Necklines vary in shape and extension and can be placed at varying distances below—or above—the base of the neck, both at the front and the back of the garment, so they can, at the extremes, either be close to the neck or fall over the shoulders and drop down almost to the bust-line in front, and to the waist or below behind.

When drawing necklines—in all views—they must be carefully aligned with the center-front of the body, as they are conspicuous, and the garment is symmetrical about this point. To make sure the alignment and curvature of the neckline around the body is correct the base of the neck should be lightly sketched in as an ellipse and the center-front line marked in. It is difficult accurately to draw the neckline curving around the body with a single line gesture—foreshortening and the exact curvature of the line can be tricky— so draw it in two halves, starting at the back, curving over the shoulder and ending at the center-front line, then repeating on the other side. Unless it happens to be one that falls at the back, a neckline will most commonly appear higher at the back of the neck than the front. Nuance the line, making it thicker as it curves over the shoulder to indicate shadow and the three-dimensional shape of the body; otherwise keep the line smooth and steady.

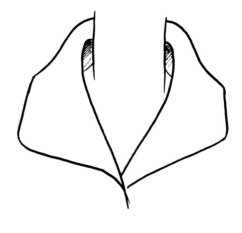

Collars are usually symmetrical and encircle the neck.

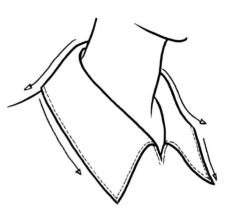

Rolled collars extend from the neckline up the back of the neck and then "roll" over; the line of the roll being higher at the back than the sides and front.

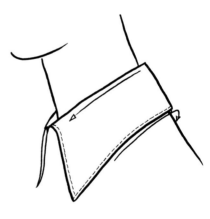

Side view of rolled collar. The silhouette of the collar slopes down from the back of the neck to the front.

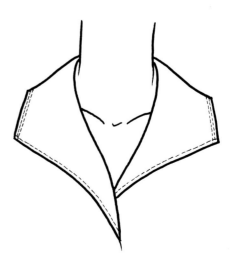

Collars are made in all shapes and sizes. Make sure the points of the collar—where it turns back towards the center-front—line up.

necklines and collars/exercise

COLLARS are important, prominent style features of garments—clear indicators of the quality of the workmanship—so must be drawn accurately to convey their intended effect. Collars frame the neck and vary in type according to their shape and where they sit in relation to the edge of the neck of the garment and the neck itself.

There are four basic types of collars: FLAT, ROLLED, STANDING and DRAPED. FLAT COLLARS lie flat on the neck of the garment, so there is practically no difference between the shape of the collar and that of the garment at the neck.

ROLLED COLLARS are tailored collars—molded to extend up the neckline and then rolling over onto the neck of the garment. The shape is achieved by attaching the upper collar to an under collar, sometimes with interfacing inserted between the two. The under collar and interfacing (if the collar is well constructed) do not show, nor do any seams at the finished edges. Rolled collars where the collar and lapels are cut as one piece are known as SHAWL COLLARS. Shawl collars are commonly found on robes and wraps, held together with a belt or sash instead of buttons or other closures.

The line of the high point of the collar, as it circles around the neck, is called the ROLL LINE, or ROLL. The roll line rises at the back of the collar as it extends further up the back of the neck. When drawing rolled collars the roll must be even and smooth as it extends around the neck. STANDING COLLARS are of many different types, constructed to stand straight up from the neck like a band around the neck; if the fabric turns down it does so almost without roll. Men's tailored shirts usually have standing collars. DRAPED COLLARS—cowls are examples—are made with excess fabric, usually cut on the bias so it falls folds as it falls away from the neckline, either in front or behind.

EXERCISE
Draw a blouse with six different collars.

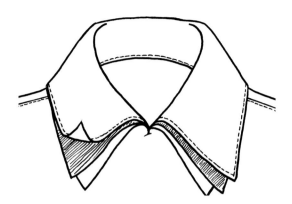

Tailored rolled collars are made with an upper collar and lower collar and often a layer of interlining between. When drawn, only the upper collar is seen.

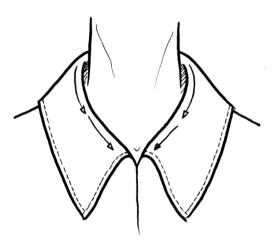

The *roll line* is the "ridge" of the collar as it circles the neck. It is higher at the back.

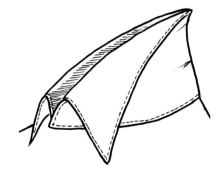

Roll collars stand up at the back of the neck. This collar has been constructed with a high stand.

necklines and collars

Note that when drawing tied garments—in this case a neck scarf—one end is seen in front of the knot and the other sits behind.

Peter Pan collar with bow. Note the shading to indicate the extensive drape.

Layering of collars. When garments are layered each layer has to be shaded individually to show depth.

Oversize asymmetrical trench collar over asymmetrical crossover shirt collar. Note that the shadow under the outer collar indicates the weight and thickness of the fabric. Note also that the top of the roll of the outer collar is shaded on both sides to make it appear rounded.

Notched collar over convertible collar. The convertible collar appears higher on the neck and covers most of the neck. The notched lapel of the jacket sits beneath the convertible collar but both collars sit above the shoulder line.

Cowl neckline

necklines and collars

Ruffle collar. These dramatic folds have to be shaded like cylinders—as they curve towards the light they get lighter and as they curve away they get progressively darker.

Leather top with funnel neckline. Note that highlights are seen on upper edge of collar, at the opening, along the side seam and along the princess seam. These highlights help convey the shininess of the fabric.

knitted sweaters/ knitted tops

KNITTED SWEATERS and KNITTED TOPS are garments that are made either directly, by knitting the yarn, which can be wool, silk, cotton or synthetics, or sewing together pieces of knitted fabric–a process known as "cut and sew". Knitted garments range from very tight-fitting to very loose-fitting and have elastic qualities: they stretch to allow limbs to enter and then resume their original form, closely fitting the body. Spandex and similar fabrics have increasingly been included in knitting yarns to allow more elasticity so that truly body-hugging fits can be achieved. When drawing sweaters, make sure to indicate the fit accurately and, if loose-fitting, show where the fullness is in the garment.

Knitted sweaters—as with other knitted garments—are constructed using a variety of methods, ranging from hand-knit to industrial knitting machines. How a sweater has been knit is clear when it is handled and inspected, but does not usually show in a drawing unless it has been made with a relatively thick yarn that produces a chunky knit. If it is important that the stitch used in a knit be clearly seen, a separate magnified detail can be included with the drawing (*see* Chapter Five: Encyclopaedia of Details for examples of knit stitches).

Besides the silhouette and detailing, the features of a knitted sweater or top that can be seen in a drawing are: (i) the different ways the hems, edges, sleeves and necklines are finished off—various types of ribbing, and rolled edges (because of the "stretch" of knits the constructional devices used to remove fullness in woven garments—tucks, seams and so on—are not required, and hems and edges are finished by changing the stitch/yarn/ pattern and knitting a ribbing or rolled, crotcheted or embroidered edge; (ii) the different textures and patterns—cables, diamonds or intricate jacquard-knit patterns—that are incorporated into the knit and (iii) if the sweater is knit with yarn made from a fiber with a distinctive appearance, such as mohair, angora or cashmere. Examples of these variations in sweaters are shown in the following pages.

EXERCISES
Draw ten knitted tops using different types of wool or stitching and different ribbed finishes to sleeves and hems.

Knit dress. To show the softness of the fabric there are no hard edges. The skirt is semi-transparent so the legs are partly visible underneath.

Designer sweaters (sweater-dress on right). Left, chain stitch; middle, braid stitch; right, braid and popcorn stitch.

knitted sweaters/ tops/ dress

Left, sweater with wide asymmetrical rib collar, cable knit down front, ribbed hem and decorative ribboned cuffs. Right, knit dress with halter neckline and layers of different stitching. Note the popcorn stitching on the bottom layer has to extend beyond the silhouette; if not, it will look like a print.

Slip over with cable stitching over tailored shirt. Flat shown upper left.

Left, rib-knit wool sweater; right, striped merino wool turtleneck sweater. Flats shown upper left and right.

knitted sweaters

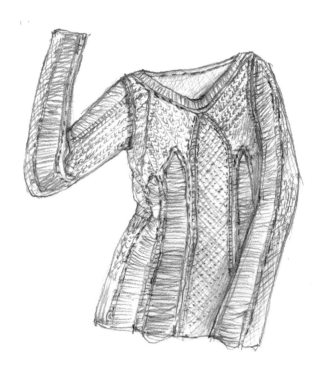

Although it can be tedious to do so, if it is necessary to render the entire garment make sure the repeat of the stitches follows the curves of the body. If several similar garments are shown it is only necessary to render a portion of the knit–usually about one-third. In these examples the knits were fully rendered to show how the stitches bend around the figure.

Cable-stitched wool sweater.

crochet-knit poncho

Building up the detailed shading of a crochet-knit poncho.

cuff/hem treatments
for knitted garments

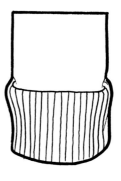

Single-ribbed cuff, folded over.

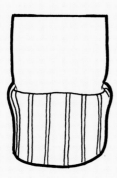

Double-ribbed cuff, folded over.

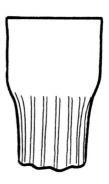

Single-ribbed cuff, unfolded.

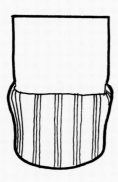

Triple-ribbed cuff, folded over.

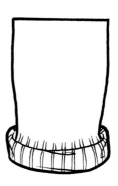

Double-ribbed cuff, folded over.

Fringed cuff.

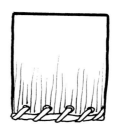

Whip stitch.

Because of the way knitted garments stretch they are finished differently to woven garments: the constructional devices needed to remove fullness in woven garments—tucks, seams and so on—are not required, and hems and edges are finished by changing the stitch and/or yarn and/or pattern and knitting a ribbing or rolled, crotcheted or embroidered edge.

dresses/
general points

DRESSES

Although dresses are one-piece garments, there is little difference in drawing them from the way a top and skirt are drawn. Dresses are usually the most feminine and sensuous of garments, with fabric draping next to the body for the full length of the figure. They often are made with large quantities of fabric, which usually implies copious amounts of drape. The fabric and how it drapes is a large part of the appeal of the dress, and a pose should be chosen that shows it off to best effect: often an "in-motion" pose with numerous diagonals will be best for achieving this.

There is a wide variety of dress silhouettes, ranging from tight "sheaths" that fit closely to the curves of the body, to, at the other extreme, forms that are almost completely independent of the shape of the body underneath. For dresses that do not fit the body closely, it is nevertheless important to know exactly where the figure is located under the garment, and to sketch in the pose of the croquis before drawing the dress. Unless the position of the body under the dress is known, the parts that emerge from the top, sleeves and bottom of the dress cannot be accurately positioned, and the drawing looks incorrect.

For dresses the pose is often also an indicator of the market the garment is designed for: for example, a dress for a younger woman might be shown with a more dynamic pose. Choose a pose that shows off the best features of the garment, and if it contains a large quantity of fabric use the full page to do it full justice.

GENERAL POINTS TO KEEP IN MIND WHEN DRAWING DRESSES

1. Be attentive to scale and silhouette. Belts often create a slim area close to the body and, when pulled tight at the waist, create a soft silhouette in the upper torso.
2. All parts of a dress have to be drawn as curving around the figure underneath. Draw the neckline around the neck, the armholes around the arms and the hem around the legs.
3. All hems bend around the bottom of the figure; collars bend around the neck and sleeves bend around the arms.

Although dresses often *cover up* a large portion of the body it is nevertheless important to know the position of the figure underneath. Unless the position of the figure under the dress is known, the parts that emerge from the top, sleeves and bottom of the dress cannot be accurately positioned so the silhouette of the dress itself cannot be correctly positioned and the drawing appears incorrect. It is often helpful to lightly sketch in the croquis before drawing the dress.

Silhouette

Drape and fit.

Dress. Points of tension/where drape forms.
Left, front view, dress drapes into long, vertical folds; center, S curve pose, front view, drape radiates from raised hip on left and across bodice; right, S curve, three-quarter view.

dresses

4. Wedding dresses and evening gowns require a full sweep and curve of the hem which can dip down at the back of the figure, in the front of the figure or perhaps off to the side. Where fabric extends along the ground it drapes horizontally rather than vertically when on the body.

5. No matter how long a hem is, it is often a good idea to show the shoe protruding underneath—it can make the drawing more realistic by providing a point of reference for the eye, and can make the drawing look graceful.

6. Tailored dresses are drawn with crisp sharp lines and fewer folds.

7. As mentioned, dresses are the garments that usually contain the most fabric, and as a result they also usually contain the most folds and drape. Design features are often incorporated specifically to show off the fabric and drape, and include such details as pleats, gathers, shirring, cowls (at front and back and on sleeves), deeply plunging necklines and backs and other features that highlight the fabric. (When dresses incorporate these design features the fabric of the dress is also often cut on the bias—on the diagonal—so it stretches more than when it is cut "on grain"—when the cross and lengthwise threads are at right angles to each other.) These design features are as a rule vital to the overall appearance of the garment and should be accurately rendered using techniques to show clearly the fabric type and the detailed way it folds and drapes. Refer to Chapter Six: Fabrics to see how to render different types of drape and different fabrics.

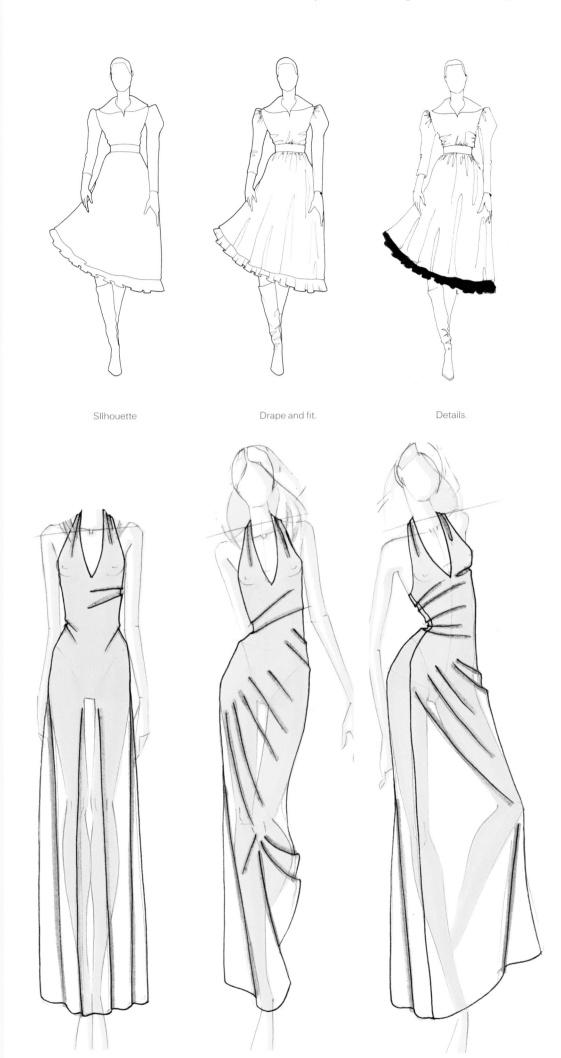

Silhouette.

Drape and fit.

Details.

Dress. Points of tension/where drape forms.
Left, front view, dress drapes into long, vertical folds; center, S curve pose, front view, drape radiates from raised hip on left and across bodice; right, S curve, three-quarter view.

DRAWING DRESSES

Dresses are best depicted with poses that show the fabric and drape to best effect, so often a walking pose is used that shows the body in an S curve with the hip up on one side, creating diagonal drape. Dresses cover the whole body so it is important to align the garment with the figure underneath, as, as in the example shown, the upper body might be straight and the hips tilted at an angle.

1. It is easiest first to lightly sketch in the position of the neckline and the hem. In this example with a walking pose the hemline tilts up on the side of the nearer leg. Make sure the neckline is aligned with the line of the shoulders. As when drawing all garments it is best to indicate the position of the center-front line to ensure the dress and details within the dress are symmetrical.

2. Sketch in the rest of the silhouette of the garment. The armholes of this dress are deeply cut and curve low under the arms. The waistline is a cinch belt—a tight-fitting belt— indicated by two curved parallel lines at the waist. This causes the fabric to billow above the waist. The silhouette of the dress clings to the hips and tops of the thighs.

3. Drape is added within the garment. The neckline has a cowl drape shown by the two diagonal lines that curve up at the bottom. More drape is created in the garment on the side where the hip is up. This is indicated by extending the curves up from the top of the waist. Lines are added to show creases in the belt. In the skirt folds are shown extending from just inside the point where the hip swings out, the point where the top of the leg makes contact with the fabric, across the front of the garment. Another fold line starts at the top of the inside of the forward leg.

4. Add final details—here trim at the hem and a self tie belt at the waist.

1. Lightly sketch in the position of the neckline and hem. In walking poses the hem curves up. Indicate the c-f line.

2. Sketch in rest of silhouette. Armholes are deeply cut and waist is a cinch belt. Note belt causes fabric to billow above waist. Dress clings to hips and tops of thighs.

3. Add drape throughout garment. Neckline has a cowl drape. .See detailed instructions in text for where drape forms.

4. Add final details—trim at hem and a self-tie belt at the waist.

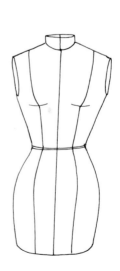
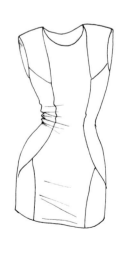

Note that when the dress moves with the body the style lines change shape.

dresses/day dresses

Day dresses. The dress on the left is a tight-fitted medium-weight silk dress or sheath with a cinch-belted waist and contrasting fabric between top and skirt. The dress on the right is made from a rayon or lightweight cotton that creates rounder, fuller folds above and below the cinched waist. Note the print on the dress follows the bend of the leg and is shaded in the area behind the leg.

Day dresses. Left, asymmetrical knit sheath with wrap at neck and gathered waist. Because it is a knit it fits snugly to the body; the bust must be indicated with shading. Center, knit baby doll dress gathered to the waist; each individual soft fold is separately shaded. Right, knit long sleeve dress with gathers at neckline and narrow waist. Note the direction of the stripes across the torso and diagonaly down the arms. All stripes follow the contours of folds.

dresses/day dresses

Knit day dresses with multiple style-lines.

Day dresses made of woven fabrics. The shading shows that the garments are made of fabrics that are fitted to the body but do not cling to the body so it is not necessary to indicate the bustline with shading. Note as with all garments the neckline bends around the clyinder of the neck, the trim on the armhole bends around the shoulder and under the arm, the yoke bends around the hip and the hems bend around the lower body.

Asymmetrical wrap short dress with belted waist. This dress is made of a luxury fabric–silk taffetta–that has a crispness that allows it to form shapes independently of the body underneath. This draping quality is used in this dress to create a fullness in the sleeve so it sits above the shoulderline. This is made clear in the drawing by shading in the interior of the fabric as it curves around the neck. Folds are wide and are drawn with straighter, more angular lines than when drawing softer, less crisp fabrics.

Sleeveless short knit dress. This dress is made from a fine, loosely woven yarn, making it transparent. The short and top under the dress are drawn with a darker value although areas are erased out to show the sheen of the outer garment.

dresses/evening dresses

Dresses with full cowl draping. The dress on the left is constructed with a long length of fabric that starts at the back, drapes diagonally across the body and wraps around the head. The cowl drape forms above the right knee. The dress on the right has a large cowl drape in the front.

dresses/evening dresses

Multi-layered transparent print dresses made of silk organza. Silk organza has an ethereal transparent quality that must be drawn with very few dark lines; the edges are defined more by tonal shading than lines, except for the pleating which is drawn with short, crisp lines. The complexity of the prints and the shading of the details require careful planning and execution. This drawing was made by first filling in the shading and then defining the body underneath and highlights on the surface of the folds using an eraser.

dresses/evening dress

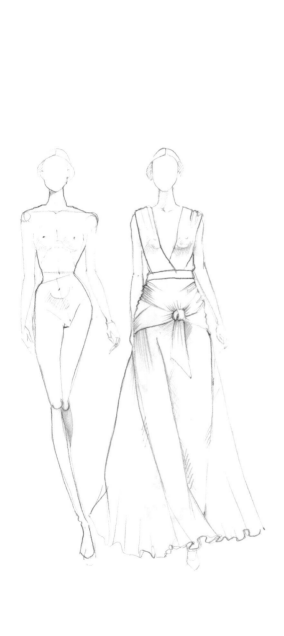

Sleeveless gown with plunging neckline and full skirt made of a finely gathered fabric that creates voluptuous drape. This dress fits tightly on the upper torso, around the bustline and at the hips. Smooth dark shading should be applied around and under the bustline to show the fabric recedes under the breasts and behind the belt. It is also applied below the tummy and into the knot of the wrap and in the drape around the left leg that is moving forward.

Shiny leather dress with trumpet silhouette. The shape of this dress is created by multiple tucks and gathers. The effect of the shine is created by leaving a thin line of the white of the paper to appear on the tops of the folds and applying a dark value immediately next to it. Tucks create a corset-like effect in the upper body and there is a succession of two-point cowl drapes in the neckline and the fitted area of the skirt. The flare below the knees is drawn in perspective, for dramatic effect, so that the area in the front appears to be flying up towards us. Not a dress to be attempted by beginners!

dresses/evening dresses

Spring/Summer dresses with fitted bodices and full skirts, made from cotton ethnic prints. The complex prints have to be planned carefully as they bend into and around folds. Note that the pattern becomes darker in the interior of the inverted pleats in the dress on the left and bends around the flounce on the bottom of the skirt on the right.

Pattern repeat across folds

Long summer dresses made of finely woven, semi-transparent fabrics. The fabric is so fine and lightweight that it appears to float. This is shown in the dress on the left by bending the flutter sleeves away from the body in a wide arc. In the dress on the right it is the hem that bends away and becomes almost transparent—indicated by the light subtle shading.

dresses/ wedding dress

Wedding dress with long full train, in Spring/Summer lightweight fabric, drawn in perspective so the full drama of the train is emphasized. Each floral appliqué is shaded individually.

dresses/ wedding
dress

Wedding dress made with Fall/Winter heavyweight fabric. The fabric of this dress falls in fuller, wider folds than the previous dress. Note the criss cross lacing has to be drawn accurately to show where laces cross over and under each other. The full billowing sleeves are created by gathering the fabric at the top and bottom of the sleeve in wide, rounded folds. The skirt is given volume by creating a huge cowl drape from the left hip to the right hip.

dresses/ wedding dress

Wedding dress with elaborate appliqués and beading. When drawing beads and appliqués it is best to space them unevenly so that each bead or appliqué reflects the light differently and the fabric appears more natural.

tailored garments/
drawing tailored jackets

TAILORED GARMENTS

Tailored garments are garments that are made using a series of sewing (both hand and machine), cutting, pressing and other construction techniques such as interfacing, interlining and use of interior materials that create shape and support.

A tailored garment is a garment that is molded to create a shape of its own, largely independent of the figure underneath. Because of this it can disguise the figure underneath. It is distinguished by sleek lines, with no hint of the underlying construction, precise fit without the apperance of stiffness, hidden seams and hems and exquisite quality and finish of all details.

Tailored garments are often thought of as a limited number of types, comprising jackets, suits, coats and other formalwear, and originally tailoring was in fact just for jackets, but now most types of garments, including tops, blouses, sleepwear, casualwear worn in the home (such as coats and robes) and underwear can be tailored. Tailored garments are also those garments that require tailoring in certain areas to provide shape and structure that the fabric alone cannot provide, for example, a roll collar on a thin summer dress.

DRAWING TAILORED JACKETS

The jacket is the classic tailored garment. Coats can be thought of as long jackets and are drawn in a similar fashion.

1. First draw the croquis, either the full croquis or the top to below the waist where the arms end. For tailored garments symmetry is essential, so it is important carefully to draw in the center-front line. First decide what the shape and depth of the neckline will be and make a mark on the c-f line where the lapels will overlap and also the position of the top button below that. The placement of the first button is a major determinant of fit and silhouette, and can be placed at the bustline, above the bustline or below the bustline, even as far down as the waist or below. Position the top button on the center-front line. Sketch in the shape of the neckline and continue the line of the outside lapel—here on the left—to the end of the lapel and then vertically downwards to the end of the jacket.

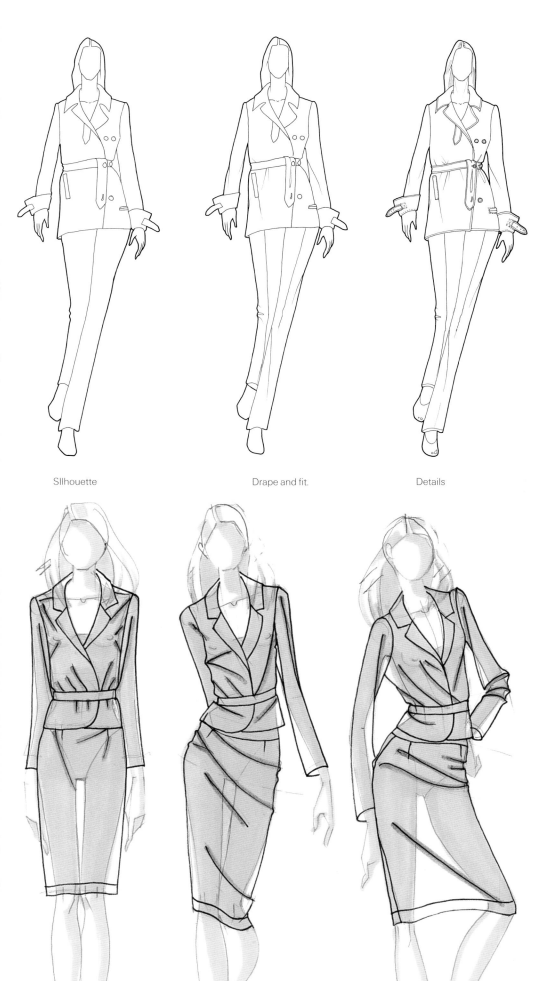

Sllhouette   Drape and fit.   Details

Tailored jacket with belt. Points of tension/where drape forms .Left, front view, belt creates folds as it gathers in the excess fabric; center, S curve pose, front view, drape shifts to left of jacket as shoulder and hip compress; right, S curve, three-quarter view.

tailored garments/ drawing tailored jackets

2. Begin drawing the collar from the back of the neck. Be clear about how high the collar will be and where it will begin at the neck and where it will meet the shoulder line. Draw the top edge of the collar to the first point on the shoulder line. From there the line of the collar drops and spreads out slightly at a diagonal then returns to meet the lapel at what is known as the gorge seam. Draw in both sides making sure that each side is symmetrical about the c-f line. Extend out the lapel along the line of the gorge seam to its widest point (planned ahead of time, as for the neckline). The lapel on the left side then returns to cross over the c-f line and meet the top edge of the lapel, bending as it crosses the c-f line (there are three layers of fabric in the lapel which means it does not lie flat but bends around the top button). After crossing the c-f line the lapel becomes the edge of the body of the jacket. Draw in the lapel on the other side. The point of the lapel on the right side is hidden under the overlapping left lapel. Be precise when determining the width of the lapel—lapel width is an important design element—and how far it extends towards the armhole, as well as the relative sizes of the collar and lapel (another important design element)

3. First draw in the hem and then the outside silhouette of the sides of the jacket from the armholes. Jackets have a large variety of silhouettes. This jacket is fitted at the waist, but jackets can be boxy, oval- or bell-shaped or of many other types. .

4. Draw in the sleeves from the shoulder to wrists. They appear more natural if drawn with a slight bend at the elbow. The bottom of the sleeve curves around the wrist. Sleeves can also vary in length; in the classic tailored jacket wrist-length is the norm. Note that in some jackets are made with two-piece sleeves; in this case a second line is drawn to indicate that seam. This jacket is sewn with princess seams, which are indicated with curving lines between the c-f line and the sides of the jacket. Princess seams also can vary in length. In this case they are long, running from the armholes to the seam.

5. This is a belted two-button jacket. Draw in the buttons on the c-f line with horizontal buttonholes. Draw in the belt and indicate the crush of the fabric above and below the belt with a few diagonal lines. Draw in the pockets extending from the princess line to the side seams. Tailored garments are made with precision and details should also be drawn in with precision.

1. Draw in top half of croquis and carefully draw in c-f line. Decide on neckline shape and depth and mark position of lapel overlap and top button. See text for detailed instructions

2. Begin drawing collar from back of neck. See text for detailed instructions on the important stage of drawing the lapels.

3. Draw in the hem and the the outside silhouette of the sides from the armholes. This jacket is fitted at the waist.

4. Draw in the sleeves from shoulder to wrist—they appear more natural with a slight bend. See text for detailed instructions.

5. Draw in the buttons on the c-f line with horizontal buttonholes. Draw in belt and indicate crush of fabric above and below it. Draw in pockets extending from princess lines to side seams.

tailored garments/ general points/buttons/belts

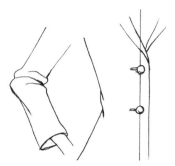

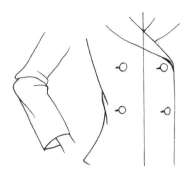

GENERAL POINTS TO KEEP IN MIND WHEN DRAWING TAILORED GARMENTS.

Tailored garments are made with precision and attention to detail, which is responsible for a large part of their overall appearance. It is important to respect this attention to detail when drawing these garments in order to capture the clean and crisp lines and detailing. Openings, hems, seams, darts and the shape and lengths of sleeves, collars, lapels and the main body of the garment must all be accurate.

1. The top button must be placed on the center-front line directly beneath the bend of the lapel. The buttonhole is horizontal.

2. Buttons must be evenly spaced vertically and if the garment is double-breasted the two lines of buttons must also be placed at equal distances from the center-front line and in horizontal alignment with each other. Pay attention to the type of button and buttonhole being drawn.

3, 4. On classic women's jackets the lapel on the left side (as viewed) crosses over the right lapel. Remember that jackets are, except for the area where the lapels cross, almost completely symmetrical, and the strong lines created by tailoring accentuate this and make it more noticeable if they are not drawn with complete symmetry. Be precise when determining the width of the lapel—an important design element. Make sure the gorges (the seams between the collar and the lapel) are the same length.

5, 6. Tailored jackets are constructed very precisely so all details must be drawn accurately. A welt pocket sits above the bustline. The cap of the sleeve is drawn at an angle from the shoulder to the bottom of the armhole. With tailored jackets, when the sleeve hangs by the side the cap is hardly visible; when the arm is bent the cap is clearly visible.. Princess lines are important in tailoring construction and should be accurately indicated.

7. When jackets are drawn over one or more garments—a blouse, shirt or sweater, for example—it is advisable to draw the undergarment first, making sure the collar is above the shoulder line, and then to draw the collar of the jacket overlapping it.

Do not draw a line under the bustline with tailored jackets; most tailored jackets smooth out the bustline rather than accentuate it.

General Points for tailored garments.1.,2. For single-breasted jacket the buttons are placed on the c-f line directly beneath the bend of the lapel. The buttonhole is horizontal. For d-b jackets buttons must align both vertically and horizontally and placed at equal distances from the c-f line. Note the sleeve bends around the arm.

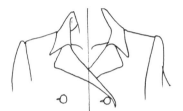

3., 4. Jackets are, except for the area where the lapels cross, almost completely symmetrical. The strong lines created by tailoring make it noticeable if they are not drawn with complete symmetry. Be precise when determining the width of the lapel—an important design element. Make sure the gorges (the seams between the collar and the lapel) are the same length. On classic women's jackets the lapel on the left side (as viewed) crosses over the right lapel.

Princess lines

5.,6 Tailored jackets are constructed very precisely so all details must be drawn accurately. A welt pocket sits above the bustline. The cap of the sleeve is drawn at an angle from the shoulder to the bottom of the arm-hole. With tailored jackets, when the sleeve hangs by the side the cap is hardly visible; when the arm is bent the cap is clearly visible.. Princess lines are important in tailoring construction and should be accurately indicated.

7. When jackets are drawn over one or more garments—a blouse, shirt or sweater, for example—it is advisable to draw the undergarment first, making sure the collar is above the shoulder line, and then to draw the collar of the jacket overlapping it.

jackets construction details/ belts & sashes/exercises

BELTS AND SASHES are frequently an important feature of tailored jackets: They are usually integral to the intended silhouette of the garment, gathering any fullness of fabric to a slim, figure-flattering waist, as well as often being attractive design details. If a belt *is* an important design detail in a jacket then it should be drawn with care.

There are numerous types of belts and sashes (less so sashes, naturally, the variation limited to the type of fabric or cord used and the trimming). Belts can be straight or contoured to follow the curves of the body and have a variety of fastenings, including prong and eyelet with a buckle, snaps, hooks and eyes and clasp buckles. Except where the fastening is positioned off-center, make sure the buckles, knots or other fastening devices sit symmetrically on the center-front line.

EXERCISES

1. Draw a tailored jacket with (i) a notched collar, (ii) a shawl collar, and then draw a double-breasted jacket with no collar.
2. Draw five jackets with different silhouettes and of different lengths. Choose a skirt or pair of pants to go with each jacket.

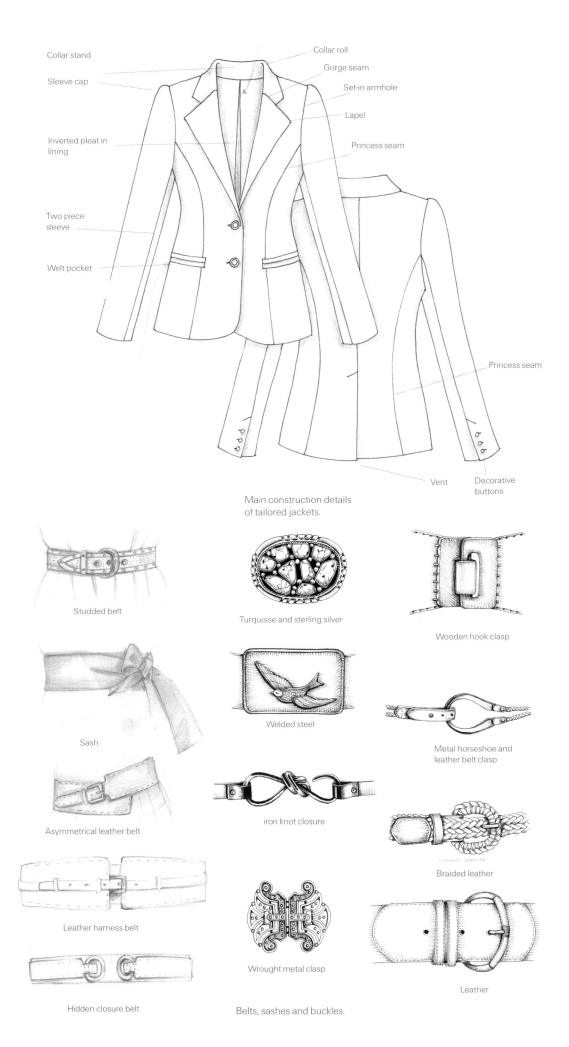

Main construction details of tailored jackets.

Collar stand
Collar roll
Sleeve cap
Gorge seam
Set-in armhole
Lapel
Inverted pleat in lining
Princess seam
Two piece sleeve
Welt pocket
Princess seam
Vent
Decorative buttons

Studded belt

Turquoise and sterling silver

Wooden hook clasp

Sash

Welded steel

Metal horseshoe and leather belt clasp

Asymmetrical leather belt

iron knot closure

Braided leather

Leather harness belt

Wrought metal clasp

Leather

Hidden closure belt

Belts, sashes and buckles.

collars/lapels/
shoulder pads/details

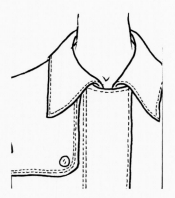

Buttoned down
yoke and fly front.

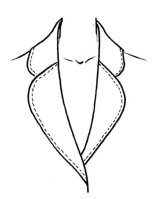

Clover leaf lapel

Semi-peaked lapel

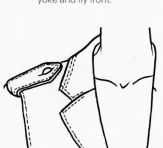

Epaulette

Notched lapel

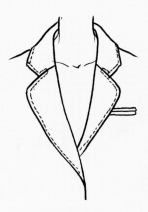

Clover leaf lapel
with slit pocket

Belted cuff

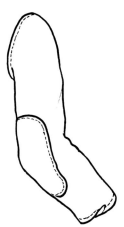

Sleeve patch

Peaked lapel

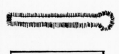

Buttonholes—top, key-
hole; bottom, bound.

Contemporary jack-
et styles.

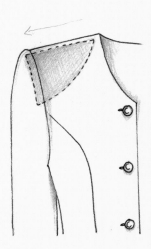

Shoulder without shoul-
der pad. Note angle
from top of neckline to
cap of sleeve.

Shoulder with shoulder
pad. Note angle from
top of neckline to
cap of sleeve.

tailored jackets/
leather/fitted/relaxed

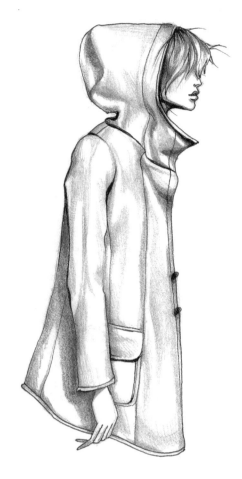

Hooded duffle jacket, side view. Note that the opening of the hood rests on the top of the head and curves around the side. The coat is shaded with soft wide areas that show the soft wide folds of the thick soft wool fabric of its construction.

Summer-weight wool jacket tied at waist. Shaded with soft wide areas to indicate the voluptuous drape.

Cropped leather motorcycle jacket with shearling collar, trim and cuffs. This shiny fabric is drawn with sharp highlights on the tops of the folds with darker areas immediately adjacent to them. The jacket is finished with shiny metalic bands at the wrists.

tailored vest/jacket

An Alexander McQueen fitted jacket with beading and gold appliqué. When drawing jackets with elaborate appliqué or embroidery it is necessary to plan the position of the pattern first before starting to shade to ensure it appears symmetrical.

Fur vest/waistcoat with zipper front closure. The fur is drawn with layers of broken lines that create the broken edge of the silhouette. Note that wide across areas of the fur indicate the volume and fluffiness of the fur.

Traditional double-breasted riding jacket. The fabric is matte in color so the range of colors in the jacket is limited and it is drawn with a limited range of values. The jacket is highly tailored so all edges must be drawn sharply and cleanly.

tailored jackets/

Three-quarter length hooded parka with tog-gled drawstring hem and self-tie waist. Note the single needle cover stitching around the lapels, wide drape above waist created by the self-tie belt and the rounded silhouette of the lower part of the garment.

Double-breasted soft-tailored jacket with Dolman sleeves, barrel silhouette. The long armhole creates a large amount of excess fabric that is crushed when the arm is straight.

Fitted jacket with novelty darts at shoulders and waist.

coat/jackets

Short-sleeved wrap jacket.

Barrel coat with kimono sleeves.

Single button long-sleeved jacekt.

coat/jacket/blazer

Jacket with gathered drawstring hood. The casing of the drawstring crushes the fabric creating multiple folds that curve around the edge of the hood and are softly shaded, as with the folds of the sleeves.

Three-quarter length coat with lantern sleeves.

Classic blazer

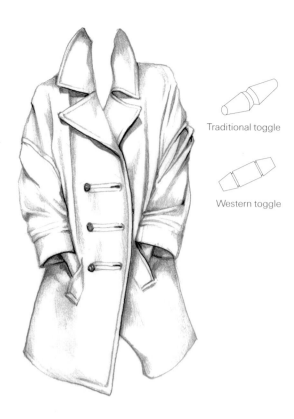

Traditional toggle

Western toggle

Double-breasted duffle coat with toggle closures

Quilted parka with hood. To indicate the fullness of the quilting make sure the silhouette puffs out from each seam of the quilt. Individual quilt panels are drawn to show the drape inside each panel–the higher parts are left white and the valleys are shaded.

Clutch coat adapted from 1920s coat with fur collar, asymmetrical closure, fur cuffs and hem, self-tie belt. Include wide areas of shadow at the edges of the fur to indicate its depth.

Long silk self-tie coat with scoop neck, raglan sleeves and wide pockets.

tailored coat

Wool plaid coat with fur collar and fur trim at cuffs and sleeves. The plaid pattern is
first planned out by defining the major horizontal and vertical stripes and then insert-
ing the details with lines and narrower bands. The fur is drawn mainly with the side
of the pencil to show the softness of the folds. Note the individual fibers of the fur
outlined at the silhouette of the collar and cuffs.

tailored coat

Fur coat. Note the size of the individual pelts used in drawing fur coats: in this coat they are smaller (probably a mink). They are drawn with the side of the pencil to indicate the softness of the fur. The belt is tied into a knot, slimmer than the rest of the belt, and then flares out into triangles on either side.

tailored coat

1. Draw the croquis and silhouette. This is a walking S curve pose. The coat is tailored in the collar and shoulder but then drapes away from the body. The bottom of the coat sweeps out from the body in a wide A line.

This coat is made out of a medium weight wool/flannel and is tailored in the collar, which stands up high above the shoulders, and in the shoulders where it is fitted. Below the shoulders it falls away from the body and is not tailored.

2. FIll in the folds of the coat with shadows and shade along where the coat touches the edge of the body.

3. Add darker shades in the diagonal parts of the folds.

Casual jacket over textured top with knife-pleat skirt. All three
pieces have volume but drape in distinctive ways.

Shawl jacket, wrap top and fringe skirt.

separates/sweater/
tops/skirts

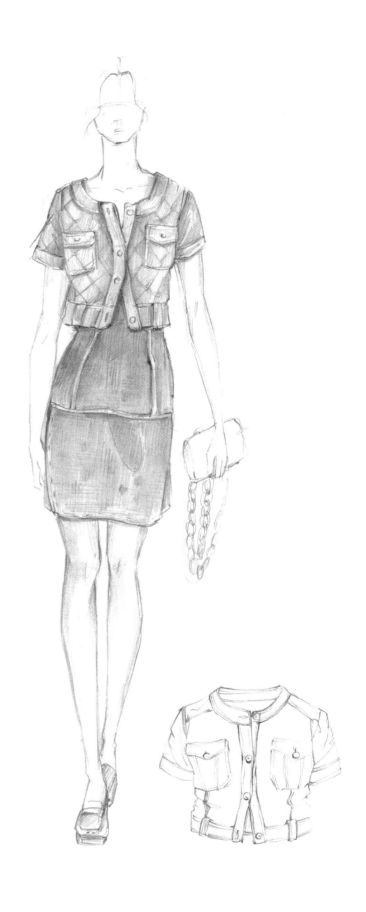

Separates are garments that are made for easy mixing and matching with other garments. They complement each other in some way—similarity or sometimes contrast in fabrics, colors, cut, detail, trim. Designers often create separates in their collections. Left, crop sweater, over-the-shoulder outlaw belt, straight skirt with c-f placket and button closures—all made from same fabric. Right, cropped casual jacket with scoop neck over simple sheath dress. The cropped jacket adds a casual tailored quality to the look.

When drawing outfits made up of separates it is important to represent each separate garment accurately: garments are often made of different fabrics that fit the body differently. Size, fabric, drape and scale of the the different garments must be taken into consideration.
Left, Cropped jean jacket with tiered ruffled hem. Note how hem of jacket is drawn away from body while pants fit snugly. Right, top made of a knit jersey that drapes fluidly across the body contrasting with a wide-leg denim pant that fits snugly until below the knee.

separates

Separates made of a variety of fabrics, showing varying silhouettes and drape.

active sportswear/ rollerblading

ACTIVE SPORTSWEAR

Active sportswear (AS)–often now also referred to as *activewear*– has become an increasingly important clothing category, worn both when practicing the sport it is designed for and also as casualwear. It used to be the case that clothing for professional athletes differed from that designed for amateurs: for performance garments function had often to be favored over design. Nowadays, though, new fabrics and materials have allowed function and design to come together and the exact garments worn by professionals can be sported by all: the stylish jacket or t-shirt worn on casual occasions will often embody professional standard performance characteristics of insulation, breathability, moisture-wicking, support and protection, while at the same time being comfortable-to-wear and often ultra lightweight.

AS has become one of the most important categories in fashion as it now influences every other category, both in style and in use of fabrics: There has been enormous innovation in fabrics for AS in terms of waterproofing, stretching, warmth and breathability.

AS clothing is, for sports not requiring protective padding, usually designed to fit close to the body, with a bias towards making the body appear sleek and athletic, especially for those who miss the occasional workout.

1. Active sportswear is drawn with many seams. Seams are introduced to create stronger areas where the fabric is subject to repeated stress and also to get thick fabric (fabric for active sportswear is often thick—e.g. neoprene, heavy nylon, spandex, tricot, stretch elastic and other technology-enhanced fabrics) to lie flat. Seams are often indicated by showing top-stitching. More padding is employed and layering is used to keep the body warm when the body begins to cool down. Snaps, elastic and velcro are often used in addition to buttons, toggles, drawstrings and laces for ease of access. Typical fabrics are waxed cotton, nylon, neoprene, fleece, gortex, lycra, rubber and canvas.

2. Because the construction materials are often man-made, the silhouettes of active sportswear are usually clear and crisp. Draw them using a clean, clear, sharp line that bends around the body.

3. Young, active poses that represent a typical movement in the sport, or a relaxed, "off-court" are advantageous. It is often helpful to include one of the main accessories of the sport—for example, a tennis raquet, skis or snowboard—in order to clearly identify the exact type of garments.

4. Accessories—gloves, hats, goggles and others— are commonly included as an important part of the outfit for function, protection and style. Accessories

Roller blading. Though not always necessary, it can be effective when drawing active sportswear to use a pose that expresses the movement of the sport, with lots of diagonals and foreshortened limbs in different planes. Including a piece of the equipment used in the sport as an accessory gives a clear indication of what the sport is that the clothes are designed for. Note that clothes for active sportswear have lots of seams as seen in the garments in this drawing.

active sportswear/
hiking

Hiking outfit. Fur-collared zippered parka with numerous pockets and
closures, cotton hiking pants with knee patches, hiking boots with
gaiters, multi-strapped nylon backpack.

Cyclist wearing multi-sectioned jacket with rib-sleeves, funnel-kneck, cargo-pockets, self-tie belted waist and hood over cotton leggings. Flat is variation.

active sportswear/ hiking

Left, contrast racing-stripe hiking jacket with cargo pockets and shoulder pouch-es, velcro closures at cuffs over high-collared t-shirt, thigh pack. Right, vest with high waist cinched with ties for warmth, buckles, zippers and patch pockets; hiking pants with gusset for ventilation, knee straps. Flats are variations.

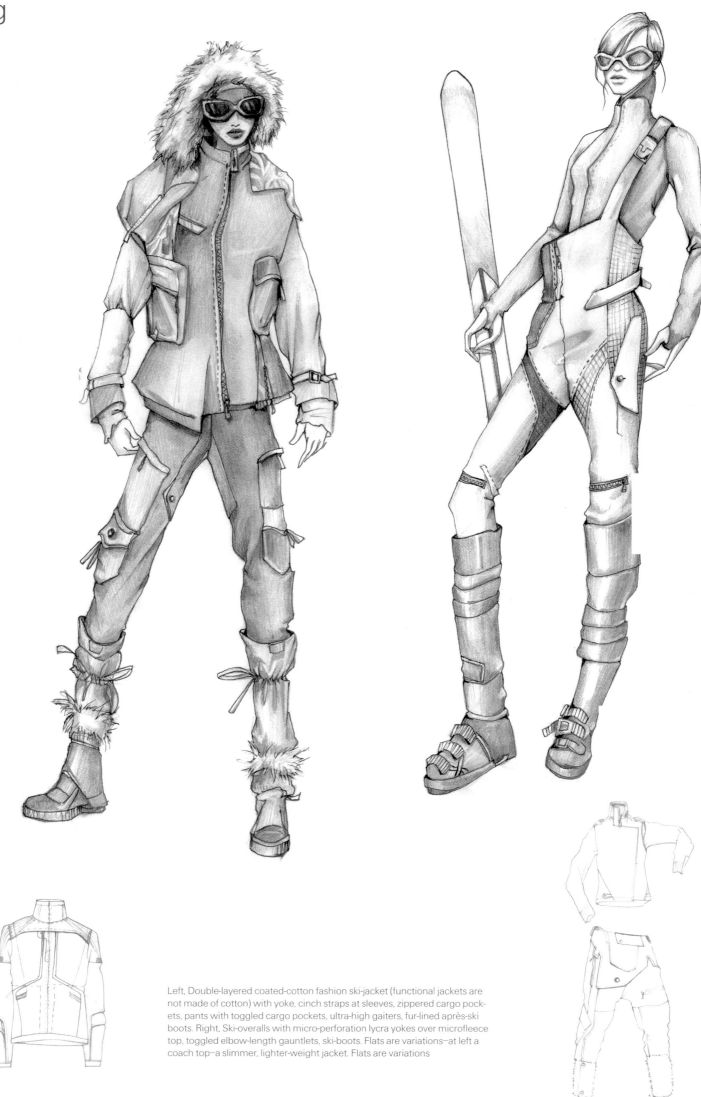

Left, Double-layered coated-cotton fashion ski-jacket (functional jackets are
not made of cotton) with yoke, cinch straps at sleeves, zippered cargo pockets, pants with toggled cargo pockets, ultra-high gaiters, fur-lined après-ski
boots. Right, Ski-overalls with micro-perforation lycra yokes over microfleece
top, toggled elbow-length gauntlets, ski-boots. Flats are variations—at left a
coach top—a slimmer, lighter-weight jacket. Flats are variations

Left, hooded jacket with gun patch, exposed railroad zippers, expedition pants with large cargo pockets and padding at crotch, gaiters, out on left, tucked-in on right. Flat is variation. Right, running outfit, cotton tank top and cotton shorts.

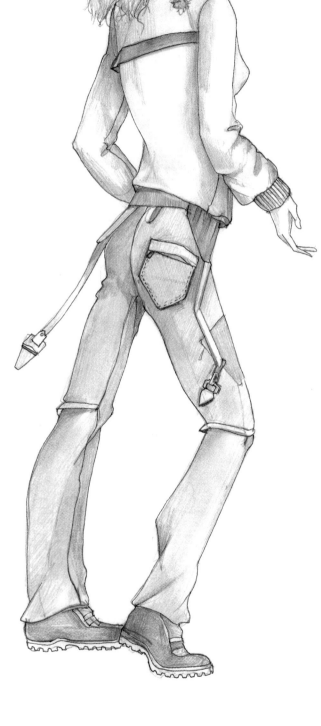

Left, yoga outfit, turtleneck with micro-mesh dry-fit, bi-stretch second skin top, cotton zippered and toggled yoga pants. Right, hiking outfit, coach jacket with rib collar and cuffs, long cotton pants with hidden-ventilation vents at thighs, zippered detachable lower legs.

sleepwear/swimwear/ lingerie/exercises

SLEEPWEAR/ SWIMWEAR/LINGERIE
Garments in these categories are made in a variety of styles and fabrics but are mostly designed to fit close to the figure, with the exception of gowns and coverups worn over them .

These types of garments are usually small (also with the exception of the robes, gowns and coverups used with them) and often designed purposely to reveal the figure, so it is important that the figure is drawn well and shaded correctly so its dimensions can be clearly seen and the garment fully understood. Care should be taken also to draw the fabric so it can be immediately recognized—whether it is silk, cotton, lace or another. Poses should be youthful, fun and sassy.

EXERCISES

1. (Active sportswear). Copy ten figures engaged in three different active sports from the sports section of a newspaper or a sports magazine.
2. Draw clothes for a sport that requires minimum protection (e.g tennis) and one that requires maximum protection (e.g.skateboarding).
3. (Sleep/swimwear). Choose two sets of sleepwear, two swimsuits and two sets of lingerie from magazines. Copy, drawing in the croquis on each.

Simple two-piece outfits that can be used as templates for swimwear. Note the shape of the bra around the breasts and the curve of the straps around the neck.

Left, seamless bra bikini; center, junior bikini with multi-tiered ruffled top and bottom; right, backless one-piece halter swimsuit.

swimwear/one piece/
two piece

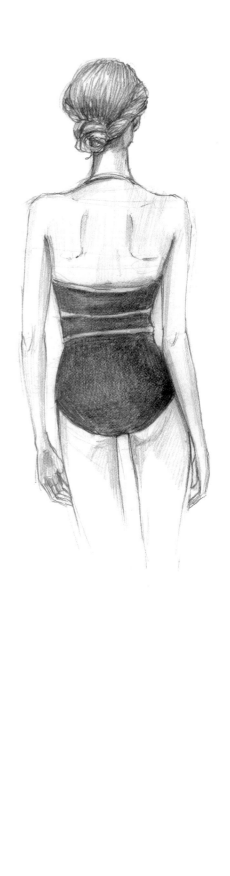

Left, maillot swimsuit; center, two piece swimsuit with high-
waisted bottom; right, one-piece maillot seen from back.

swimwear/one piece/
two piece

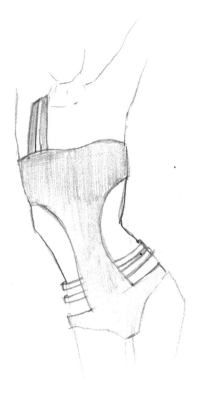

When drawing swimwear it is important to ensure that garments line up with the bodies underneath—that the center-fronts of both are closely matched up. The garments fit very close to the body so their lines must closely follow the body's curves.

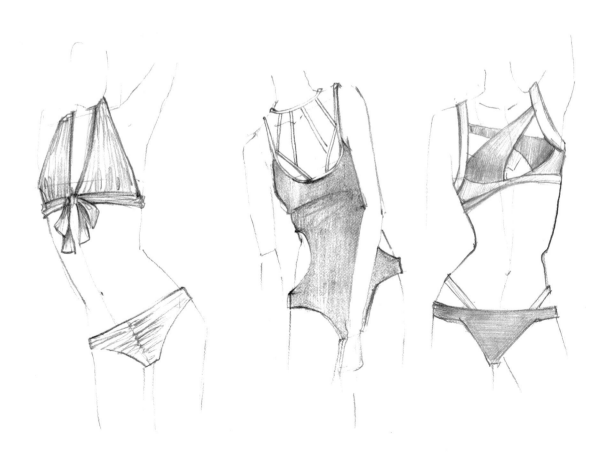

Strap variations in one and two-piece swimsuits.

swimwear/bikinis

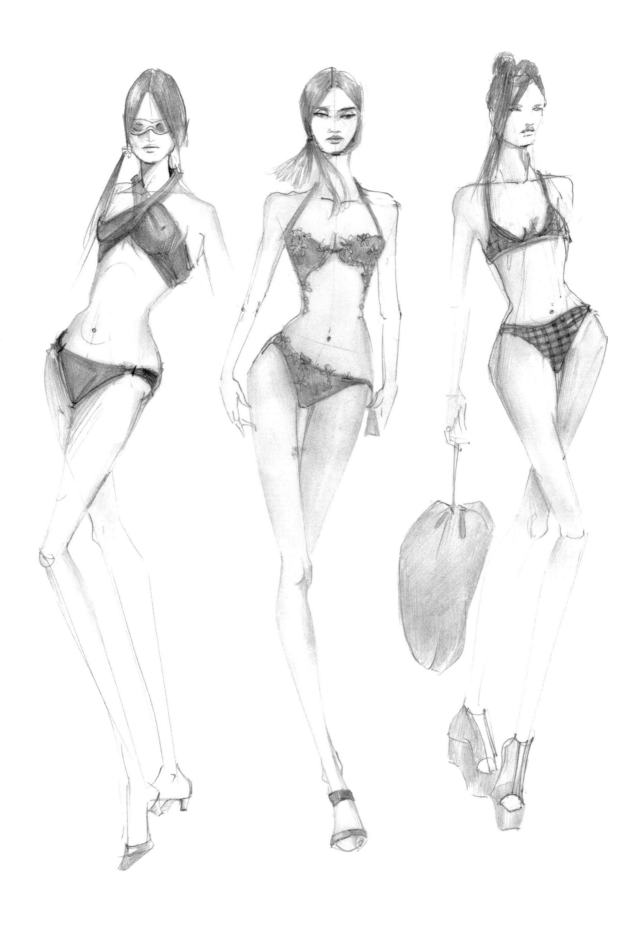

Bikinis with varied straps—criss-cross, halter and spaghetti.

Left, asymmetrical cotton coverup; center, semi-transparent
sarong; right, cape coverup over bikini with ornamental detail.

Lower left, semi-transparent cotton blouse with cap sleeves over
two piece bathing suit; top left, man's shirt over two piece
bathing suit; top right, cotton sweatshirt over boy shorts.

Left, oversized hooded jacket with dolman sleeves; center and
right, front and back views of transparent coverup.

Left, low-rise cotton pants with wide pockets; center, hooded top with flutter sleeves over soft cotton pants; right, skinny low-rise jeans.

lingerie

Left, baby doll top with criss cross straps; center, comfort bra with lace detailing and transparent lace briefs; right, underwire bra, embroidered panties.

lingerie

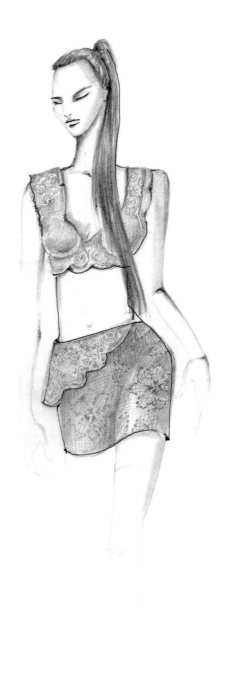

Left, cotton separates sleepwear. Right, cotton lace separates with underwire and cotton lace slip.

lingerie

Left, bra and girdle with suspenders and gown; right, transparent-sleeved bra top, lace panties.

lingerie

Left, corset with satin yoke and silk briefs; center, strapless bra with
lace trim and lace briefs; right, full underwire bra, boy-cut shorts.

Color adds a new dimension of information to a fashion drawing. To be able to draw well in color, though, it is best first to master how to use line and shading in black and white so that the silhouette, drape and fit ,and details of a garment can be presented in a clear, accurate and attractive way.

chapter three:
accessories

drawing accessories/ hats

Accessories are items of fashion worn or carried in addition to the primary articles of clothing in an outfit. Accessories are usually functional but are also chosen for the fashion message they convey. Like clothes themselves accessories work with the outfit in a number of ways, acting as adornments, color complements and focal points among others. They include such items as hats, gloves, jewelry, bags, umbrellas, shoes, scarves and bows, belts, watches, socks, nylons, eyeglasses.

Today the range of accessories is wider than ever because of the numerous gadgets of the modern age—cell phones, pagers, sophisticated watches, laptop computers, hand-held electronic devices, cameras, binoculars, videocams, tape recorders, roller skates, skateboards. Accessories used to be made from a limited choice of materials. Today they are made from a far greater range, both naturally occurring and man-made, including plastics, nylon, natural and synthetic fabrics, rubber, metals, papers, leathers and animal skins.

When drawing accessories first pay attention to the material they are made from. If the accessory is made from a solid material, e.g. metal, plastic, glass, wood or gemstone, it should be drawn with a crisp, clean outline. Use a very sharp pencil point or thin ink line. When drawing cut gems (diamonds, sapphires, rubies, emeralds etc.) be sure to leave a tiny separation at the corners where the different facets meet. This gives the illusion of reflection and shine. Draw pearls with a tiny highlight and a dark area where each individual pearl is connected to its neighbor. Be sure that all jewelry when worn appears to go around the body.

HATS

Hats come in many shapes and forms and have many different functions; they can be decorative, protective or part of a uniform. Hats are also made from a large variety of materials. The hat must fit around the head, with the brim usually extending down the forehead, often as far as the eybrows. Since hats actually change the scale of our heads, they are a significant and important accessory.

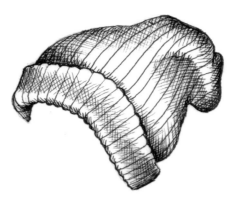

Beanie

Wide-brim hat

Bowler hat

Hunting cap

hats

Chinese-inspired
straw hat

Garbo hat

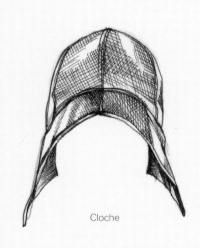

Cloche

Vintage hat with feathers

Beret

Cossack

Fedora

Cowboy hat

hats on heads

HATS ON HEADS. Don't let hats levitate—they cannot float in space. Note that all hats are *elliptical*—they are *not* round, the elliptical curves tiltling up or down according to the angle of the hat.

SHAWLS
Shawls require a large amount of fabric and are often drawn framing the head and shoulders. To show the luxury and fullness of the drape, use sweeping, voluminous lines. Shade with wide, soft tones. Add fringe and pattern as desired.

Don't let hats levitate, they cannot float in space. Note that all hats are elliptical—they are not round—the elliptical curves tilting up or down according to the angle of the hat.

Baseball cap

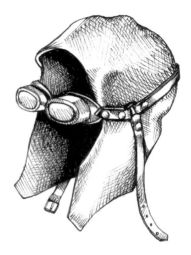

Aviator hat and goggles

Sun visor

Riding hat

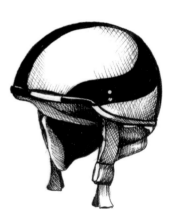

Motorcycle helmet

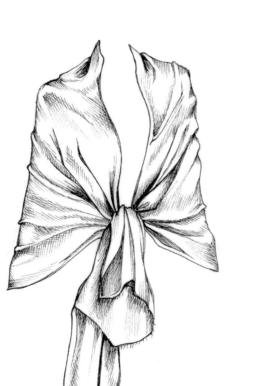

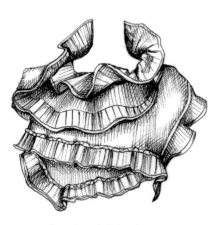

Complex spiral shawl.
It is essential to note the
direction of each layer as
it spirals down.

All the folds of this shawl
radiate from the tie.

Folds extend from left hand side of
the shawl. Note that size of drape
varies considerably within the
shawl.

bows/belts

BOWS

Begin with a simple butterfly shape consisting of two triangles touching in the center. Add the knot , which bends around the center of the two triangles and often has a little fold. Bring the ties or streamers out of the sides of the knot. Remember the streamers cannot come out of the center of the knot. This is a do-not do! Shade with a soft pencil or ink wash. Drawing the streamers in a soft scarf or bow requires more curves and fluid lines as if the wind has softly whisked the scarf into the air.

BELTS

When drawing belts it is essential to express the way the belt bends around the figure. Darkest shading will often be at the sides where it is recedes from the light. Buckles should be carefully placed– aligned with the c-f of the garment where in the middle of the belt. Pay attention to the material of the belt and draw accordingly. If the belt has a bow or tie drape should emanate from that area.

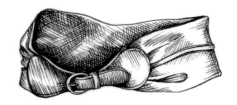

Bows are not easy to draw. The knot must look as though it is compressing its interior and one of the tails must be drawn in front of the knot and the other behind. The tails must also appear to be the same width as the rest of the bow. Belts must appear to bend around the figure. The buckle must be correctly placed on the c-f line.

bags and necklace/
exercise

BAGS

The best angle from which to draw a bag to
show its design details to the best effect is the
three-quarter view. Start with a cube or cylinder, whichever is closest in shape (refer to
Chapter One for how to draw these three-
dimensionally); add shading and design details.

EXERCISE

Begin by drawing twenty ovals. Divide a piece
of paper into four sections. Choose four
favorite accessories from your wardrobe. Draw
each of these accessories carefully, paying
attention to the materials they are constructed
from and how shadows form on them and light
is reflected. Work slowly and with great precision so you will have a piece good enough for
your portfolio.

bags in the hand

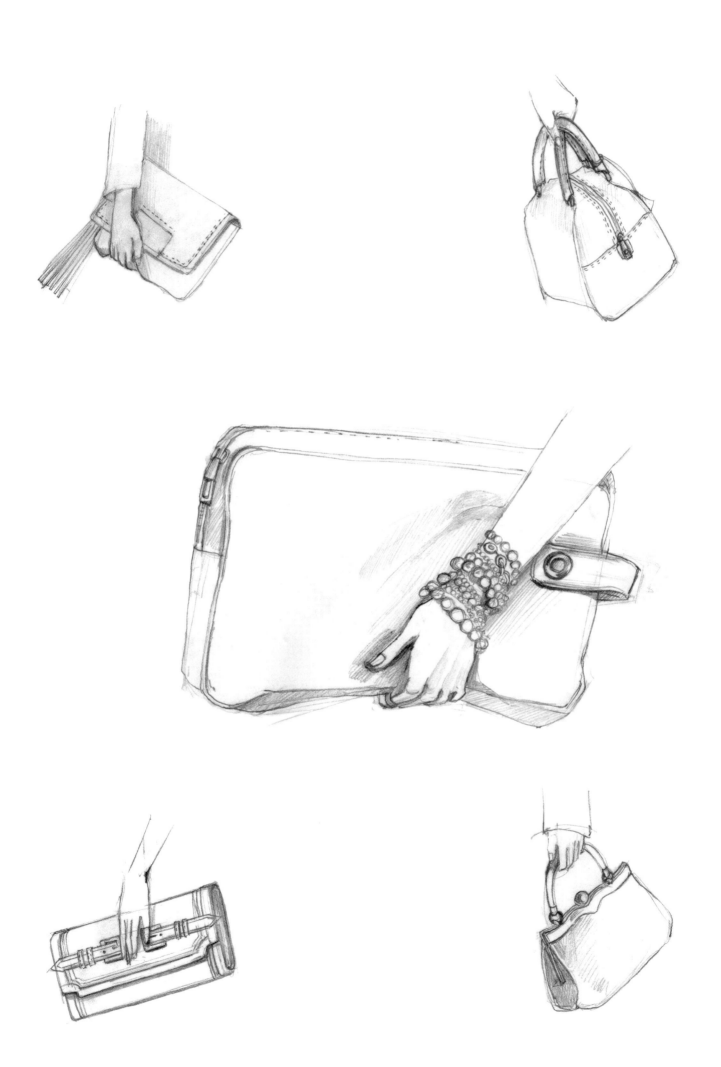

jewelry

JEWELRY, BRACELETS AND WATCHES
When drawing these items, think about simple ovals. A bracelet may be drawn using two parallel ovals, connected at the ends. Shading is darker in the interior of the bracelet. Add additional elements such as beads or indentations using a dark tone. Watches must be drawn with care so that the face and the frame of the watch remain distinct. Surface reflections may be drawn by adding an even tone of pencil. To add the appearance of a reflection on the face of a watch, use a sharp eraser, such as a pink pearl, quickly make a streak across the drawing. This gives the illusion of reflected light.

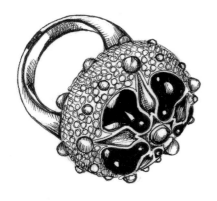

gloves

GLOVES

Gloves are often made of plastic, fur, fabric, leather or are knitted. They add volume to the hand so must be drawn with care and an elegant line to avoid a bulky sausage-like shape. Fingers and wrist can be tapered to enhance the beauty of the drawing. Remember to add stitching, especially round the thumb.

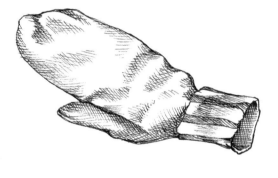

gloves

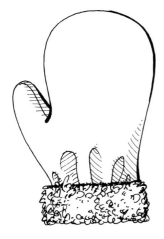

Mitten with fur cuff

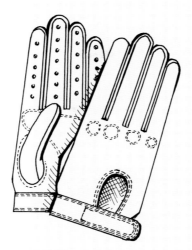

Walking /golf glove

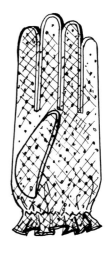

Lace glove with elastic wrist

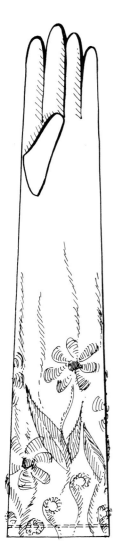

Arm length with embroidery

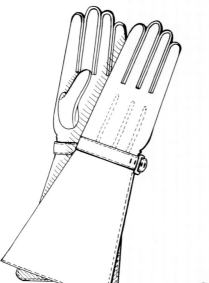

Gauntlet

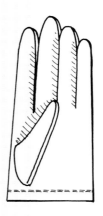

Shortie

Opera glove with trim

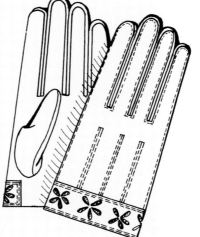

Slip-on with burn out
flower design

Knit glove with rib cuff and
jacquard inset

Fingerless sports/workout glove

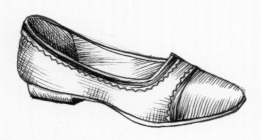

Flat

Open-toe high heel

Open-toed evening shoe

Prada inspired high heel

Sandal

Ankle bootie

Wedge bootie

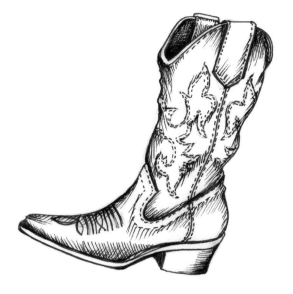

Cowboy boot

Casual oxford

Stiletto platform shoe.

High-ankle strap day shoe

Tennis shoe

Cold weather work boot

Running shoe

Strapped designer boot

Velcro strap bootie

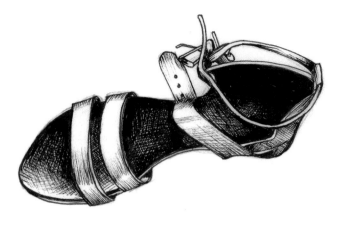

Sandal

Buckle work boot

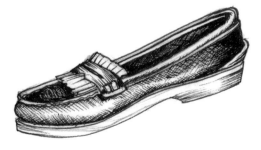

Penny loafers

Fur-lined tie mocassin

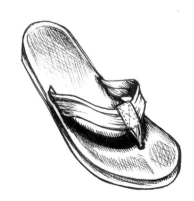

flip flop

Ankle strap high heel

Self-tie high heel

Ballet shoe

Evening slide

Strappy stiletto

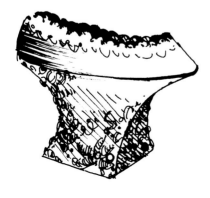

Chopines (17th c.
Venetian lady's shoe)

Ballet shoe

Costume jewelry ring

accessories on the figure

Hat/glove ensemble

Necklaces, bracelets and rings

accessories on the figure

Multiple rings

Veil and floral hat

chapter four:
flats

flats

FLATS

Flats are two-dimensional drawings of garments with all proportions and measurements made exactly to scale, like architectural blueprint drawings. In flats the garments are drawn alone, without the figure. When accompanied by the vital measurements and details of a garment flats are known as "specs" (short for specifications) and provide a definition exact enough to allow a garment to be constructed. These flats are known as "production flats".

Flats are usually complements, rather than substitutes, for concept drawings of garments: For a completely new design for a garment it is important to know the intended mood, fit and drape of a garment, and these aspects are best shown in a concept drawing. Where new designs are evolutions of, or are closely related to existing garments, however, and the look and feel of the garment are well known, flats alone often can communicate all the information required. This is especially so for active sportswear garments, where silhouettes, fit and drape are usually familiar, and new designs are often simply changes of superficial detailing.

Because flats are scale drawings used directly in the construction of garments they must reflect actual body proportions—a length equivalent to eight heads— rather than the idealized proportions of the nine-head fashion croquis. The croquis template used for flats is also fuller-figured than the slim nine-heads croquis.

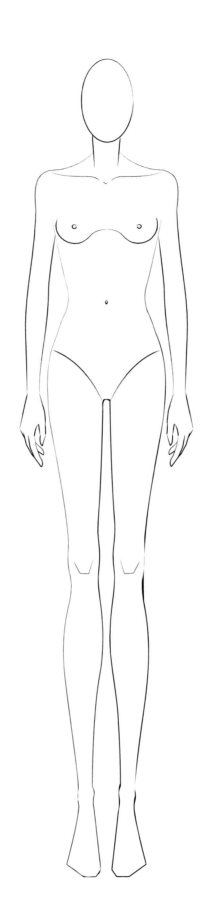

The original nine heads croquis used in concept drawings.

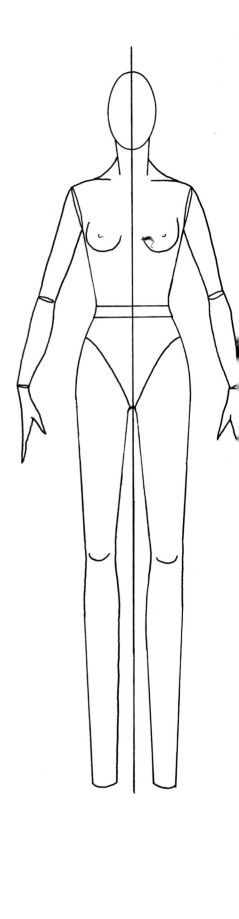

The template for flats based on the eight heads figure. Besides being shorter it is fuller than the nine heads figure.

precision of line/ materials for drawing flats

PRECISION OF LINE

In concept drawings lines can be free and expressive, and artistic license can frequently be taken: although proportions and details must be accurate, conveying exactquantitative information is often not as important as conveying mood and overall appearance. In concept drawing lines are also frequently nuanced—their thickness and weight varied— to indicate shading and fabric type. This is not the case with flats: Lines used in flats have to be precise, smooth and with no jagged edges or wobbles so that the exact shape of the garment is made crystal clear. Flats, particularly when learning to draw them, are first drawn in pencil, but the final presentation is made using a fine point ink pen that produces a smooth, even line.

When drawing flats, any tool or device that helps produce better drawings can and should be used: rulers help in drawing straight lines and French curves help in drawing smooth curves. While making full use of these tools, it is also useful to develop the ability to draw lines freehand from an early stage; this will make the process of drawing flats quicker and easier. A good exercise to develop this skill is to fill a page with dots and practice joining them with as straight a line as possible using a single fluid movement of the wrist without pausing partway. Practice drawing curves freehand by copying curves produced with a French curve and tracing over garment outlines.

In concept drawing lines can be free and expressive and are frequently nuanced. Garments are often shaded using dense flat applications of pencil. These techniques contrast strongly with. the precise use of line required when drawing flats.

materials for drawing flats/
line weight/stitches

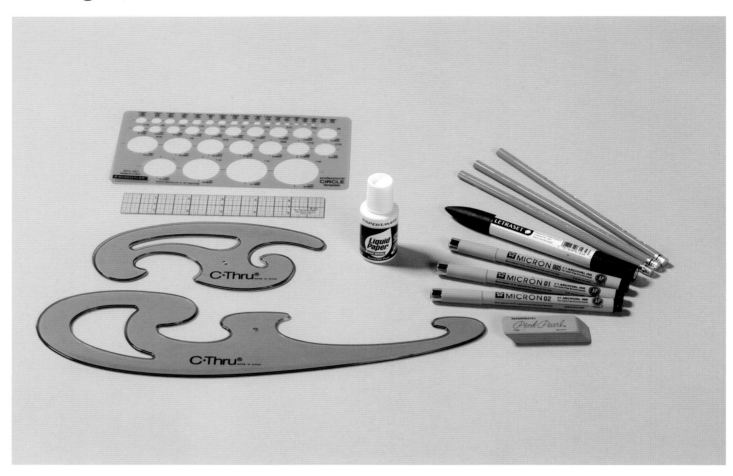

Materials for drawing flats.

PENS: .005 for silhouettes
             .003 for detailing
             .05 for shadow on buttons,
             pockets, collars etc.
PENCIL :   2H lead pencil
PAPER :   Layout or copy paper
             Tracing Paper
MARKER   (for shading)–10% Cool grey
RULER: 6″ Transparent plastic
FRENCH CURVE
ERASER
WHITE-OUT CORRECTING FLUID
PENCIL SHARPENER (Electric sharpeners are best)

Marks used on knitted garm-
nets to show where parts of
the garment are sewn to the
main body.

Usual lineweight for drawing flats, made with a .005 pen.

Blind stitching, made with a .005 pen.

Usual lineweight for shading flats, made with a .03 pen.

Saddle stitching, made with a .03 pen for the horizontal line and .005 pen for the stitches.

Top stitching, made with a .005 pen.

Double-needle top stitch, made with a .005 pen.

Lineweight and use of line when drawing flats.

templates/knitwear/
bodysuit/general points

DRAWING FLATS: TEMPLATES

Flats are based on the actual proportions of the figure. The eight-head croquis that is the basis for flats can be used as a guide, placed directly underneath the flats being drawn, to ensure the proportions are correct. Rather than working with the croquis, though, it is more usual to work with templates based on the eight head figure and made for different garment types. In this chapter these templates are used as the starting points for explanations of how to draw flats and work out specs for a number of basic garments. The templates included here are examples of near-generic garments. In the garment industry, particularly for sportswear, templates are developed in-house, and new designs worked out quickly and easily using the templates derived from existing garments.

There are a number of characteristics common to all flats, as well as techniques and helpful tips that should be considered before beginning to learn to draw flats, and kept in mind whenever drawing flats. These are:

1. Flats are symmetrical: the left and right sides match exactly, except in those cases where the garment contains an asymmetrical design element. One method to make sure flats are drawn symmetrically is to draw one side of the garment up to the center-front line, trace over that drawing, flip it over and trace over it again to give a mirror image for the other side.

2. As mentioned, flats are eight heads, reflecting real proportions. All proportions are the same as the nine-head figure but the legs are shortened by one head. Flats appear slightly wider and larger than garments drawn on a nine-head figure.

3. Flats should be first drawn in pencil (always use a very sharp pencil) and then inked in when correct. French curves and rulers should always be used.

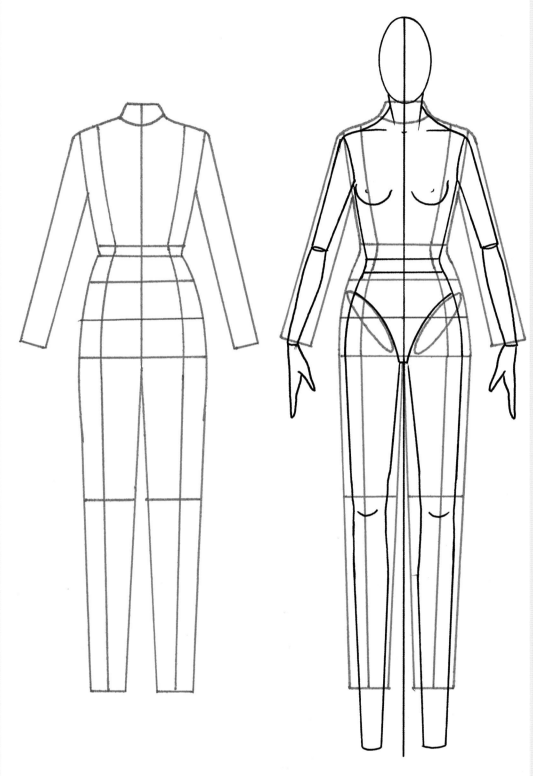

Bodysuit/knitwear template.

Bodysuit/knitwear template over 8 head croquis.

how to draw skirt/pant flats

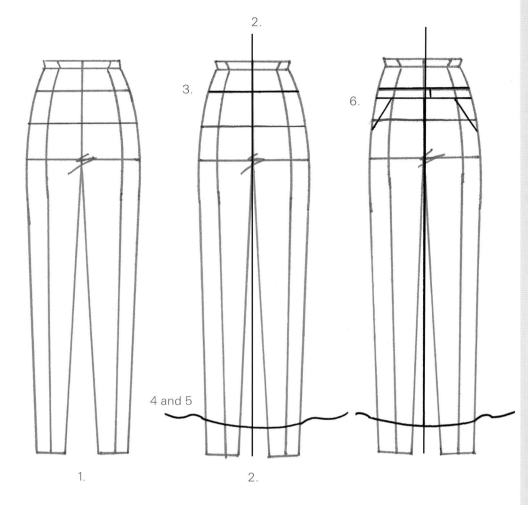

1.

2.

3.

4 and 5

6.

2.

4. Especially when beginning to draw flats, sketch on top of the eight head croquis template or one of the basic garment templates included in this chapter. *Always* indicate the center-front line and make sure measurements are symmetrical on either side of that line.

5. All seams and other constructional details must be included in flats, drawn to the scale of the garment. For garments with sleeves, arms are shown away from the body so the silhouette of the sleeve can be clearly seen. If sleeves contain details on the underside, one or both arms can be shown bent at a 45° angle so the detail is revealed.

SPECS

Methods for measuring specifications for the garments described in this chapter is included in an appendix at the end of the book.

PANTS

Flats for pants should be drawn with the legs about shoulder-width apart so the silhouette of the legs can be clearly seen. The template shown in the illustration is taken from the full-body template for flats and is for relatively close-fitting pants but can be used to develop any number of variations. The fit in the waist and hip area is close, and fullness in the legs of the pants can be varied by changing the line of the outer edge below the lower hip line; the inseam remains near-vertical for all shapes of pants.

SKIRTS

The skirt silhouette is almost the same as that of pants with the obvious difference that skirts do not have legs. The flat is drawn by indicating the position of the hem and then finishing the silhouette by joining the hem to the pants template where the fullness starts, at the lower hip line, as with pants (unless the skirt is gathered at the waist, in which case the fullness starts at the waist). A breakdown for drawing skirt flats is shown at right.

Drawing skirt and pant flats.
1. Start with the skirt/pant flat template.
2. Establish the axis/center-front line.
3. Determine position of waist (options :high waist/on waist/natural (just below)/high hip (hipsters)/low hip (low riders.)
4. Decide on the length of the garment.
5. Decide on the fullness of the garment. The fuller the skirt the more curves it will have at the hem. How far down does the fullness start?
6. Determine the width of the waistband and indicate the position of the pockets.

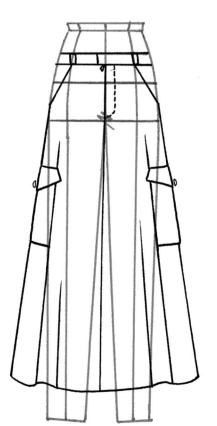

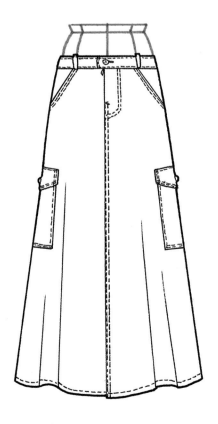

7. Flesh in waistband styling. Draw in pockets. Draw in the center seam and princess seams if necessary. Indicate the position of the zipper pull and the stitching of the zipper seam.

8. Add details (for example, double needle stitching; zippers; shading; hem treatments; belt loops, buttons/buttonholes).

pant and skirt lengths/
pant and skirt widths

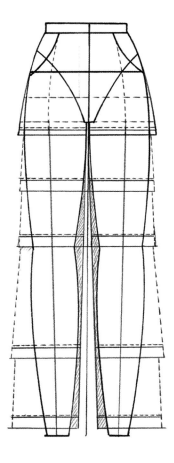

Pant lengths.

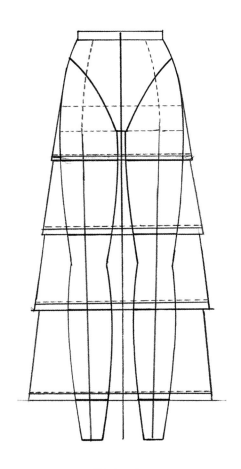

Skirt lengths..

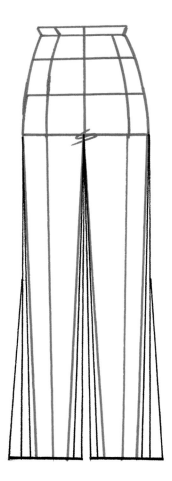

Pant widths.

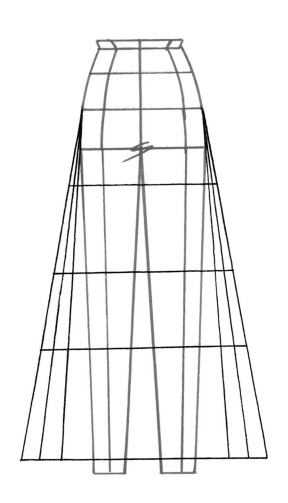

Skirt widths.

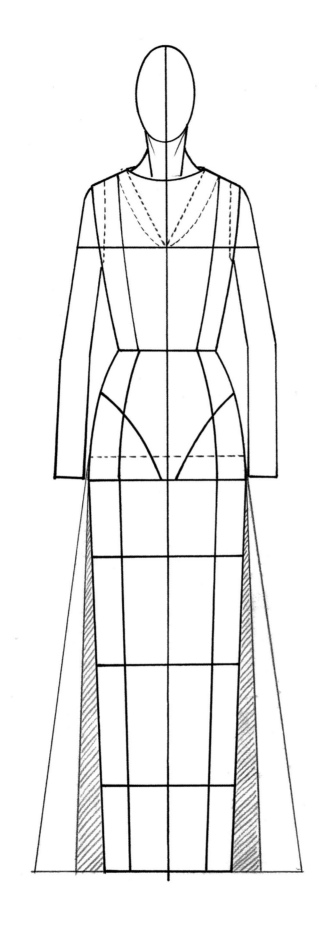
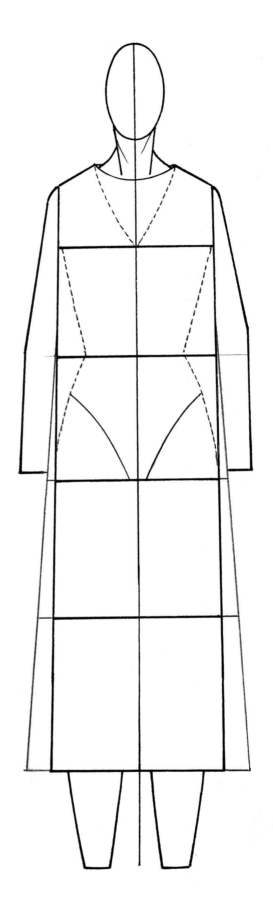

how to draw fitted
garment flats

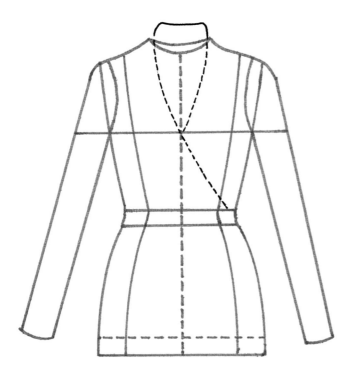

1. Draw in the center-front line. Draw in the collar opening to the wrap point Define the length and indicate the arm-hole/sleeve adjustment.

2. Flesh in the "shell" of body and the ties.

3. Add drape.

4. Add shading/ stitching details/ indi-cate construction at back of the neck.

how to draw tailored jacket flats

1— Establish the center-front line and the position of the buttons on it. If the jacket is single-breasted the buttons will sit on the center-front line. Space the buttons evenly by marking the center of each button and measuring from center to center.

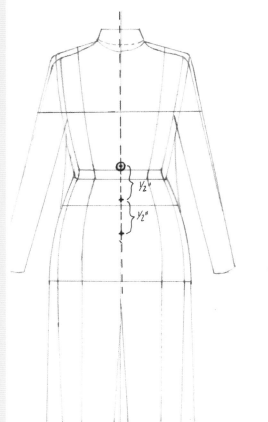

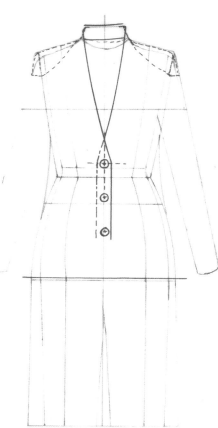

2— Draw in the opening of the jacket by extending lines from the center front to the break-points of the collar on each side.
−Add buttons.
−Add the roll of the collar , hugging the neck , and drawing slightly curved line from the neck to the break point.
— Repeat on the other side. Note:that this line will extend to the imaginary break point on the other side of the jacket. If this is done correctly the ends of the collar rolls will be at center front.
— Establish the finished length of the coat.
—Make allowance for the thickness of the shoulder pads (incorporate into the croquis

3.—Establish the position of the lapels (below the collar) first then add the shape of the collar.

4.— Pencil in the internal details of the jacket i.e..welts, princess seams etc.

5.— Establish the hem line shape at the front and pencil in. Again measure from center - front line to check symmetry.

6. —Add in the "shell" of the jacket
— Ink in details and add button holes (usually keyhole on tailored jackets).
—Add top stitching (if any)
— Add lining details (if any)
— Add shading to give depth under the collar, lapel & b.

Note: Tailored jackets usually two-piece sleeves. Do not forget to show the seams.

fitted dress/square jacket templates
positions for showing sleeves

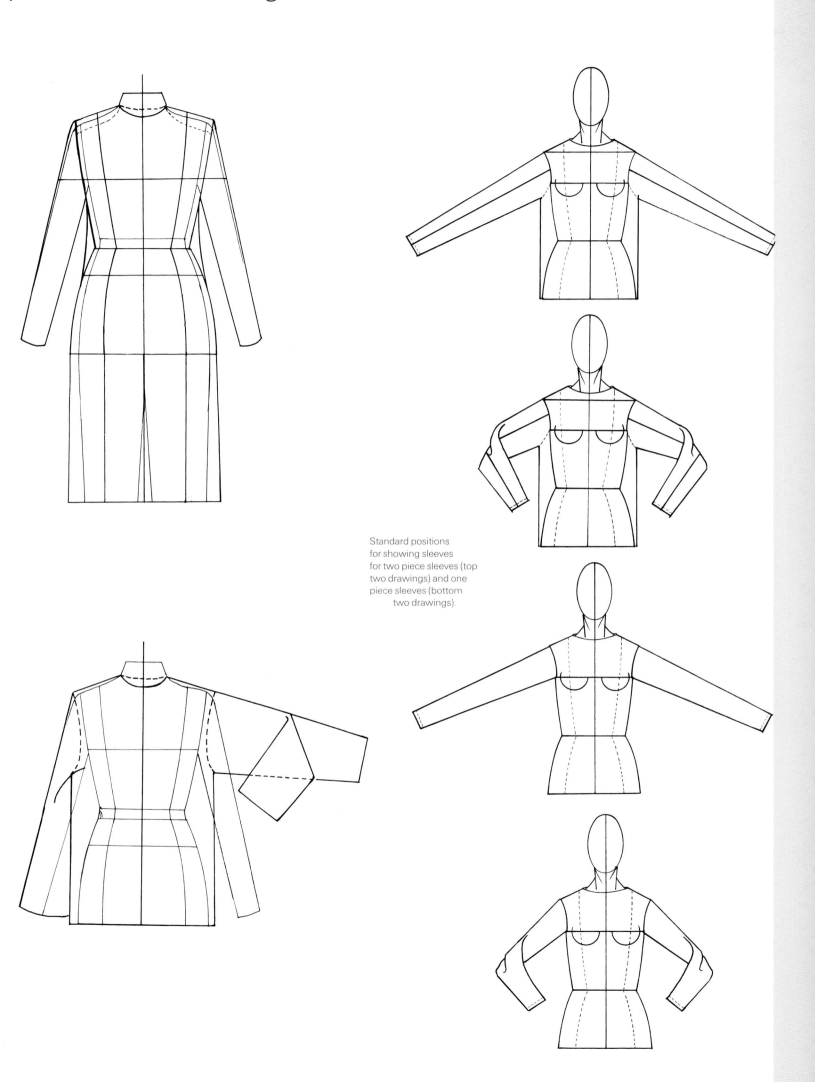

Standard positions for showing sleeves for two piece sleeves (top two drawings) and one piece sleeves (bottom two drawings).

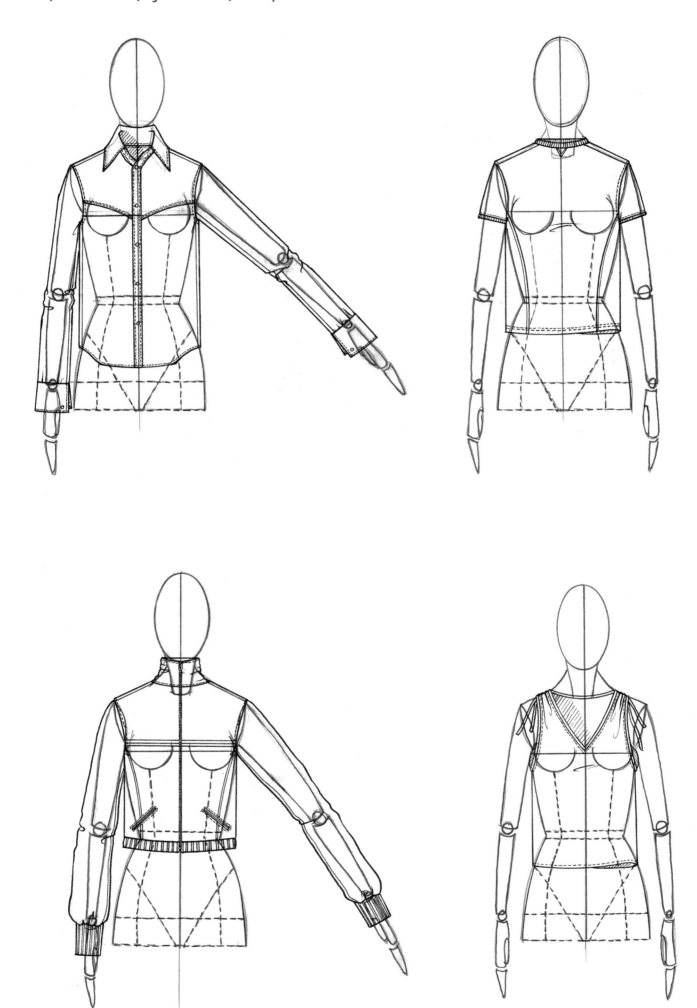

flats drawn over templates/
jackets/do's and do not do's

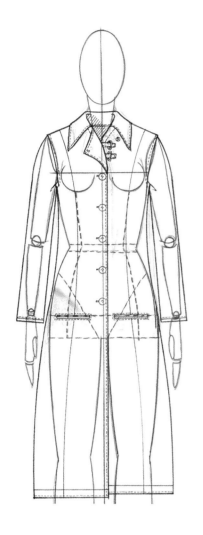

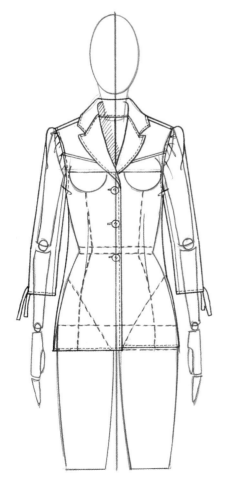

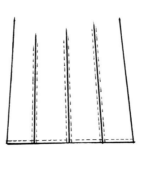

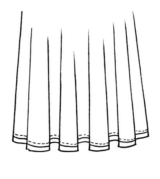

Skirt Do's and Do not Do's. The middle drawing is correct, the other two are incorrect. Where hems end in folds these should be drawn as cylinders; attempts at shorthand two-dimensional graphic representations will often be misinterpreted as seams.

Pant waistlines. Top, correct; bottom ,Do not Do. Gathers at the waist must be drawn to show the fullness of the fabric or will be misinterpreted as flat bands.

Pant Do's and Do not Do's. Top two drawings are correct; bottom two are incorrect. The break in pants can be shown by a squiggle or horizontal line but not by "frown" or "smile" V-lines.

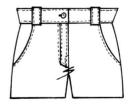

Do not Do. Waistbands must be drawn with square edges and for female pants fly should be on left (unless denim jeans, which are unisex right.

flat drawings on templates
jackets/do's and do not do's

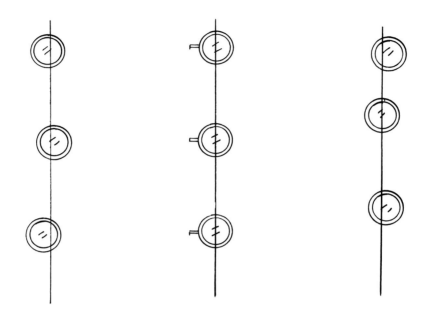

Button Do's and Do not Do's. Left and right are incorrect, center is correct. Buttons must be drawn on the center-front line and equally spaced. When the buttons have buttonholes the buttonholes should always be drawn. Buttons can be an important fashion feature and the drawing should show their detailing.

Collar Do's and Do not Do's. Left, correct; middle and right, incorrect. The edge of the collar and roll line meet at the silhouette of the shoulder of the garment (the drawings on the right suggest that angles have been introduced into the shape of the collar). The curve of the collar around the back of the neck should be indicated and the top and bottom lines of the band should be parallel.

flipover flaps

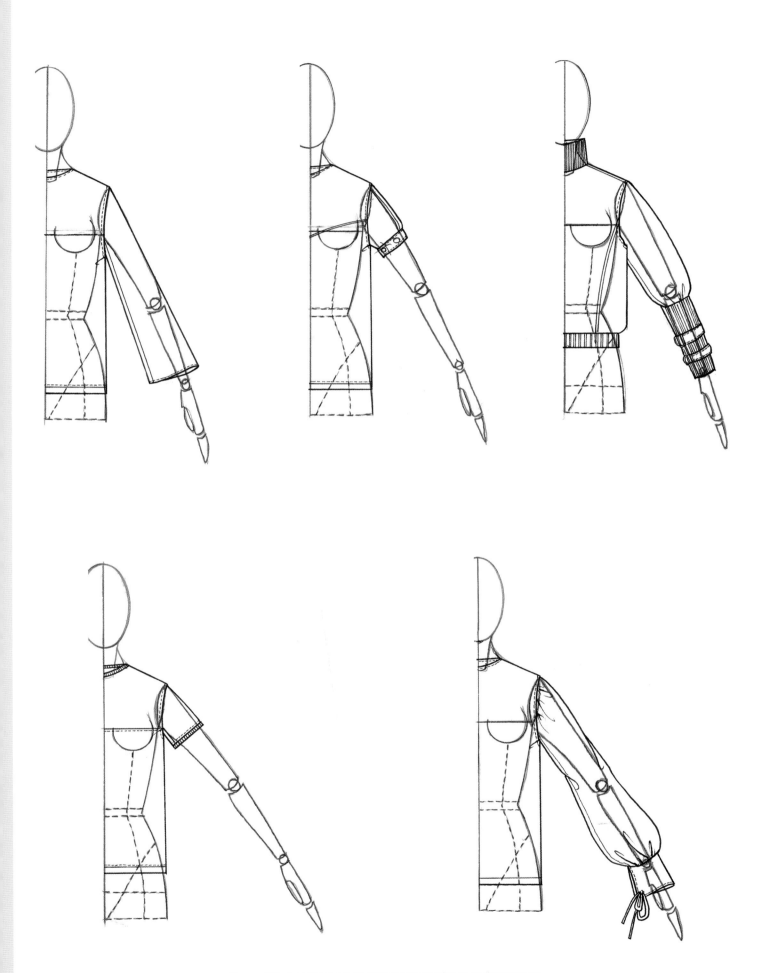

Flipover flats. A common way to draw flats is, drawing on tracing paper, to draw half the flat, fold the drawn half under the paper so it becomes its mirror image, trace over that onto the other half of the paper and open out the paper with the complete flat. This technique can save time and ensures the flat will be symmetrical about the center-front line.

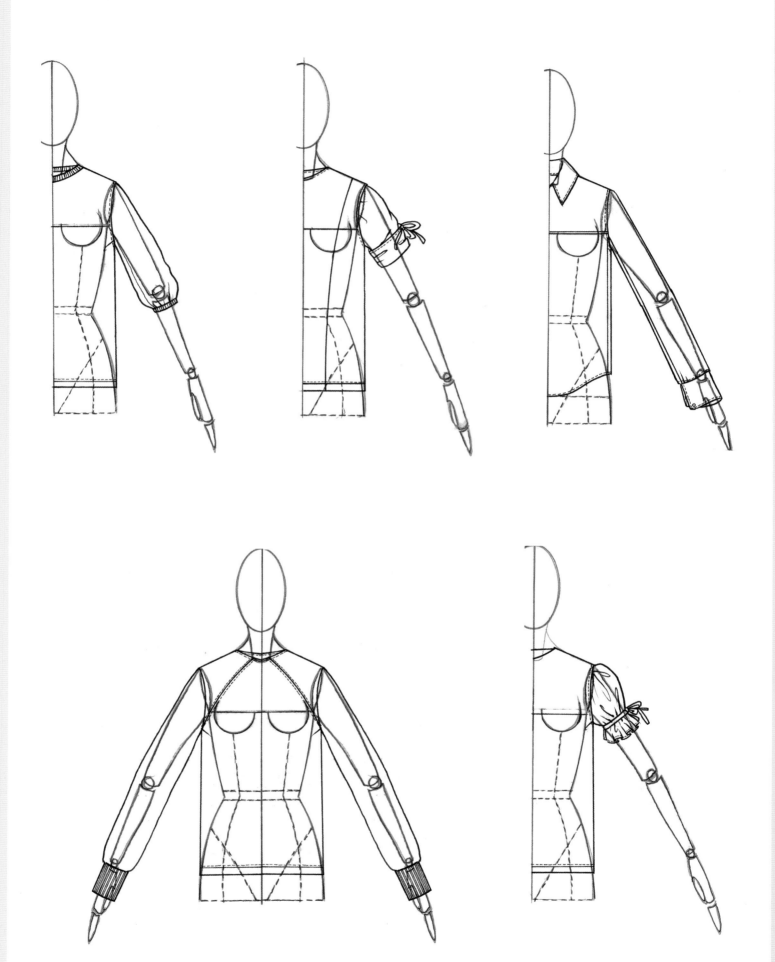

The finished flat created by flipping
over and copying one half.

freehand flats

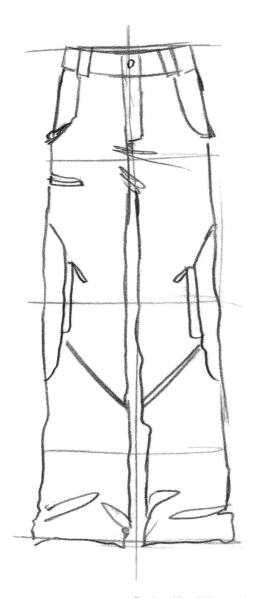

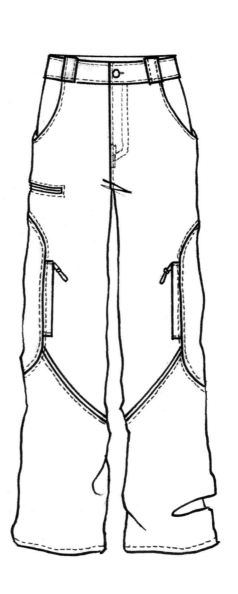

Freehand flats. With experience it is possible to sketch flats "freehand" with pencil without drawing in the template and with little use of rulers and curves. The sketches are then inked in and tightened up to produce the final flat, as shown in these illustrations.

flats with figure

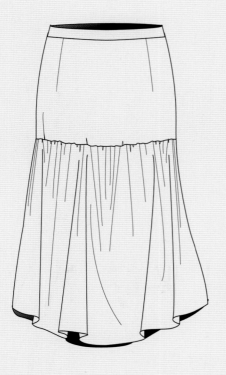

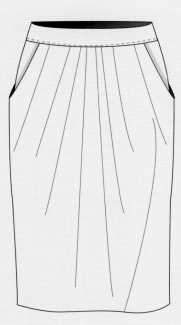

flats with figure

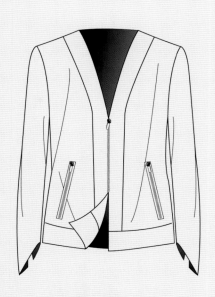

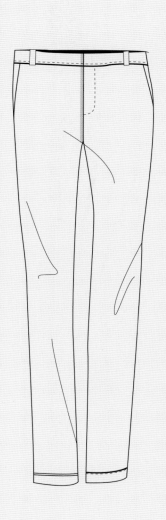

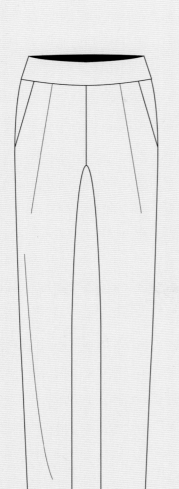

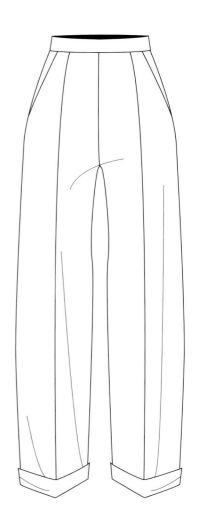

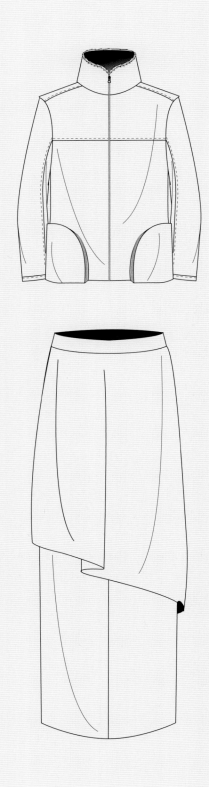

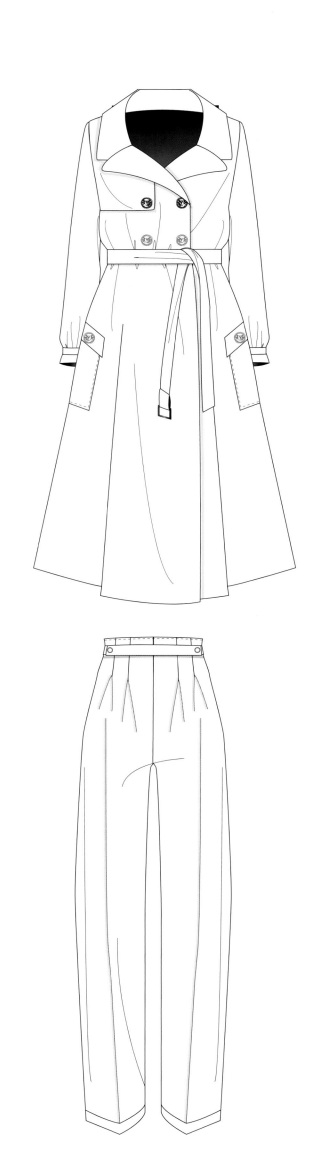

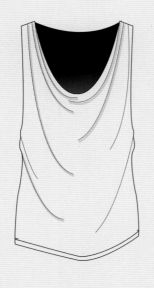

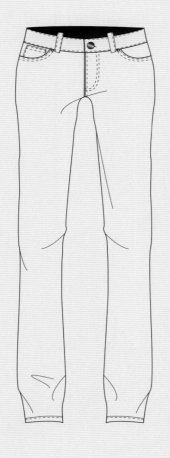

chapter five:
encyclopaedia
of details

fashion details/
collars

A large part of the process of designing new fashion involves creating variations from garments that already exist. This is done by combining the different elements of fashion in new ways, using new fabrics and colors and altering shapes and proportions. In most cases all the individual details of a new fashion garment are familiar and instantly recognizable to the fashion expert but are now presented in a fresh and unique new design combination.

Fashion details—known also as construction details (though some details are purely decorative)—are the different ways that the different parts of fashion garments can be made. Together the body of details forms a visual vocabulary from which the designer can freely choose and combine into new designs, both in the process of drawing new designs and in the actual construction of the new garment. When learning to design fashion it is most important to become familiar with a wide range of fashion details, to root them deeply in the memory so they are instantly recognized and can immediately spring into the imagination when a new design is being created.

This chapter is a mini encyclopaedia of (mainly) modern fashion details (many of the details have in fact existed for several centuries or more, but are still in common use and are regarded as "classics"). It can be used as a reference guide (all the different details are listed in the main index) or as a source of inspiration when working on new designs. The details have been drawn as accurately as possible mostly in two-dimensional flat-style form, but they can be used as references to create accurate three-dimensional concept drawings also. Careful note should be made of the way that line weight is used in the drawings to convey information about different types of details and the different parts of those details. Line weight is used here to indicate a number of different variables, including fabric type, weight and thickness and garment construction.

Included in this chapter are drawings of different types of closures, buttons, collars, tucks, darts, folds, fabrics, stitches, knitting stitches, knots, bows, sequins and other jewels and various other accessories. Also included are some classic styles for skirts, jackets, tops and other coats; a further range of these and other garments can be found in the Appendix of women's flats and Chapters Seven and Eight on Men and Children, respectively.

Funnel

Square

Shirt—basic rolled collar

Round roll-back & buttoned

Cowl—stand style— high

Button-down collar

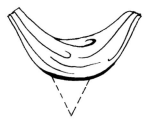

Draped neck

Stand-up/banded collar

Fichu-tie front

Turtleneck

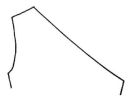

One shoulder

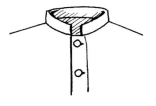

Mandarin

collars/hoods

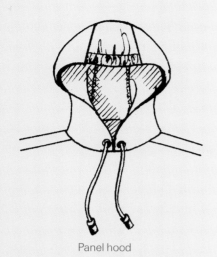

Panel hood

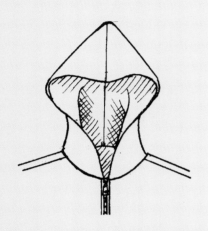

Panel hood/zipper

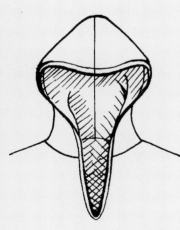

Panel hood/neck opening

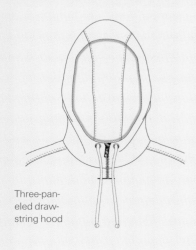

Three-paneled drawstring hood

Hooded—drawstring

Basic

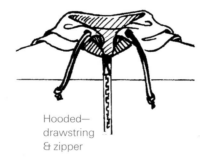

Hooded—zipper

Round zipper/bobber

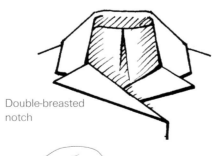

Hooded—drawstring & zipper

Peter Pan

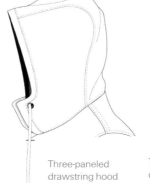

Double-breasted notch

Polo

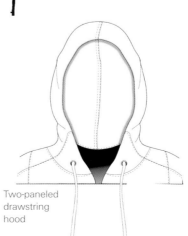

Three-paneled drawstring hood side view

Two-paneled drawstring hood

Multi-paneled drawstring hood

collars

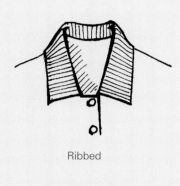

Ribbed

Sweetheart

Round—basic

Stock tie

Round—jewel

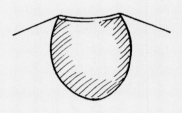

Scoop—basic

Wing—Chelsea

Round—bound/banded

V-neck

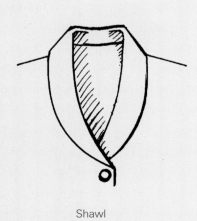

Shawl

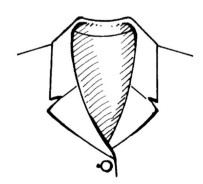

Notched

Boat/bateau

collars

High rib with
railroad stitch

Funnel with
invisible zip

Off neck

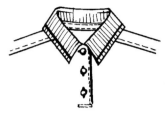

Polo with tipped collar
& back neck taping

Turtle with knit neck

Mock turtleneck with
coverstitch

French turtle—clean

Boat neck—faced

Peter Pan with
picot trim

Bertha with zip back

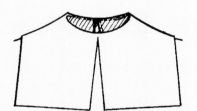

Pilgrim with button loop

Puritan with button loop

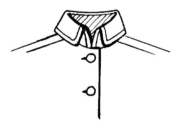

Convertible collar/high stand

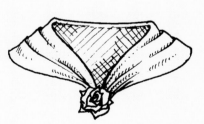

Fichu with rosette

Scarf/ascot

Stole collar

Notched Bertha

Buster Brown (Bertha)

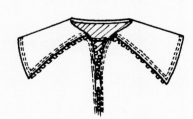

Zip-up Bertha

Bertha with knotted end

Cross muffler collar

Cowl

bottle

Roll with cover stitch

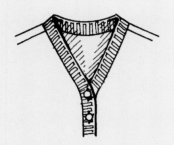

Cardigan—2x2 rib
Y neck

Drawstring

Convertible collar

Wing

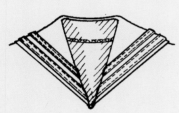

Sailor

Mandarin with edge-
stitch

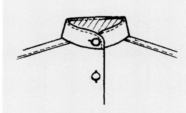

Cape

Chinese with frog

Bow

Clerical

Stand

Tab

Cascade

Double fold cascade

Tie front

Capelet—basic

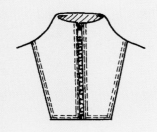

Zip front inset.
Mock turtle

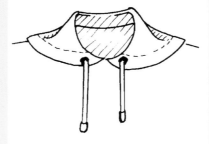

Drawstring hood

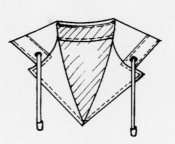

Hooded collar

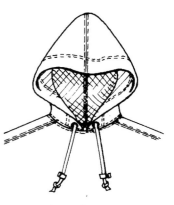

Hood F.V. upright

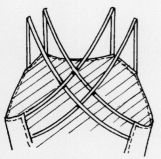

Criss-cross strap (back) version 1

Cross strap (back)

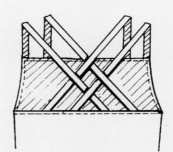

Criss-cross strap (back) version 2

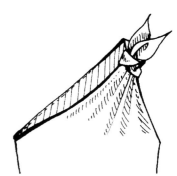

Asymmetrical with knotted shoulder

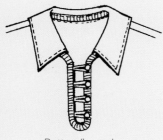

Button/loop closure

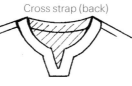

Round neck
Bound key hole

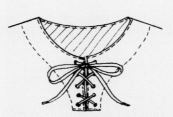

Lace-up front with facing

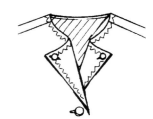

Fold-back collar

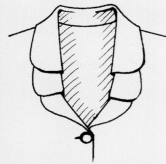

Triple

Shawl with fringe

Notched shawl

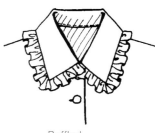

Ruffled

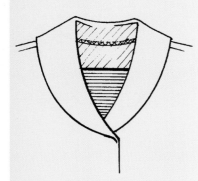

Shawl with inset

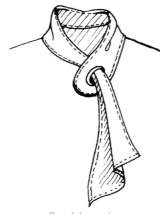

Scarf through

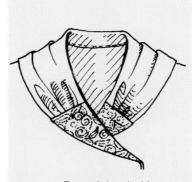

Draped shawl with embroidered panels

Pierrot

Wide hood with
blanket stitch (front)

Wide hood with blanket
stitch (back)

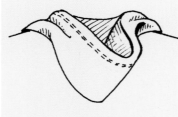

Alternate back view—
hood

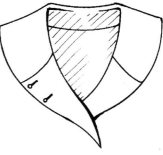

Roll back shawl collar

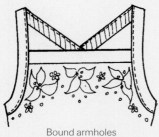

Bound armholes
with embroidery

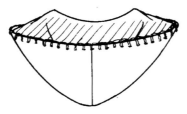

Spaghetti straps with
beading

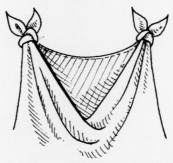

Knotted shoulders

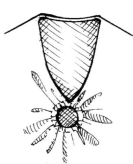

Center front ring

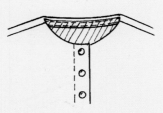

Snap front with twill tape
& back neck

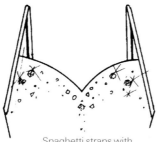

Chanel-style round neck

Button over collar

Zip front stand collar

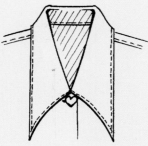

Wing—Chelsea

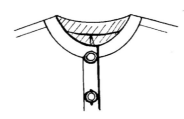

Round with shell stitch

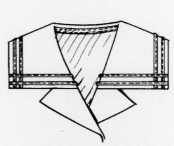

Square sailor with braid

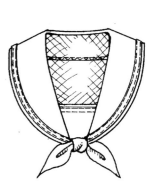

Shawl sailor with braid

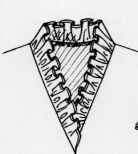

Flounce V-neck

Off-the-shoulder double
flounce

Cowl stand/turtle

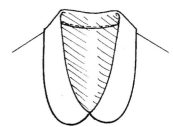

Rounded Chelsea

collars

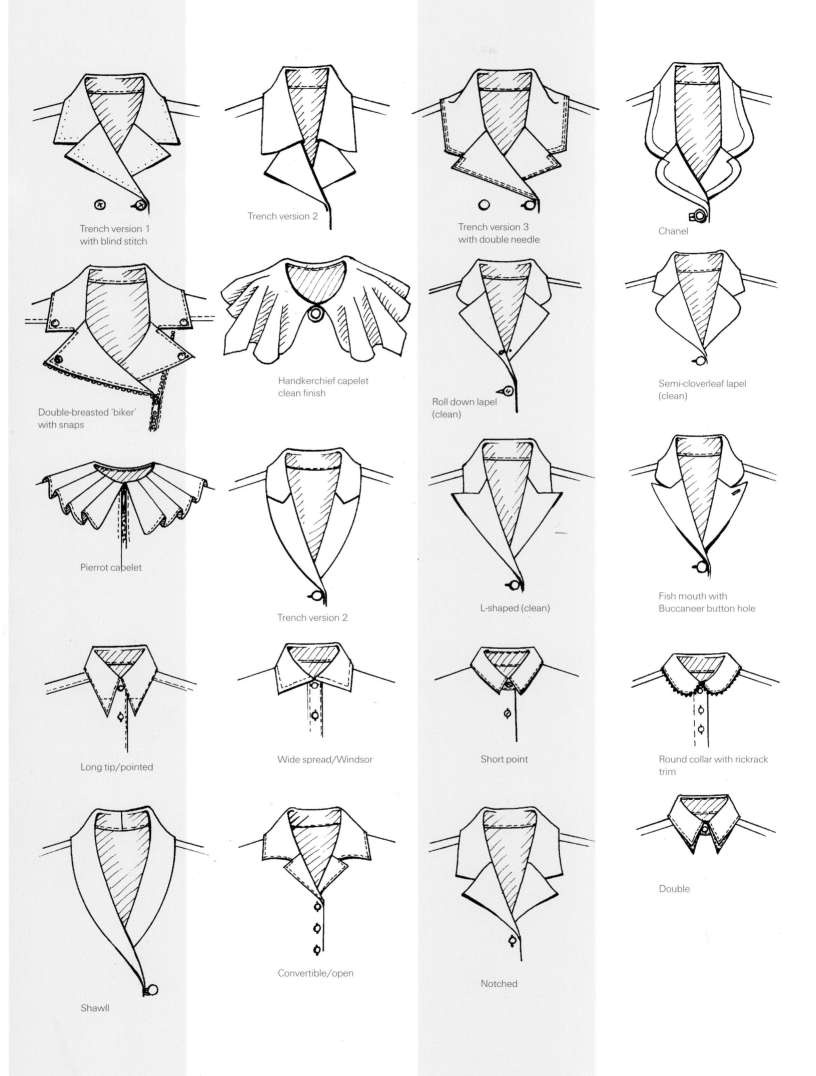

Trench version 1
with blind stitch

Trench version 2

Trench version 3
with double needle

Chanel

Double-breasted 'biker'
with snaps

Handkerchief capelet
clean finish

Roll down lapel
(clean)

Semi-cloverleaf lapel
(clean)

Pierrot capelet

Trench version 2

L-shaped (clean)

Fish mouth with
Buccaneer button hole

Long tip/pointed

Wide spread/Windsor

Short point

Round collar with rickrack
trim

Shawll

Convertible/open

Notched

Double

collars

Novelty shawl with
single needle

Notched shawl
clean finish

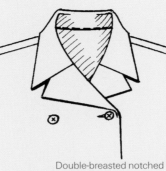

Double-breasted notched
clean finiish

Double-breasted
notched shawl

Semi-peaked with blind

Notched with blanket
stitch

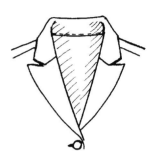

Bullied with novelty
embroidering

Semi-notch clean

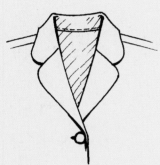

Clover field

Sword/peaked

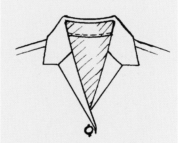

T-shaped

Flower

Wing version 2

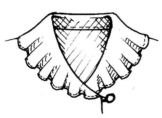

Ruffle

Low point collar

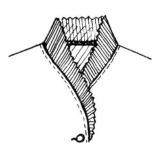

Frill

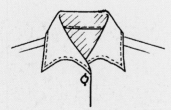

Italian/triangle/one piece

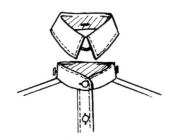

Detachable

Buttondown

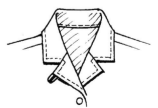

Hama/one nap

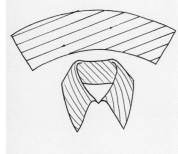

Bias cut

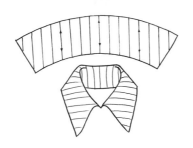

Straight grain

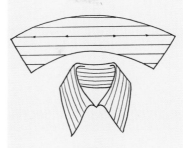

Cross grain

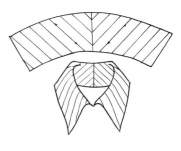

Mitered

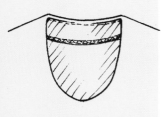

Oval—clean finish

Crew—clean finish rib

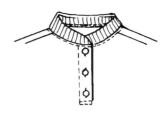

U-neck—clean finish faced

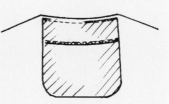

Henley

Spoon with picot edging

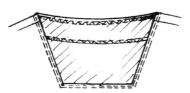

Keystone squared V
with 2n topstitch

Oblong

Round with button/loop
at LB

Scallop with zip opening
facing clean finish

2x2 rib scoop neck

Sculptured sweetheart

Halter—keyhole

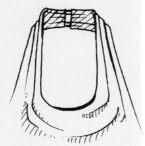

Halter—cowl with two
buttons at back

Halter with bow

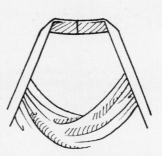

Halter—draped cowl

Halter—crossover

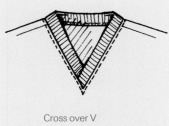

Cross over V

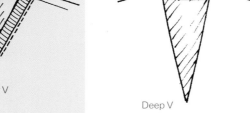

Deep V

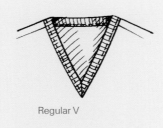

Regular V

V-shaped crew

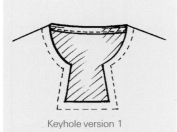

Keyhole version 1

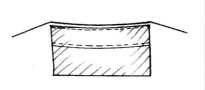

Square with facing
clean finish

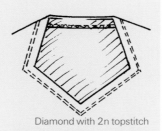

Diamond with 2n topstitch

Heart with facing
clean finish

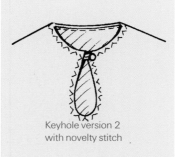

Keyhole version 2
with novelty stitch

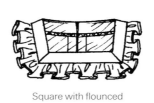

Square with flounced
Merrow edge

Halter-cut out shoulder

Sweetheart

Halter with tie at back

Halter-rib turtleneck

Halter—twisted

Halter—piped square front

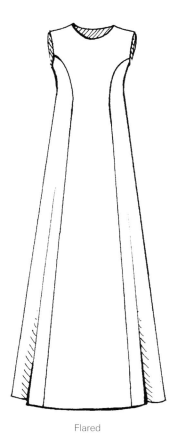

Flared

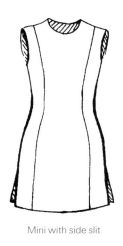

Mini with side slit

Full flared

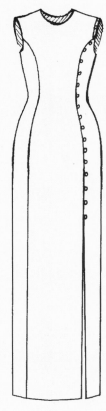

Fitted at waist

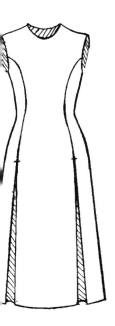

Princess seam with
inverted pleats

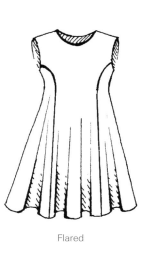

Flared

A line

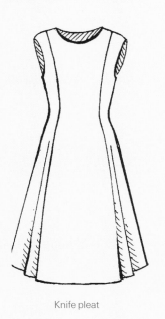

Knife pleat

Belted

skirts

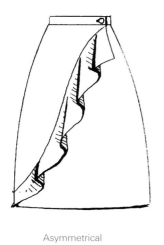

Asymmetrical

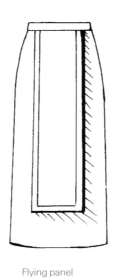

Flying panel

Granny

Culottes

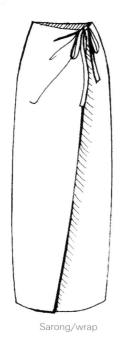

Sarong/wrap

Yoke skirt

High-waisted

Handkerchief hem

skirts

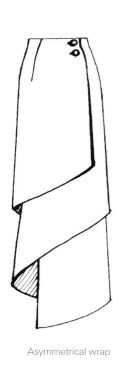

Asymmetrical wrap

A line

Dirndl

Draped

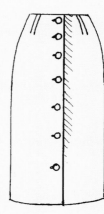

Button front

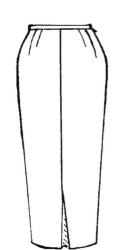

Peg top skirt

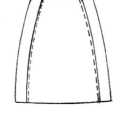

Miniskirt

Fly front micro mini

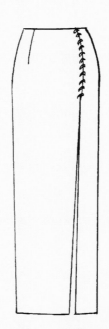

Slit skirt

Prairie

skirts

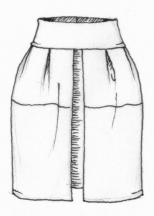

High waist short skirt

Two-tiered short skirt

Skirt with half peplum

Bias draped miniskirt with
decorative waistband

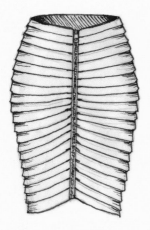

Multi-tiered fitted
skirt/railroad zipper

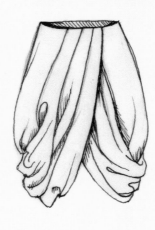

Asymmetrical
draped skirt

A-line skirt with button closure c-f

Pencil skirt with
asymmetrical detail

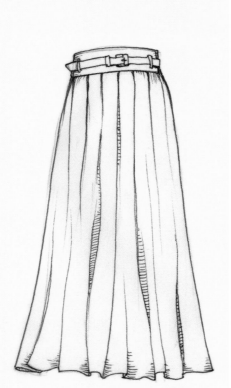

A-line skirt with belted waist

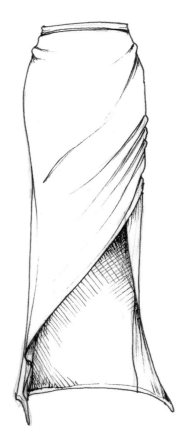

Long skirt with asymmetrical drape from ss

pants

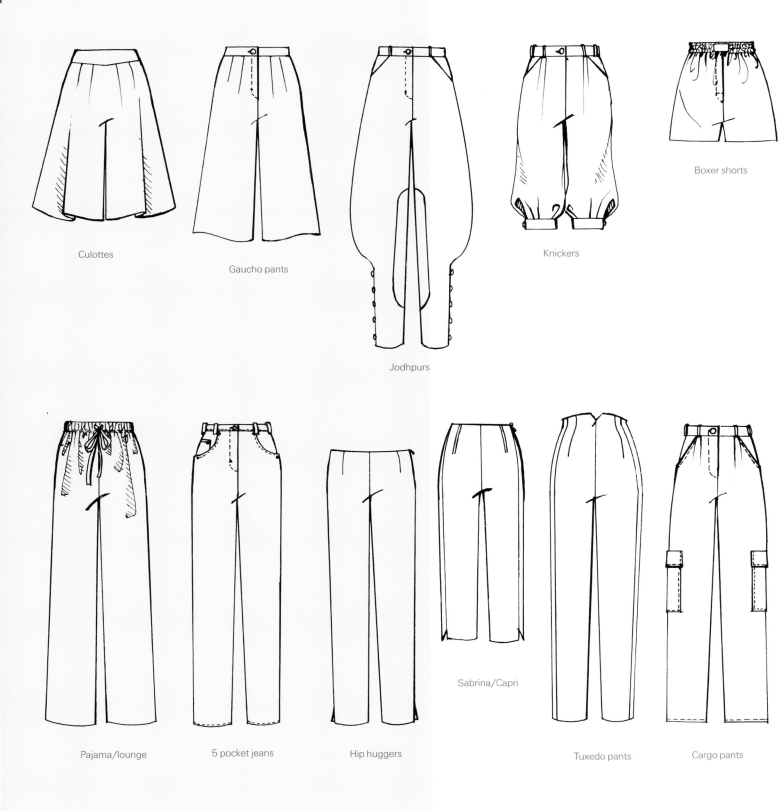

Culottes

Gaucho pants

Jodhpurs

Knickers

Boxer shorts

Pajama/lounge

5 pocket jeans

Hip huggers

Sabrina/Capri

Tuxedo pants

Cargo pants

Daisy Dukes/cut-offs

Hotpants

Board shorts

Bike pants

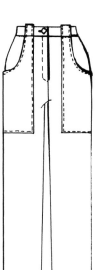
Bush pants

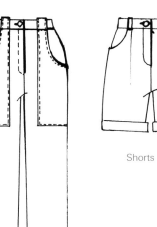
Shorts

pants

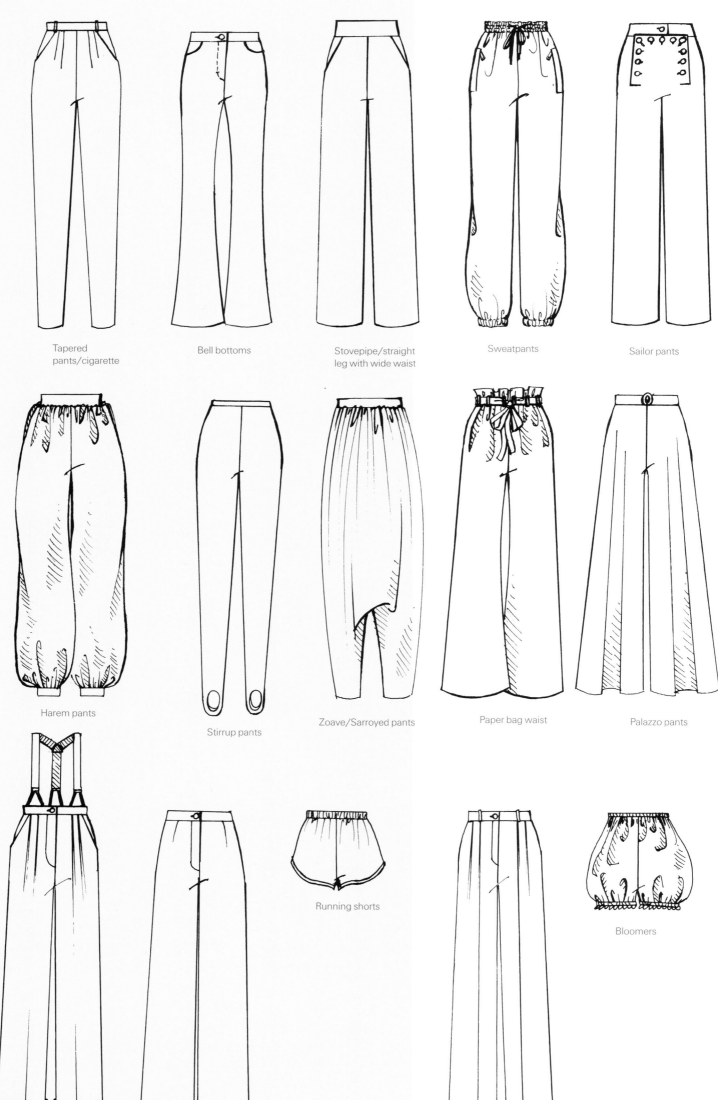

Tapered pants/cigarette

Bell bottoms

Stovepipe/straight leg with wide waist

Sweatpants

Sailor pants

Harem pants

Stirrup pants

Zoave/Sarroyed pants

Paper bag waist

Palazzo pants

Wide leg

Running shorts

Pantaloons

Bloomers

waistlines

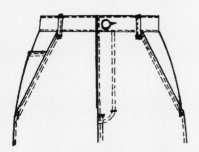

Unisex 5 pocket jean with
2n & bartacks

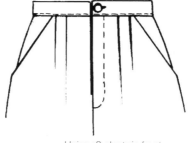

Unisex 2 pleat zip front
with slash pockets

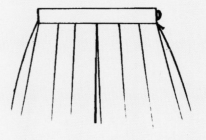

Pleated with set on waist
band—side seam zip/ button
opening

Pleated with back opening

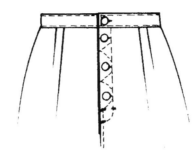

Button front pant

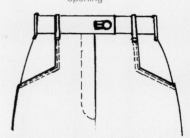

Belt loops, welt buttonholes
and novelty slash pockets

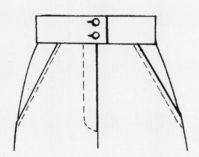

Wide waistband with 2-button
closure and slash pockets

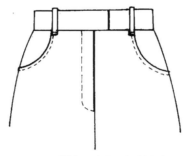

Wide waistband with belt
loops and bar/hook closure
and rounded pockets

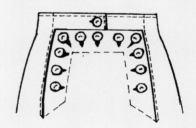

Sailor front 12 button opening

Elastic waist surge set
with"tearaway" side seam
snap closure

Faced waist with bow knot
at front

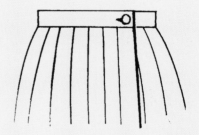

Asymmetrical button closure

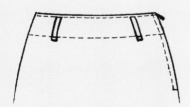

Faced natural waistline with
railroad side zipper

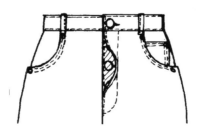

Womens 5 pocket jean with
button fly and rivet details

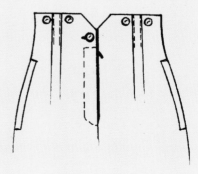

High-waisted 2 pleat pant with
single on seam welt pockets

waistlines

Invisible spider and yoke set

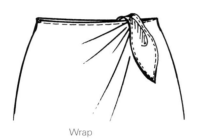

Wrap

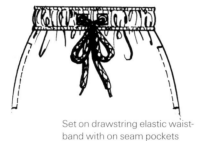

Set on drawstring elastic waistband with on seam pockets

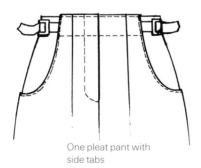

One pleat pant with side tabs

Button front waist band with drawcord and slash pockets

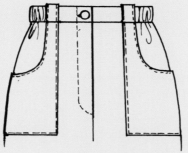

Half elastic waist with zip front and novelty pockets

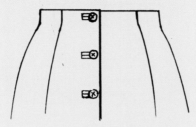

Fitted high waist with button closure

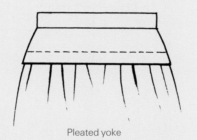

Pleated yoke

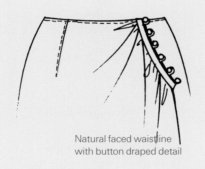

Natural faced waistline with button draped detail

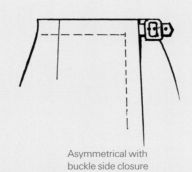

Asymmetrical with buckle side closure

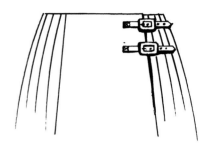

Kilt style with buckle side closure

Flat front pant with bound waist and button side closure

2 pleat pant with double welt zipper pockets and belt loops

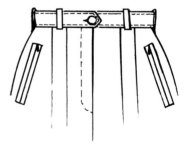

High waist with skinny belt tied at center front and belt loops

Novelty belting

waistlines

Denim belted waistband

Gathered paper bag waist

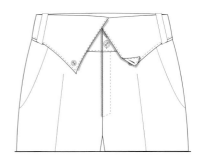

Overwrap button down

D ring wrap waist

D ring pleated waistband

Pleated attached belt waistband

Overlap rib

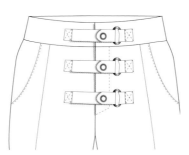

Triple belted waistband

Sarong waistband

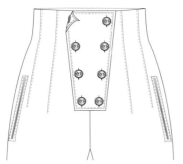

Vintage high waist wrap over

High waist pearl hook

lingerie

Half underwire bra

Full underwire bra

Panty girdle

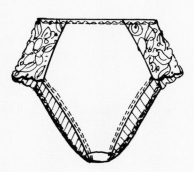

High cut control brief

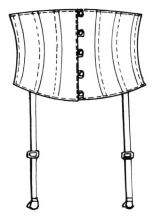

French cinch guepiere

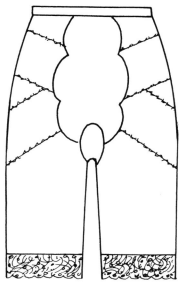

Knee length panty girdle

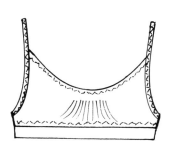

'Seamless' bra

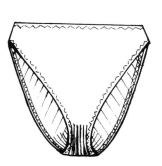

High cut brief

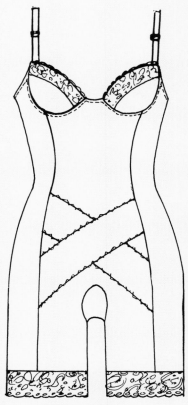

Full body slimmer

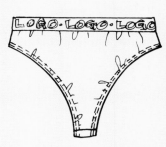

Sports bra with racer back

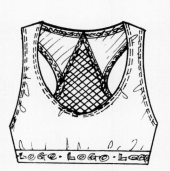

Sport thong front view

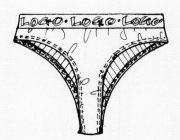

Sport thong back view

Standard 4 dart

French dart

Armseye darts

Armseye princess seams

enter front seam parts

H dart princess

Princess seams

Princess seams

Underwire bra and panty
set with lace trim

Cotton wireless bra and panty

Cami and bikini set

High waist girdles

Panty girdle

Poet/pirate style

Wrap around surplice

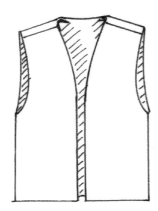

Straight vest

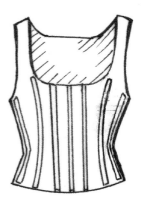

Boned bustier

Tie front

Fitted with puff sleeves

Fitted ruffle-front blouse

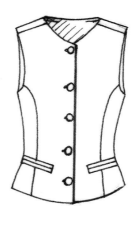

Fitted princess vest

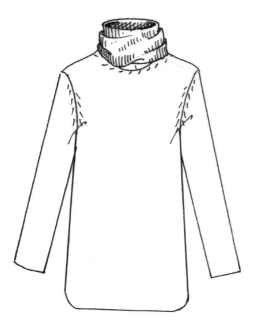

L/S tunic with cowll neck and
fully fashioned arm well

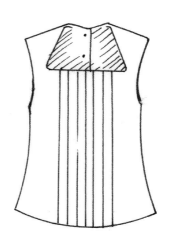

Sleeveless with front tuck
detail

Basic unisex 1 pocket shirt

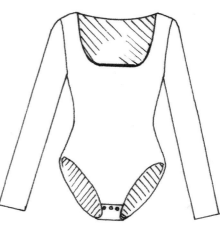

L/S bodysuit with open neckline

Dress shirt with pleated front

Fitted ruffle front

Shirt with hidden placket

With snap front

Bishop's sleeves and fold
backcuffs

Peplum and bell sleeves

Basic short-sleeved polo

Basic short-sleeved
pocket t

With pin tuck front

short sleeve shirt

Military style

Western style

Short sleeve—basic button down

Hidden placket

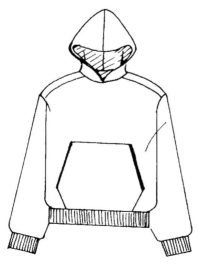

Hooded sweatshirt with kangaroo pocket

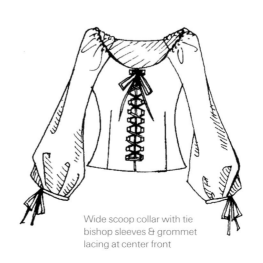

Wide scoop collar with tie bishop sleeves & grommet lacing at center front

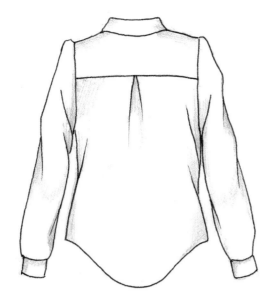

Inverted pleat yoke

yoke with shirring

v yoke

Closed pleat yoke

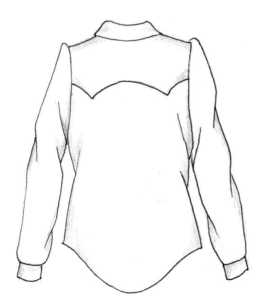

Western style yoke

Window pane yoke

jacket styles

Single-breasted cutaway. Single button.

2 button single-breasted. Round hem.

2 button roll-down single-breasted with regular front hem.

3 button single-breasted with regular front hem.

6 button double-breasted with square hem

4 button double-breasted

jacket styles

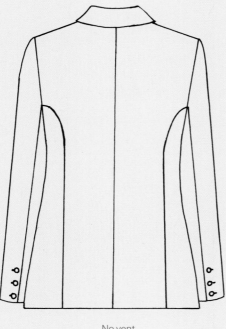

No vent

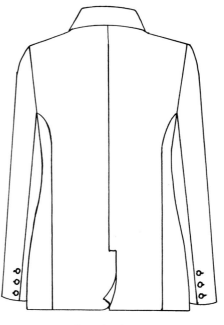

Center hook vent

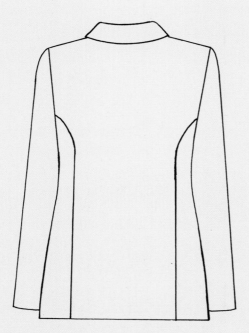

One piece back

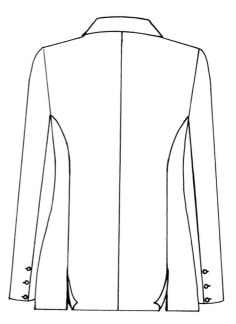

Side vents

jackets

Stadium jumper/
letterman's jacket

Zip front bomber with
tipped ribbing

Tie locken or wraparound

Nehru

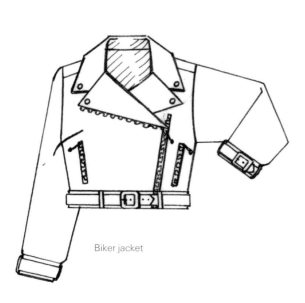

Biker jacket

Riding jacket

jackets

Denim jean

Blouson

Safari

Tuxedo/smoking jacket

Spencer

Chanel style

Quilted hooded jacket

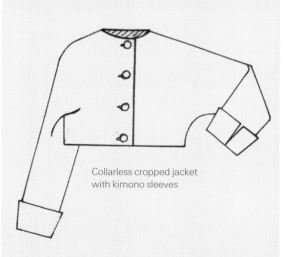

Collarless cropped jacket
with kimono sleeves

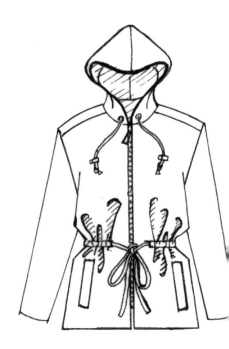

Hooded anorak

jackets/coats

Fur and suede duffle

Belted cape

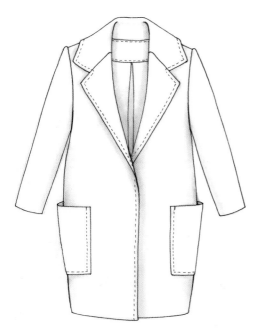

Wool barrel coat

Three-quarter length
shearling and leather

Double-breasted military style

Cinched waist fitted coat
with complex yoke

Trench coat

Cape

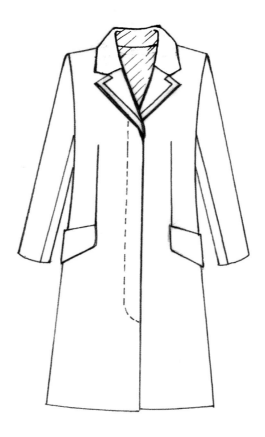

Chesterfield

Princess

Duffle

Pea coat

Double-breasted

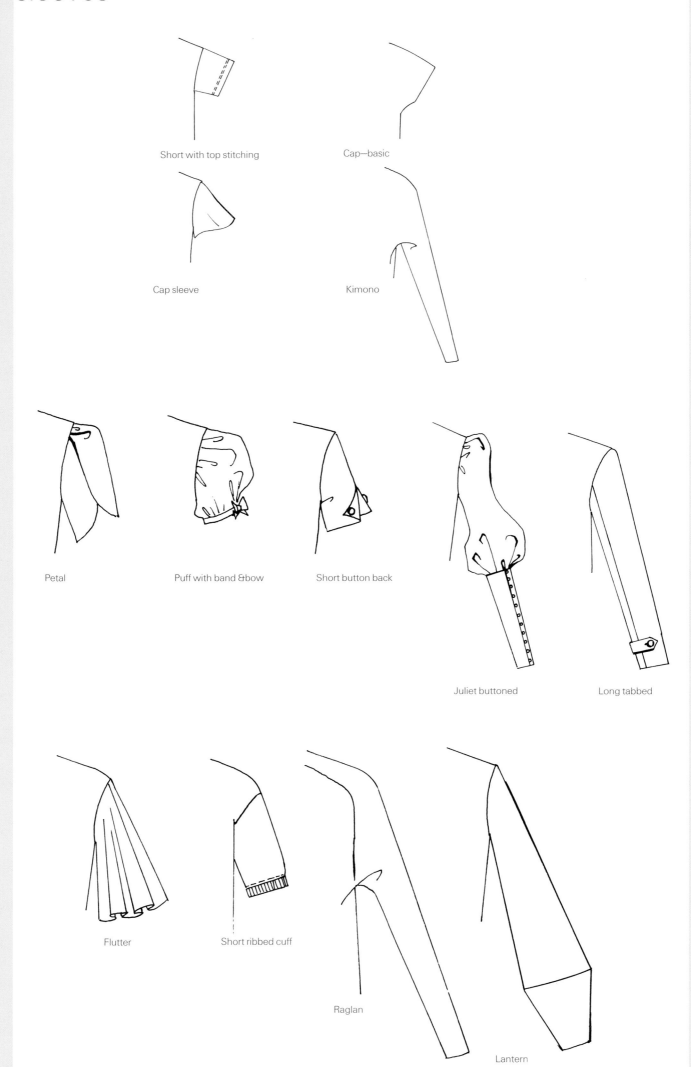

Short with top stitching

Cap—basic

Cap sleeve

Kimono

Petal

Puff with band &bow

Short button back

Juliet buttoned

Long tabbed

Flutter

Short ribbed cuff

Raglan

Lantern

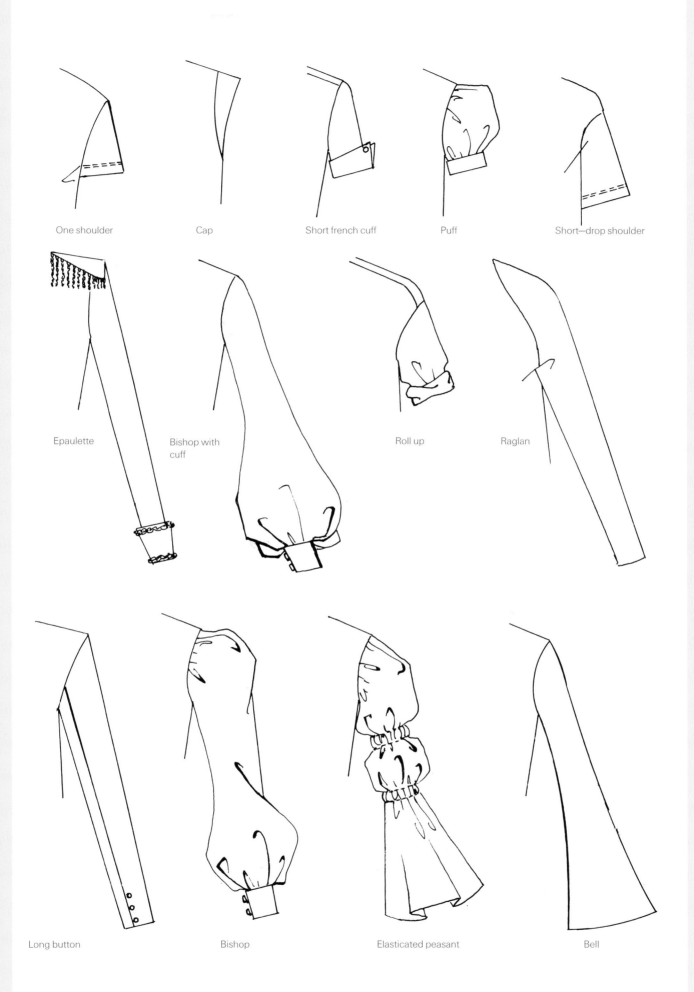

One shoulder

Cap

Short french cuff

Puff

Short—drop shoulder

Epaulette

Bishop with cuff

Roll up

Raglan

Long button

Bishop

Elasticated peasant

Bell

cuffs

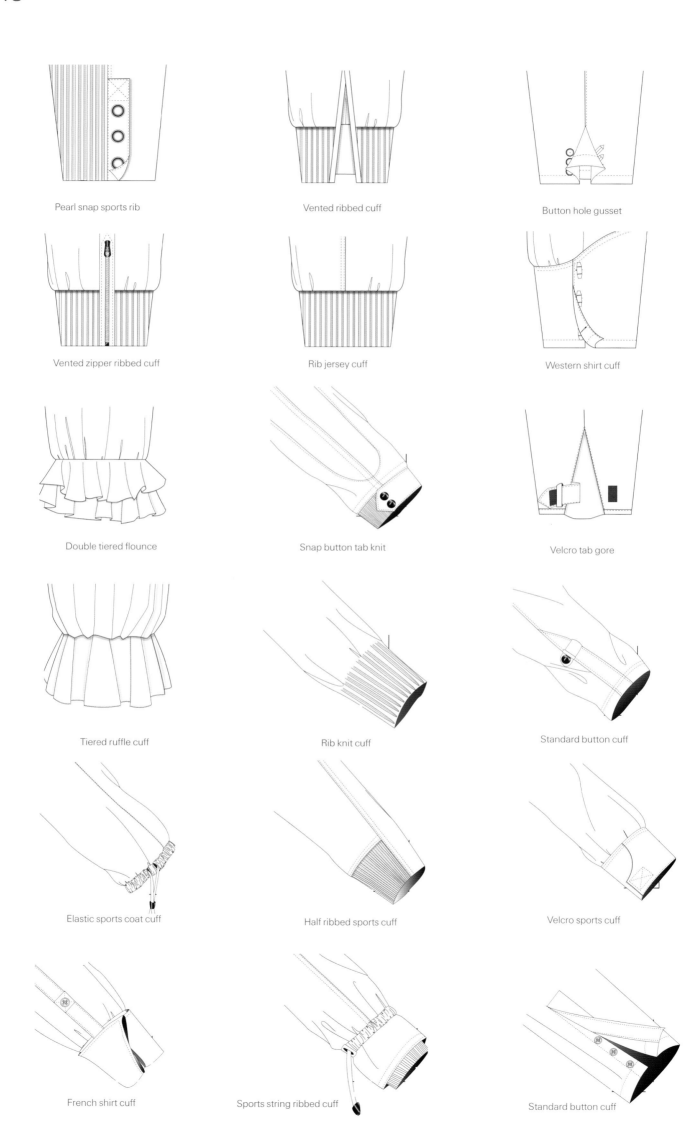

Pearl snap sports rib

Vented ribbed cuff

Button hole gusset

Vented zipper ribbed cuff

Rib jersey cuff

Western shirt cuff

Double tiered flounce

Snap button tab knit

Velcro tab gore

Tiered ruffle cuff

Rib knit cuff

Standard button cuff

Elastic sports coat cuff

Half ribbed sports cuff

Velcro sports cuff

French shirt cuff

Sports string ribbed cuff

Standard button cuff

shoes

Low-cut stiletto boot

Plastic jelly shoe

High heel sculptured designer sandal

Flower encrusted flat

Finger shoes

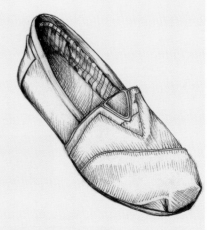

Slip ons

shoes

Suede high sneaker

Metal cleated shoe

Teva hiking sandal

Soccer cleats

Sandal flats

Slip on bootie

eyeglasses

Wellington

Aviator

Oxford/Lexington

Oval/Ben Franklin/Granny

Queen

Square

Half moon

Bevelled

Foxy

Pentagon

Boston

Round/Lloyd

Half/reading glasses

Flip up

Pince nez

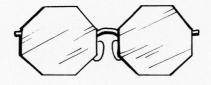

Octagon

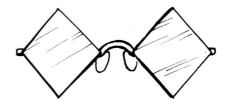

Harlequin

Tear Drop

Wrap

Flat top

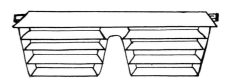

Lounge

John Lennon

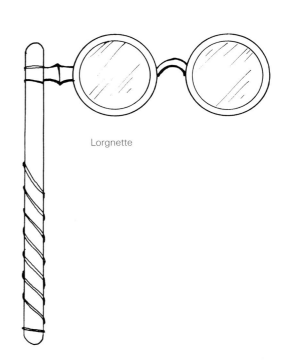

Lorgnette

Monocle

eyeglasses

Round horn-rimmed

Cat eye

Wire rimmed

Aviator

Lolita

Designer ribbed frame

Horn rimmed

Half frame glasses

Thick frame

Round frame

stitches

Top side	Underside

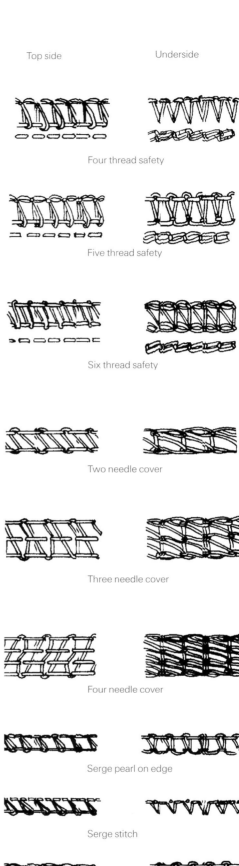

SN chain stitch

SN blindstitch

SN saddle stitch

SN modern saddle stitch

SN lock stitch

SN zig-zag lockstitch

Two thread chainstitch

Cording for permanent crease

Converse stitch

Zig-Zag chainstitch

Modified multi zig-zag chainstitch

Top side	Underside

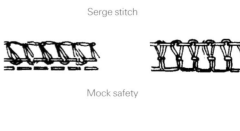

Four thread safety

Five thread safety

Six thread safety

Two needle cover

Three needle cover

Four needle cover

Serge pearl on edge

Serge stitch

Mock safety

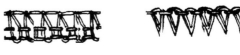

Hosiery stitch

buttons/buttonsholes/closures weaves/details

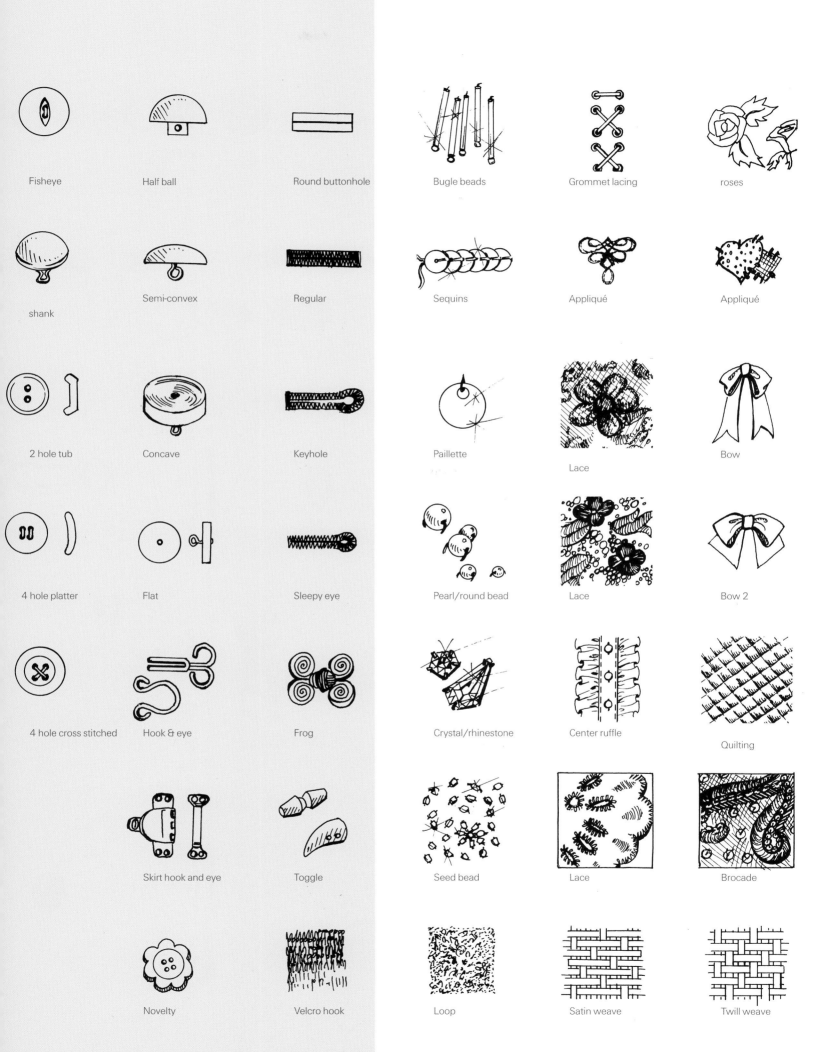

Fisheye	Half ball	Round buttonhole
shank	Semi-convex	Regular
2 hole tub	Concave	Keyhole
4 hole platter	Flat	Sleepy eye
4 hole cross stitched	Hook & eye	Frog
	Skirt hook and eye	Toggle
	Novelty	Velcro hook

Bugle beads	Grommet lacing	roses
Sequins	Appliqué	Appliqué
Paillette	Lace	Bow
Pearl/round bead	Lace	Bow 2
Crystal/rhinestone	Center ruffle	Quilting
Seed bead	Lace	Brocade
Loop	Satin weave	Twill weave

buttons/closures

Novelty star button

Novelty flower button

Novelty heart button

Vintage brass confederate button

Tack button

Hook and eye

Traditional four hole

Toggle

Pearl snap details

Clasp snap button

Vintage jewel button

Pearl snap

Plastic four hole button

Sports toggle

Sports toggle

Metal hook

Vintage portrait porcelain button

Knit button

Brass zipper pull

Elastic sports toggle

Leather button

Vintage YSL crystal pearl button

Wooden cross stitch button

Vintage sailorl button

Rectangular toggle

Traditional toggle

Western toggle

Plastic novelty button

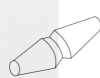
Leather detail button

Vintage Victorian jewel button

Elastic sports pull

Plastic pull zipper

Zipper crocodile leather wallet

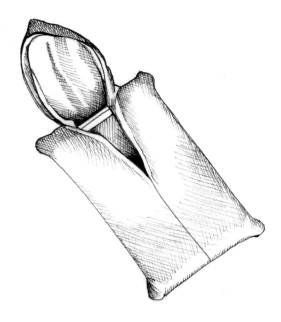

Ipod hoodie

Leather clutch

Leather art portfolio

Sparkle metal clutch

Laptop sleeve

bags

Envelope bag

Clutch purse

Lunch box

Backpack

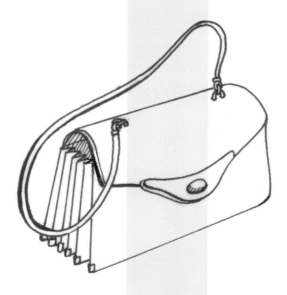

Accordion bag

Straw bag

bags/cases

Soft leather shoulder bag

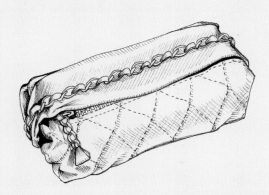

Quilted purse

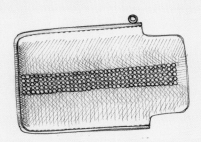

Pavé phone case

Zippered handbag

Laptop sleeve

Fringe money purse

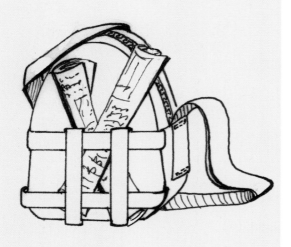

Newspaper bag

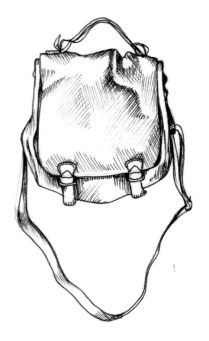

Messenger bag

Tote

Evening clutch

Cosmetics purse

Shoulder bag with chain

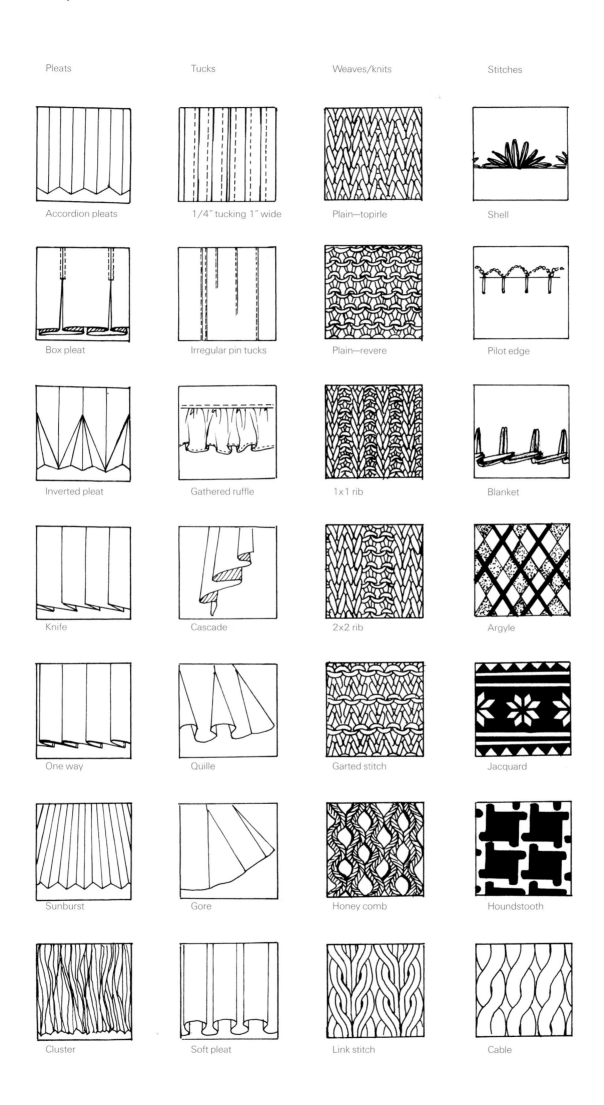

Pleats

Accordion pleats

Box pleat

Inverted pleat

Knife

One way

Sunburst

Cluster

Tucks

1/4" tucking 1" wide

Irregular pin tucks

Gathered ruffle

Cascade

Quille

Gore

Soft pleat

Weaves/knits

Plain—topirle

Plain—revere

1 x 1 rib

2 x 2 rib

Garted stitch

Honey comb

Link stitch

Stitches

Shell

Pilot edge

Blanket

Argyle

Jacquard

Houndstooth

Cable

Garter	Bulky chunky yarn	Plain weave
Crochet	Sport yarn	Popcorn stitch
Cable	Cable	Micro rib
Crocodile	Zebra	Terry cloth
Short fur	Leopard	Houndstooth
Long fur	Silk	Lace
Sequins	Animal print	Bouclé

pockets

Patch pocket

Western flap
pocket

Welt pocket

Kangaroo zip

Cargo pocket

Sports pocket

D ring cargo
pocket

Welt pocket

Basic cargo

SIde pocket

Patch flap

Sports cargo
pocket

Patch pocket

Rounded
patch pocket

Western welt
flap

Sports kanga-
roo

Patch pocket
with flap

Sport draw-
string pocket

Inverted
sports pocket

Tabbed button
flap

Overlap flapp-
pocket

Inverted
cargo pocket

Kangaroo
basic

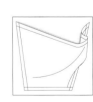

Inverted

Bucket

Basic welt

Cargo pocket

Ribbed cargo

Formal welt

Buttoned
patch pocket

pockets

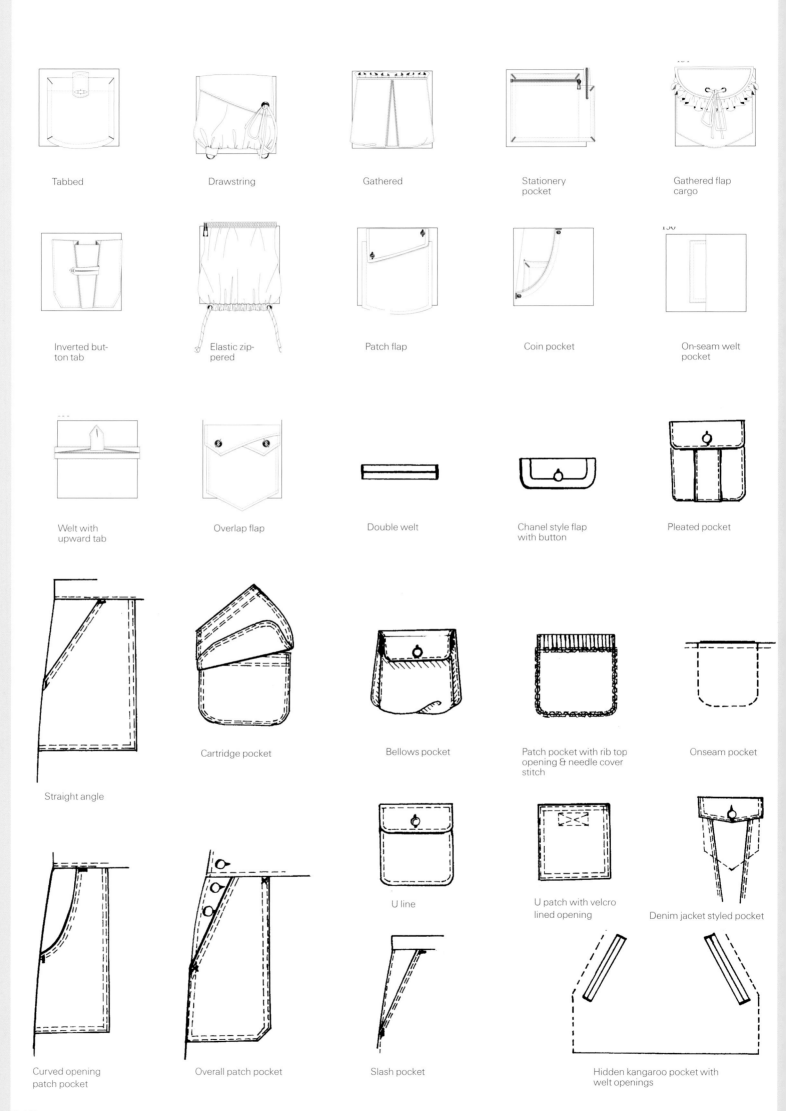

Tabbed

Drawstring

Gathered

Stationery
pocket

Gathered flap
cargo

Inverted but-
ton tab

Elastic zip-
pered

Patch flap

Coin pocket

On-seam welt
pocket

Welt with
upward tab

Overlap flap

Double welt

Chanel style flap
with button

Pleated pocket

Cartridge pocket

Bellows pocket

Patch pocket with rib top
opening & needle cover
stitch

Onseam pocket

Straight angle

U line

U patch with velcro
lined opening

Denim jacket styled pocket

Curved opening
patch pocket

Overall patch pocket

Slash pocket

Hidden kangaroo pocket with
welt openings

Feather trim

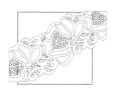

Venice lace

Bullion crest

Folded flower ribbon

Taffeta Bow

Pearl snap epaulette

Fringe

Beaded bridal motif

Iron-on flower fringe

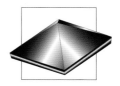

Metal stud

Metal stud

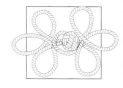

Beaded bridal trim

Elastic zip-pered

Fringed Concha

Suede fringe

Gathered

Leather braid trim

Swarovski motif

Beaded Venice appliqué

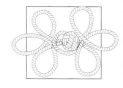

Frog closure

Safety pins

Gimbalt ring

Military emblem

Military emblem

Coin medallion

Metal zipper

Chain trim

Bullion crest

Eyelet

Reinforced buttonhole

Loop buttonhole

Square buttonhole

Overstitch buttonhole

Buttonhole

Reinforced buttonhole

Piikaboo buttonhole

Keyhole buttonhole

Secure buttonhole

Peekaboo buttonhole

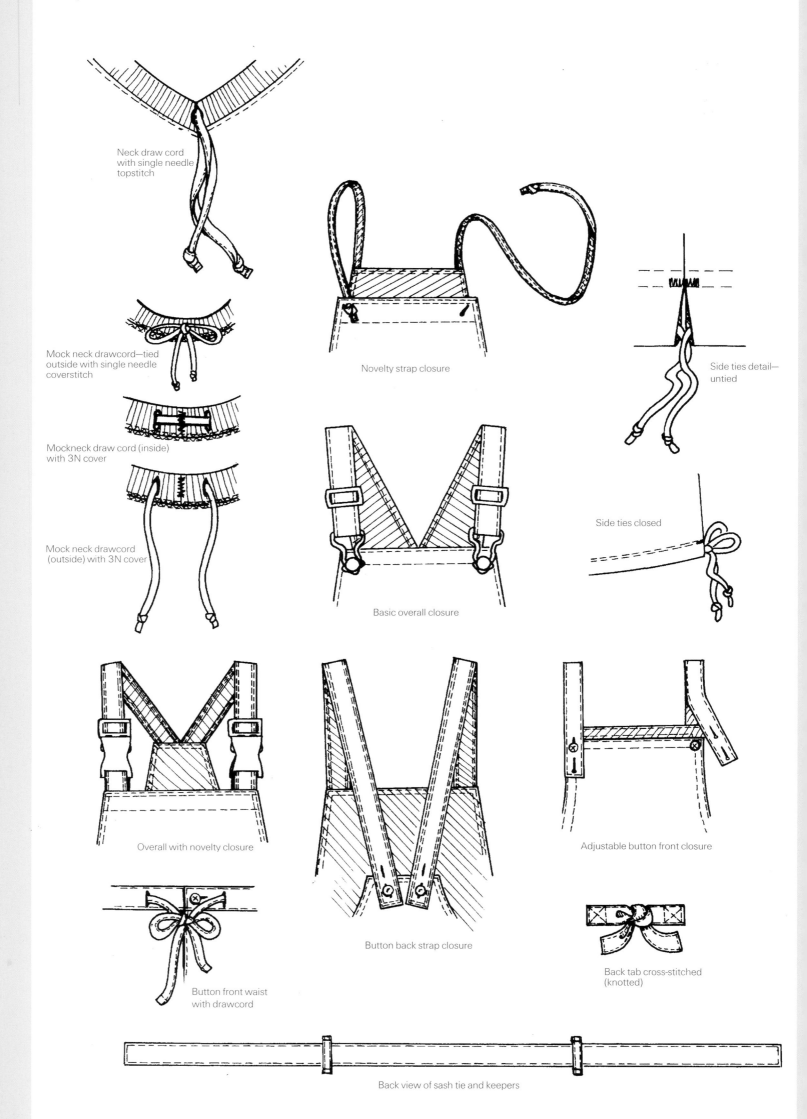

Neck draw cord with single needle topstitch

Mock neck drawcord—tied outside with single needle coverstitch

Mockneck draw cord (inside) with 3N cover

Mock neck drawcord (outside) with 3N cover

Novelty strap closure

Side ties detail—untied

Side ties closed

Basic overall closure

Overall with novelty closure

Button back strap closure

Adjustable button front closure

Button front waist with drawcord

Back tab cross-stitched (knotted)

Back view of sash tie and keepers

zippers/closures/do's/ do not do's

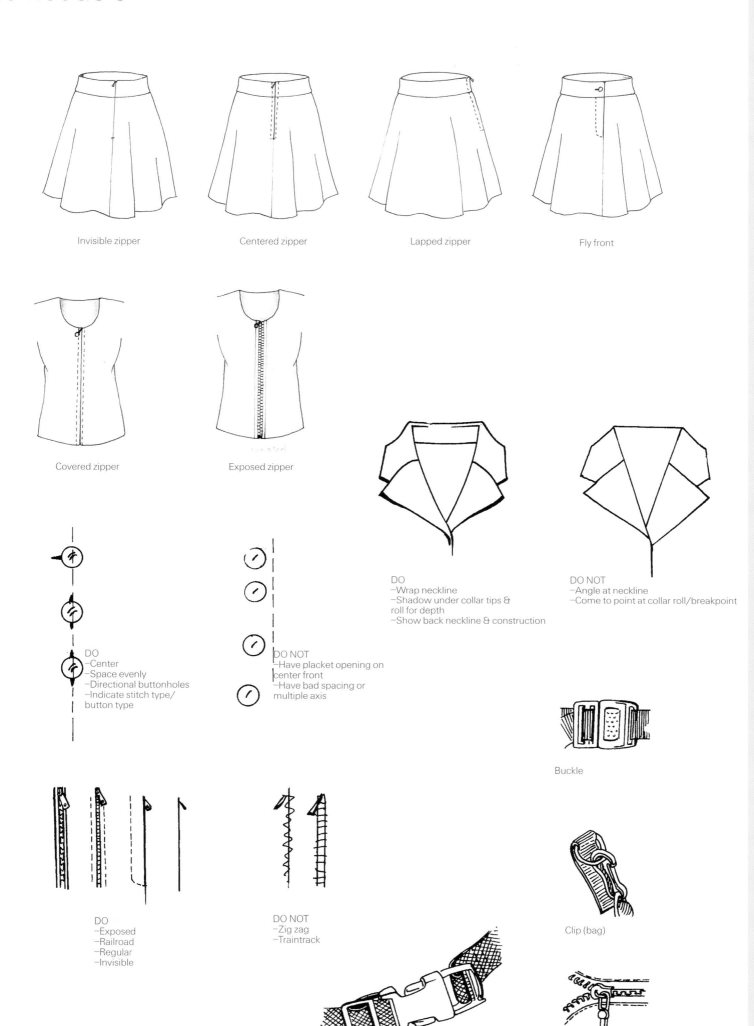

Invisible zipper

Centered zipper

Lapped zipper

Fly front

Covered zipper

Exposed zipper

DO
–Center
–Space evenly
–Directional buttonholes
–Indicate stitch type/ button type

DO NOT
–Have placket opening on center front
–Have bad spacing or multiple axis

DO
–Wrap neckline
–Shadow under collar tips & roll for depth
–Show back neckline & construction

DO NOT
–Angle at neckline
–Come to point at collar roll/breakpoint

Buckle

DO
–Exposed
–Railroad
–Regular
–Invisible

DO NOT
–Zig zag
–Traintrack

Clip (bag)

Parachute clip

Zipper

drawing fabrics/ fabric on the body

DRAWING FABRICS

This chapter completes the range of techniques we have learnt for accurately representing the defining features of a garment—silhouette, drape and fit and details—by showing how we can achieve similar standards of accuracy and realism in our depiction of the other defining feature, the fabric.

A drawing of a garment in which we can see at once and with a high degree of certainty what fabric the garment is made of is a highly effective fashion drawing. Such a drawing makes us feel (assuming of course that the garments are well drawn in all other respects) an immediate familiarity with the garments, an instinctive understanding of how it will feel, fit, drape and look; we will instantly form a clear idea of what markets, occasions and age ranges it is designed for and are free to switch our attention to the finer points of design and construction. Drawings like these can take a little longer to produce (though surprisingly less than might be thought) but in terms of the accuracy and immediacy of the information they convey they can be considered as being well worth any extra effort.

There are two aspects to drawing fabrics so they appear realistic and immediately recognizable. One is the accurate rendering of the actual surface appearance of the fabric. Leaving aside color, the surface appearance consists of, predominantly, (i) the surface texture (which depends on the size of fiber, yarn, weave, composition or natural texture of the fabric) and (ii) how light is reflected from the surface (whether it is shiny or matt or perhaps has a sheen). The second aspect of drawing fabrics is the accurate depiction of how the fabric folds and drapes on the body. Color is obviously a distinguishing feature of fabrics, but it is important to know how to represent the other visual aspects before adding color to a drawing; remember, color can improve a good drawing but can make a poor drawing look terrible, and color is not that helpful as additional information if the fabric type itself cannot be identified. The tools used in drawing to capture these two aspects of the appearance of fabrics are, as in the other parts of fashion drawing, line and value.

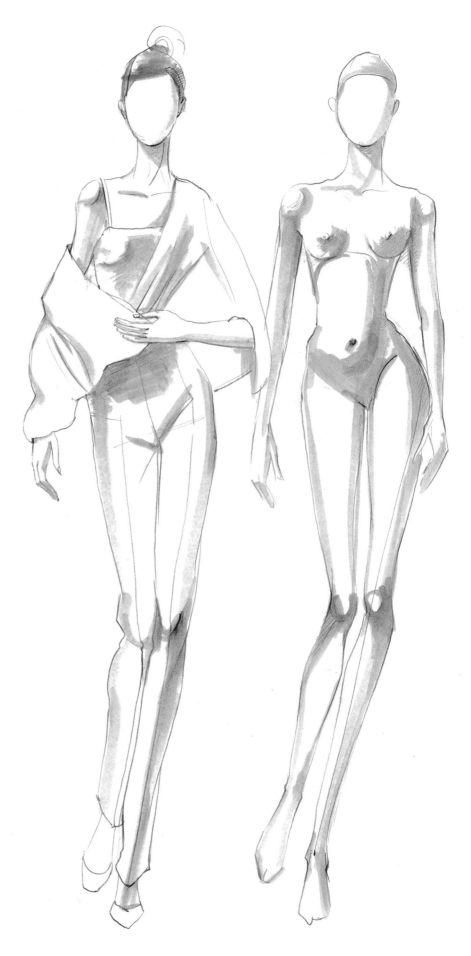

Shadow maps. Where shadows form on the unclothed figure (right) and when fabric is draped on the figure (left). Fabric draped close to the body forms shadows in the same way as they form on the unclothed body. Where the fabric fits loosely on the figure it forms folds and drape which create deeper shadows in the folds with light areas on the tops of the folds and a gradual change of the value of the shadow betweeen.

fabric on the body/
shading fabric/value scale

This chapter begins by examining the relation between construction and drape—how drape is formed by garment construction and how to shade drape correctly. Then the characteristics of different fabrics and how they are drawn is covered. Value—the degree of light and dark—is an important factor in a drawing. The value range used in drawings is usually indicated next to the drawing.

FABRIC ON THE BODY

In fashion drawing we are interested in giving a realistic impression of how clothes will look when worn on the figure. In order to do this it is necessary to understand the shading of the body under the fabric and then to understand the shading of the *fabric* in the parts where it fits and where it falls away from the body. The drawings overleaf show these two sets of shadows.

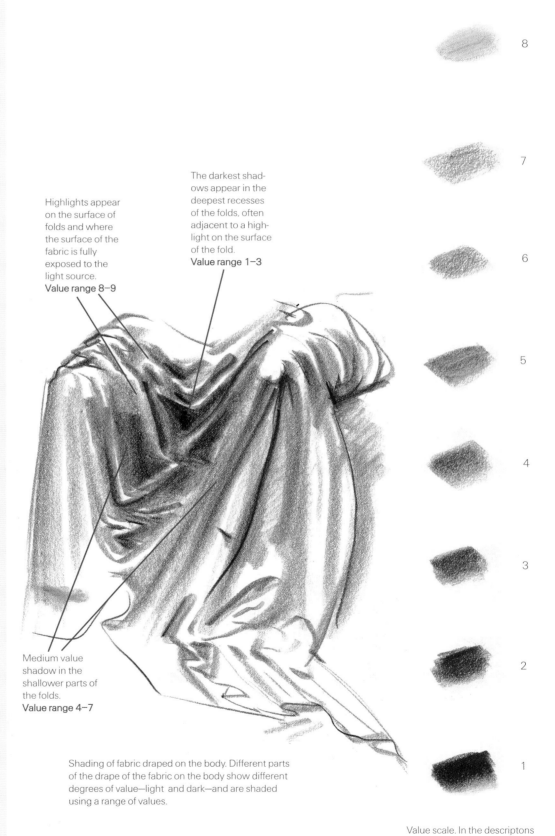

Highlights appear on the surface of folds and where the surface of the fabric is fully exposed to the light source.
Value range 8–9

The darkest shadows appear in the deepest recesses of the folds, often adjacent to a highlight on the surface of the fold.
Value range 1–3

Medium value shadow in the shallower parts of the folds.
Value range 4–7

Shading of fabric draped on the body. Different parts of the drape of the fabric on the body show different degrees of value—light and dark—and are shaded using a range of values.

9

8

7

6

5

4

3

2

1

Value scale. In the descriptons of shading fabrics included in this chapter reference is made to a **value range.** This refers to the value—the darkness or lightness—of the shading to be used. The numbers refer approximately to the values shown above, with 9 the white of the paper and 1 close to black.

355

use of line for fabrics/jacket

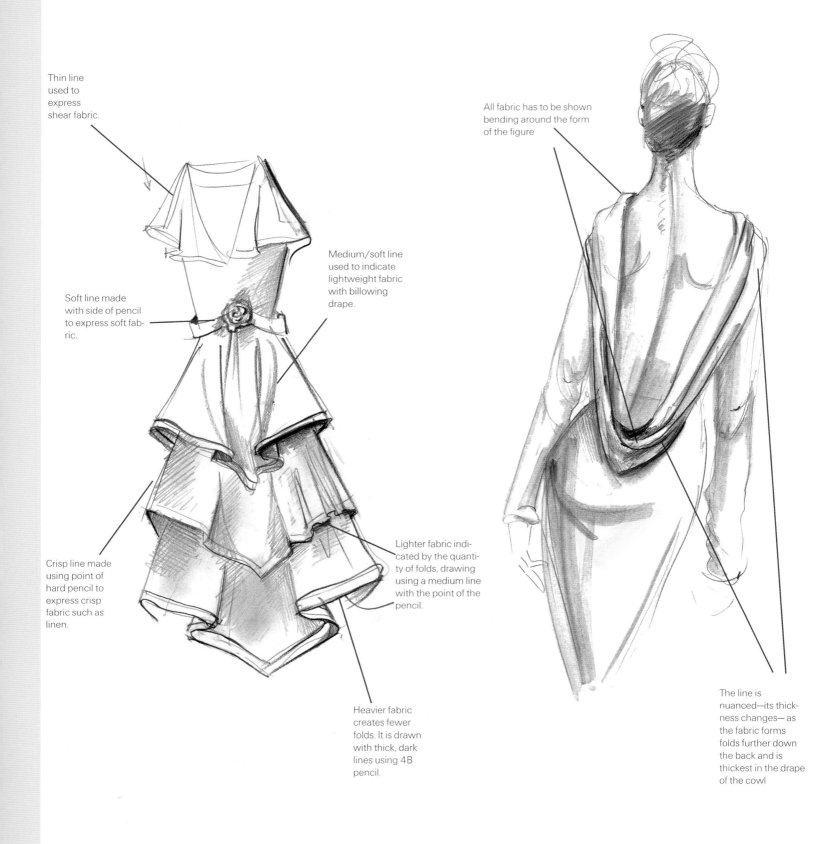

Thin line used to express shear fabric.

Soft line made with side of pencil to express soft fabric.

Medium/soft line used to indicate lightweight fabric with billowing drape.

Crisp line made using point of hard pencil to express crisp fabric such as linen.

Lighter fabric indicated by the quantity of folds, drawing using a medium line with the point of the pencil.

Heavier fabric creates fewer folds. It is drawn with thick, dark lines using 4B pencil.

All fabric has to be shown bending around the form of the figure

The line is nuanced—its thickness changes— as the fabric forms folds further down the back and is thickest in the drape of the cowl

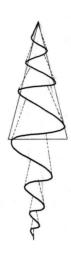

Cascade drape, vertically suspended
1. Draw an inverted cone shape.

2. Draw the outline of the drape as a line snaking dorwn between the sides of the traingle and extending beneath.

Draw in the shapes of each section of the drape with sides sloping towards the center-top. Shade in the interior of each fold.

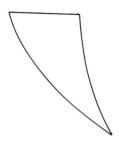

Cascade drape, diagonally suspended
1. Draw a dagger shape

2. Draw in the shapes of the drape, bending diagonally towards the suspension point.

3. Shade in the interiors of the folds.

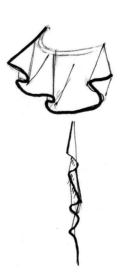

DO NOT DO. Incorrectly drawn cascade drape. The folds are drawn at different angles. The sections of drape must all be aligned in the same dirrection.

DO. Correctly drawn cascade drape.

Cowls are examples of two-point drape. The fabric is suspended from two points and drapes fluidly with wider folds at the bottom. Here the drape of the cowl is correctly drawn.

DO NOT DO. Incorrectly drawn cowl—there are too many lines. Lines relate to individual folds and cannot intersect other lines.

Side cowl, correctly drawn..

DO NOT DO. Incorrectly drawn side cowl. The cowl is not drawn to bend around the figure and appears stiff. Both the silhouette and the interiors of the folds should curve round the figure.

Gathered fabric. When fabric is gathered into a seam it flares out from the seam into a series of cone-shaped folds, radiating from the center of the seam. At the edge of the fabric these cones curve out and then back in on themselves. The cones left of the center radiate out to the left and those right of center radiate right. When drawing, first draw a second line parallel to the hemline to mark the height of the folds, and draw the folds between that line and the hem.

The gathers are drawn as loops, also radiating to left and right.

DO NOT DO. Here all the folds face to the right and the gathers are not drawn radiating from the seam; gathers must be drawn emerging from the seam.

drape and shading/

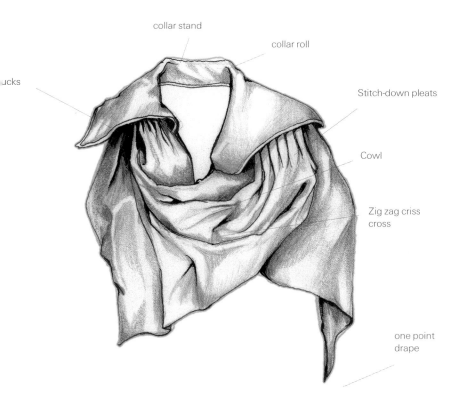

collar stand

collar roll

ucks

Stitch-down pleats

Cowl

Zig zag criss cross

one point drape

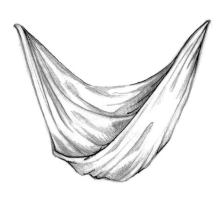

Half lock drape

Cowl drape

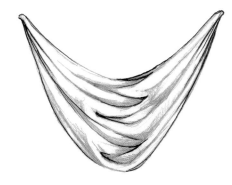

Zig zag criss cross

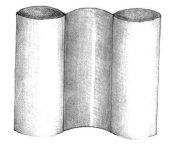

Skirts with wide folds. Note that each fold is drawn like a cylinder and the area between the folds is drawn like the inside of a cylinder.

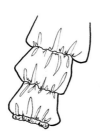

Ruching (also spelt rouching) is where areas of bunching and rippling in the fabric are caused by gathers on both sides of a seam.

DO NOT DO. Here the silhouette does not accurately reflect the gathering. With this amount of gathering there would be more fabric in the sleeve and it would puffout more.

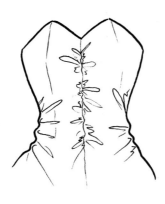

Ruching .

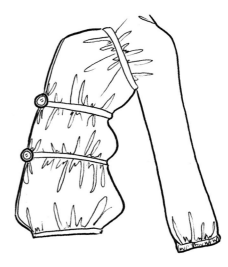

Ruching .

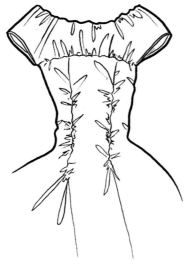

Ruching .

DO NOT DO. Here also, as above, the silhouette does not accurately reflect the construction of the garment. Fashion drawings are technical drawings and all parts must be consistent with each other.

drape and shading/
do not do/do's

DO NOT Do. No seam is drawn for the sleeve to connect to the main body of the garment. The position of the seam connecting the sleeve to the body of the garment contains essential information on the drape–and how it is shaded– of the garment.

DO. Note in the skirt, which is correctly drawn,that a large amount of fabric in the body of the garment means the hem will be wide.

DO. Note the correctly placed shadow along the overlap of the opening of the jacket, indicating depth and that the shading on the right side of the jacket and the left side of the skirt indicates that the garments are larger than the body underneath , i.e. they are loose-fitting in these areas.

crisp fabrics/cotton voile/
silk organza/linen

CRISP FABRICS

A thin line is used when drawing the silhouettes of garments made of crisp fabrics. The slight stiffness of crisp fabric causes it to drape in folds that are more angular than softer fabrics: soft flowing curves are not present.

Dress made of cotton voile, a light open-weave fabric that is crisp and has a wiry feel. Note the angular appearance of the points of the handkerchief hem indicate the crispness of the fabric. The lightness of the fabric causes numerous folds to form; these are drawn in with a light touch. :
Value range; 8–6

Tiered skirt with unpressed pleats made of silk organza with paillettes. Fabric is lightweight so can be gathered into numerous narrow pleats that form numerous folds. Draw with sharp lines using the point of the pencil.
Value range: 8–6

Handkerchief linen scarf with rayon velvet ties. The gathers are drawn with thin crisp lines.
Value range; 7–6, Velvet, 8–7

crisp fabrics/
cambric/sateen

The top is cambric, a closely woven, smooth cotton fabric; the skirt is made of canvas linen, a heavier weight linen with a soft finish, with stitched-down pleats. The skirt is drawn with heavier straight lines to indicate the flatness of the stitched-down pleats and the weight of the fabric. Note the beads are drawn with a crisp edge to indicate the hardness of the material they are made of.

Value range : skirt , 6–4; top and beads, 7, 3,2,

Sateen dress. Sateen is a smooth, tightly woven fabric with a sheen that drapes with numerous crisp folds that are rendered using a light line.
Value range: 7–3

prints, plaids and stripes

PRINTS, PLAIDS AND STRIPES

Prints are designs that are printed onto a range of fabrics,including cotton, silk, wool but also many others. Prints can be applied in numerous ways, as repeating patterns or randomly, in the body of the garment or along a border.

There are no fixed rules, but generally if a print is larger, with a limited number of repeats on the garment, it can be fully rendered. If the design is small and with large numbers of repeats then, both from the point of view of the ease of rendering and also ease of viewing, it is usually best to render only a portion of the overall printed surface.To gauge the size of the repeats for repeating patterns it is easiest to hold the fabric to the body and count the number of repeats. This is the number that will appear in the drawing.

When drawing garments made of printed fabrics, it is best first to draw the outline of the garment and then to shade it so it will be clear where the folds will appear. The garment is shaded in the same way as a plain unprinted garment in the same fabric would appear, for example, wool/ mohair is shaded with soft, broad shadows, silk taffeta with sharp, angular, highly contrasted shadows. Once the shaded garment has been drawn the print design is plotted onto it. A simple shape is chosen to represent the design of the repeat—for example, flowers might be represented by circles. It is easiest to plot the position of the pattern repeats using a grid system, making sure that it is adjusted to follow the curves of the body. The hem provides the horizontal axis for the grid and lines should follow its curves.

Remember that patterns on printed fabric break up and fall out of register in the folds of the drape. Surprisingly, it is actually easier to draw prints on fabrics with abundant drape as it is not as necessary to be as precise as when rendering a print on a flat surface, where every tiny error of measurement can be noticed.

Both coats are wool cashmere, and the top and skirt are cotton shirting.
The print on the coat is only partially rendered: it is usually too time-consuming to render the whole garment, and often makes the drawing look too busy. The coat on the left is apaisley print that *has* been fully rendered: sometimes the final result is worth the effort! Print designs must always be positioned parallel to the curve of the hem of the garment, as seen in both garments here.
Value range: Coats, 7–6; skirt/top, 8–5

Stripes. Left, the horizontal stripes of this dress follow the curves of the bust, waist, hip and all the folds. In the ruffled collar the stripes are parallel to the edges of each ruffle; on the sleeves the stripes bend around in a diagonal. Right, the skirt and the body of the top are printed with vertical stripes that change width below the yoke; the sleeves have horizontal stripes. Note that the stripes follow the drape of the fabric as it curves over the bustline and into the seam of the yoke. The stripes form a v-shape where the fabric is gathered into the seam at the princess line and bend around the pockets and into the folds of the skirt.

prints, plaids and stripes/
silk crepe/cotton/jersey

This dress is made of floral-printed silk crepe. The design on the print is randomly placed; the repeats are irregular. The skirt of the dress is full, with numerous folds; the top is more fitted with fewer folds. It is important that the print repeats correspond with the drape of the fabric: they break up in the folds of the skirt and are seen bending around the bust in the bodice.
Value range: 6,5,1

The plaid design of this cotton top is made up of a mesh of vertical and horizontal lines of different widths. The easiest way to draw plaids is first to sketch in the position of the widest vertical and horizontal lines and then to place in the secondary lines.
Value range: 9–1

The collar of this sleeveless jacquard jersey dress has diagonal stripes that bend in towards the knot; on the tie the stripes change angle and on the belt are again parallel to those of the collar. The stripes on the body of the dress are vertical and wider-spaced. With stripes of varying widths and directions it is important to make sure they appear even. This is done by first drawing in the center stripes and then drawing in the number of stripe repeats making sure they are evenly spaced.
Value range: 7–5

shiny fabrics/
silk velvet

SHINY FABRICS

Shiny fabrics, as part of their own definition, show values at the high end of the scale—the highlights are bright white, shown in a drawing by leaving the white of the paper unmarked (and occasionally enhanced with the use of white-out or similar). For dramatic effect, the bright highlights are often juxtaposed with the darkest shadows, so the contrast of values is most extreme.

A number of different types of fabrics are shiny, for example: velvet, taffeta, leather, fabric with metalic thread, satin and others. Although they are all shiny they do not all reflect light in the same way: as they drape differently, with folds of different widths, angularity and softness, so they reflect light in different patterns. *Shine* should also be differentiated from *sheen*. Shine is a sharper reflection of light, often in highlights, whereas sheen is a broader diffusion of light across a larger surface. Examples of fabric with sheen are: silk charmeuse, velour, cotton velvet, jersey, cashmere.

When drawing garments made of shiny fabrics it is best to plan out where the areas of light and dark will fall before beginning the drawing. Remember that light is reflected at its brightest on the top of the folds and shadows are darkest in the interiors of folds. As mentioned, to highlight the contrast of dark and light, the darkest shadows of folds are often place next to the lightest highlights on the tops of the folds.

Silk velvet or crepe asymmetrical top and long skirt with train drape.
Value range: 9–6, 3–1

shiny fabrics/cashmere/ velvet

Wool cashmere long-sleeved designer jacket with mandarin collar and gothic novelty trim, fitted at waist with large pouch pockets
Value range: 9–6, 3–1

This sleeveless, knee-length dress is made of crushed velvet, a fabric with a slightly textured surface that reflects light unevenly across its surface. Light is reflected more as *sheen* than shine, with a broader area of light forming on the tops of the folds. The uneven quality of the surface texture is drawn by making short strokes with the side of a soft pencil slightly raised to the tip, creating a smaller mark, and using a tapping motion. This technique is used in all the areas of the garment. A 4B pencil is used in the darker areas and a 2B in the lighter, and the white of the paper shows through in the lightest areas.
Value range: 7, 6, 2

In this ensemble the skirt is jacquard taffeta, the jacket is felt, trimmed with hand-crocheted balls; the hat is also felt and the muff is faux fur. To draw the jacket and hat use the side of a 4B pencil; the folds are soft and rounded and the highlights on the tops of the folds are narrow. The skirt, by comparison, has crisper, more angular folds.
Value range: 9,3–1

Duchesse silk satin dress. SIlk satin is a highly reflective luxury fabrics. The sheen of the duchesse silk satin used in the dress is enhanced by the use of a continuous filament yarn. The dress has crisp folds with thin highlights across the top and wide areas of very dark shadow, the contrast between the two creating the illusion of shine.
Value range: 7,6,1

shiny fabrics/cottons/ sequins

Different decorative elements. The sleeve is tied with rat tail cording; it is very black, drawn with a 6B pencil leaving a little light on the surface of the bows. The belt is studded with sequins and seed pearls. These are both drawn as half-circles, with the sequin as a flat circular shape and the pearls as spheres. Both have round highlights. The flowers on the sleeveless shirt have interlocking petals that cast soft shadows creating a spiral effect.
Value ranges: 9,2,1

The garments in this gypsy outfit are made of a variety of fabrics: the blouse is cotton gauze, the vest is cotton felt, the skirt is cotton. Sequins are sewn onto the border of the vest, belt and skirt. The fabrics themselves are *not* shiny, but the numerous sequins are, and each has its own bright point of light. The sequins are drawn as a half circle with the point of the pencil (the other half is left undrawn to represent the reflection of light). Place a dot in the middle of each sequin to show the thread securing them to the garment. Each sequin has its own small cast shadow also in the shape of a half-circle.
Value range: 9,6,5

shiny fabrics silk velvet/ leather

Left, viscose silk velvet jodhpurs; right, leather outfit of various leathers. In the outfit on the left, 100% silk velvet is rare and highly expensive so silk is usually blended with rayon viscose to achieve a beautiful drape and a more durable garment. This fabric has a soft body so forms round, soft folds. The outfit on the right is made of various leathers: glove leather is used in the gathered area of the top and around the sleeves, patent leather is used in the binding of the legs and torso, leather lacing is used in the grommets down the front of the skirt. The challenge in drawing predominantly black outfits is to work with values that are close together, ranging only from grey to black plus the white used as highlights on the surface of the folds. Subtle variations in pressure on the pencil are needed to ensure that a range of values is achieved.
Value range: Left, 9,8,2,1, right, 9,8,2,1,

shiny fabrics/silk knit/ beading

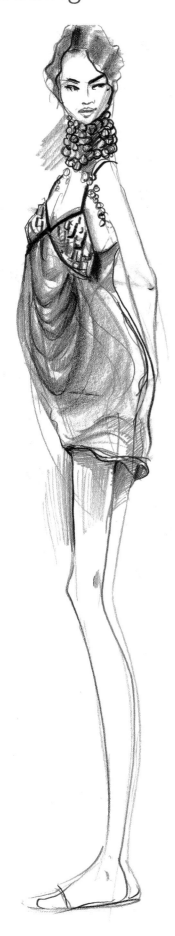

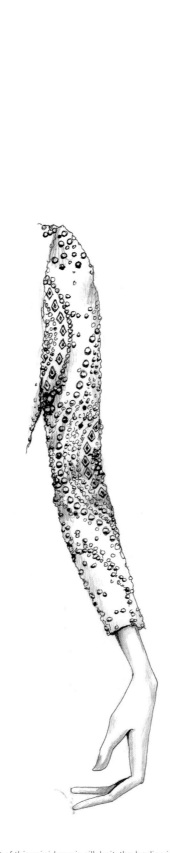

Left, minidress. The skirt part of this minidress is silk-knit, the bodice is metallic brocade. Silk yarn is shiny and when knitted into fabric displays a sheen across the surface. It is lightweight, forming soft folds, and is shaded using the side of the pencil to avoid hard lines; shadows should be rounded. The metallic brocade bodice is shinier and has a wider range of values; shadows in this part of the garment appear more angular and geometric. The surface texture of the metallic brocade is not smooth and this creates numerous uneven areas of shadow and light. Here it is lit from the left side which has the effect of creating deeper, more dramatic shadows. Shading is drawn in with the point of the pencil to pinpoint precisely the small areas of shadow. Center, Beading. Note that each bead is shaded individually. Where the beads sit right on the edges of the sleeve they are seen in profile and break up the silhouette. Right, brocade. Shadows are drawn under the pattern to creat the "relief" effect of another fabric sitting on top of the main fabric

Value range: skirt, 6, 5, 3; bodice, 9, 2; beading 9,5,3,2, 1, brocade, 8,5,4,3

matte fabrics/
wool georgette

Jacket and jodhpur-style pants made from wool georgette. This jacket has asymmetrical closure and feather trim at closure and hem. Both jacket and pants are made of a fabric with soft drape that has a matte surface; when drawing it the shadows in the folds are of a medium value. The deepest shadows are only slightly darker than the medium values in the folds.

transparent fabrics/
chantilly lace/exercises

So-called transparent fabrics (also called "sheer" fabrics) are in fact rarely fully transparent; they range from partly or semi-transparent to almost fully transparent.

Generally speaking transparent fabrics are more opaque in the parts where they fold over themselves—in the drape, hems and seams—and more transparent on the flatter areas. The more transparent parts of garments made of these fabrics are shown by indicating the presence of the shaded body underneath; the less transparent parts are shaded with subtle value ranges depending on the fabric.

Note that a common mistake when drawing transparent fabrics is to omit the constructional detailing: these features are in fact made even more pronounced by the transparency, so all seams, hems and tucks should be clearly shown.

EXERCISES
1. Draw on the croquis a leather jacket with fur trim over a lace blouse, matched with cotton pants. Draw twice over varying the fabrics of each of the garments.
2. Draw a tiered skirt with the top tier made of a shiny fabric, the middle of a matt fabric and the bottom of a transparent fabric.
3. Draw a tailored suit using plaid fabric for the jacket and a textured fabric for the skirt or pants.

This sleeveless party dress is made of a fine Chantilly lace. Chantilly lace is the finest of laces, often appearing in the shapes of leaves or floral motifs. It is drawn with the finest point of a hard pencil and a very light touch. Refer to the description of the Alençon lace dress in this section.
Value range: 9,4,3,

transparent fabrics/alençon lace/silk chiffon

This evening dress is made of Alençon lace—a handmade French lace that has solid patterns where the lace is more tightly woven and bordered with cording (*cordonnet*). The garment is drawn by first outlining the repeat of the lace pattern on a grid, in a similar way to drawing a print. The design of the pattern is then drawn using a hard pencil to give clear, precise lines. Most patterns in lace are so complex that they can be drawn abstracting much of the actual detail, while preserving the overall scale and shape, and indicating the thickness of the lace by the thickness of the line used to draw it. The net ground beneath the lace is indicated with very fine cross-hatching. This does not have to be rendered across the whole surface; it can be effectively shownby drawing in those parts where the garment touches the body and the shadow of the body underneath shows through.
Value range: 9,4,3,

This high-waisted, sleeveless evening gown is made of silk chiffon, an extremely light and soft, transparent fabric. The lightness of the fabric makes it billow and flow across the body. All the curves of the drape are rounded, and shadows are thin and soft. The whole garment is drawn using a very light touch. The silk has a slight iridescent quality that can be accentuated by using the sharp edge of an eraser to bring out the thin lines of light on the tops of the folds.
Value range: 9,7,6

transparent fabrics/
vinyl

Transparent vinyl raincoat. The fabric has angular, rigid folds that must be clearly seen in the silhouette. Shadows are drawn to express the body under the garment with a light touch and even value. Do not outline the body under the garment. The reflective areas of the vinyl at the tops of the folds are drawn in by erasing the pencil to leave the white of the paper to show through. Darker shadows are applied in the deepest parts of the folds.
Value range: 8, 5, 4

textured fabrics/
faux crocodile/faux fur

TEXTURED FABRICS

Textured fabrics range from all kinds of knits, to furs and other animal skins, to fringe, beading, quilting, cording and numerous other natural and man-made fabrics.

Of all fabrics, textured fabrics are those with the most direct impact on a garment's silhouette. The surface quality of the fabric is uneven, in varying degrees, and this can be clearly seen in the fabric, so has to be clearly reflected in the silhouette.

When drawing textured fabrics more line and shading is used than other fabrics as the surfaces are often broken up and more edges are seen. These outlines generally require the use of harder, HB or 2H pencils.

This faux crocodile/alligator jacket with faux fur collar is drawn with two contrasting techniques: Once the silhouette of the garment is drawn the fur is rendered using the side of a soft pencil with long strokes. The pressure of the strokes lightens towards the end of each stroke (here from left to right) to show the lighter area of the fur on the right side where it is closest to the light source. The silhouette and interior texture of the fur is brought out using the point of the pencil to show the individual fur fibers (different animal or faux animal skins have different lengths of individual hairs). The body of the jacket is drawn using the side of the pencil to create the squares that represent the individual crocodile scales. Only one pencil is used—a soft, 4B, for example—but the squares cover a wide range of light to dark values that represent the shiny parts and darker areas, so the pencil must be used with a correspondingly wide range of pressures to capture this variety.
Value range; 9,3–1

textured fabrics/
wool/fur

Vintage belted wool coat with fur lined neckline. The wool fabric is soft and matte so folds are soft and wide and are rendered with only subtle changes in value. The fur of the collar is drawn with wide dark areas of shading near the neck and at the outer edges and the interior of the collar is left light so the overall effect is of the collar as a wide cylinder. The individual strands of the fur are created with lines drawn closely together at the edge and further apart in the interior.
Value range, coat, 7,6,5,2,1; fur, 9,4,3,2

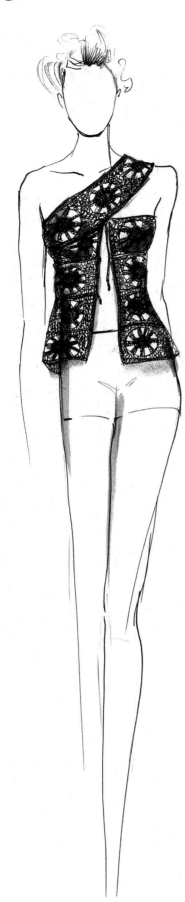

This short dress has a fitted bodice with fagoting—an open, decorative stitch used here along the side seam—and a fringed skirt. Fringe and fagoting are textures made up of linear elements. Fringe can be drawn with a more fluid, diagonal stroke, indicating that it can move freely. The fagoting is drawn with more control to indicate its precise structure that is an integral part of the garmen. Value scale 9, 5,4.

This top is made of crocheted mohair "granny" squares with rosette appliqués of the same fabric attached to the center of each square. The crochet pattern is drawn with the point of the pencil using a circular motion; denser applications are made where the crochet is thickest and appears darkest.
Value range 9, 7,6,2,1

The texture of denim is due to its twill weave—a weave with diagonal ridges—that gives the fabric a slightly rough surface. Denim is a medium-weight fabric that drapes in wide folds. It is drawn by first filling in the silhouette of the garment with an even application of shading of a medium value using the side of a soft pencil and then indicating the darker values of the folds using smaller, circular strokes. Indicate the twill—the white cross yarn—by removing thin lines from the rendering using the fine point of an eraser.
Value range: 6,5,4,3

soft fabrics/suede

SOFT FABRICS

Soft fabrics include wool, angora, cashmere, suede and felt, and other fabrics that are soft but without the distinctive texture of furs or some bulky knits. As their name suggests, everything about soft fabrics is soft. Soft fabrics generally do not have shine, but can have a subtle sheen, so their value range are closer together than those of shiny fabrics. They are usually drawn using the side of a soft pencil.

Suede is a very soft fabric that forms wide shadows. In the finished garment no lines are visible except those of constructional details; the silhouette is defined by the edge of the shadows. Suede is drawn by applying successive layers of pencil to express first the value of the intrinsic color of the garment and the shadows and subtle sheen on the surface of the folds. Using a blending (smudging) technique with a stump or cotton swab, layers of tone are then added inside the folds to create the shadows. The sheen on the top of the folds is created by lightly removing some of the pencil with the sharp point of an eraser.
Value range: 6, 4, 2

soft fabrics/gabardine/
suede

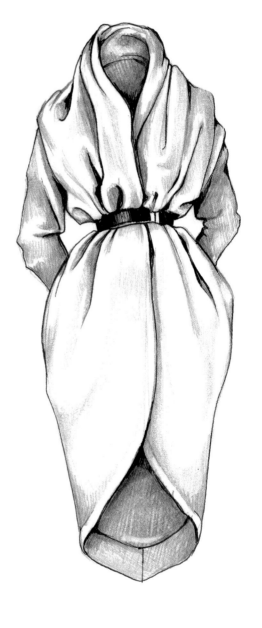

Gabardine has a tight weave with a flat surface so drapes in shallow folds that form wide shadows with relatively little contrast with the color of the body of the garment. The silhouette is drawn with clear edges but avoiding sharp lines. Fill in with an allover even value and apply shadows into the interiors of the folds with wide pencil strokes.

Suede has a similar surface quality to gabardine but is drawn with wider shadows and has a slightly softer edge than gabardine.
Value range: gabardine, 8–5; suede, 6–3

Wool cashmere cocoon coat with cinched waist. Wool cashmere is an extremely soft fabric that drapes in wide folds. The soft feel of the fabric is conveyed in the drawing by using soft, wide shading with only subtle variations of value except in the deep shadows in the creases, particularly above and below the belt. The interior is shaded slightly darker to indicate depth.
Value range: 2,4,5,9

soft fabrics/faux fox/ lambswool

Left, faux fox fur vest. The garment is made of many rows of fila-ments. Each filament is drawn individually; they are not aligned with each other and each point at slightly different angles. The thickness and depth of the fur is indicated by using wide shadows. Right, lambswool stole. The fur fil aments are drawn with a curved line to show the corkscrew shapes of the fur.
Value range: Left, 7,6,3,2 Right, 7,6.

chapter seven: men
and men´s clothing

drawing men/men and women/men's poses

DRAWING MEN

It is important not to confuse men with women, and vice-versa. Women often draw men that look like women and men often draw women that look like men. Like fashion itself, looks come in and go out of style, and one season men's looks can be masculine and muscular and the next thin, sensitive and more feminine. Despite these seasonal variations, though, there are clear physical differences between the sexes that are independent of fashion, and these must be clearly shown in drawings. As a rule, the male of the species is built more for "fight and flight" than the female, and is larger, harder and more angular. Although the figure is still a nine-heads one, a few of the proportions are slightly different. Here are the main differences:

1. The male head is slightly larger than the female head. It is squarer, with flat planes and more prominent features. The jaw is wider, the nose stronger, the forehead more prominent, cheekbones higher. The mouth is wider and the lips, particularly the upper lip, are not as full as in the female face; the eyes are less rounded. The neck is thicker than the female's.
2. Men's shoulders are wider and straighter than women's, closer to two heads wide as opposed to a woman's one and a half heads. In contrast to women the shoulders are also wider than the hips. The arms are thicker and more muscled and the hands are larger.
3. The chest is wider than a woman's, as is the back.
4. The torso is slightly longer than a woman's. The waist is lower and not as tapered; the hips are not prominent and the pelvis area is smaller.
5. Male legs are slightly shorter than women's, with much larger muscles, knees and feet. Hands are wider and fingers thicker than women's.

MEN'S POSES

With the exception of active sportswear poses, where it is effective to use poses from a "frozen moment" when legs and arms can be extended in a number of planes typical of the sport, filling a large portion of the page, men's poses tend to be straighter and more conservative than women's, with arms and hands closer to the sides of the body: Men are angular and poses

Men should be drawn to look like men.

men and women/
men's clothing/exercise

do not have the same sensuous curves of women's bodies. This is not to say that men's poses are not graceful and sophisticated, however: men should not be drawn stiffly; rather, their poses are more "ready for action", often with legs slightly apart to balance the body weight (rarely seen in female poses except for younger women)

MEN'S CLOTHING

Although the variety of men's clothing continues to grow rapidly, there is still not the same range of garments as is available for women. Tailored suits and other garments continue as important staples of men's wardrobes—basic uniforms with a long lineage dating back to heraldic times when they were a form of body armor. Increas- ingly, though, tailored garments have come to be adopted for less formal occasions or to be worn in combination with more casual clothes; for example, a tailored jacket might be paired with a t-shirt.

When drawing men's tailored garments, other than the differences in silhouette corresponding to the different body poportions, there are remarkably few differences from women's tai- lored garments, the main one being that closings on men's clothes are from right to left on the drawing (left to right on the body). Suits are often drawn worn with formal shirts and ties. When drawing the shirts, make sure that the shirt collar covers most of the neck and is placed above the jacket collar. In front view, little, if any at all, of the neck is visible between the jaw and the top of the collar: long, elegant necks do not feature in fash- ion poses for men.
The same attention to detail, precision of line and symmetry are present in men's tailored garments as in women's.

EXERCISE

Study the croquis over the next few pages and then copy three front, three side and three three-quarter views.

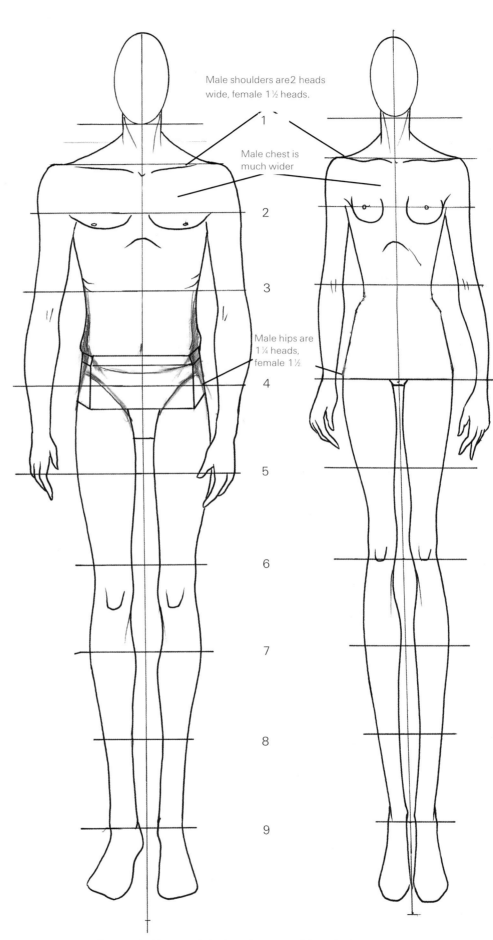

Male shoulders are 2 heads wide, female 1 ½ heads.

Male chest is much wider

Male hips are 1 ¼ heads, female 1 ½

The male fashion croquis is about the same height as the female but most of the features are bigger and broader. The torso is longer but the legs shorter than a woman's. Men should be drawn to look like men, and it is worthwhile to study the main physical differences between the sexes in order to draw them accurately.

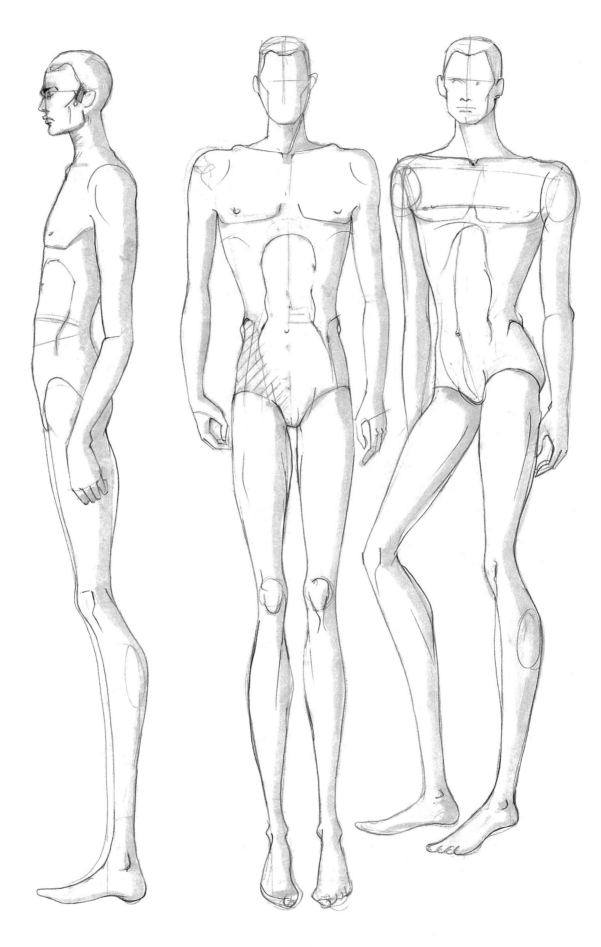

Male croquis—side, front and three-quarter view.

male croquis/front/back view/three-quarter S curve

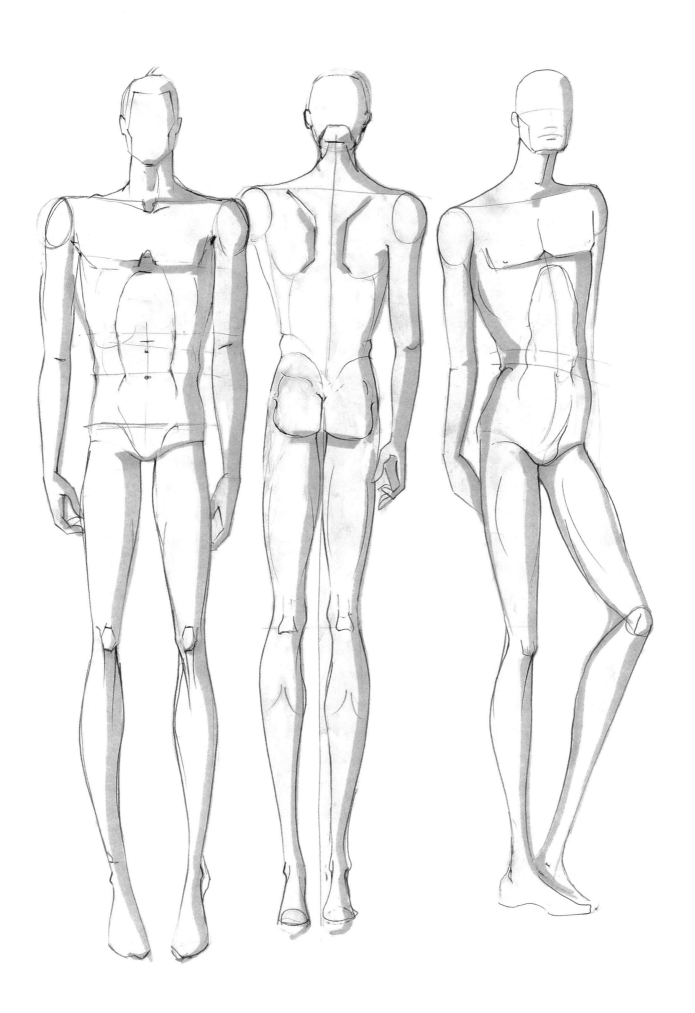

male croquis/three-quarter back
view/front S curve/front view

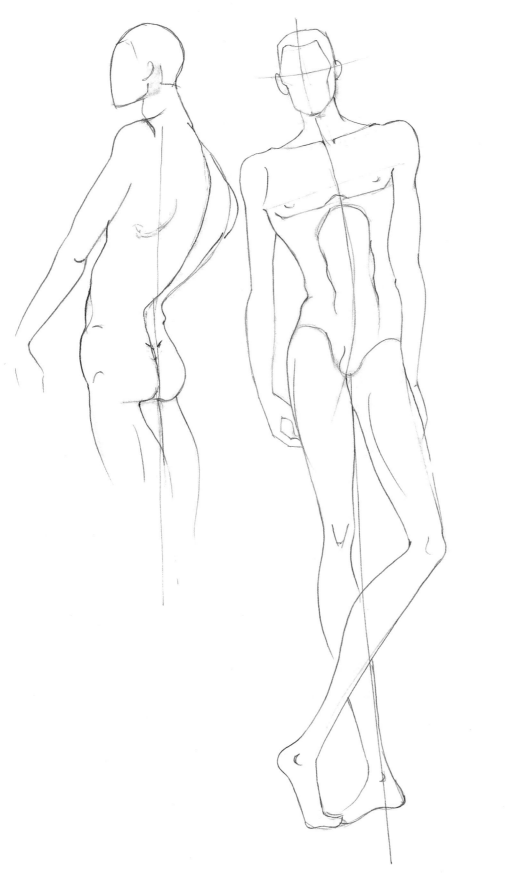
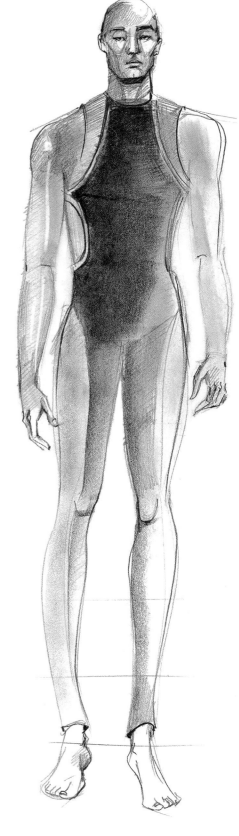

male croquis/ front view— fleshed-out

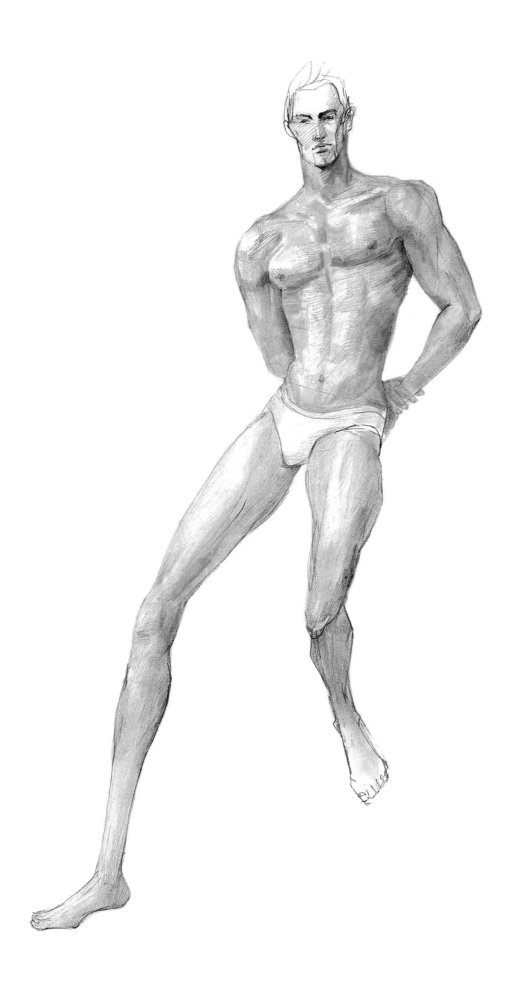

male face v.
female face

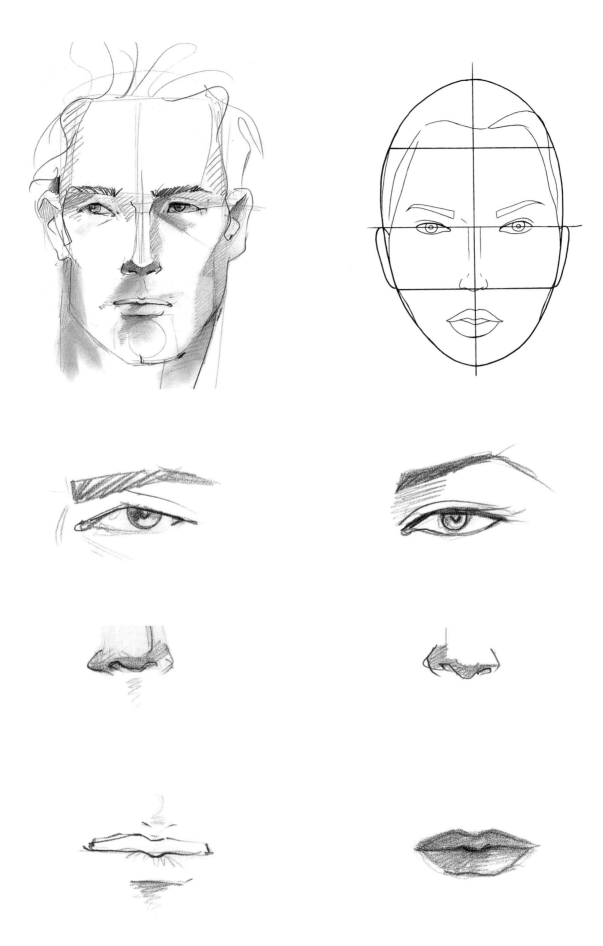

Male face v. female face. The male face is more rectangular, with a wider brow, larger chin and squarer and lower jawline. The features are in the same locations but are more horizontal. To give a particularly masculine look the planes of the face can be drawn in, from the sides of the eyes to the nose, and then straight down to highlight the cheekbones. **Eyes/eye-area**. The male eyebrow and eyelid are more horizontal than the female and the eye is more recessed—there is more shadow under the eyebrow. **Nose**. The male nose is more horizontal at the bottom—it does not turn up. **Mouth**. The male mouth is more horizontal. If the upper lip is drawn then it is more squared off at the edges.

male face/three-quarter view/exercises

EXERCISES

1. Copy three front, three side and three three-quarter view faces from this section.
2. Choose pictures of different types of men from a magazine or newspaper (e.g. college student, businessman, soldier) and draw their faces.
3. Fill a page with men's eyes, noses and mouths.
4. Draw a three-quarter croquis wearing an outfit (i) for the weekend, (ii) for a business meeting (iii) for travel and (iv) to play a sport.
5. Draw a young man dressed to go out to a club in leather and denim.

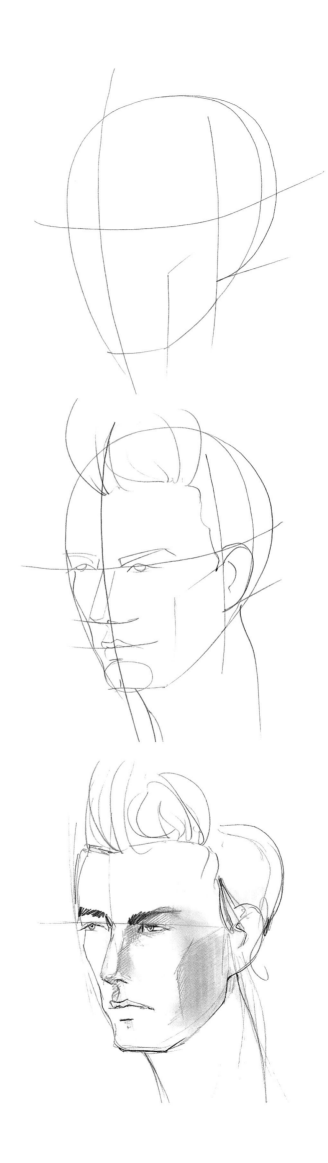

male face/
various views

male face/
front view

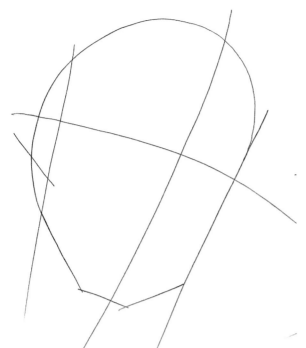

male face/
various views

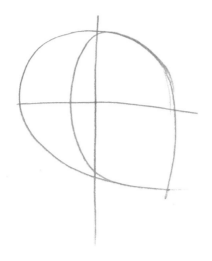

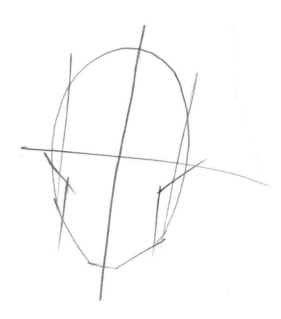

Position of lapels in front and three-quarter figures. Make sure the lapels are correctly placed in relation to the center-front line in all angles of poses.

Men's suits do not always have to be drawn with stiff, formal poses.
Relaxed poses are often effective for showing off more formal garments.

man in suit/duffle coat contemporary poses

Left, two button business suit with contemporary jacket. RIght, casual wear duffle coat and pants. Note the different poses chosen for the different types of garment. The tailored suit is more structured and has fewer folds than the garments on the right.

young man in jacket/pants
contemporary pose

This figure is seen from a slightly lower eye level, making the line of the jacket bend upwards and giving the drawing a more dynamic feel, almost as though captured in a walking pose by a camera.

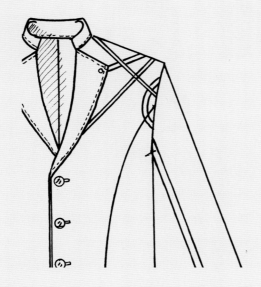

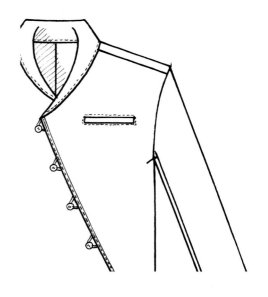

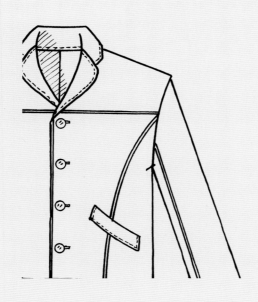

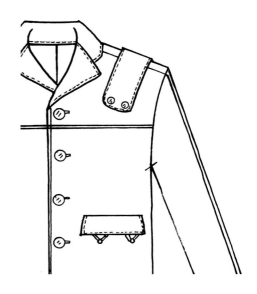

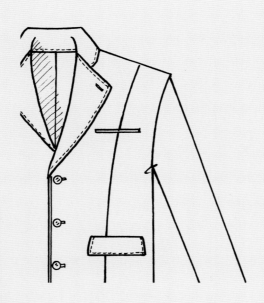

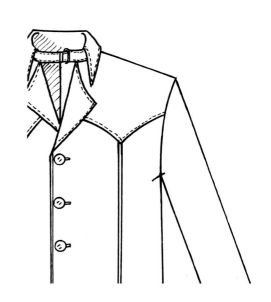

mens' jacket styles— designer and retro

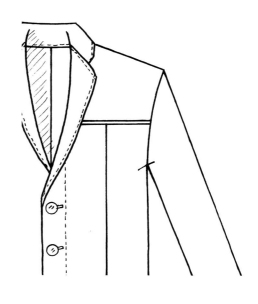

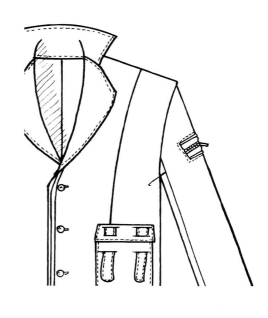

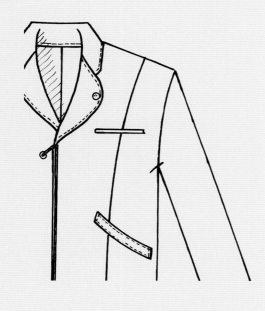

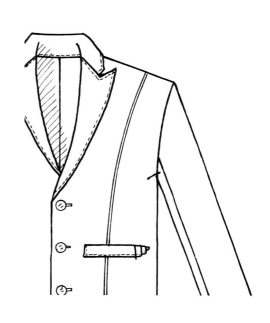

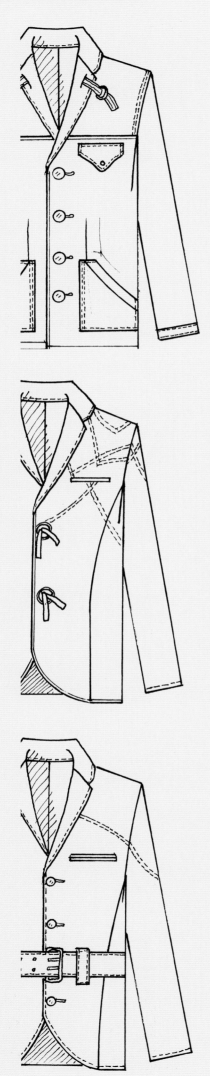

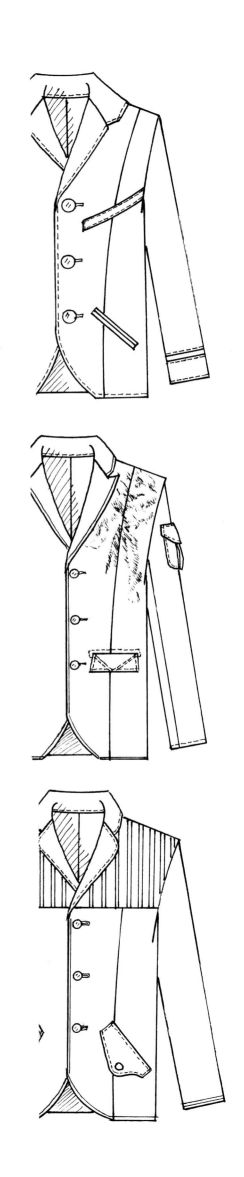

mens' jacket styles— designer and retro

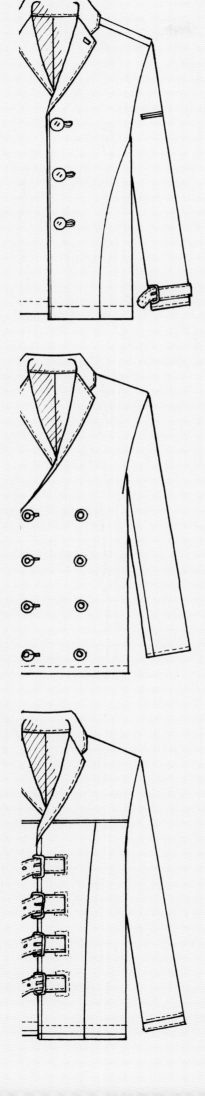

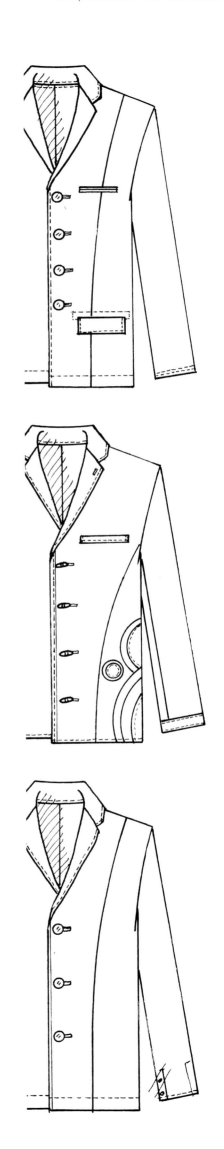

shirts

SHIRTS

Shirts, though now often worn by women, are traditionally one of men's staple garments and are worn in a wide variety of formal, informal, casual and active sporting occasions. Traditional shirts close in front, others close behind or pull on over the head; some shirts have long hems that tuck inside the pants and others have hems of varying lengths worn either in or out of the pants. In men's shirts long hems are common, in women's less so (though they sometimes imitate men's). Remember that men's shirts button left over right, women's right over left.

Most shirts contain some degree of tailoring: dress and formal shirts are fully tailored, and other less formal shirts have less. The constructional details common to most shirts are the following:

YOKES.

The yoke is the part of the shirt that fits across the shoulders. Yokes extend in varying lengths down the front or back of the garment, or both, and the back and front parts of the shirt are attached to them.

COLLARS

Shirts are made with a wide variety of collar types—they continually change shape and size with fashion trends. Some shirts are made with detachable collars and others without collars. Collars are usually attached to the yoke with a neckband that allows the collar to stand up over the body of the garment. The collar neckband is closed either with a button or stud aligned with the buttons on the band that runs along the placket—the opening—at the front of the shirt. (A placket is the name for any of the slits inserted into shirts or blouses to make them easier to put on and take off; they can be located at the sides, front, neck, back or wrists.)

BANDS/BUTTONS/BUTTONHOLES

As a rule the buttons are sewn onto the extension, or band, that extends down the front of the shirt from the neckband to the hem. Buttons should be placed at equal distances down the band; the size of the buttonholes varies with the size of the buttons. Men's dress shirts usually have small buttons and buttonholes.

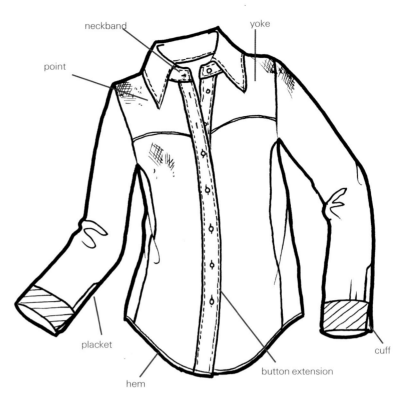

Parts of shirt with tailored, rolled collar.

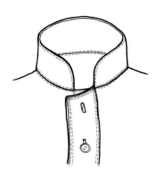

Band collar

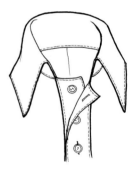

Rolled collar

Rolled collar

wing collar

Spread collar

CUFFS

Sleeves end in cuffs, either made of a separate piece of fabric sewn onto the sleeve or formed by folding over the end of the sleeve. Cuffs are a prominent fashion feature of shirts and there is a large variety of types. Make sure that cuffs are curved—drawn as ellipses around the arm—and are seen peeking out of the bottoms of jacket sleeves, sometimes adorned with cufflinks.

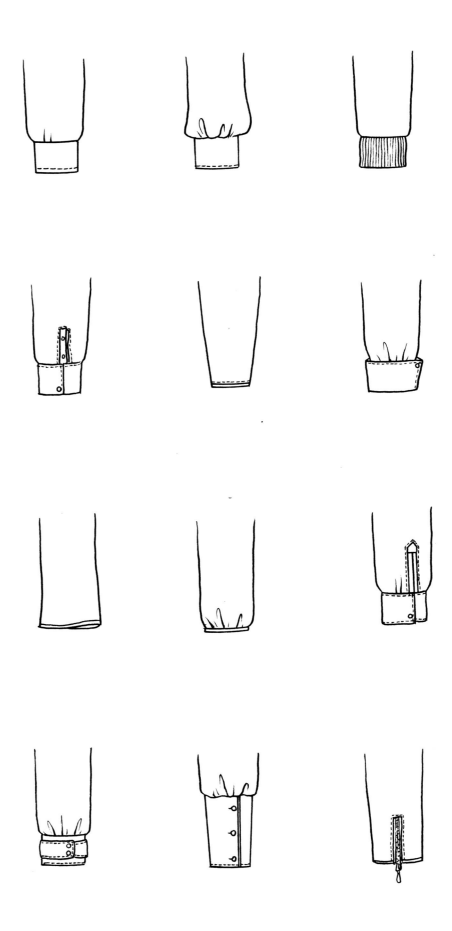

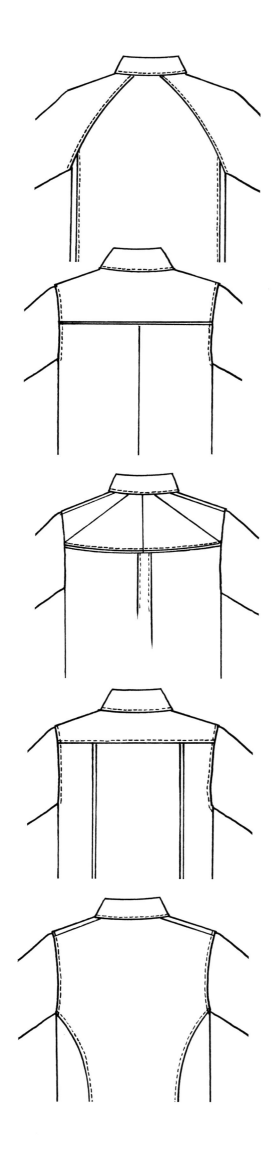

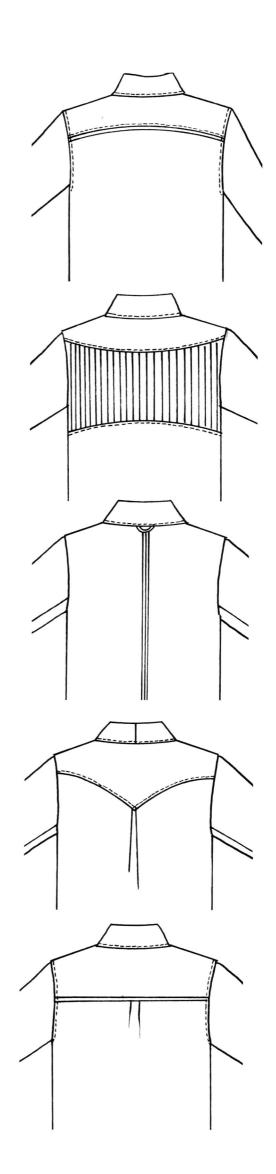

young man/ contemporary pose

A typical male pose—hand-in-pocket. Note how this pose affects the shape of the jacket: it opens up the front of the jacket, revealing the siilhouette of the pants and their fit at the waist and the details of the shirt.

The variety of poses for young men's fashion reflect the variety of young men's attitudes: youthful, energetic, athletic, happy, tough, nonchalant, street-wise, thoughtful and more.

young men/
contemporary poses

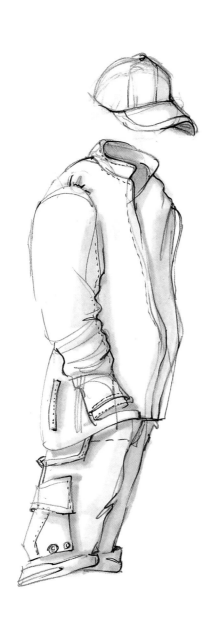

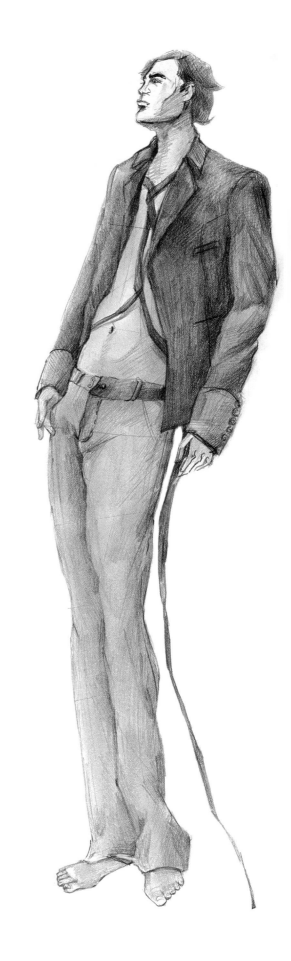

young men/ contemporary poses

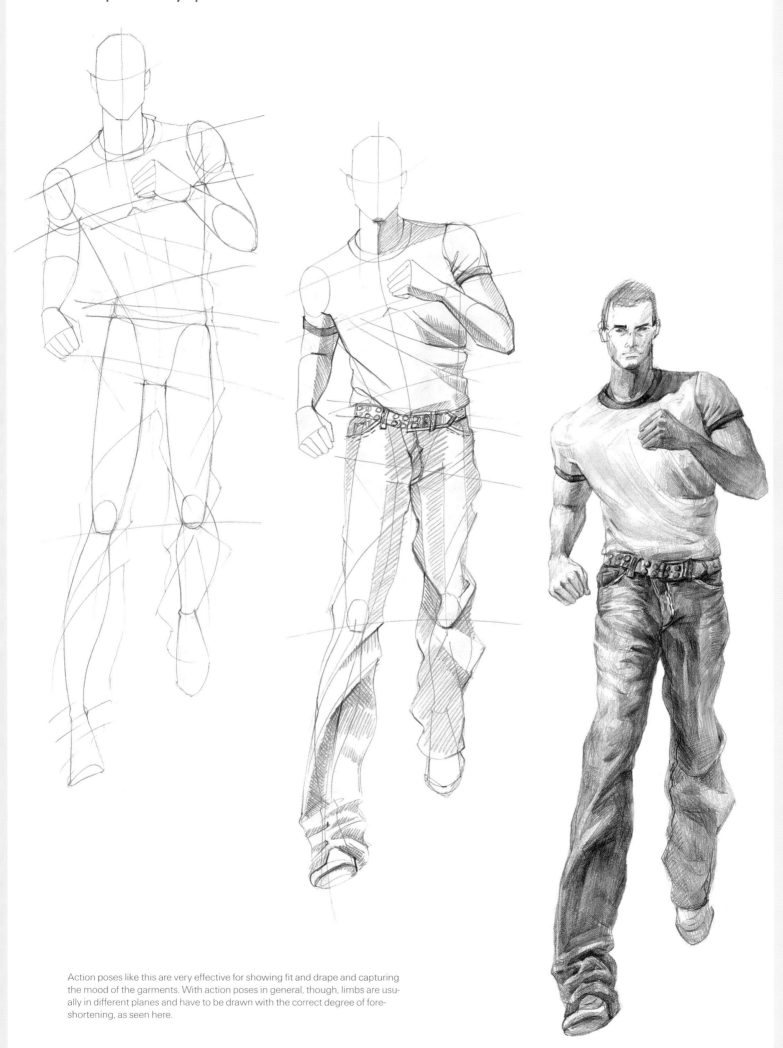

Action poses like this are very effective for showing fit and drape and capturing the mood of the garments. With action poses in general, though, limbs are usually in different planes and have to be drawn with the correct degree of fore-shortening, as seen here.

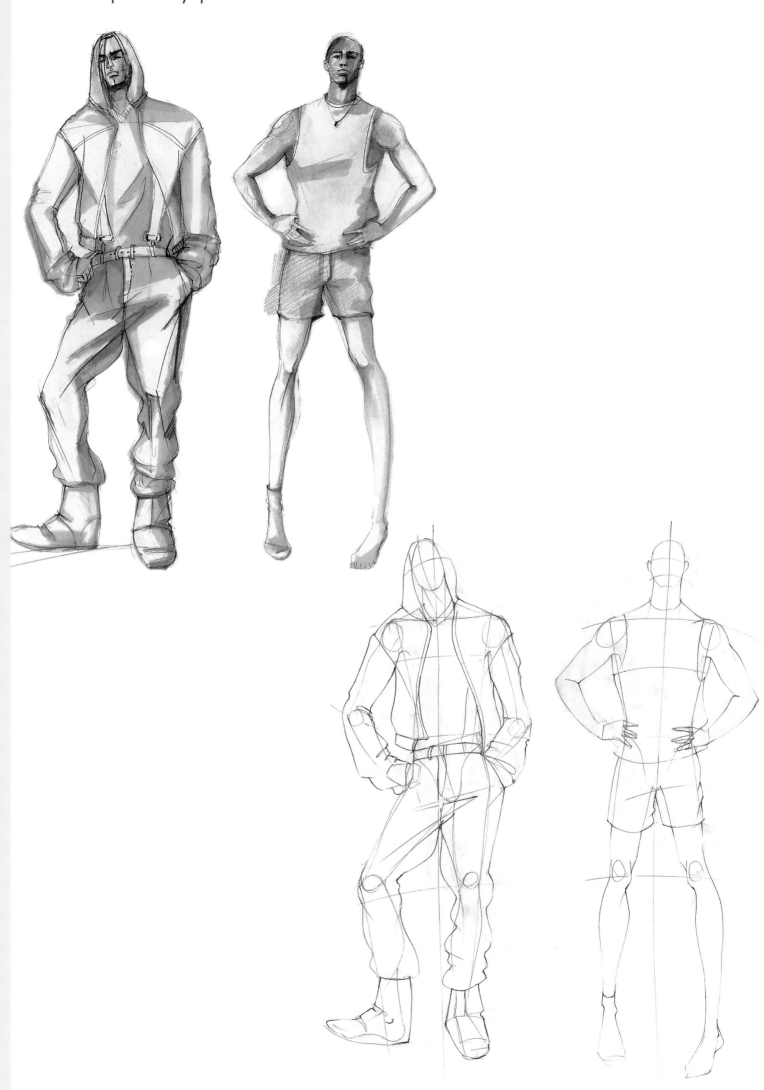

men´s accessories

men's flats/
templates

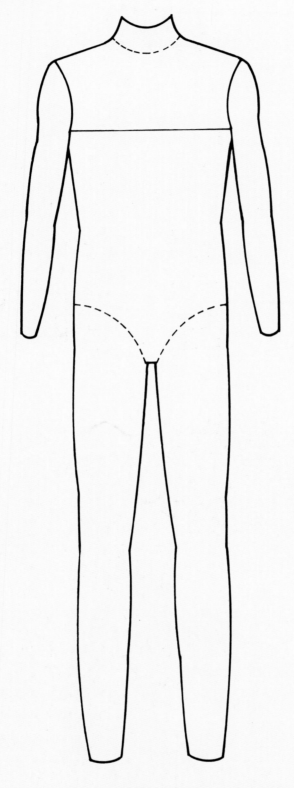

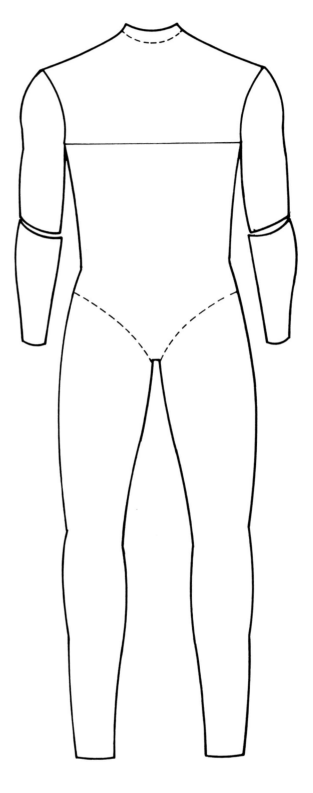

Traditional men's eight-head flat template. Most of the examples of flats included in this section are developed on croquis of this size or a slightly slimmer young man's template..

Contemporary men's eight-head flat template. The chest and shoulders are broader and waist relatively slimmer than the traditional template. Used frequently when drawing active sportswear.

men´s flats/
jackets

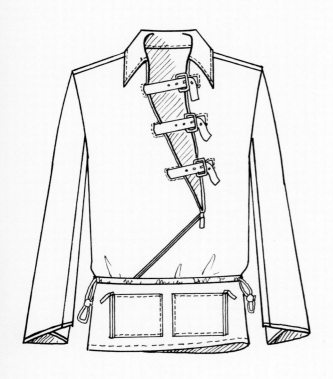

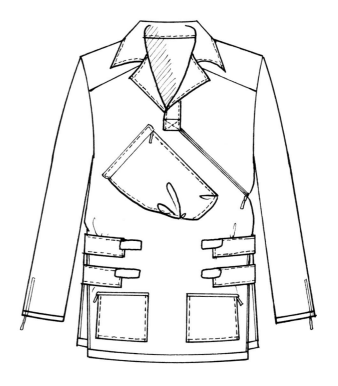

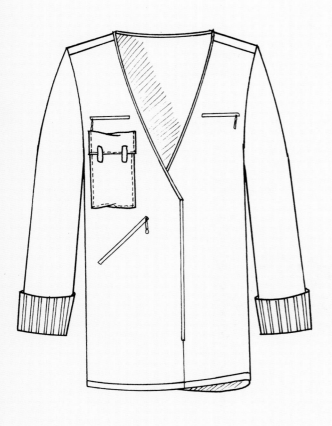

men's flats/ jackets

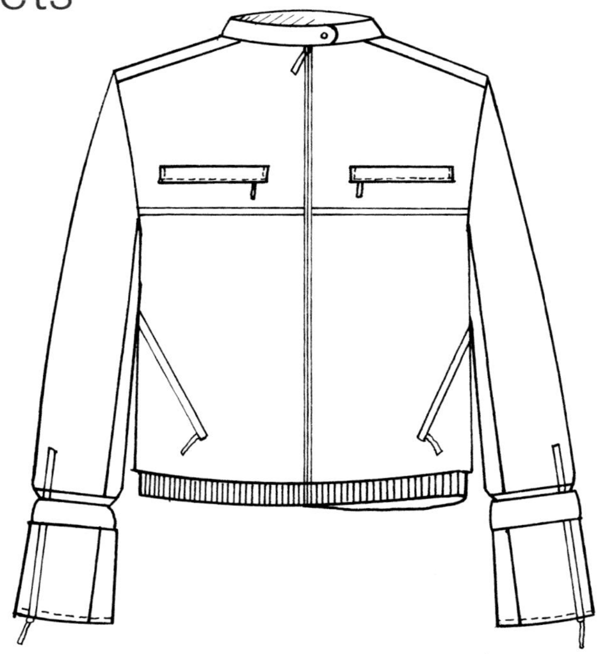

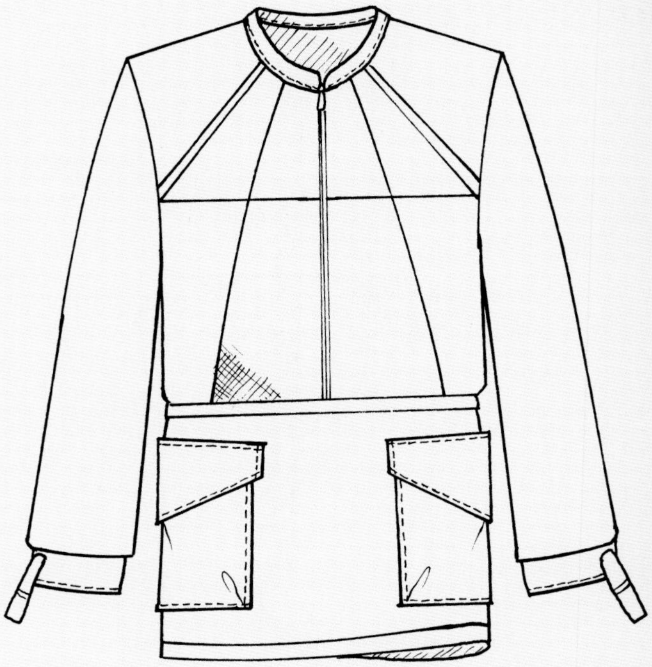

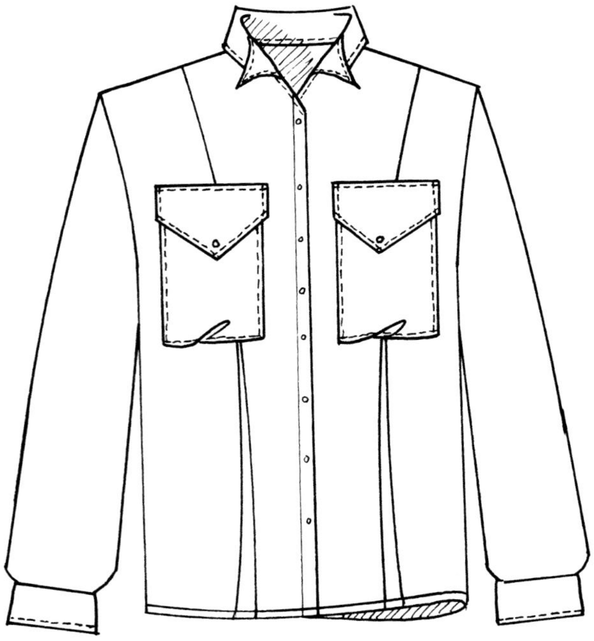

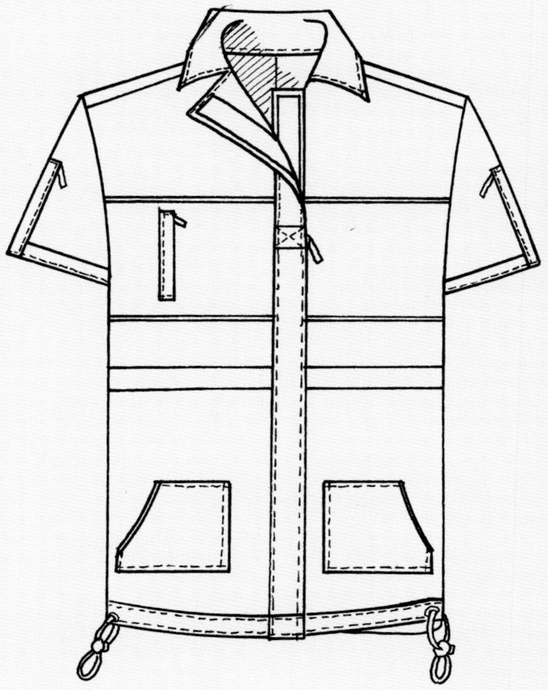

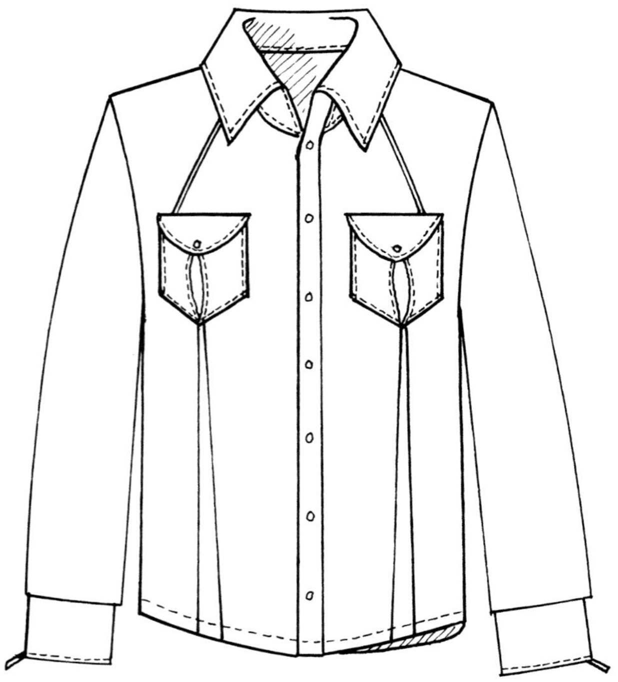

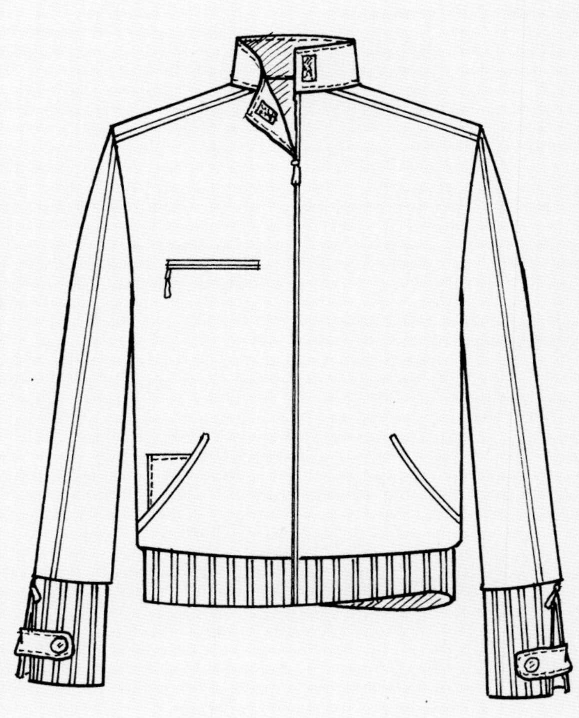

men's flats/ jackets

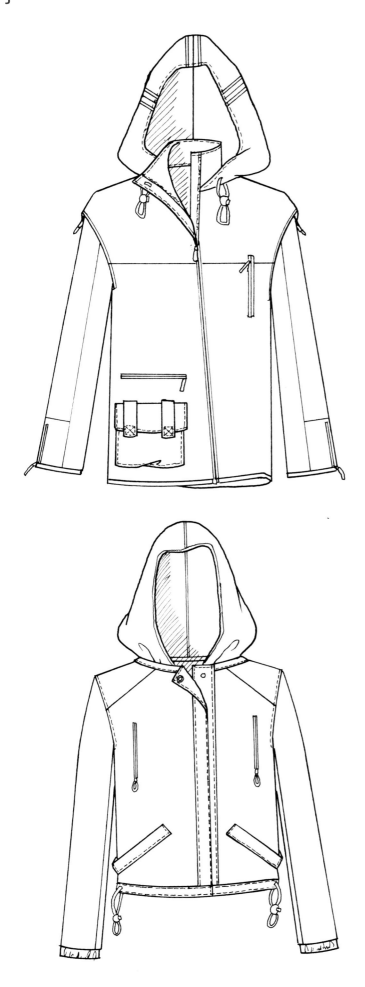

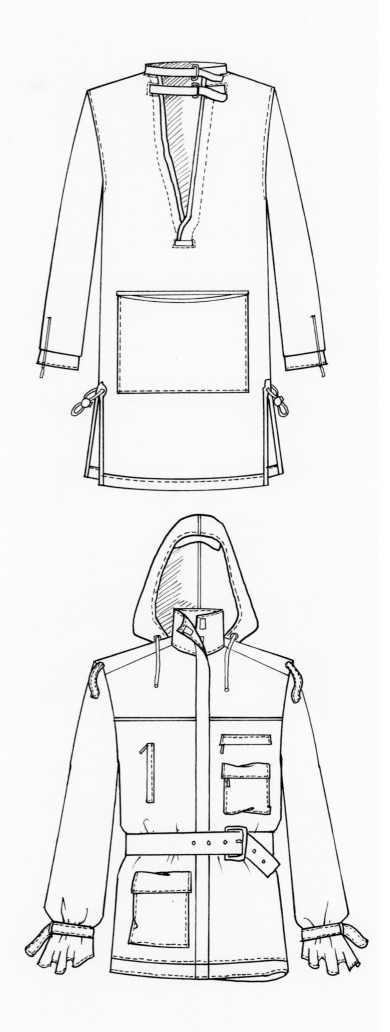

men's flats/
shirts

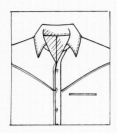

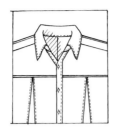

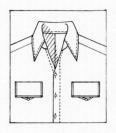

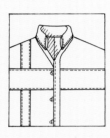

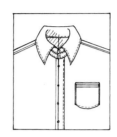

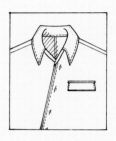

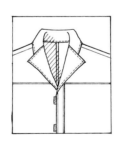

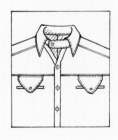

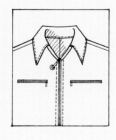

men's flats/
shirts

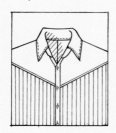 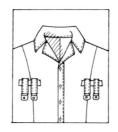 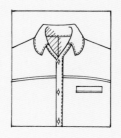

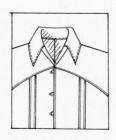  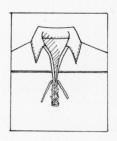

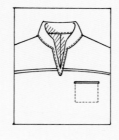  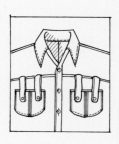

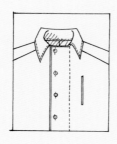  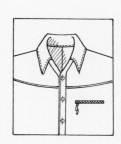

men's flats/
underwear/swimwear

chapter eight:
children and
children's clothing

drawing children/
young children's croquis

DRAWING CHILDREN

Renaissance artists—the great Leonardo da Vinci just as much as lesser artists—were able to master the complexities of perspective drawing and drawing the adult figure and face, but for the most part, for some unexplained reason, never mastered the art of drawing children: most of the children in Renaissance paintings look like little old men and women. Children do not really look like old men and women, of course, and artists in following centuries were able to capture their likenesses admirably, but we must avoid the Renaissance (or any other approach) that distorts how children actually are; children are different from adults in many ways, and must be drawn with care if they are to look natural and convincing.

Children's bodies and faces have different proportions, shapes and textures to adult bodies and faces. Children's faces and facial features are soft and round with few planes. Until they are almost into their teens, little bone structure can be discerned in their faces, or muscles on their bodies (That was the main mistake the Renaissance artists made—they drew scaled-down, developed "adult" facial and body features rather than real children's features.) Because of this, children should be drawn with a light touch to convey the softness of their features. The shapes of the accessories—toys, bags and so on—that children favor at different ages can often be used effectively in a drawing to echo the rounded shapes of their faces and bodies. Children's bodies change quickly from year to year and so care has to be taken to draw the croquis that corresponds to their age. The different croquis are shown here and the differences between them should be studied.

The ways children differ from adults other than the purely physical are also significant when portraying them in fashion drawings: Children are not sophisticated in their facial expressions and bodily poses; they are loose-limbed and playful and often pose in ways that

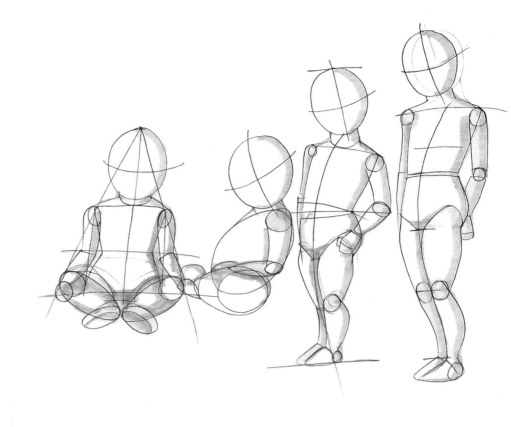

Young children's croquis: infants; toddler, small child.

older children's croquis/exercises

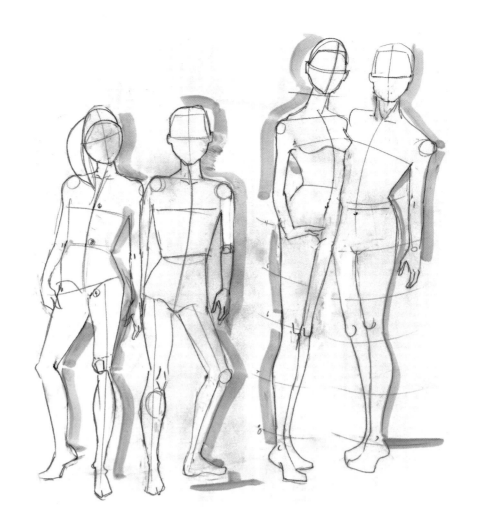

would look silly or awkward in an adult. This is not to say, though that they do not have personalities: children are (usually, but not always!) sweet and innocent, but also complex and multi-dimensional: modern designers create beautiful garments for children that recognize and respond to this. To do justice to them, then, children's croquis should be drawn with typical natural poses and attention to detail.

EXERCISES

1. Copy photos of babies, toddlers, small children, older children and teenagers from magazines and copy.
2. Draw a page of babies and children of different ages and sexes.
3. Select five garments from the flats at the end of this chapter and draw on children of three different ages.
4. Draw a group of children in pants and sweaters and the same group in party dresses.
5. Show a little girl and a little boy of different ages going to (i) school, (ii) a party, (iii) the beach and (iv) to church or a wedding.

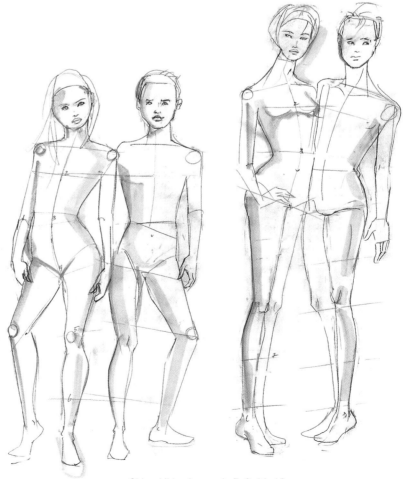

Older children's croquis: 7–9; 11–12.

children/characteristics of different ages

PHYSICAL CHARACTERISTICS OF CHILDREN OF DIFFERENT AGES
The usual age group categories for children are INFANTS/LAYETTES, TODDLERS, YOUNG GIRLS AND BOYS (3–6), OLDER GIRLS AND BOYS (6–12), JUNIORS/TEENAGERS (12–18).
The croquis and main physical features corresponding to the different categories of children are as follows:

INFANTS/LAYETTES.
Generally drawn with 3 – 3½ head croquis. Small children have low eye levels—about two-thirds way down from the top of the head (adult eyes are half way down the head). Heads and limbs are rounded so they will bounce off hard objects. No necks are visible. As they do not yet walk, crawl or stand infants are usually shown sitting or laid down with feet pointing inwards. Infants have little hair, and the little hair they *do* have is fine and close to the head.

TODDLERS.
The croquis is about 4½ heads. Growth from infant has occurred mainly in the legs. The face is round and there is very little definition in the features. The eyes appear disproportionately large as they are the same absolute size as adult eyes. The limbs are rounded and well padded; still no necks are visible. Hair is thicker and more evenly spread over the head. Toddlers can be shown sitting or in rather awkward standing or "toddling" poses.

Top—infant/layette. Small babies cannot sit or hold up their heads and have to be supported in any position. Note that there are no hard edges to any of the features. Bottom—infant, 3–6 months. By this age infants can support their own heads and sit comfortably. Note the position of the legs—they splay out from the body and then bend back in from the knees so the feet are together.

children
children's clothes

YOUNG GIRLS AND BOYS: The croquis is about 5½ heads. This age group has become longer in the torso than toddlers and necks are defined. Children start to participate in decisions about their clothes around this age. Accessories start to become important–bows, hair pieces, backpacks, belts, shoes and so on. Small boys start to have angles and planes in their faces (up until this age there is very little difference in the physical appearance of the sexes). Although still awkward in many poses, children of this age are now fully mobile and can be shown in a range of standing, walking and running poses.

OLDER GIRLS AND BOYS: The croquis is 6½–7 heads. Girls especially start to grow in their legs around 8 or 9 years old. Bone structures become more defined, poses are more graceful. Eye levels have moved up to about the same level as adults—half-way down the head. Vanity reigns: clothes become extremely important and a wide and increasing range caters to the children's and parents' whims.

JUNIORS/TEENAGERS: The croquis is 8 heads. The appearance is almost exactly like an adult except the facial features are slightly more rounded. Poses are generally more exuberant than adults, with arms and hips akimbo and considerable attitude displayed. Colors in general are saturated and vibrant; skin tone is healthy and rosy.

CHILDREN'S CLOTHES

The variety of children's clothes has grown enormously. Children wear a full range of clothes designed exclusively for them as well as miniaturized versions of adults' clothes. The market for children's clothes continues to grow rapidly with parents' increasing affluence and generally lower cost of clothing.

Children's clothes are usually made from soft and simple fabrics. Head openings are usually proportionately larger than in adult clothes, otherwise there is little difference between children's and adult's clothes.

Top—positions of babies' legs; bottom-study of (high fashion) toddler's face.

429

Toddlers have little sense of balance. They are very naughty and make cute, awkward poses. Feet turn in and limbs are akimbo. All limbs and features are rounded.

children/
toddlers' poses

More toddlers. Note that at this age children are still wearing diapers; clothes have to be roomy enough to accomodate them, and they should be indicated by fullness around the bottom.

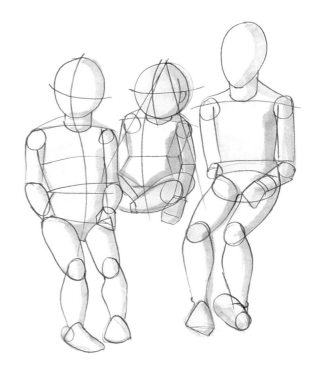

Top, little children—2, 3 and 4. Attitudes are playful with mouths turned up in smiles. Bottom, left and right, slightly older children—4 and 6. Limbs and features are still rounded at these ages.

children/
little children´s poses

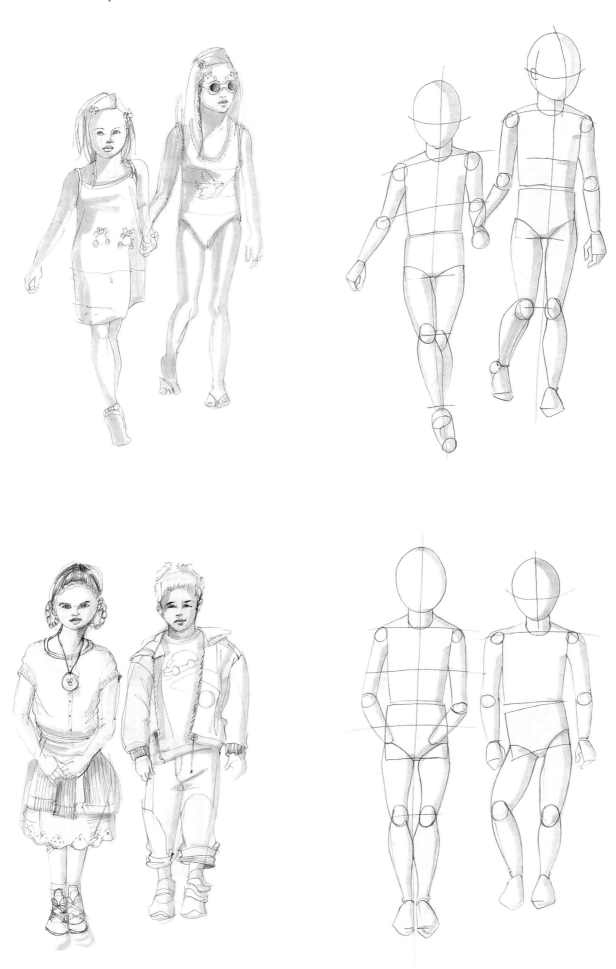

Clothes for different seasons. Top, summer clothes; bottom, autumn clothes. Children about 6.

11–12 year olds

Party clothes, 11–12 year olds.

Fashionable outfit, 12 year old.

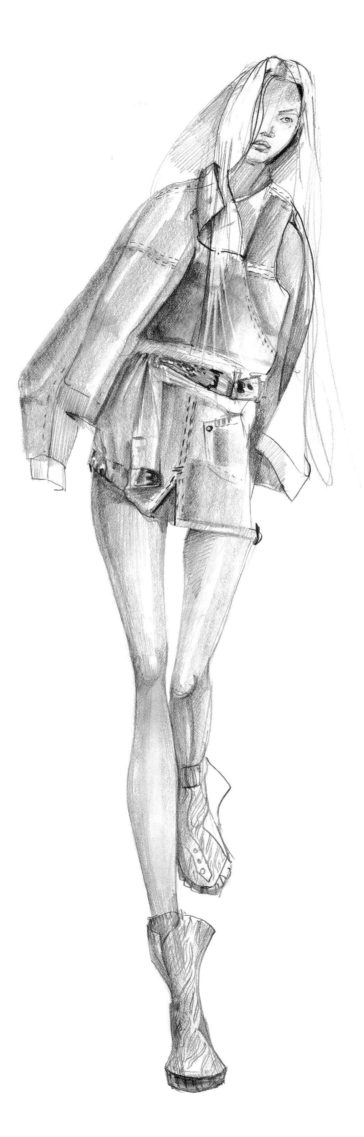

teenagers

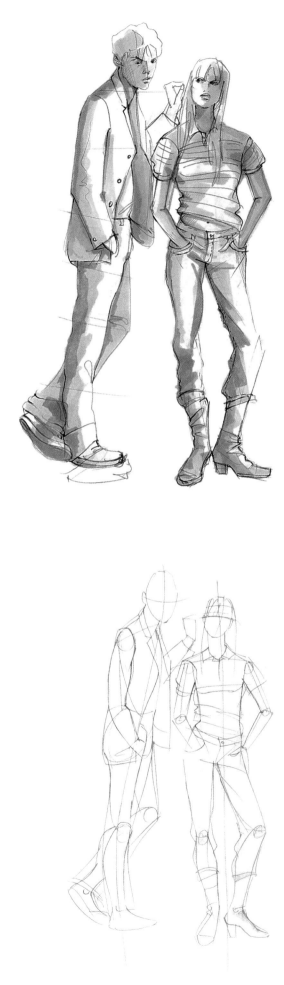

Teenagers. Note that men's faces start to
square up in mid to late teens.

children's flat templates/ younger children

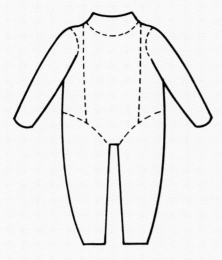

Layette—0–9 months.

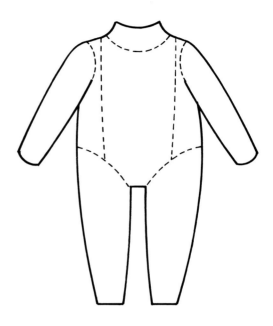

Infant—9–24 months.

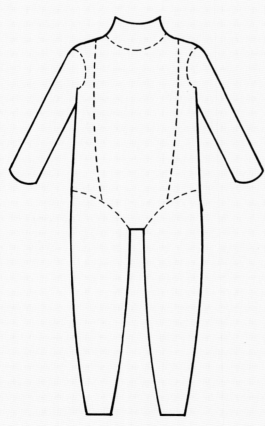

Toddler—2–4 years.

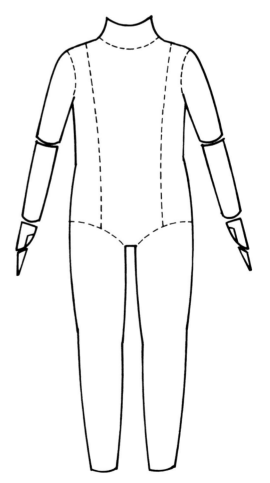

Boy/girl—5–8.

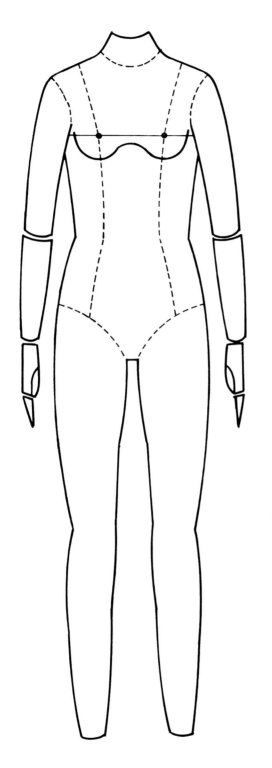

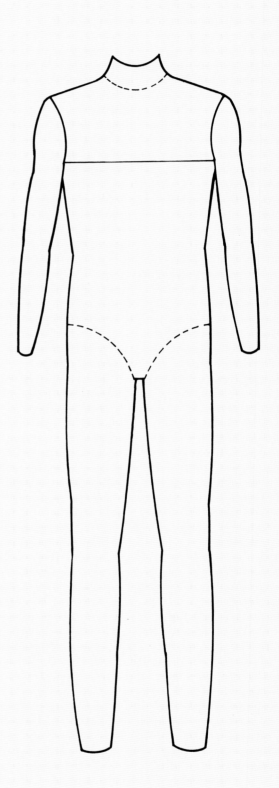

Junior girl and boy flat templates.

children's flats/
pants/dungarees

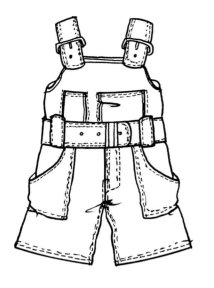

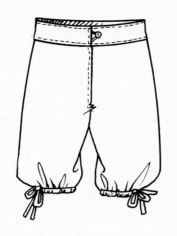

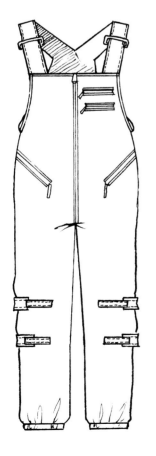

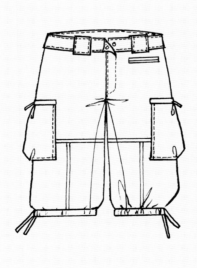

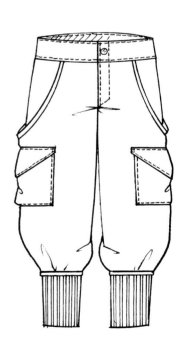

children's flats/ jackets/tops

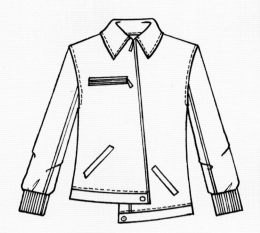

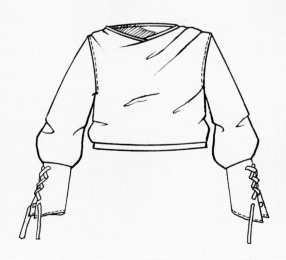

chapter nine:
composition and
fashion shorthand

composition/fashion shorthand/ single figure composition

COMPOSITION AND FASHION SHORTHAND

This chapter covers two more advanced types of drawing that are not closely related but are included together here because they are two of the most important drawing skills the student of fashion can and should master. The first of these skills is composition—how to "compose" fashion drawings so the clothes are displayed to best effect. The second is how to take fashion shorthand, the ability to record or communicate the essential elements of a garment's design quickly, in a time-restricted situation. Both these techniques allow the basic skills of drawing fashion garments and the fashion figure to be used to best effect in often-encountered "real life" situations. These "real life" situations can be, for fashion shorthand, situations such as job interviews (where concepts have to be communicated quickly to interviewers) or when working in a design team and other members need to see one's ideas or working for a private client. For composition, these real life situations include preparing a student or professional portfolio and presenting a design collection—how to present one's design drawings so they have most impact.

COMPOSITION: FROM FASHION DRAWING TO DESIGN DRAWING PRESENTATION

Up to this point we have been learning how to draw fashion garments on the fashion figure, the croquis. Now we have learnt how to draw fashion garments on the figure the final step is to learn how to prepare our design drawings for presentation to others. This is the final stage of the fashion drawing process, coming when all the individual designs have been finalized in detailed concept drawings and accompanying flats, where appropriate, and are ready to show to the outside world (whoever that might be!).

In fashion, as in all art and design, presentation is always important: On the runway, a new garment must be presented so it is seen at its best and catches the eye; it must look new and freshly pressed and fit the runway model to perfection, who must walk and twirl to show off the cut and drape of the fabric and direct attention to the special design features. A good runway presentation can never fully compensate for a poorly designed garment but it captures the viewer's attention and pre-disposes her to give the garment a fair evaluation.

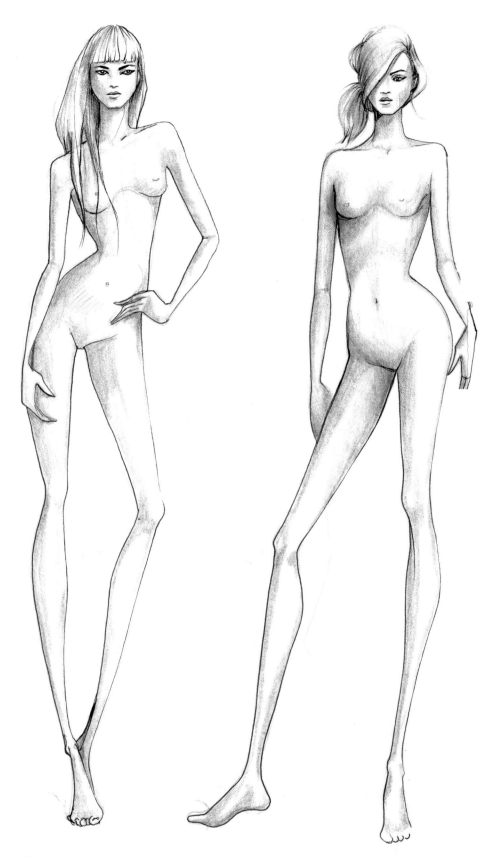

With single figures the number of design variables is limited: it is possible to vary the size of the frame to achieve different effects, but most of the elements that make up the design are in the pose. In this asymmetrical S curve pose there are 3 interesting negative spaces of almost perfect triangles of different sizes within the body— between each arm and the torso and inside the legs. The angling of the shoulder causing the compression of the body on the left and the shapes in the hair, styled asymmetrically to the left of the head also accentuate this theme of triangles and diagonals which give dynamism to and lead the eye around this single figure. The variation in the pose of the hands also adds interest.

An excellent pose for showing pants or activewear as the figure is open to show off the full silhouette. The asymmetrical hairstyle adds interest and points to the arm which leads the eye to the leg and around the composition.

composition/single figure composition

A fashion drawing, like the first appearance of a designer's garment on the runway, is, for those who do not yet have their own runway shows, how most fashion designs are presented for the first time—to colleagues, clients, teachers or interviewers. And also just as clothes have to be displayed so they make the maximum impact on the runway, in drawings they should also be displayed to achieve maximum effect.

Design drawings are presented in a number of different ways, from drawings of a single outfit on a single figure to drawings of a number of garments from a collection (or "line") on a number of figures. It is usual not to exceed five figures (wearing five outfits) in a single drawing—more figures than this and the drawing begins to look cluttered and it becomes difficult to take in all the information. Whether the drawing contains a single figure/outfit (which might be the case if the outfit is not part of a collection, or if it is part of a collection but has no obvious similarities to the other pieces in the collection) or several figures/outfits, it still has to be "composed". to best effect on the runway, drawings on paper must also be presented in such a way as to capture the viewer's attention and interest. Whether that interest is held or not will depend largely of course to a large extent on how good the fashion design is, but unless we can capture that interest in the first place our design drawings will not even receive a proper appraisal.

Once the choices have been made for styling, pose, facial expression and background/setting have been made, then for single figures/outfits on a single page the decisions left to be made are how to place the drawing on the page. Surprising as it may sound, the placement of a single figure on a page does involve some compositional decisions: the page will consist of the figure and the space around it, known to artists as negative space. How the figure and the negative space around it fit together will determine whether the composition is effective or not. Where two or more figures/outfits are shown on the page then there will be decisions about the placement of the figures on the page, the negative space around them and also the compositional interactions among the figures and the negative space. These interactions have to be considered in making sure the composition works. There are no hard and fast rules for composition in a drawing, but applying basic design principles as used in art and graphic design usually improves the results.

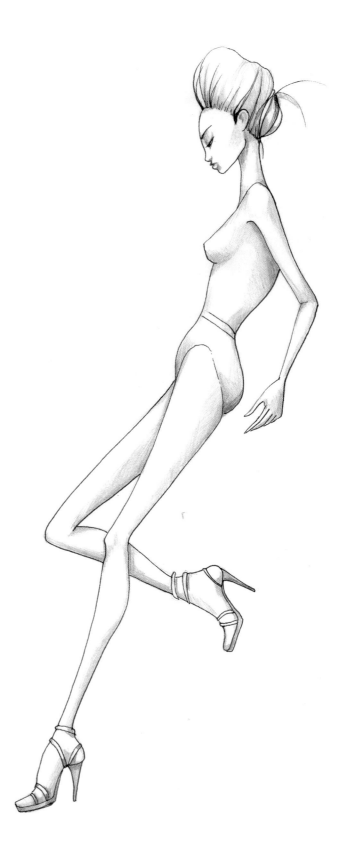

This side view is composed of dynamic diagonals and angles: the body reclines at an angle, the head echoes that angle while the upper arm bends back and the forearm is parallel to the body. The left leg bends back at the knee to bring the eye to a focal point at the shoe in the center of the page, vertically below the head, and then to the arm and back to the body.

planning the composition/ two figures

The principles most relevant for achieving good composition in fashion design presentation are illustrated and discussed in the drawings in this section, which will hopefully encourage students of fashion to focus on this important aspect of the presentation of their work and explore compositional options. The discussion is limited to poses and spatial relations among the figures in the composition; what is not discussed here is the use of backgrounds, particularly now it is easy to insert photographic or graphic backgrounds using software programs such as Adobe Photoshop. Once you have become sensitive to the importance of presentation and composition then your own eye—a feeling of whether a composition looks right or not— will usually lead the way to the best compositional decisions.

PLANNING THE COMPOSITION

The composition of fashion design drawings has to be planned in two steps: First, the design aspects of the garments that are thought to be the most important and have to be emphasized in the drawing should be clearly identified. This involves analyzing the garments and deciding on the relative importance of silhouette, cut, proportion, fabric, detailing and accessorizing, the mood and "look" of the garments, and which market segment they are designed for. Also, for drawings where two or more outfits from a collection are to be presented together there will usually be some similar element that unifies the garments in the collection; it might be that this unifying element is obvious and speaks for itself or it might be necessary to draw some attention to it. Once the most important design aspects of the garments have been identified then the compositional elements of the drawing have to be planned that will best show off these important fashion design aspects. These elements include: styling—what is the best choice for hairstyle/color, makeup/color (styling in color is not covered here but is covered in detail in the companion book Colors for Modern Fashion); pose and facial expression; background/setting (usually not more than a simple graphic element, often inserted using Photoshop). These elements have to be considered even where only a single figure/outfit is shown on the page. Where two or more figures/outfits are to be shown in the drawing then those elements have to be considered for each separate figure/outfit.

Study the drawings and comments in the captions in this section and refer to them when preparing final drawings for a presentation or portfolio.

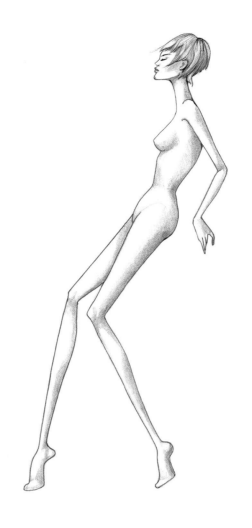

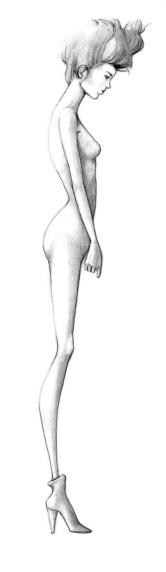

Above. It often seems to be easier to create interesting dynamic figure compositions where there are an odd number of figures. It is also often not easy to make compositions with back to back figures work well as the figures can appear isolated and unrelated. In this composition one of the figures has a static pose and the other a dynamic one. In the figure on the right, though, although the pose is static the head is inclined at the same angle as the body in the reclining pose on the left, so that element, plus the arm and leg of the left figure pointing to the figure on the right create a connection between the two figures. Small details such as an interesting facial expression, an extended finger or similar device can create just the right amount of interest in the figure to hold the gaze while not distracting attention from the garments.

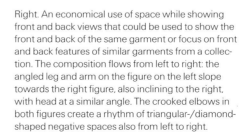

Right. An economical use of space while showing front and back views that could be used to show the front and back of the same garment or focus on front and back features of similar garments from a collection. The composition flows from left to right: the angled leg and arm on the figure on the left slope towards the right figure, also inclining to the right, with head at a similar angle. The crooked elbows in both figures create a rhythm of triangular-/diamond-shaped negative spaces also from left to right.

composition/
three figures

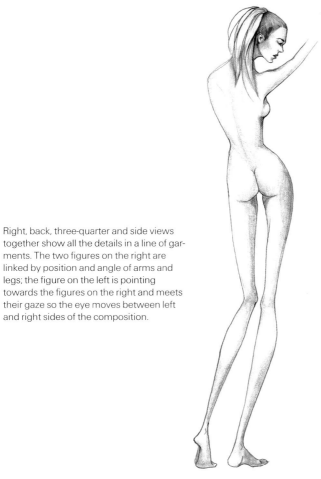
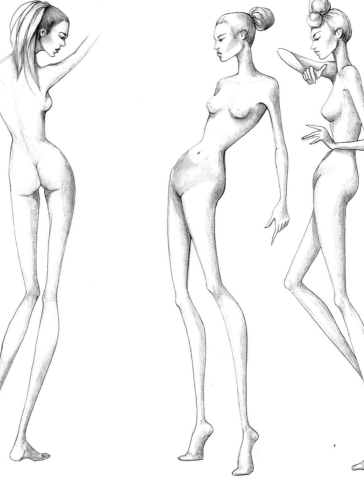

Right, back, three-quarter and side views together show all the details in a line of garments. The two figures on the right are linked by position and angle of arms and legs; the figure on the left is pointing towards the figures on the right and meets their gaze so the eye moves between left and right sides of the composition.

Left, teenagers, usually shown with less sophisticated poses, younger hair styling and perky facial expressions. The subtle variations in position and angle of the legs, arms and shoulders make for a variety of different shapes of negative space. The figures on the right overlap at arm and leg and the figure on the left is leaning towards them, helping to unify the composition.

composition/
three figures

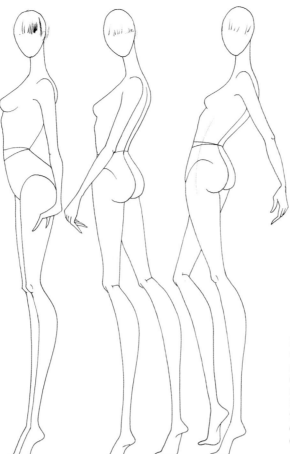

Left. Although these are similarly posed figures they each show subtle variations in positions of hands, arms, legs and feet that engage the eye. There is also a feeling of rhythm as the figures lean further back from left to right and the bodies turn from a front three-qaurter view on the left to back three-quarter, center, and back three-quarter/side on the right and the legs change position.

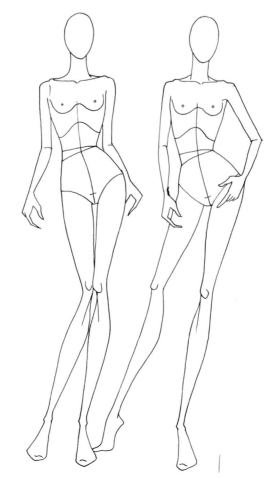

Right, a composition that does not work. The front view poses of the figures on the left feel static and there is no feeling of connection between them. There is also no feeling of connection between the pair on the left and the single figure on the right, which appears completely uninterested in the group, gazing outside the composition, a pose that does not encourage the eye to linger.

composition/
four figures

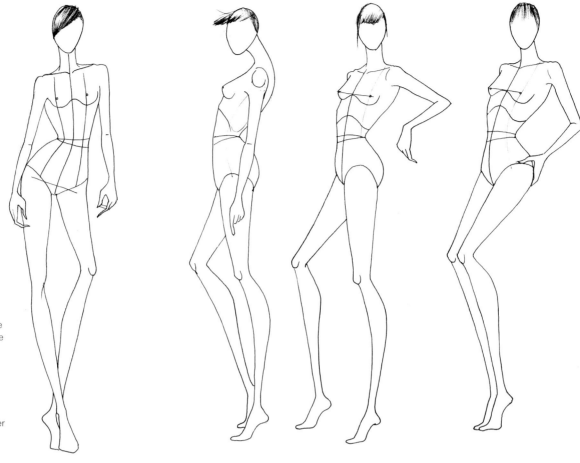

The three figures on the right are leaning (and the first figure of the group has leaning hair also) towards the figure on the left, which has a solid, front-view pose and acts as an anchor for the drawing. These are unusual poses and energy for showing garments designed for a younger market.

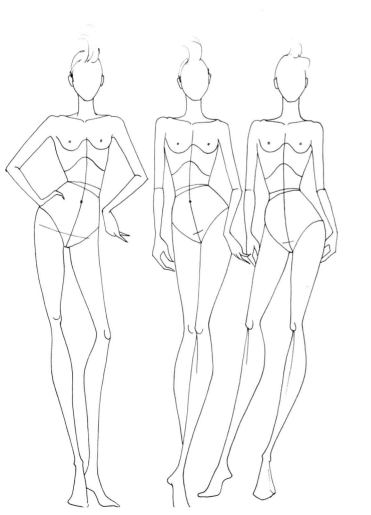

This composition is effective because the figure on the right has limbs extended and occupies a similar amount of total space and negative spaces to the three figures on the left, which are drawn in classic front view poses with limbs closer to the body. This gives a sense of balance between the two sides of the composition, even though there is a disparity in numbers on each side.

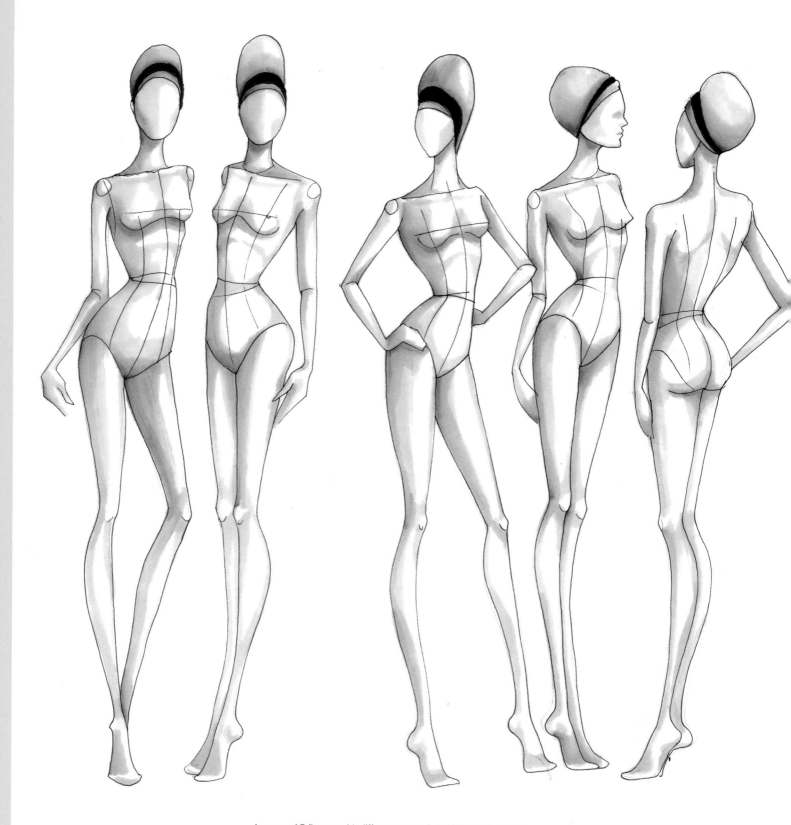

A group of 5 figures with different poses that might be chosen to show off garments with important details in all views, such as those in tailored garments (seen in fact later in the chapter). Subtle variations in positioning of limbs, angle of heads and and shoulders add interest and there is a variety of different shapes of negative space. The middle figure acts as a bridge between the two subgroups of figures by leaning and gazing towards the subgroup on the left. The group is also unified by the similar hairstyles and headbands

composition/
three figures

In this presentation of three outfits from a collection the core outfit is shown on the figure in the foreground which is the focal point of the drawing. The other two figures face each other behind the main figure and also frame the main figure. The common elements running through the collection are the sleek silhouettes and the print repeat of the fabric used as trim at collar and cuffs on the core garment and as a skirt and a panel of the dress of the others. The composition is further unified by using the same hairstyle on each of the figures and the relative sizing of the purses.

Compositions with even numbers of figures are more difficult to design than odd numbers. Here again the core outfit is featured by bringing the figure to the foreground. The outer figures face each other, looking into the drawing and the other figure looks at the main figure so the eye is kept within the drawing and led to the main figure. Hairstyles further unify the drawing as do the shiny black shoes. These garments are separates with sleek fitted silhouettes above the waist and more fullness below.

fashion shorthand

FASHION SHORTHAND

There are a number of situations where fashion information has to be either communicated or recorded quickly, where the amount of time available is limited. Situations like this can arise, for example, at a runway show (one where photography is not permitted, as is quite often the case) or in an interview with a prospective employer, client or supplier or a meeting with other members of a design team where we wish to convey our ideas about fashion garments. If we are able in these situations to make a quick sketch that records or conveys key fashion information clearly and accurately this is a valuable and extremely useful skill that greatly enhances our professional effectiveness.

A large part of what is involved in becoming effective in sketching quickly and finding the short cuts for recording or communicating information is not as much learning a new drawing skill as it is learning to be able to sort out different types of information and decide which information should be conveyed in a drawing and which information is best conveyed in another way, mainly verbally, through language. This is like learning a type of " fashion sketching shorthand".

What are the characteristics that define a fashion garment, the variables that make it different from all other garments? These characteristics are, as we have discussed at length in this book:

garment type (i.e. jacket, pant, blouse etc.)
silhouette,
fit,
proportions,
fabric,
color,
details,
styling.

How do we describe those characteristics of a garment, either to record or to communicate them? Well, as an exercise let us attempt to describe those characteristics in words. We will use one of the drawings from the companion book to this one-Colors for Modern Fashion. The purely verbal description of the outfit, consisting of three garments and accessories is shown at right. This verbal description took several minutes to work out (and that was looking at the finished drawing; on the runway one sees a garment for perhaps fifteen or twenty seconds). See how accurate a picture of the garment the words conjure in your mind's eye before turning the page and seeing the actual garment and looking at how much better it can be described using a combination of quick sketches and key information points— a type of fashion shorthand.

garment description

garment type:

a. knitted scoop neck t-shirt with ¾ length sleeves under
b. sleeveless knit v-neck empire waist draped top, contrast yoke attached at seam under bustline, self-tie belt at front, gathered waist and hip area, ruched at side seams, gathered miniskirt over
c. palazzo pants
d. neck scarf
e. flats with patterned uppers

colors:

a. fuschia and white
b. orange with printed pink yoke, yellow, pink, orange and red mid-section, black miniskirt with embroidered striped band of several colors on green (upper) and white (lower) backgrounds
c. forest green with black print
d. red with white dots
e. red stripe pattern on white background, green soles

hair: multi-colored mop wig

market: designer (Custo Barcelona)

Can you visualize this outfit?

fashion shorthand

FASHION SHORTHAND CONTINUED

The outfit seen at the right is the outfit of the verbal description of the previous page. How close was the picture you developed in your mind's eye from the verbal description to the actual outfit? If you were close then you have a powerful imagination and intuition, great powers of interpretation and deduction and an in-depth knowledge of fabrics and fashion garment construction. If your idea of what it looked like did not turn out to be close to the actual outfit then you are one of the vast majority of people who work in fashion who are visually rather than verbally oriented.

The finished drawing itself took a couple of hours to complete, obviously a great savings in time compared with the process of trying to find fabric samples and produce mock ups. What if we only have a few seconds, as a model walks down a runway, or a couple of minutes to convey our ideas to the rest of our design group, a client or interviewer? The answer is to develop a type of *fashion shorthand* as shown in the example on this page and the following pages.

As can be seen, the key here is to make a quick sketch that will act as a diagram. The sketch records shapes: the shape of the outer silhouette of the garment(s) and the main internal shapes—the different sections of a garment and the drape caused by construction details such as pleating, gathering or, as in this example, ruching. Once we have that sketch then, if we are recording information we wish to use later, we can make it into a simple diagram and indicate the colors in different parts of the outfit as well as any other noteworthy aspects relating to proportions or fit, and jot down the type of fabric and market segment. If we are in a face-to-face meeting we can quickly articulate our ideas for the other aspects of the garment. All that information can be conveyed in one or two spoken or written words. The end result is an effective way of storing or communicating information on a garment or outfit that is not immediately available as a photo with a considerable degree of accuracy.

Study the examples of fashion sketching shorthand included in the remaining pages of this chapter. To master this technique practice converting favorite drawings or photos into fashion shorthand.

The outfit corresponding to the verbal description on the previous page. Not so easy to describe using words alone!

Fashion shorthand. The exterior and interior silhouette can be quickly sketched and notes made jotted down on fabric, construction, color and styling.

fashion shorthand

These are designer knit dresses, with ample soft drape that could be the result of bias cut or fabric with easy drape. The silhouettes and areas of drape are the most important features to be conveyed in the drawing and notes.

Designer knits

Soft fabric with ample drape or bias-cut

Tight in parts, loose elsewhere

rust, green, greys, black

Wool/silk jersey, almost any knit

fashion shorthand

These are fitted designer dresses or "sheaths". The shorthand sketch focuses on capturing the variations in the treatment of the neckline, sleeves and hem lengths.

Designer knits

Sheaths

Variations in sleeve and neckline treatments

Jewel tone colors

fashion shorthand

In conveying the essence of these designer winter jackets the volume of the garments and their round puffiness must be clearly captured in the shorthand sketch. Fabric and colors can be quickly noted.

Designer knitted sweaters

Fair Isle wool or similar

Natural, off-white colors

Complex collars/full drape

Varied stitches (sketch)

The identifying features of these three designer knitted sweaters are each of their bulky silhouettes. Attention should be paid to recording the shapes of the elaborately designed collars and hood and the patterns of the stitching. The shorthand drawing of the silhouettes should be supplemented with a quick sketch of the stitches; together they give an accurate view of the garments.

Quilted jackets.

Nylon, silk, goose-down

Browns, greys

Railroad zipper, long sleeves

These drawings show how a free-thinking stream of design ideas has been quickly jotted down, in these cases for tailored garments. Recording our design ideas in a quick sketch can speed up the overall creative design process as new thoughts react to and build on preceding thoughts.
These designs were sketched over templates of groups of croquis that had been copied, saving the time of drawing them separately. Designers often create hundreds of sketches like these before honing in on their final designs.

Fabrics: gabardine, wool crepe, silk, other suiting fabrics

Colors: Muted blues, greys, black

fashion shorthand/
using templates

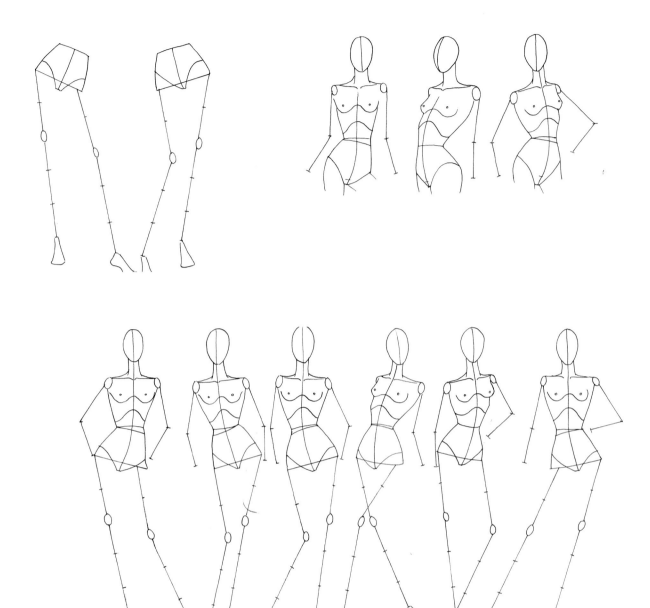

Where speed is important we should only draw the essentials. If we are focusing on garments for the top part of the figure we do not need to spend time on drawing the bottom part. We can develop a number of templates of croquis of the figure above the waist in different poses that we can use as mannequins onto which to drape our clothes. It *is* necessary to flesh out the figures in the torso area, above and below the waistline, which is where the garments fit. It is *not* necessary to draw the arms in detail as they are likely to be covered by sleeves, so they can be indicated as lines with the bend at the elbow shown. Similarly, if we are focusing on garments for the lower part of the figure we can develop some below-the-waist croquis in different poses. If we know the legs are going to be hidden under pants or skirts it is also not necessary to draw them in detail; we just need to know how long they are and which way they angle above and below the knees. Keep a series of different types of templates reflecting different requirements for different types of garments.

appendix a:
fashion drawing in the digital age/
introduction to using Adobe Photoshop

fashion in the digital age/
introduction to Photoshop®

FASHION IN THE DIGITAL AGE

As as happened in elsewhere in everyday life, computers are now used in every area of the fashion business, from design to production to marketing and distribution. This has occurred as much in the areas of fashion drawing and design as in the other areas. With the rise of the internet and the web and the ability to create instant high quality digital images that can be transmitted almost instantaneously, whether photos or digital scans of freehand drawings, digital images are now used more widely than physical versions of images. As a result, a knowledge of the techniques used in the creation, presentation and communication of those images is nowadays essential for all students of fashion.

This chapter of the book is intended as a brief introduction to the field, focusing mainly on the use of one the principal software programs used to create and manipulate digital images—Adobe Photoshop. If, after reviewing these introductory tutorials the reader wishes to learn more about techniques for using Photoshop, which is a complex and deep application, then it is recommended that the subject is pursued further by studying one of the general texts in the field, such as *Photoshop CS5 Digital Classroom*. The information supplied in these books is more accurate and comprehensive than the books written specifically on digital fashion illustration, and once the reader has become familiar with the basic techniques shown in this section of the book it will be easy to grasp intuitively how more advanced techniques can be applied in fashion drawing.

This section on Photoshop was designed on a Mac and so all the screen shots and command instructions are for the Mac. PC users will however easily be able to follow the instructions.

INTRODUCTION TO PHOTOSHOP

Photoshop is the most popular software program for editing digital images—images that are usually created either by scanning an image on paper, taking a photograph with a digital camera or downloading images from the internet. Photoshop is used by graphic designers, photographers and designers of all types, including fashion designers.

Photoshop works using *bitmap* images, or *raster* images as they are also called. Bitmap or raster images are images comprised of thousands of pixels–little squares of illumination on the computer screen. The quality of the image–how sharp and detailed it is–varies according to the total number of pixels it contains, called its "resolution" and measured in dots per inch (dpi). The higher the density of pixels in an image the higher the resolution and the better the quality. For the applications of Photoshop shown in this section the resolution should be set to 300 dpi; if higher then the processing power required to manipulate the images will be higher and the program will run more slowly; if lower, then the quality of the image, especially for larger images, will be inferior. When printing 150 or 300 dpi can be used.

Photoshop works in three main areas: correcting and touching up images' manipulating images and digital painting. In these tutorials we will focus on the first two.

EQUIPMENT NEEDED

The software program Adobe Photoshop should be purchased. It is part of a suite of digital imaging products called Creative Suite but is also available separately.

COMPUTER

Either a Mac or PC, with at least 2 GB of RAM and at least 300 GB of memory on the hard drive is required. All computers produced over the last few years can run Photoshop. Larger screens will make manipulating images easier.
Photoshop files are quite large, so it is useful to also have an external hard drive for extra storage and backup as well as a flash drive for easy transportation of images.

SCANNER AND PRINTER

A scanner is the device that allows us to convert our hand drawings into digital form so we can manipulate them in Photoshop as well as email them or print them. A relatively simple scanner that scans up to 600 dpi is all that is necessary and a printer that prints up to 720 dpi.

GRAPHICS TABLET

A graphics tablet is not needed in order to complete the tutorials in this chapter,but can help in digital painting as it is easier than using the mouse and brings the computer drawing experience closer to hand drawing. The reader does not need to consider acquiring a graphics tablet until she has developed a proficiency in using Photoshop and can better judge if a tablet will be helpful.

workspace/tools

Workspace menu

THE PHOTOSHOP WORKSPACE

MENU BAR
Location of all the main commands organized by task.

OPTIONS BAR
Allows settings to be chosen for the tool in use.

TAB WINDOW
Allows different windows to be opened by tab

TOOLBAR
Contains tools needed to create, edit, and manipulate images. Tools are selected by clicking on the icon. "Hidden tools" are tools with similar uses to the main icon tool and are displayed by clicking on the small triangle in the lower right corner of the particular tool. The most commonly used tool groups are discussed below.

DOCUMENT WINDOW
The image currently being worked on, title shown in the tab window.

PASTEBOARD

APPLICATIONS BAR
The Applications bar contains various controls to manage and make adjustments to the image in the Document Window. Clicking on the Workspace menu on the Applications Bar gives the option of using a different workspace setup. To customize and save an individual workspace, position the palette windows then click on the Workspace menu and assign a name in the Save Workspace box. Helpful when working on a shared computer.

PALETTES
Palettes are different windows—Colors, Swatches, Styles, that are used to control and change an image. Palettes can be positioned anywhere in the workspace and collapsed into icons to save space.

SHOW TOOL TIPS
The Show Tool Tips is a helpful feature of Photoshop. When the cursor rests over any tool, function, palette, etc. a small yellow box pops up on the screen indicating the tool name. It is usually a default setting but might need to be activated in Photoshop Preferences.

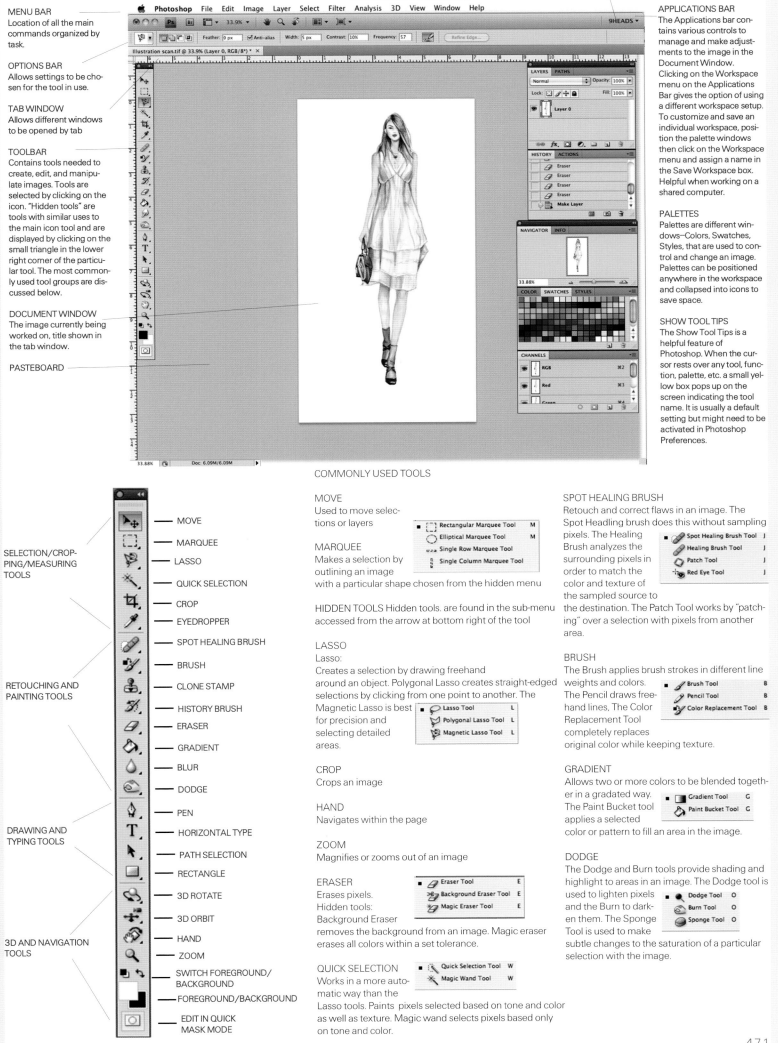

COMMONLY USED TOOLS

SELECTION/CROPPING/MEASURING TOOLS
- MOVE
- MARQUEE
- LASSO
- QUICK SELECTION
- CROP
- EYEDROPPER

RETOUCHING AND PAINTING TOOLS
- SPOT HEALING BRUSH
- BRUSH
- CLONE STAMP
- HISTORY BRUSH
- ERASER
- GRADIENT
- BLUR
- DODGE

DRAWING AND TYPING TOOLS
- PEN
- HORIZONTAL TYPE
- PATH SELECTION
- RECTANGLE

3D AND NAVIGATION TOOLS
- 3D ROTATE
- 3D ORBIT
- HAND
- ZOOM
- SWITCH FOREGROUND/BACKGROUND
- FOREGROUND/BACKGROUND
- EDIT IN QUICK MASK MODE

MOVE
Used to move selections or layers

MARQUEE
Makes a selection by outlining an image with a particular shape chosen from the hidden menu

HIDDEN TOOLS Hidden tools. are found in the sub-menu accessed from the arrow at bottom right of the tool

LASSO
Lasso:
Creates a selection by drawing freehand around an object. Polygonal Lasso creates straight-edged selections by clicking from one point to another. The Magnetic Lasso is best for precision and selecting detailed areas.

CROP
Crops an image

HAND
Navigates within the page

ZOOM
Magnifies or zooms out of an image

ERASER
Erases pixels.
Hidden tools:
Background Eraser removes the background from an image. Magic eraser erases all colors within a set tolerance.

QUICK SELECTION
Works in a more automatic way than the Lasso tools. Paints pixels selected based on tone and color as well as texture. Magic wand selects pixels based only on tone and color.

SPOT HEALING BRUSH
Retouch and correct flaws in an image. The Spot Headling brush does this without sampling pixels. The Healing Brush analyzes the surrounding pixels in order to match the color and texture of the sampled source to the destination. The Patch Tool works by "patching" over a selection with pixels from another area.

BRUSH
The Brush applies brush strokes in different line weights and colors. The Pencil draws freehand lines, The Color Replacement Tool completely replaces original color while keeping texture.

GRADIENT
Allows two or more colors to be blended together in a gradated way. The Paint Bucket tool applies a selected color or pattern to fill an area in the image.

DODGE
The Dodge and Burn tools provide shading and highlight to areas in an image. The Dodge tool is used to lighten pixels and the Burn to darken them. The Sponge Tool is used to make subtle changes to the saturation of a particular selection with the image.

getting started/setting up the workspace

OPENING A NEW PHOTOSHOP DOCUMENT
Photoshop documents (PSDs) are the files that store and allow images to be stored and worked on using Adobe Photoshop.

Launch Photoshop and from the Menu Bar, click on File > scroll down to New (Keyboard Shortcut: Command + N). From this screen, there is a choice of paper size, image resolution, color mode, and background contents. Working in 300 dpi resolution is recommended but If storage space is limited a lower resolution will lower the file size. Set the Color Mode to RGB Color, 8 bit.

Background Contents provides three options for the background. There is a choice of using white, the background color currently displayed in the Toolbar, or transparent background content. For editing purposes, transparent content is helpful as the image created doesn't have a background layer. This allows for more freedom when editing the image as a transparent background allows adjustments in opacity and blending modes to be made (blending modes, which change the way that layers interact or "blend" with each other are discussed in detail further on). Using a white or colored background content creates a locked background layer that cannot be edited. If one particular document and resolution size is frequently used, then there is the option of saving those measurements as a preset. This is done by clicking Save Preset. Name the Preset and make sure that all the Saved Settings are checked.

SCANNING AN ILLUSTRATION
There are a number of ways to access the scanner. In the Photoshop Menu Bar, go to File > scroll down to Import > click on the scanner listed. This method does not always work, however, and sometimes the scanner is not listed. On a Mac, go to the application Image Capture, Preview or the dedicated scanner software program (Finder For Windows, use the application Microsoft Scanner and Camera Wizard.)

There is the option of Flatbed or Document Feeder for the scan mode. Flatbed allows for easier manipulation of the image being scanned. Set the resolution at 300 dpi. The size of the image can be adjusted using the dotted bounding box. Checking the box Detect Seperate Items is helpful for scanning multiple swatches of fabric or any image with multiple components that need to be scanned separately. For a single image, uncheck the box. Choose the destination for the image to be scanned, name the file, and use a TIFF format. Under Image Correction, make sure that None is selected. Clicking on Overview will show a preview of the scan, allowing corrections to be made to the placement of the paper or to the outline of the scanned image.

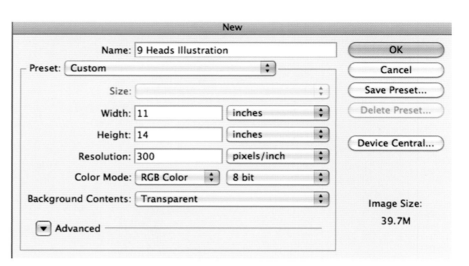

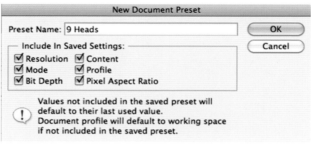

Saving a custom preset will save time when creating new documents.

WHY DO WE CHOOSE A TRANSPARENT BACKGROUND FOR OUR PHOTOSHOP DOCUMENT?
When a drawing is scanned in, the background paper is scanned as well and is usually white. If the background layer in Photoshop is already white and a scan is opened that was drawn on a white background, no difference will be seen when attempting to erase white pixels from the scan because the background layer is white–a white background scan on a white layer background. A transparent background (the gray checkered boxes) allows the user to see every manipulation that is done.

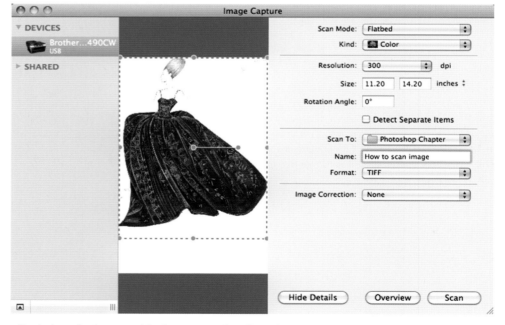

Set the bounding box around the figure to scan. Scan illustrations into the computer at 300 DPI in TIFF Format. Saving a custom preset will save time when creating new documents.

OPACITY
Opacity is the amount of transparency that exists in an image. 100 percent opacity would make the image not transparent at all. As the amount of opacity is decreased, the image become more transparent.

SCANNING TIPS
Always try to place the edge of the paper completely straight against the guides on the scan/ flatbed. When scanning an illustration drawn on transparent paper, placing a few white sheets of blank paper behind the image will help reflect the light and generate a higher quality scan.

opening a scan/ saving work

OPENING A SCANNED ILLUSTRATION

There are two ways to open a scanned illustration. If Photoshop is open, go to the Menu Bar > File > Open > find the location of the scanned file (Keyboard Shortcut: Command + O). If Photoshop is not open, the first step is to locate the file for the scanned image on the computer hard drive. Once found, Right Click on the file and scroll down to Open With. Select Adobe Photoshop to open both the image and program simultaneously.

THE IMPORTANCE OF SAVING

A most important rule when using Photoshop is to remember remembering to save work frequently. Unlike other applications, Photoshop does not have an automatic saving feature. Getting in the habit of saving a document after every few changes will prevent a complete loss of work in the event that the program unexpectedly quits. It is also recommended to save a copy of the original scanned sketch for easy reference. If saving a document for the first time, go to the Menu Bar >File > Save As. After the document has been initially saved, it can be re-saved by going to the Menu Bar > File > Save (Keyboard Shortcut: Command + S).

FORMATS FOR SAVING

Photoshop provides a number of options for saving a document. For this chapter, only three will be necessary: PSD, TIFF, and JPEG formats as described below.

PHOTOSHOP PSD FORMAT

Use the PSD format when saving a layered composition. Saving as a PSD document willpreserve the layers, enabling them to be manipulated further at anytime in Photoshop. After clicking Save As, an option screen will appear with a maximum capability option. If planning to open the image in other applications, leave this box checked. If the image will be used exclusively in Photoshop, the box can be left unchecked. If it is necessary to save a document as a JPEG or TIFF for printing or some other reason but the document will be further manipulated in Photoshop in the future, save the document as a Photoshop document as well as a document in the other format.

JPEG FORMAT

Use the JPEG format when saving flat images without layers. JPEG is the ideal format for Web output, archiving work, or emailing digital artwork. Saving as a JPEG file will retain a high-quality image with a smaller file size. After clicking Save As, an options box will appear. The image quality should be between 10-12 and the Baseline Options Format selected. To flatten the layers of an image for saving in a JPEG or TIFF format, go to Menu Bar > Image > Flatten Image prior to saving. This will merge all of the layers into a single background layer.

TIFF FORMAT

The TIFF format is the standard used for commercial printing. From the options box, select LZW for Image Compression.

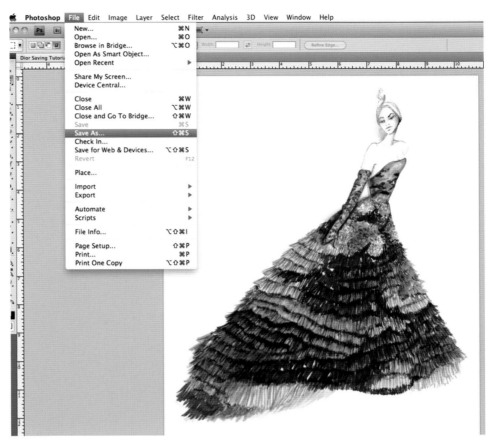

Photoshop has no autosave function so it is helpful to develop the habit of frequently saving work in case the application unexpectedly quits. Saving in the PSD format allows images to be saved with their component layers. For output for other uses such as web images or printing, JPEG or TIFF should be used.

Use the PSD format for saving images with multiple layers.

Use JPEG for archiving, emailing or printing.

TIFF is the standard format for files destined for commercial printing.

tutorial 1/hand drawing to digital

TUTORIAL 1:
CREATING A DIGITAL ILLUSTRATION

This first tutorial will show how to transfer a port-folio-ready hand drawing into a digital form so it can be archived, emailed, uploaded to the internet, transported on a flash drive or printed on paper. Being portfolio-ready means that the free-hand drawing was created with great care and attention to detail. The figure is proportionally drawn with carefully applied color, highlights, and shadows. The final outcome of this first tutorial is a digitized illustration that is only slightly edited for color contrast definition and is presented on a solid white background.

1. Open the previously scanned illustration in Photoshop. If there are any smudges on the page, the quickest way to remove them is to eliminate the part of the background where they are present using the Crop tool. The Crop tool creates a box around the image and removes the selection from the background. Select the Crop tool from the Toolbar (Keyboard Shortcut: Command + C). Starting from a corner slightly higher than the top of the image, click and scroll down to form an outline around the entire image. The area being cropped can be adjusted by moving the squares on the outside of the outline. Click the check mark in the Options Bar or simply press the Return key to crop the image.

2. An illustration that has been scanned into Photoshop often has less contrast than the original illustration. This can be corrected by adjusting the contrasting levels of black, white, and gray in the image to achieve the darkest blacks and whitest whites. To do this, go to the Menu Bar > Image > Levels (Keyboard Shortcut: Command + L) making sure the box next to Preview is checked in order to view the changes to the image as they are being made. To adjust the color and tonal range, toggle the sliders under Input Levels to achieve the desired intensity. The black lever corresponds to the dark tones, the gray lever to the midtones, and the white lever to the highlights. There are also a number of Presets already available that can be explored. Using Levels also eliminates most smudges or marks that appear on the white background of the scanned image.

The original scan opened in Photoshop

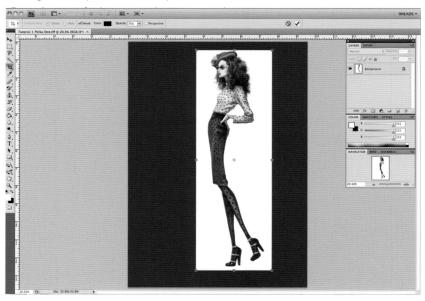

Use the Crop tool to remove an image from the background.

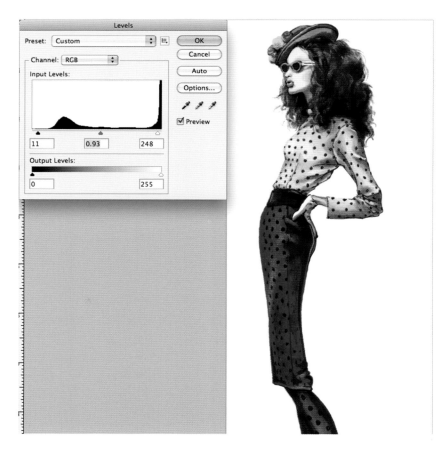

Use Levels to adjust the highlights, lowlights, and midtones of an image. Be careful not to overuse the Levels as doing so will result in a loss of definition from the original scanned drawing.

tutorial 1/hand drawing
to digital

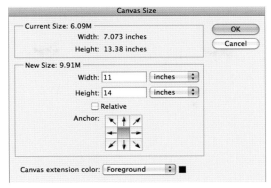

3. The next step is to set the Canvas Size for the illustration. The Canvas Size refers to the size of the layer which the image is on. (Photoshop works with *layers* that can be thought of as like separate imges printed on transparent cellophane that sit on top of each other. Layers will be used from the next tutorial onwards.)
Adjusting the Canvas Size does not change the size of the image, rather, it simply enlarges the borders of the working space that surround the image. The Canvas Size will also set the paper dimensions for printing. For a portfolio illustration, a Canvas Size of 11″ x 14″ is suggested. To access Canvas Size, go to Menu Bar > Image > Canvas Size. To pick a specific size, make sure the Relative box is unchecked. To add on to the current size of the canvas, check the Relative box. The new size can be added to the current size by using values for a variety of options. For example, the size can be added as a percentage, pixel quantity or an amount of measure. Enter the new dimensions and click OK. To create a border around an image, choose the new size and select the color of the border under Canvas Extension Color. Anchor indicates the location of the border in relation to the image. The center shadowed square represents the image and the arrows display the possible directions for the border. Note that a Canvas Extension Color can only be added to the Background Layer.

4. For this tutorial, the Canvas Size was set to 11″x14″ with a center anchored white Canvas Extension Layer. If there are any stray pixels remaining around the figure, use the Eraser tool to eliminate them. Select the Eraser tool from the Toolbar and erase pixels by clicking and dragging the mouse.

PHOTOSHOP TIPS
ACTUAL PIXELS VIEWPOINT: Refocuses the image to the highest level of magnification for the pixels without distortion (Keyboard Shortcut: Command + 1).
TO MANIPULATE VIEWPOINT: Hold the Space bar key down at any time to temporarily access the Hand tool.
TO GO BACK A STEP: Go to Menu Bar > Edit > Step Backwards (Keyboard Shortcut: Command + Z).
TO GO BACK MULITPLE STEPS: Use the History Palette and click on which the desired action.
TO DESELECT: Go to Menu Bar > Select > Deselect (Keyboard Shortcut: Command + D).

Canvas Size set to 11″x14″ with a center anchored gray Canvas Extension Color.

Canvas Size set to 11″x14.″ The Canvas Extension Color was selected from the color palette. The imageis anchored using the lower left arrow.

The finished digital illustration placed on a white background.

tutorial 2/joining scans

TUTORIAL 2: JOINING SCANS

Fashion drawings, especially if made on a large sheet of drawing paper, 12" x 17" or more, are often too large to fit onto a standard size flatbed scanner. Large bed scanners are expensive, and sometimes even they are not large enough to scan an entire image, as was the case for the image shown on this page which is included in Chapter Two of this book. This difficulty can be overcome by joining two or more scans of different overlapping parts of the image together in Photoshop resulting in one single image. This process, often known as "stitching" the images together, results in a single image with no visible "seam" that can be imported into Photoshop for manipulation or become available for other uses, such as printing. In the example shown here on the opposite page, two scans were made of the drawing with overlap between the two images and then joined together using the steps outlined below. Either horizontal or vertical scans can be joined in this way in any number.

1. Line the image up exactly with the scanner edges so the different scanned sections are scanned at the same angle.

2. Scan the sections of the image at 300 dpi and save as TIFF files. Make sure there is some overlap between the scans of the different sections, as seen in the scans on the right.

3. Open a new Photoshop document (Menu Bar > File > New) and make it the same dimensions as the original drawing with a 300 dpi resolution. Open the two (or more) scanned files in Photoshop. They appear as tabs in the tab window. Open each in turn, copy and paste one by one onto the new document. Use the Move tool to arrange the scans so that they fuse into a single image that resembles the original drawing (Levels Palette will have the top part of the drawing at the top as Layer 1, the bottom part of the drawing in the Middle as Layer 2, and the white background layer listed on the bottom).

4. Set the blending mode for the top layer to multiply so that the scan below is visible and you can see exactly where the lines on each scan overlap. Enlarge the image if necessary.

5. After fitting the image together, set the top layer (Layer 1) back to Normal blending mode. You might notice a dark band over the image where the two scans overlapped. If so, use the eraser to remove the band. As one part of the image is superimposed over the other, you can erase the band from one layer without erasing the drawing.

7. Join all layers together by Merging Down to produce a single image (Menu Bar > Layer > Merge Down).

8. Further adjust the levels if necessary.

9. Use the eraser to clean off any visible stains or marks.

10. Print the image to make sure that it appears as desired.

The first partial scan, of the top part of the drawing

The second partial scan, of the bottom part of the drawing. The drawing was lined up with the edge of the scanner in both scans to ensure the same angle.

The final joined image. Showing a complete drawing of the dress
allows the scale and beauty of detail in the train to be fully appreciated.

tutorial 3/cleaning up a hand drawing

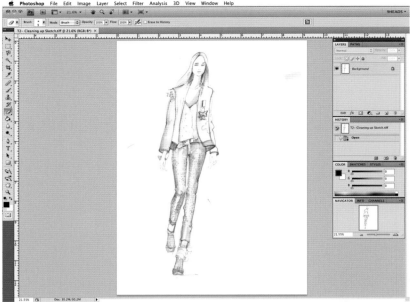

The original scanned drawing.

TUTORIAL 3: HOW TO CLEAN UP A SCANNED FREEHAND SKETCH

This tutorial will show how to "clean up" a drawing so that smudges or other marks are quickly eliminated and, if the drawing was created without a clearly defined edge of the figure, that will be remedied so it can be more easily manipulated (as will be seen further on). The ending result is a free-form figure that is placed on a gradient background.

1. Scan the sketch and open in Photoshop. The image automatically appears as the "background layer" as seen in the layers palette. When editing an image, it is always best to preserve the original layer and make a copy layer on which to work from. This ensures that the quality of the original scan is maintained. In this case, the Background Layer will serve as the original scan. To create the copy on which to work off, Right Click on the Background Layer and scroll down to Duplicate Layer. Name the layer 'Working Sketch' and position the layer at the top of the Layer's Palette. The Background Layer is always a locked layer which means that it cannot be edited. (Individual layers can be viewed by checking the box next to the thumbnail sketch of the layer image: an eye appears when the layer is visible.) Uncheck the eye next to the Background Layer to hide the layer's visibility. To finish setting up the sketch to be cleaned, use the Levels adjustment as in the previous tutorial to manipulate the contrast of the image.

SELECTION IN PHOTOSHOP

Photoshop operates on a process of selection: in order to edit something, it must first be selected, both layers and the image being manipulated. When working with multiple layers, the layer outlined in blue in the layers palette is the "live" layer—the layer currently in use. When making a selection directly on the image, blinking black and white dots will surround the selected area. These are also referred to as "Marching Ants."Once the intended layer is selected, there are three varieties of individual selection tools that enable the artist to manipulate the image. These tools are the Marquee tools, the Quick Selection and Magic Wand tools, and the Lasso tools. For this chapter, the Lasso tools will be used most frequently. This tutorial incorporates use of the Polygonal Lasso tool, which creates freehand straight-edged selections.

2. Select the Working Sketch Layer from the Layers Palette and the Polygonal Lasso from the Toolbar. Adjust the viewpoint to Actual Pixels. To use the tool, click next to the image and drag the mouse around the figure, depositing anchor points by clicking to alter the direction of the straight edges. To close the selection, position the cursor over the first anchor point. A small circle will appear next to the Lasso icon to indicate the correct place. Click on the circle and Marching Ants will appear around the figure. The figure has now been entirely selected.

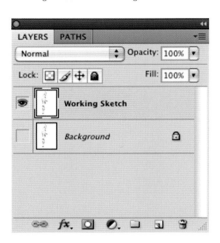

Always save a copy of the original image. Here the original is locked as the Background Layer and a new Working Sketch Layer is created.

Using the Polygonal Lasso Tool, move closely around the figure until the entire image is selected. The marching ants will indicate that a closed selection is made.

tutorial 3/cleaning up a hand drawing

3. Once the figure is surrounded by the Polygonal Lasso, the selection can be inverted. This switches the selection from the figure to the background surrounding it so we are now manipulating the background. From the Menu Bar > Select > Inverse. Press Delete on the keyboard to erase the background, leaving the figure on a transparency. Now the figure has been removed from the marked and smudged background the edges of the figure itself need to be cleaned up. This is done using the Eraser tool. Erasing will get rid of pixels to reveal the transparent background layer, creating the outline of the figure separate from its scanned background. The Eraser tool removes pixels in a brush-like way, at a rate that varies with the opacity percentage selected; a 50% flow removing half the number as a 100%. Depending on the project, it is a good idea to experiment with the opacity and fill of the tool. (These features are controlled with sliders in the layers palette.) Adjusting the opacity will alter the transparency of the pixels being erased, the level of transparency increasing as the opacity percentage is decreased. The flow (or fill) relates to the amount of paint that the eraser causes to flow out of the image. For example, a 50% flow would erase 50% of the pixels in a given area.

After using the Inverse Selection function to delete the background, use the Eraser tool to get in closer to the image. Erase any areas that extend beyond the natural borders of the image.

ERASER TIPS
-To erase large areas at a time, hold down the mouse and move the cursor across the image.
-Press the Space Bar key to access the Hand tool while using the Eraser.
-Adjust the size of the brush and the level of hardness from the Options Bar or by Right Clicking with the mouse.

4. A good method for revealing any stray pixels which might not be noticed (but might, if not removed, become visible later, such as when printing) is to create a brightly colored background layer. This is only to assist in editing process and will be removed later. Go to Menu Bar > Layers > New Layer > Layer 1. This can also be done directly from the Layers Palette by clicking on the icon of a small square inside a larger square. Once created, drag the layer below the Working Sketch Layer. To fill the layer with color, Select All of the layer. Go to Menu Bar > Select > All (Keyboard Shortcut: Command + A). Next, click on the Foreground Color in the Toolbar. Choose a color, then select the Paint Bucket tool. Click on the document to paint the background. Use the Eraser tool to completely erase any remaining pixels. After the pixels are erased, use the Paint Bucket tool (located with the gradient tool under the eraser on the toolbar) to color Layer 1 white. This prepares the image for creating a gradient background.

To quickly erase any stray pixels, create a colorful background layer and place it beneath the Working Sketch Layer. Select the Working Sketch Layer and continue using the Eraser to delete the remaining pixels. Now the image can be placed on a gradient background layer.

5. Once the outline of the image has been cleaned up, sections in the interior of the image can be adjusted. As the drawing was initially created in pencil, various parts of the figure can benefit from additional color contrast manipulations. (Perhaps, for example, the figure was for time considerations only rendered in part, or one part was drawn more lightly than others.) To do so, outline the desired area with the Rectangular Marquee tool. This selects only the pixels within the shape. Go to Menu Bar > Edit >Levels and re-adjust the tonal quality.

6. Now the freehand sketch is completely cleaned up. At this point, the figure exists free-floating on the Working Sketch Layer. The figure is ready to be presented on any type of background layer. For this tutorial, the background will consist of an individually created *gradient* layer. Gradients are visual effects where a color changes in a continuous sequence of changes into another color (whether in black and white or color). This can be a change from one color to a completely different color or a more subtle tonal change occuring in a single color, for example from 50% to 20% dilution with white of a given color (like the color field behind this text which is 25% to 15%). Numerous types of gradient are possible, with changes taking place in different ways and rates and the variable itself also changing. In Photoshop many gradient types are possible. Each color can be individually selected and placed anywhere on the gradient bar.

CREATING A UNIQUE GRADIENT
In order to accurately see the level of transparency of the gradient while it is being created a white layer can be placed under the Working Sketch Layer. If this was not done in Step 4, create a new white layer now. From the Layers Palette, select the circle icon that is half white and half black. Select Gradient from the pop-up Options window.From the Gradient Fill dialog box, decide on the style and angle of the gradient. In this example, a Linear style with a 90 degree angle is used. Next, click inside the Gradient box to open the Gradient Editor dialogue box. Photoshop offers a number of Gradient Presets that can be used as the basis for the new gradient. To create an original gradient, set the Gradient Type to Solid and begin changing the colors of the gradient stoppers. Click on the left-most gradient stopper and a black triangle will appear over it, indicating the color is currently being edited. Double click the stopper and choose a color. Choose colors for the remaining stoppers to the right. Note that as the color is being selected, the changes and ways in which the colors blend together are visible in the Document Window. The top stoppers can be manipulated to apply opacity in a given area of the gradient. Once finished, name the gradient and click New to add it to the list of Presets.

7. To complete the illustration, go to the Layers Palette and set the Working Sketch Layer to Multiply mode. (From the layers palette, change the blending mode from Normal to Multiply. All blending modes are listed in a drop-down menu located at the top of the Layers palette.) The Multiply mode treats the white pixels as transparent and adjusts the black pixels to opaqe. This allows the background to blend together with the drawing, rather than having the drawing appear on top of the background.

Use the Marquee selection tools to focus on specific areas that need additional manipulation using Levels.

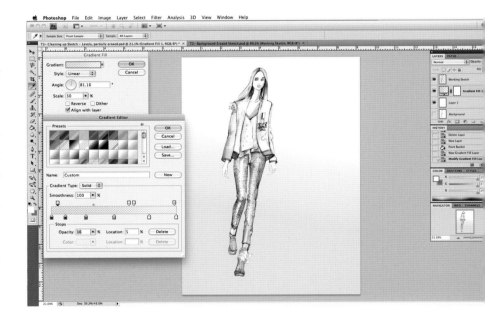

Use the Gradient Editor to create custom gradients. The changes will be visible as they occur in the Docume

The final result. The drawing has been cleaned up and presented on a unique gradient layer background created by the artist.

tutorial 4/adding color to a drawing

The original scanned drawing

TUTORIAL 4: INTRODUCTION TO DIGITAL COLORING

Photoshop allows color to be added to or altered in a freehand drawing, a technique that is extremely useful in situations where final color choices for a garment have not been made or where a garment or outfit is to be made in a number of different colors. As always, it is necessary to begin with a well drawn sketch. Including light shading in the drawing will carry through to the final illustration. To make the process more efficient, take care make sure the drawing does not contain areas where the outline is broken: if the line is not continuous then the color to be applied will seap out into the parts lying outside the figure. This is also the case for different areas inside the figure that are to be colored differently, and also for the different parts of the body such as skintone, hair and lips, if they are also to be colored differently from the garments.

1. Scan the image into Photoshop. As in the previous tutorials, create a copy layer to work from, lock the original layer, and use Levels to make adjustments. These adjustments should be made on all drawings that are manipulated in Photoshop. Going forward with the chapter, these steps will be referred to as "Setting up the Sketch."

2. For images with a clear, well-defined outline, the Magic Wand tool will quickly remove the figure from the background. The Magic Wand tool selects all pixels that are similar in color to the original pixel selected. As the original drawing has a sharp, dark pen outline around the figure, the Magic Wand can easily differentiate between the background pixels and the figure's edge. To start, select the Magic Wand tool from the Toolbar. Click on the background and notice the Marching Ants appear around the outline of the figure. If there are Marching Ants inside the figure, this means that there are gaps in the outline of the figure. To remedy this adjust the tolerance of the Magic Wand in the control in the Options bar until only the exterior of the figure is outlined. Make sure to check Anti-alias and Contiguous. After the white background has been removed certain areas, such as the space between arm and torso might persist. To add these areas select by Shift-clicking while making the additional selections. After all the selections are made, simply press the Delete key to remove the white background.

Use the Magic Wand to delete the scanned background. For this image a tolerance value of 15 was used.

The figure is left with a crisp, solid outline on a background of transparent pixels.

tutorial 4/adding color to a drawing

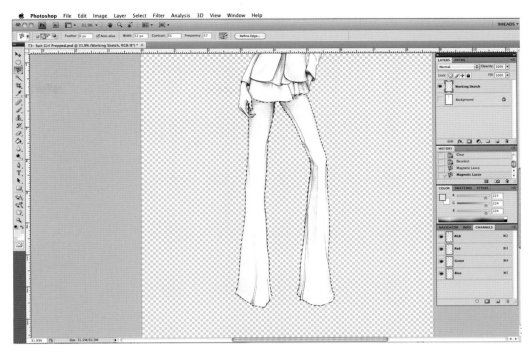

3. The next step is to select the different areas where color is to be added. The Magic Wand, which selects all pixels of a similar color, would not be the best tool in this situation, as the shading in the drawing would prevent it from making an accurate selection. In this case the Magnetic Lasso tool is best suited for the job. The Magnetic Lasso will select the outlining edge of an image by looking for differences in value and color between the image and the background. Select the Magnetic Lasso from the Toolbar. Once selected, adjust the settings in the Options Bar. Set the viewpoint to Actual Pixels and begin using the tool to outline sections of the image to colorize. A selection is complete when all like-colored areas on the figure are outlined in Marching Ants. To add additional selections, Shift+Click when starting to outline another selection.

Use the Magnetic Lasso tool to select the individual areas of the figure to be colored. For example, the pants that are selected will be a different color than the rest of the figure. First, select one leg of the pants and then, Shift+click to begin selecting the other leg.

MAGNETIC LASSO OPTIONS BAR

FEATHER: Creates selections with blurred edges. Leave unchecked for sharp, non-blurry selections.
WIDTH: The width can only be adjusted prior to using the Magnetic Lasso. It refers to the size of the area that is analyzed to locate the edge of the image. Experiment with different width settings to get a feel for how they are best employed.
EDGE CONTRAST: The level of contrast between the image and the background.
FREQUENCY: The Frequency refers to how often Photoshop places anchor points along the edge of the image. The default setting is 57. Rather than increasing the frequency, anchor points can be added manually by clicking on the line as the target is moved along the figure.

The Options Bar allows the user to control the settings of the Magnetic Lasso. Keep Feather at 0 pixels to create a sharp outline for the selection.

MAGNETIC LASSO TIPS

-For greater ease of use with the tool, press the Capslock key to change the icon from a magnet to a target icon.
-Drag the target over the edges, trying to center the icon between the image edge and the background.
-If the target selects unwanted areas, click Delete on the keyboard to go back.
-To manipulate the viewpoint while using the tool, hold the Space bar down to temporarily access the Move tool.

4. Next, save the selection so it can be colored at a later time. From the Menu Bar > Select > Save Selection. Name the selection and save it as a new channel under the current document name. Make sure the Channels Palette is visible from the Interface. If not, it can be opened from the Menu Bar > Window > Channels. The newly saved selection should appear in the Palette. Click on the eye next to the channel to verify that all the pixels were selected. Repeat this process until every section of the figure has been selected and saved. When making selections, always keep in mind that each individual color will be grouped together. For example, the face would be selected and placed on a skin layer. To add lipstick, the mouth would have to be selected separately.

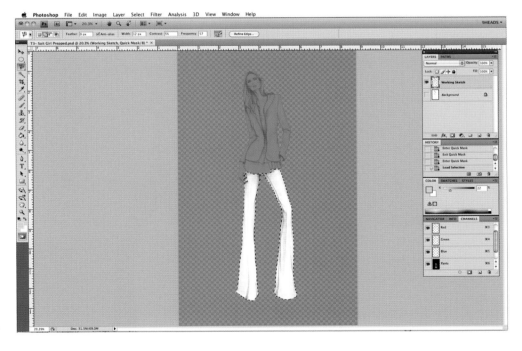

After making a selection, save the selection in the Menu Bar > Select > Save Selection. This allows the selection to be re-loaded at any time. The selection will appear in the Channels Palette. In this example, the pants are saved as an individual selection. Clicking the eye next to the Pant Channel will display the pixels that have been selected.

tutorial 4/adding color to a drawing

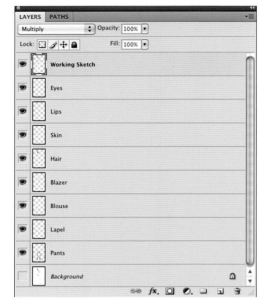

5. Now the saved selections can be individually loaded for color to be added to them. To load a selection, go to the Menu Bar > Select > Load Selection. Marching Ants will appear around the selection, indicating that it is now active. Every individual color will be on it's own layer. For example, all the sections that will be colored as skin-tone are selected together and colored on the "skin" layer. Create a new layer in the Layers Palette and name it to correspond with the area currently being filled with color. Going forward, arrange the Layers Palette so that the Working Sketch layer is at the top and all additional layers are below. Set all the layers to Multiply Mode so that the shading in the original sketch will show through the color.

6. To add color to a selection, go to Menu Bar > Edit >Fill. Select Color from the dialogue box. Choose a color from the Color Picker. If the color is one that will be used often, a particular skin tone for example, save the color as a swatch. Click on Add to Swatches, name the color, and it will appear in the Swatches Palette. After coloriz-ing a selection, adjust the level of Opacity in the Layers Palette. This small adjustment works won-ders in combining the delicate lines of the free-hand sketch with the enhancement of digital color. To deselect a section, go to Menu Bar > Select >Deselect.(Keyboard Shortcut: Command + D). Continue to create new layers, load addition-al selections, and fill them with color until the entire drawing is fully rendered

.

7. Since every individual color is on its own layer, it is very easy to change the color of something. To do so, click on the layer and load the selection (Menu Bar > Select > Load Selection). Go to Menu Bar > Edit > Fill and choose a color. This is also a great way for designers to analyze color combinations while designing a garment. As a designer you can create a custom library of color swatches that relate to a particular season or col-lection.

When coloring a drawing, remember that every color has to be on its own separate layer. The Layers Palette should be arranged with the "Working Sketch layer on top, set to Multiply mode, with each additional layer below.

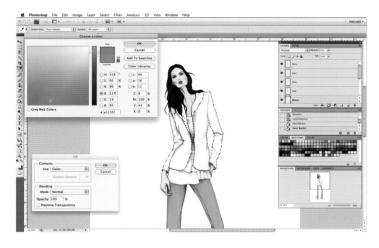

When coloring a section of a garment, first create a new layer. Next, load the selection on to the newly created layer. Finally, go to Menu Bar > Edit > Fill and choose a color. Adjust the opacity if necessary.

In Photoshop it is relatively easy to change the colors of garments. As Photoshop is compatible with the main color selection systems like Pantone® it is possible to create numerous relevant color variations of the subject garments in a fraction of the time required by hand.

The final illustration fully rendered in one of the preferred color combinations.

tutorial 5/correcting/ repairing drawings

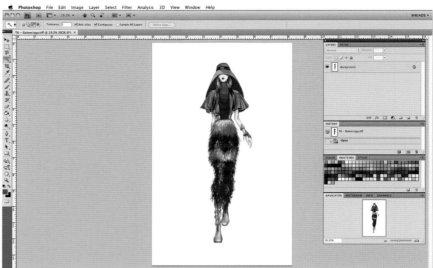

The Original Scanned Drawing

TUTORIAL 5: FIXING SMALL MISTAKES AND IMPERFECTIONS IN A FREEHAND DRAWING
Digital has become the standard format for presenting and sharing hand drawings, and Photoshop allows for minor corrections or alterations to be made easily and effectively to ensure drawings are of the highest possible standard before release. Smudges, crease marks and other defects are quickly removed and changes to a garment's fit or sizing can made without major re-draws.

1. To begin, set up the sketch that is to be worked on. In the selected example color has spilled over in three different parts of the drawing. The first two are the bracelet colors which are smeared on the skin in two places. All of these areas can be repaired using the Clone Stamp tool. The Clone Stamp tool is an excellent method for retouching an illustration. The tool samples pixels from a designated area and then, using those same pixels, it paints them over the area to repair. To start, select the Clone Stamp from the Toolbar. From the Options Bar, adjust the size and hardness of the brush. To use the tool, hold the Alt key while clicking on the location from which the tool will sample pixels. Next, move the cursor over the pixels to repair and click again. Note that the selected sample pixels will follow the cursor as it moves around the figure. Repeat this process by re-sampling from different locations. Be careful not to just continuously click on an area to repair without re-sampling pixels. Doing this will result in a distorted image where the repair appears to be composed of circles, rather than pixels blended seamlessly together. Experiment with adjusting the Opacity and Flow for the tool in order to achieve the desired level of image correction. The last location of spilled color for this example, is on the section of the blouse where it meets the skirt. Continue using the Clone Stamp until all the sections of spilled color have been repaired.

On the Original Drawing, both bracelets have color that smeared over the black line onto the skin. The Clone Stamp tool will repair this.

To use the Clone Stamp, Alt-Click on the desired area to sample from. In the example, the Clone Stamp used the whiter section of the hand as the sampling pixels. Note that when the cursor is moved over the discolored area, the selected pixels will follow the cursor.

The Clone Stamp is a quick and effective method for repairing the drawing.

tutorial 5/correcting/
repairing drawings

2. The next repair to be made is to the mouth of the figure which was drawn off-center and slighly tilted. To correct the positioning, using the Magnetic Lasso tool, outline the shape of the mouth. Next, select the Move tool from the Toolbar and move the mouth into the correct position. To correct the tilt–the angle– of the mouth go to Menu Bar > Edit > Transform > Rotate. Rotate the corners of the bounding box until the mouth appears straight. Click the Check icon in the Options Bar or press Enter to fix the mouth in place. Finally, use the Clone Stamp tool to repair the transparent area where the mouth was previously located.

The mouth in the original drawing was created tilted and slightly off-center on the face. To correct this, first select the mouth using the Magnetic Lasso.

With the mouth selected, move it so that it is symmetrical on the face. To straighten the mouth, go to Menu Bar > Edit > Transform > Rotate. Use the Clone Stamp to fill in any transparent areas of the face that are left from moving the mouth.

The final result from moving and rotating the mouth.

tutorial 5/correcting/ repairing drawings

3. The final section of this tutorial will show how Photoshop can be used to alter the shape of a garment. To do this, first decide upon the parts of the garment to be altered, in this case where more volume is to be added. To begin, select the Magnetic Lasso tool and outline a section of the garment where the fullness is to be increased. To recreate the area selected, first Copy the selection (Menu Bar > Edit > Copy, Keyboard Shortcut: Command + C). Now Paste the copied selection (Menu Bar > Edit > Paste, Keyboard Shortcut: Command + V). Notice that when a selection is Copied and Pasted, the selection will appear on a new layer. Select the Move tool and transition the selection into the desired place. Use the Transform functions to Rotate the selection so that it merges better with the other parts of the skirt (Menu Bar > Edit >Transform > Rotate). When finished, press Enter to set the selection. If necessary, go back in with either the Eraser or Clone Stamp tool so that the rest of the skirt will blend in with the new selection. Continue repeating this process until all of the desired fullness has been added. Remember that to select a new selection, the Working Sketch layer must be selected in the Layers Palette.

4. When all the added selections have been manipulated into their final positions, the layers can be merged together so that the entire illustration is on a single layer. To do this, hold the Shift key while selecting all of the newly created layers. Go to Menu Bar > Layer > Merge Layers. Now all of the newly created layers are merged into one. Next, Merge Layers again so that all the layers have been combined with the Working Sketch layer.

Use the Magnetic Lasso tool to select an area on the original skirt. Once selected, Copy and Paste the selection. With the Move tool, manipulate the selection so that it blends in with the rest of the skirt. If necessary, apply the Transform functions to Rotate the selection.

Volume was added to the original skirt in four different locations along the edge of the figure.

tutorial 5/correcting/
repairing drawings

The final illustration, having been retouched and repaired by making selections and using the Clone Stamp.

tutorial 6/simple alterations

TUTORIAL 6: BASIC ALTERATIONS AND DIGITAL MANIPULATIONS

This tutorial will detail a few easy methods for altering a freehand sketch using Photoshop. It will demonstrate how to use the Brush tool to fill in gaps that may appear in the outlining edge of the figure. The lesson will also explore how to duplicate a figure and flip the direction of the figure. Lastly, the tutorial will demonstrate how to use the Warp transform to shift the position of an arm.

1. Set up the sketch to begin. To have complete freedom when manipulating a freehand sketch, it is best to eliminate the scanned white background. As in Tutorial 2, use the Polygonal Lasso tool to make a close outline around the figure. Inverse the selection (Menu Bar > Select > Inverse) and press Delete. Set the viewpoint to Actual Pixels and select the Eraser tool from the Toolbar. Work around the figure, using the Eraser to create an outlining edge. To fix gaps that are in the figure outline, select the Brush tool from the Toolbar. The size and style of the brush can be selected from the Options Bar or by Right-clicking on the screen. Choose the size to best match the line weight in the drawing. Adjusting the Fill level will help the line blend better with the original sketch line. Click and drag with the brush to create a line that blends into the drawing.

2. To be able to see the next transformation more clearly, create a new white layer and place it beneath the Working Sketch Layer. Rather than using the Fill command, the Paintbucket tool can also be used. Create a new layer (Menu Bar > Layer > New Layer) and select the Paintbucket from the Toolbar. The Paintbucket will paint using the current Foreground color displayed on the Toolbar. The color can be changed by selecting a color from the Swatches Palette or by double-clicking on the Foreground color to bring up the Color Picker box. Use the Paintbrush by clicking anywhere in the document window to fill the selected layer with color.

3. Use the Transform options to create an interesting composition of figures. To create additional figures, duplicate the Working Sketch Layer. This can be done either by going to the Menu Bar > Layer > Duplicate Layer or by Right-clicking on the Working Sketch Layer and scrolling down to Duplicate Layer. Name the new layer Copy and position it underneath the Working Sketch Layer. Select the Copy Layer and move the figure out from beneath the original figure. To rotate the position, go to Menu Bar > Edit > Transform and scroll down to Flip Horizontal.

Use the Brush tool to fill in gaps in the outline of the figure. Note on the Left image there are gaps on the index finger and on the knuckle. Select the Brush tool and, using a click and drag motion, fill in the lines. For this image, a brush size of 3 was used with 100% hardness and a 71% fill level.

To duplicate a figure, first duplicate the Original Sketch Layer (Menu Bar > Layer > Duplicate Layer). Next, flip the position of the figure by going to Menu Bar > Edit > Transform > Flip Horizontal.

tutorial 6/simple alterations

4. This step will show to how take a straight arm and manipulate it so that the hand is resting on the hip. Uncheck the eye next to the Copy Layer so that only the Working Sketch Layer and the white Background Layer are visible. Using the Magnetic Lasso tool, select the entire arm. Go to Menu Bar > Edit > Transform > Warp. This will divide the arm into 9 equal sections that can be individually warped. The Warp command allows the control points to be drag to manipulate the shape of the image. This step can be a little tricky and it may take a few tries until it's right. Make sure to maintain the shape of the arm as closely as possible to the original, otherwise the arm will look distorted. Be especially careful not to pull the fingers too far in one direction. In the event that a section of the arm begins to look misshapen, gradually pull back on both outside corners of the bounding box until the arm resembles a more realistic shape. Press Enter to fix the transformation.

5. After the arm has been repositioned, there are spaces and markings left on the figure and in the background. If the area that needs repair is small, the Healing Brush tool can be used. While the Clone Stamp tool paints an exact replica of pixels over a given area, the Healing Brush analyzes the surrounding pixels and tries to match the destination to the source by using texture, lighting and shading. Use the tool in same manner that the Clone Stamp is used. First, select the Healing-Brush from the Toolbar. Use the Options Bar to adjust the size and hardness of the brush. To use, Alt-Click on the area to sample and, using a click and drag motion, move the cursor over the destination area.

6. Since the figure has already been removed from the original scanned background, the marks that are left over from the original arm position can easily be erased. Uncheck the eye next to the white background layer to hide the layer's visibility and select the Working Sketch Layer. Use the Eraser tool to erase any marks that remain on the transparent background.

Use the Warp tool manipulate the position of the arm. First, select the arm using the Magnetic Lasso.Go to Menu Bar > Edit > Transform > Warp. Use the corners of the warp boxes to slowly move the arm into a new position. Press Enter when finished.

Use the Healing Brush tool to repair the damaged area. Select the Healing Brush from the Toolbar and Alt+Click over the area to sample. Click and drag, using the tool in fill in the area of transparent pixels. Use the Eraser tool to erase the remaining marks from the original position of the arm.

tutorial 6/simple alterations

7. If there was shading used around the original location of the hand, that can be transfered to the new hand position. Use the Magnetic Lasso to outline the section of shading. Select the Move tool and move the shading into position under the thumb. Go to Menu Bar > Edit > Transform > Rotate and rotate the section until it blends in with the thumb. Press Enter to set the transformation. This is also a good method for double checking the correct proportions of the hand. The shading should fit directly underneath the thumb and above the index finger just as in the original sketch. If the size of the thumb is disporportionate to the amount of shading, the thumb has been warped too much. If this is the case, select the over-warped area with the Magnetic Lasso. Go to Menu Bar > Edit > Transform > Warp and use care to shift the thumb until it fits with the shading. Use the Clone Stamp tool to match the area around the edge of the shading with the color of the skirt.

8. To complete the transformation, the skirt still needs to be repaired. In order for the final result to resemble an authentic freehand sketch, the skirt will be repaired using other sections from the same side. This ensures that the outside line will blend evenly down the newly created side of the skirt. Select the Magnetic Lasso and begin outlining along the edge of the skirt, beginning at the section below the lowest cutout. Make the selection large enough to cover the area from below the hand to the top of the lowest cutout. Once selected, Copy and Paste the selection. Move the selection over the area to repair and use the Rotate transform to adjust the position. When the new outside line blends in with the original line, press Enter to set the transformation. Go to Menu Bar > Layer > Merge Down to combine the copied skirt with the Working Sketch Layer. Use the Clone Stamp to fill in the area so that it matches with the rest of the skirt. Refrain from using a small sized brush as the ending result will look like it's comprised of pixilated circles. Instead, use a large sized brush and experiment with the level of Flow until the newly created section of the skirt blends seamlessly into the original skirt.

9. Now that the transformation is complete, make one final comparison to ensure that the proportions of the warped arm are correct. Click in the box next to the Copy Layer and the white Background Layer to make both layers visible. Compare the size of the figure arm in the Copy Layer to the warped arm of the Working Sketch. If any further adjustments are needed, select the section with the Magnetic Lasso and use the Warp transform until both arms are symmetrical.

Match the shading from the hand's original position to the new one. Select the shading using the Magnetic Lasso and Move it into place. Go to Menu Bar > Edit > Transform > Rotate and manipulate the shading so that it blends in with the outline of the thumb. Press Enter to set the transformation. Use the Clone Stamp to match the edges of the shading to the color of the skirt.

Fix the skirt by using a section from below the cutout. Use the Magnetic Lasso to select an area of the skirt that includes the outlining edge. Move the selection and use the Rotate transform until the outside line is blended together. Select the Clone Stamp and, using a large brush, fill in the rest of the area so that it matches with the skirt. Experiment with adjusting the Flow level of the brush until the repaired section looks cohesive with the rest of the skirt.

The final image is flipped horizontally and the arm is manipulated to rest on the hip.

tutorial 7/picture backgrounds/ creating shadows

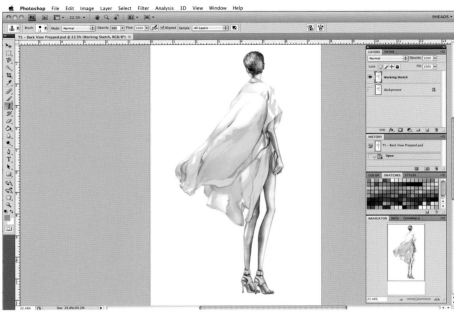

The original scanned drawing

TUTORIAL 6: USING A PICTURE BACKGROUND AND CREATING A FIGURE SHADOW

Adding a picture as a backdrop for an illustration is a creative way to combine digital art with freehand drawing. This tutorial will use a fully rendered color illustration that has significant movement in the garment. This movement allows the drawing to blend seamlessly into an unconventional backdrop. To increase the realistic nature of the finished illustration, a shadow will be added behind the figure.

1. Open the drawing in Photoshop and set up the sketch to be manipulated. To place the figure in front of a picture, the figure has to first be removed from the scanned background. For this tutorial, the Magic Eraser tool will quickly separate the figure from the background. The result is a single figure surrounded by transparent pixels. Select the Magic Eraser from the Toolbar and use the Options Bar to adjust the behavior of the tool. Click anywhere on the background to erase. For enclosed areas, such as the space between the legs, click again to eliminate most of the remaining white from the scanned background.

MAGIC ERASER OPTIONS BAR

TOLERANCE, ANTI-ALIAS AND CONTIGUOUS are separate options located on the OPTIONS BAR. Their functions are as follows:

TOLERANCE. The tolerance value defines the range of color values to be erased. A low tolerance will erase pixels with similar color values to the pixels selected with the Eraser. A higher tolerance encompasses a larger range of colors to erase.

ANTI-ALIAS: Selecting Anti-alias will generate smooth, blurred edges for the erased area.

CONTIGUOUS: Select Contiguous to only erase pixels that are adjacent to one another.

2. As this drawing is going to be positioned on a photo background, it is important to make sure the edges of the figure are perfectly clean and smooth, otherwise the imperfections will stand out against the background. In the Original Drawing, color is overlapping the black outline on many edges of the figure and there is a light shading around the figure. While this effect looks great on paper, in Photoshop it can cause the outline of the figure to appear with jagged pixels. (The bottom left drawing on the right shows this effect in the lower leg/feet area.). Also, as the shading is only faintly darker than the white background, many of the pixels will remain stuck to the figure's edge. This can be remedied by going around the outside perimeter of the figure with the Eraser tool. Use the tool to create smooth, clean edges around the figure. As in a previous tutorial, creating a temporary solid background layer will greatly assist in viewing which pixels need to be smoothed out along the edges. Experiment with the hardness/softness of the Eraser to achieve the perfect outer line for the drawing.

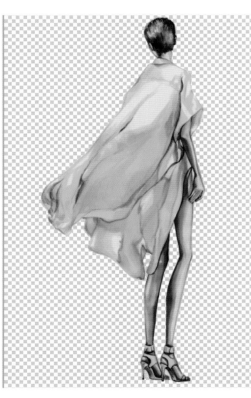

With the Magic Eraser, the majority of the white background is quickly deleted. For this image, a Tolerance Level of 8 was used to preserve the white sections of the garment. Use a higher Tolerance if there is a greater difference between the image color and the background color.

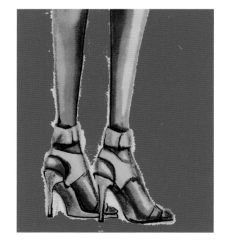

Depending on how the original drawing was created, the Magic Eraser can leave jagged pixels around the edge of the figure.

Use the Eraser tool to work around the figure edge, softening the rough pixels. This pro a crisp outline that will transition seamless into the photographic background.

tutorial 7/picture backgrounds/ creating shadows

4. When deciding on a background, the first step is making sure that it will be suitable for the image. It is important to consider how the content of each drawings go together rather than attempting a literal match between photograph and drawing. The image in this drawing has a light, feminine feel. The colors are high value lime green, yellow and white. In order to create an interesting juxtaposition, a dark neutral background has been selected with a gritty urban feel. When searching online for a suitable picture, always select a large sized image. Open the picture in Photoshop. Go to the Menu Bar >Image > Image Size. If the image will be printed, adjust the size to accommodate for the printing paper size and make sure the resolution is set at 300 dpi. Next, adjust the Levels of the image.

5. Once the background is prepared, the Working Sketch image will be copied from its original file and pasted onto the photo background. Before beginning, it is best to save the Working Sketch so that it can be manipulated later, if necessary. If a temporary colored background was used to assist in cleaning up the figure's edges, click on the eye next to the layer to turn off the visibility. Next, use the Rectangular Marquee tool to outline the figure and then Copy the figure by going to Menu Bar > Edit > Copy (Keyboard Shortcut: Command> + C). From the tabs below the Options Bar, select the file with the background photo and Paste the figure (Menu Bar > Edit > Paste or Keyboard Shortcut: Command + V). The figure will appear on the photo in a new layer as Layer 1. Rename the layer 'Working Sketch'. If the figure needs to be Scaled within the photo, use the Rectangular Marquee tool to outline the figure again and go to Menu Bar > Edit > > Transform. Scroll down to Scale and the figure will be outlined in a bounding box. Make sure to hold the Shift key down as the figure is scaled so that the original proportions of the figure remain the same. Position the figure in the desired location and use the corners of the box to Scale the image appropriately. When finished, click on the Check icon in the Options Bar or press Enter.

6. The figure will be manipulated further so that it appears more realistic standing against its new selected photographic background. To do this, use the Transform editing options (Menu Bar > Edit > Transform). As the figure has already been Scaled, the next step is to Rotate it. Shift the figure so that her heels appear to be resting in the gravel, as opposed to sitting on top. Right+click on the screen to toggle between transformation options. Take the time to experiment with all of the different Transform functions in order to determine the best use for each individual manipulation. Using these transformations can provide subtle changes to an artist's work that greatly impact the final result. For this tutorial, a combination of Scale, Rotate, Skew, and Perspective were utilized to achieve the intended result. The color of the figure can be readjusted at this point, if needed. To do so,

Using a photograph as a background, the figure is Pasted into the photo of the wall (Menu Bar > File > Paste).Hold the Shift key while scaling the figure to a realistic size. To secure the placement of the figure, click the Check icon from the Options Bar. To go back, click on the Cancel icon from the Options Bar.

Using the Transformation options, manipulate the figure so that it appears the most naturawhen standing in the background. This example used a combination of Scale, Rotate, Skew, and Perspective.

tutorial 7/picture backgrounds/ creating shadows

6.(CONTINUED)

select the figure. Use the Levels function to adjust the color of the figure. For the image, further adjustments were made under Exposure so that the figure has more of a cooler color quality to blend in with the cool tones of the Background (Menu Bar > Image >Exposure)

7. The next step is, to make the final result appear more realistic, to give the figure a shadow. Turn off visibility for the Background Photo layer and select the Working Sketch layer. Use the Magnetic Lasso tool to trace the outline of the figure. As the figure edges were previously smoothed by the Eraser, this should take very little time. Once complete, save the selection as Shadow Outline (Menu Bar > Select > Save Selection). Create a new layer, name the layer Shadow, and place the layer beneath the Working Sketch layer. Now, Load the Shadow Outline selection (Menu Bar > Select > Load Selection). To color the Shadow black, go to Menu Bar > Edit > Fill and select black. To provide a greater sense of realism and depth to the picture, adjust the opacity of the shadow so that the background wall is visible from underneath the shadow.

8. The final step is to transform the shadow so that it appears to be extending outward from the figure. The shadow will reflect back along the wall and expand in size. With the Shadow layer selected, go to Menu Bar > Edit > Transform.
Start by experimenting with the various options in order to achieve the desired result. The Warp transformation in particular, can be very useful when creating movement within the shadow. As pictured in the screen shot, the Warp transformation can be individually applied to any nine equal sections of the image. For the shadow in the example, all of the Transformation options were used in order to create the final desire result. To quickly change from one Transformation option to another, right-click on the image and choose from a drop-down menu. If necessary, one can now go back and further transform the figure placement so that it better matches with the shadow. To do so, select the top layer with the figure, and go to Menu Bar > Edit > Transform.For this image, the perspective and warp transformations were used to further manipulate the figure.

9. When all the transformations have been performed save the image so that if necessary, it can be manipulated again in the future. In order to prepare the image for different saving formats, flatten the image layers by going to Menu Bar > Layer > Flatten Image. This will reduce the file size by merging all the visible layers into the background. Note that this operation cannot be undone which is why saving a PSD
copy with the individual layers preserved is recommended. After the image is flattened, it can be saved in all formats.

To create a figure shadow, first outline the original image with the Magnetic Lasso. Save the selection and create a new "shadow" layer. Load the selection and fill with black. Adjust the opacity the shadow until the details of the wall appear beneath the shadow.

The Warp transformation is especially helpful as it allows for manipulation to individual sections of the figure. Experiment with all of the different Transformation options in order to achieve the desired result for the placement of the shadow.

tutorial 7/picture backgrounds/
creating shadows

The final illustration on a photograph background with an added figure shadow.

tutorial 8/coloring with opacity and gradient

The Original Drawing

TUTORIAL 7: CREATING OPACITY AND GRADIENT IN DIGITALLY COLORIZED ILLUSTRATIONS

This tutorial will detail the process of adding color to a garment with transparency. The end result is a dress with an opaque bodice and a gradual increase in opacity from the waist down to the hem. When creating the original drawing be sure to show what portion of the figure will remain visible underneath the opacity. In this example, the skirt of the dress is very sheer on the bottom hem but gradually gets less so where the figure is pulling on the skirt at the waist. This lesson will expand on the digital coloring skills and techniques learned in Tutorial 3. This tutorial will also use Gradient Fills to achieve the desired gradient effect.

1. Set up the sketch to be manipulated. As in the 3rd tutorial, use the Magic Wand tool to erase the scanned background. Next, use the Magnetic Lasso to select like-colored selections and save those selections as channels (Menu Bar > Select> Save Selection). For all the areas that are covered with a transparent layer, take care when making the selection to ensure that it is accurate .In this example, the legs were more difficult to outline as they are covered with the skirt and there is no definitive outline for the tool to latch on. For this situation the frequency of the Magnetic Lasso was increased to 77 while the width of the target was decreased to 5. These adjustments allowed the tool to locate the delicate outline of the legs. Make sure to select the legs separately from the rest of the skin in the event that additional color manipulation is needed. For the dress, as only the skirt will have opacity, select the skirt separately from the bodice of the dress.

Take care when selecting the legs as it can be difficult to see the outlline through the dress. Increase the frequency and decrease the width of the Magnetic Lasso tool in order to have a more accurate selection. Remember, one can always add to or delete from a selection if the user is unable to get the entire leg upon the initial selection.

tutorial 8/coloring with opacity and gradient

2. After all the selections are saved, begin the process of creating new layers for each selection. For the moment, do not create layers for the legs or the skirt yet as that will be done on the next step. Remember to arrange the Layers Pal-ette with the Working Sketch Layer on top, set to Multiply mode. It is important to begin coloring the layers that will not be affected by the trans-parency. The method used for coloring in Tutorial 3 will be the same. Beginning with the Hair, load the selection (Menu Bar > Select > Load Selection > Hair). Next, fill with color (Menu Bar > Edit > Fill > Choose color). Work down the figure until every-thing from the waist upward is colored.

3. Create a new layer for the legs and fill the legs with the same color that was used on the rest of the skin. Adjust the opacity of the color so that the legs are just barely visible. This may need to be re-adjusted after color has been added to the skirt.

Starting at the top of the figure, begin coloring all of the layers above the transparency section.

After the top portion of the figure is colored, create a new layer for the Leg selection. Load the selection and fill with the same color as the rest of the skin. Adjust the opacity so that the skin tone is just visible underneath the skirt. This can also be done after the gradient skirt layer has been added.

tutorial 8/coloring with opacity and gradient

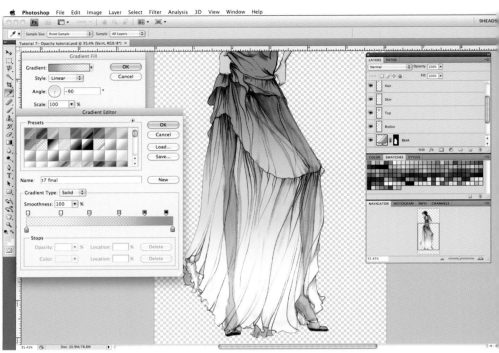

4. Next, create a new layer for the skirt and name it Skirt layer. Position the Skirt layer in the Layers Palette so that it is directly above the Leg layer. With the Skirt layer selected, load the Skirt selection. To fill the skirt with a transparency, create a gradient fill layer that will apply on the Skirt layer. Go to Menu Bar > Layer > New Fill Layer > Gradient. This can also be done directly from the Layers Palette by clicking on the circle icon and scrolling to Gradient. The gradient is made in a similar way to the background gradient in Tutorial 2 but there are a few changes. The Gradient Fill dialogue box will open. The gradient style should be set at Linear, however, the angle needs to be adjusted. In this example, the skirt will be the darkest at the waist and gradually become transparent at the hem. Set the Gradient Angle at -90 degrees. Next, click inside the Gradient box to bring up the Gradient Editor. To make the color match with the dress bodice, select the bottom stopper and, using the eyedropper cursor, click on the bodice of the dress. Repeat so that all the bottom color stoppers are the same color. Next, adjust the Opacity stoppers to reflect the desired amount of opacity. For this example, five seperate Opacity stoppers were used in varying levels to create the gradient. When finished, name the gradient and click on New to add it to the gradient library.

5. The last step is to color the shoes. Create a new layer for them and place it underneath the leg layer. Load the Shoe selection and Fill with color.

In the Gradient Editor, change all of the bottom color stoppers to the same color. Next, adjust the top opacity stoppers, positioning each one at a different level of opacity. Continue to experiment until the desired opacity is achieved. Then, Name the Opacity and click New to save it as a Preset.

The final step is to color any other items left on the figure, like the shoes. If necesary, adjust the opacity of the Leg Layer so that it blends in evenly with the gradient skirt.

tutorial 8/coloring with opacity and gradient

The final illustration, fully rendered, with a gradient-filled skirt.

SPECS

Included in this section are flat drawings of the main women's and men's garments, with indications of where measurements are usually taken to provide specifications—specs— to manufacturers. These diagrams have been adapted from systems presently in use by major garment manufacturers. It should be noted however that the location of measuring points varies between companies. If specs are accompanied by flats showing the exact location of measuring points, as here, the risk of confusion is minimized.

The letters on the drawings show the places where garments are measured. The tables below give the description of the measurement and if it is a front or back measurement or both. Garment measurements are made with the garment spread out flat on a flat surface.

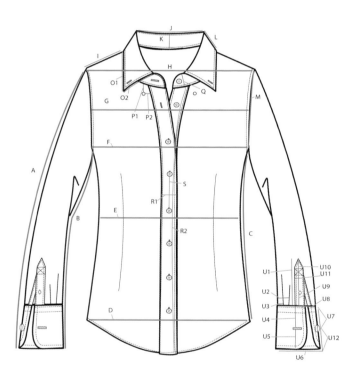

	Front	Back
A Outside sleeve	x	x
B Inside sleeve	x	x
C Side seam	x	x
D Waist	x	x
E Rib cage	x	x
F Lower torso	x	x
G Mid chest	x	x
H Across shoulder	x	x
I Shoulder length	x	x
J Back collar length	x	x
K Collar width	O	x
L Side collar width	x	x
M Armhold length	x	x
N Yoke length	O	x
O1 Front collar length	x	
O2 Front collar width	x	
P1 Button placement vertical	x	
P2 Button placement horizontal	x	
Q Stand up collar width	x	
R1 Placket width	x	
R2 Placket spacing	x	
S Placket length	x	
T Back collar bottom length	x	

CUFF	Front
U1 Placket length	x
U2 First tuck location	x
U3 Second tuck location	x
U4 Cuff length to button hole	x
U5 Cuff length from bottom to button hole	x
U6 Cuff width	x
U7 Button location from top of cuff	x
U8 Top cuff width	x
U9 Button location from top	x
U11 Placket width	x
U12 Button placement from bottom of cuff	x
V Cuff length	x

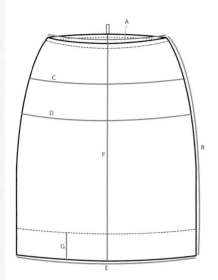

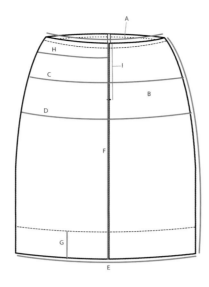

	FRONT	BACK
A Waist width	x	x
B Side-seam	x	x
C High hip	x	x
D Lower hip	x	x
E Hem width	x	x
F Skirt length	x	x
G Hem length	x	x
H Zipper location from side- seam	O	x
I Zipper length	O	x

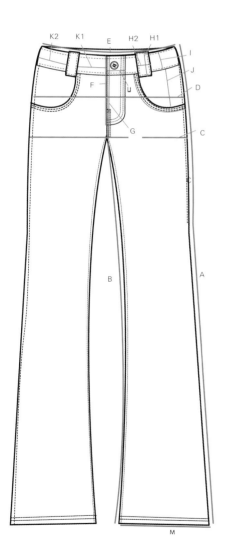

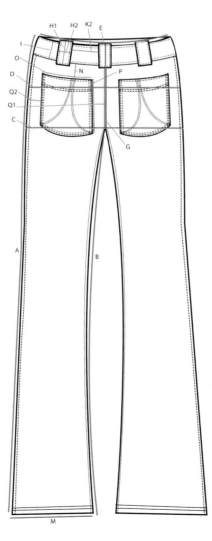

	FRONT	BACK
A Outside side- seam	x	O
B Inside side- seam	x	O
C Lower Hlp	x	x
D Pocket opening	x	O
E Waistband	x	x
F Crotch length	x	x
G Zipper placket length	x	O
H 1 Belt loop height	x	x
H2 Belt loop width	x	x
I Waistband width	x	O
J Length to pocket placement	x	O
K 1 Center front to belt loop	x	O
K2 Spacing between belt loops	x	x
L CF zipper width	x	O
M Bottom width	x	x
N Waist band to top back pocket	O	x
O Pocket width	O	x
P Pocket length	O	x
Q1 Pocket to center back	O	x
Q2 Pocket to side-seam	O	x

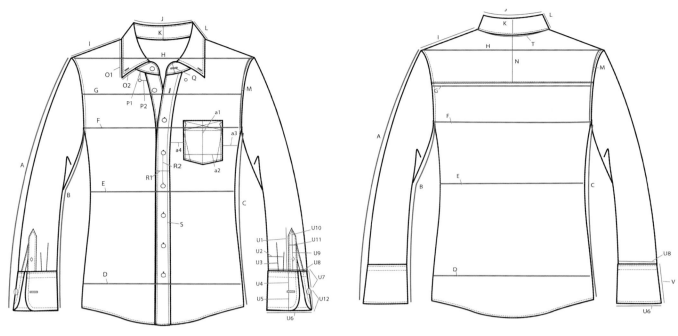

	FRONT	BACK
A Outside sleeve	x	x
B Inside sleeve	x	x
C Side- seam	x	x
D Waist	x	x
E Rib cage	x	x
F Lower torso	x	x
G Mid chest	x	x
H Across shoulder	x	x
I Shoulder length	x	x
J Back collar length	x	x
K Collar width	x	x
L Side collar width	x	x
M Armhold length	x	x
N Yoke length	O	x
O1 Front collar length	x	O
O2 Front collar width	x	O

	FRONT
P1 Button placement vertical	x
P2 Button placement horizontal	x
Q Stand up collar width	x
R1 Placket width	x
R2 Button spacing	x
S Placket length	x
T Back collar bottom length	x

CUFF	
U1 Placket length	x
U2 First Tuck location	x
U3 Second Tuck location	x
U4 Cuff length to button hole	x
U5 Cuff length from bottom	O
to button hole	x
U6 Cuff width	x
U7 Button location from top of	x

	FRONT
U8 Top cuff width	x
U9 Button location from bottom	x
U10 Button location from top	x
U11 Placket width	x
U12 Button placement from	x
bottom of cuff	x
V Cuff length	x

POCKET	
	FRONT
a1 Pocket length	x
a2 Pocket width	x
a3 Placement from side-seam	x
a4 Placement from center placket	x

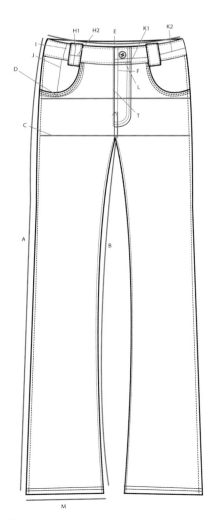

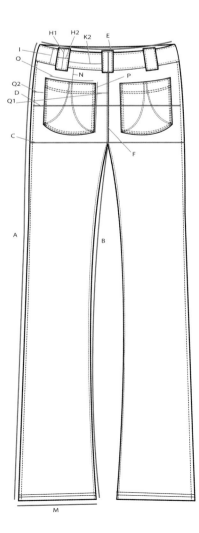

	FRONT	BACK
A Outside side- seam	x	O
B Inside side- seam	x	O
C Lower Hlp	x	x
D Pocket opening	x	O
E Waistband	x	x
F Crotch length	x	x
G Zipper placket length	x	O
H1 Belt loop height	x	x
H2 Belt loop width	x	x
I Waistband width	x	x
J Length to pocket placement	x	O
K1 Center front to belt loop	x	O
K2 Spacing between belt loops	x	O
L CF zipper width	x	O
M Bottom width	x	x
N Waist band to top back pocket	O	x
O Pocket width	O	x
P Pocket length	O	x
Q1 Pocket to center back	O	x
Q2 Pocket to side-seam	O	x

women's flats/skirts

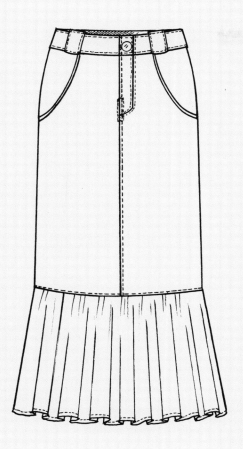

Ruffled jean skirt

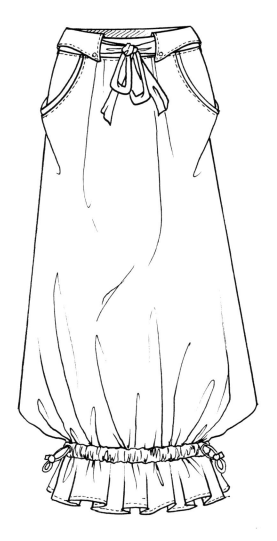

Sash tie bubble skirt

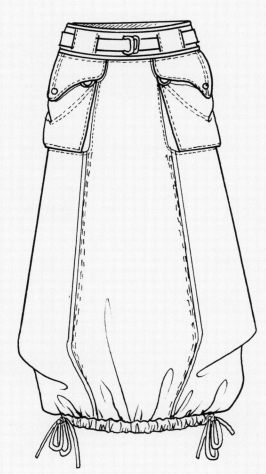

Toggle lock bubble skirt

Tiered ruched skirt with
string ties and cargo pockets

Whip stitch pockets

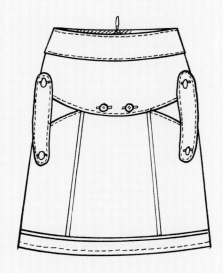

Yoke with button tab detailing

Saddle pocket mini with fringe

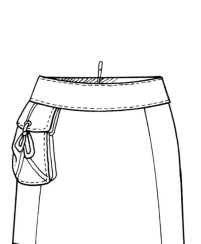

String tie novelty pocket

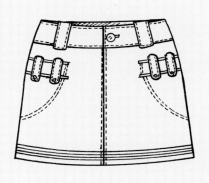

Tab pocket mini

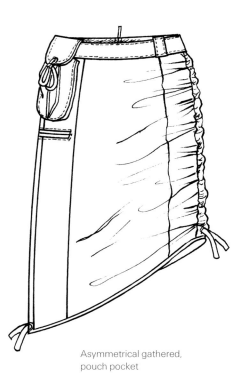

Asymmetrical gathered,
pouch pocket

Spaghetti wrap broomstick

Ruched dropped yoke

Mini with fringe

women's flats/skirts

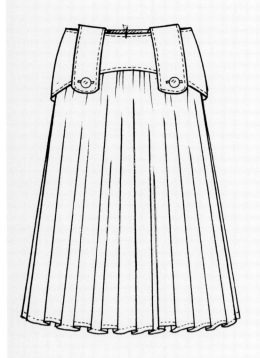

Tabbed yoke

Spaghetti tie broomstick

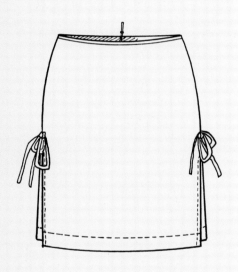

Short, side tie detail

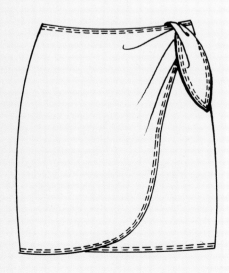

Sarong

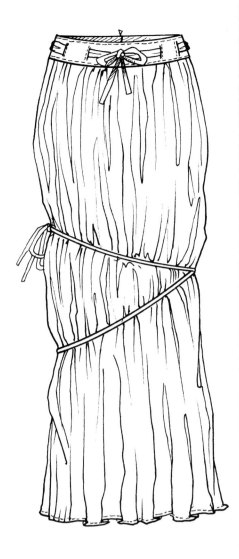

Asymmetrical layered

Embroidered yoke, drawstring

Asymmetrical

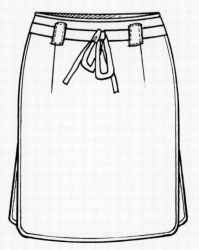

Self tie belt side slit

Fringe

Short flounce

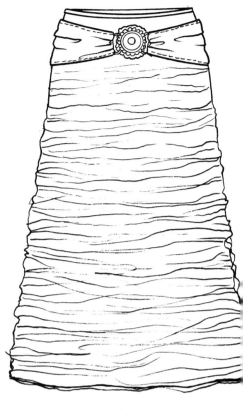

Crystal-pleated

Asymmetrical layered

Yoke floral print

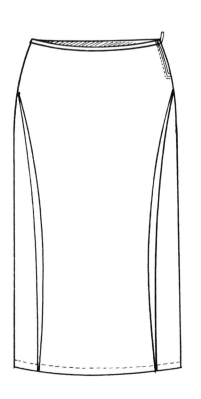

Paneled, slim

String tie wrap mini

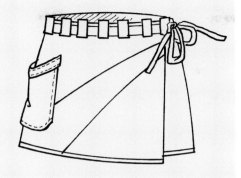

Ribbon tied mini
sarong, patch pocket

Mini with flounce

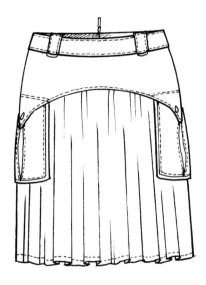

Yoke with bellows pockets

Buttoned wrap

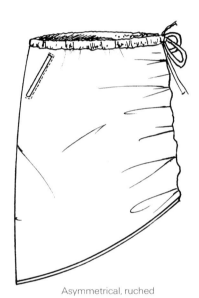

Asymmetrical, ruched

Tiered yoke

Loop detail dropped yoke

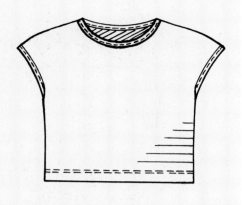

Cropped sleeveless T

Sleeveless pullover

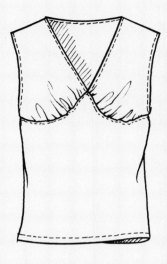

V-neck pullover, slip-inspired shell

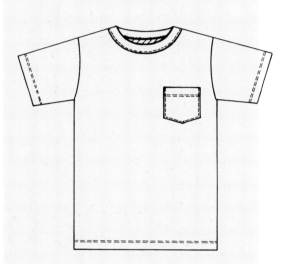

Patch pocket sleevless T

Halter

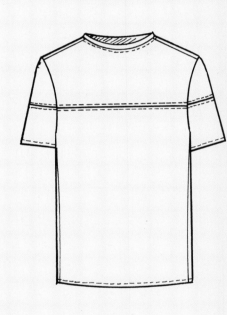

Short sleeveyoke T

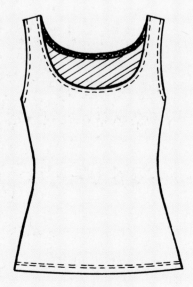

Tank

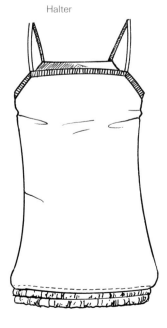

Blouson cami

Halter

Lace-up cami

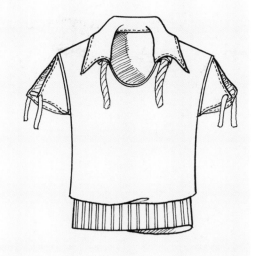

Tie detail pullover

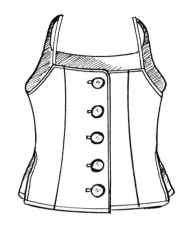

Button front spaghetti strap

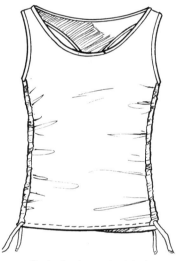

Ruched swimmer-back tank

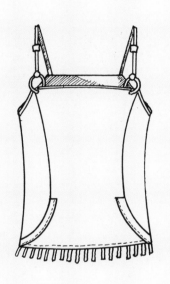

Beaded and fringed cami

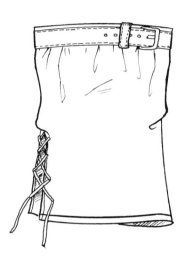

Belted, side-laced, off-the-shoulder

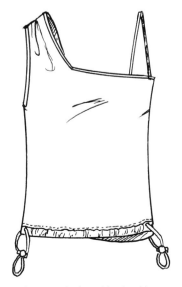

Asymmetrical cami/tank with drawstring waist

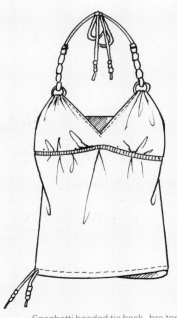

Spaghetti-beaded tie back , bra-top halter

Ruffle scoop neck

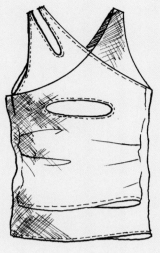

Layered cut-out crossover tank

Spaghetti-laced short cami with ruched brassiere

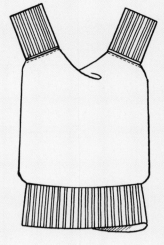

Rib-strapped and waisted tank

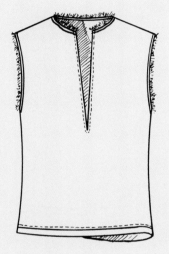

Deep split mandarin neck pullover

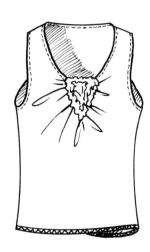

Medallion front tank

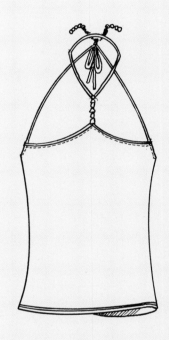

Beaded spaghetti-laced cami

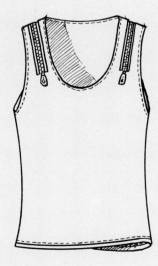

Zipper tank

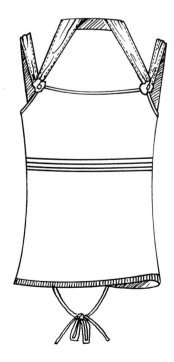

Halter neck tank

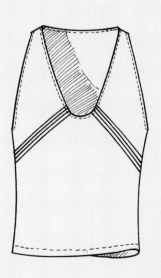

Deep v-neck tank

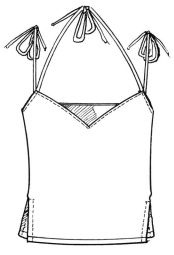

Spaghetti tie cami/halter

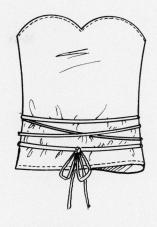

Bustier with spaghetti tie at waist

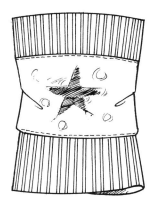

Tube with ribbing panels

Asymmetrical cami/halter

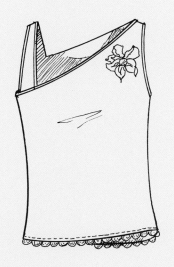

Asymmetrical with appliqué

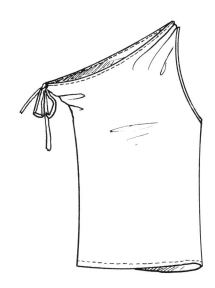

Asymmetrical off-one-shoulder

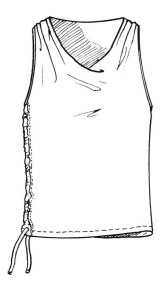

Tank with beaded side detail

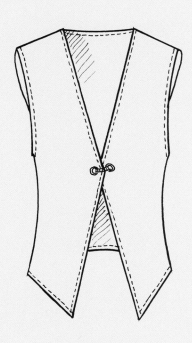

V-neck vest

Vest with frog closing

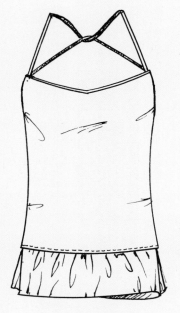

Spaghetti strap gathered
hem cami

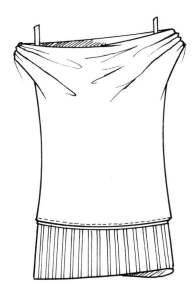

Off-the-shoulder cowl neck

Slip style cami

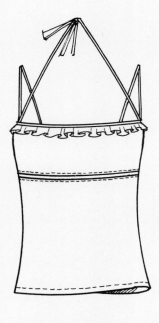

Ruffle-trim spaghetti-tie cami

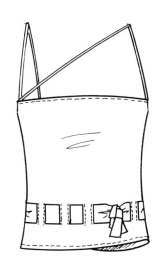

Enclosed ribbon sash cami

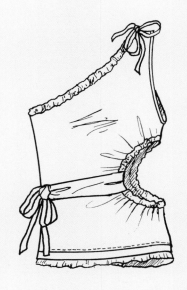

Single shoulder cut-out tank

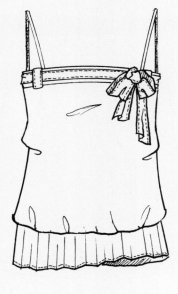

Cami with flounce

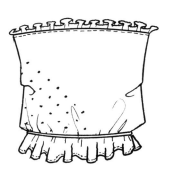

Ruffled tube top

Cap sleeved,tie detail pullover

Chinese lounging jacket

Rib trim short sleeve
pouch pocket pullover

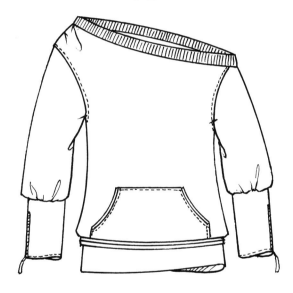

Asymmetrical neckline with
bound kangaroo patch pocket

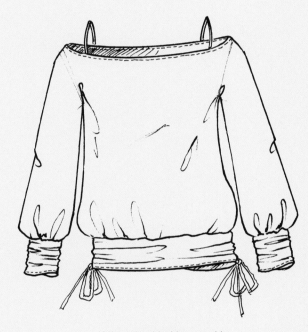

Off-the-shoulder blouson with
sash belt and matching cuffs

Split neck long raglan sleeve

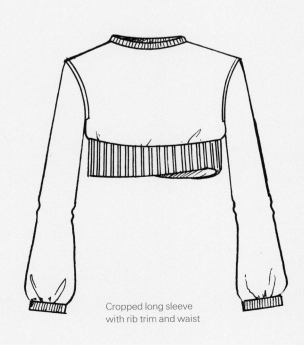

Cropped long sleeve
with rib trim and waist

Ruffle neckline/cuff

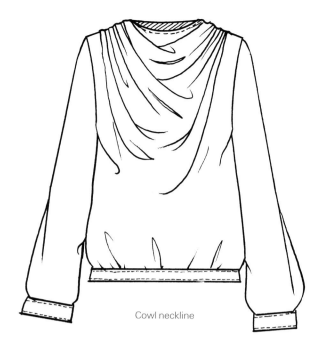

Cowl neckline

Retro housecoat with
patch pocket detail

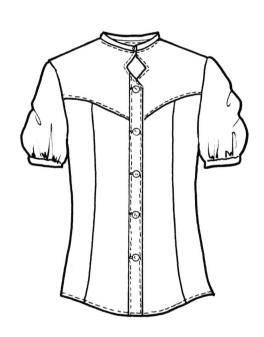

Cut-out puff sleeve blouse

Tie-front shirt

Off-shoulder raglan sleeve top

women's flats/tops/blouses

String tie flutter sleeve top

Cropped blouson

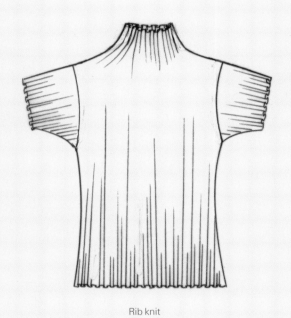

Rib knit

Cropped puff sleeve

Baby doll v-neck pullover blouse

Puff sleeve wrap blouse

Tie string ruffle trim empire

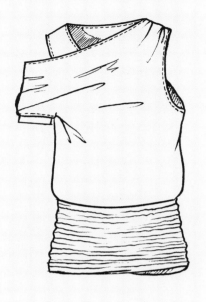

Asymmetrical wrap pullover

Wrap neck pullover

Off-the -shoulder yoke asymmetrical sleeved string tie top

Short sleeve lace trim

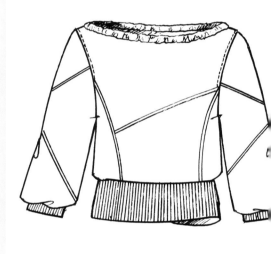

Asymmetrical paneled

Empire-waisted wrapped spaghetti detail

Grecian one shoulder flutter sleeve

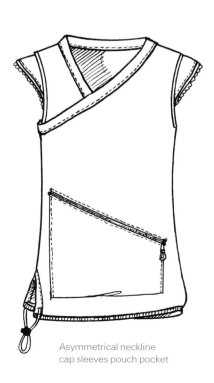

Asymmetrical neckline cap sleeves pouch pocket

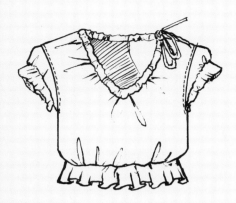

V-neck short puff top

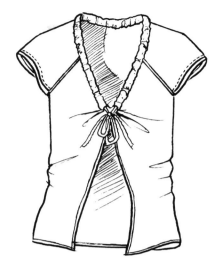

Ruched tie-front v-neck top

Shaped tube top

Double slash neckline puff sleeve

V-neck puff sleeve shirred empire

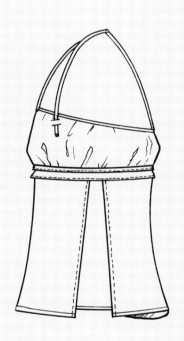

Bandeau halter

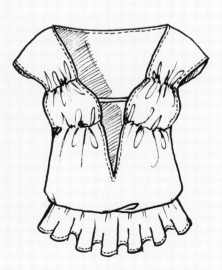

Grecian style plunging neckline pullover

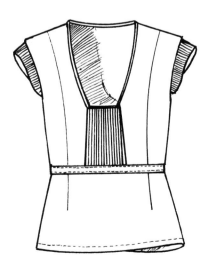

Drop sleeve square neck

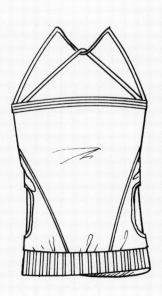

Spaghetti tie halter

Jewel neck short sleeve T

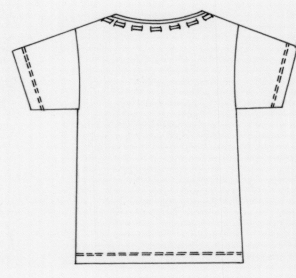

Back view

Ruffle trim Paris graphic

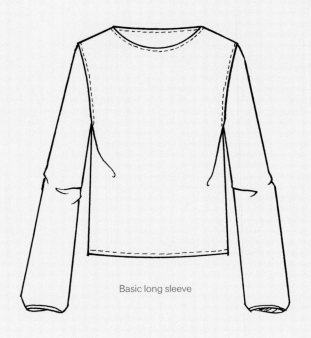

Basic long sleeve

Long sleeve turtleneck graphic

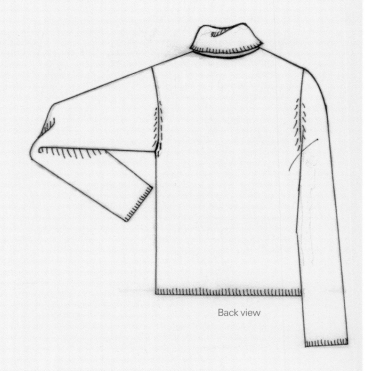

Back view

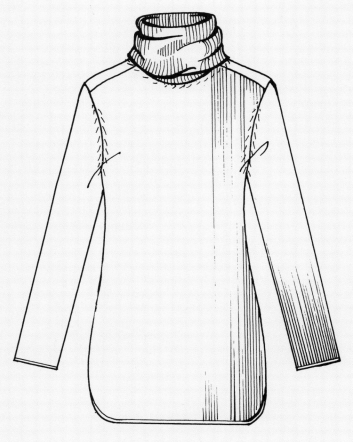

Ribbed turtleneck tunic pullover

Pirate shirt

Bandeau

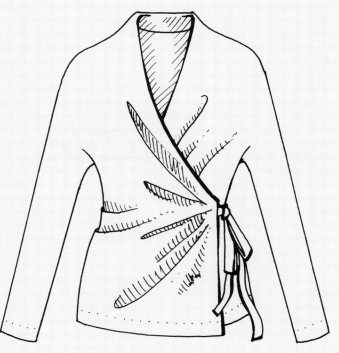

Dolman sleeve wrap

Ruffle front vest yoke shirt

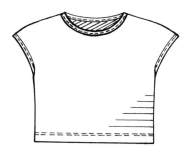
Cropped sleeveless T

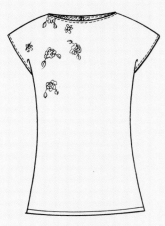
Sleeveless pullover

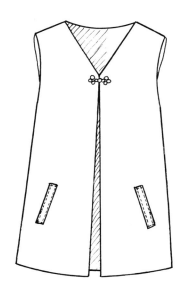
Frog closure vest

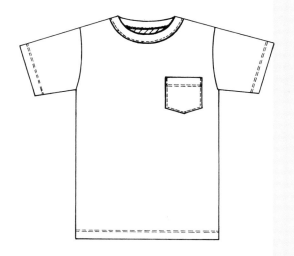
Classic pocket T

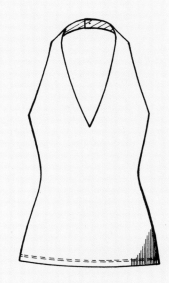
Sleeveless halter

Bolero sweater

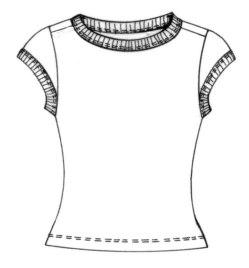
Cap sleeve T

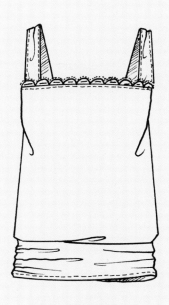
Lace trim sun with
gathered waistband

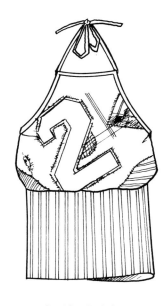
Graphic print halter
deep rib waistband

Beaded string halter

Button front sun

Back view showing
gathered back

String-laced cami

Tie detail pullover

Rib trimmed short
sleeve pouch pocket

Ruched swim-
mer back tank

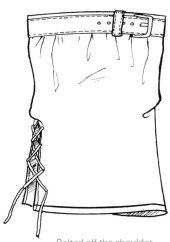

Belted off-the-shoulder

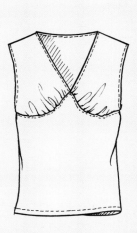

Lingerie-inspired shell

Mock wrap graphic pullover

Ruffled short
sleeved blouson

V-neck short sleeve pullover

Tie closure long-sleeved

Cropped blouson

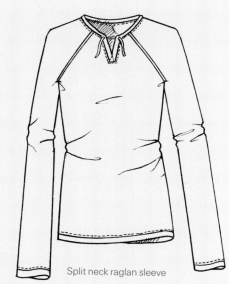

Split neck raglan sleeve

Puff sleeve empire

Floral print tie-belt blouse

Cut-out layered

Spaghetti-laced
short sleeve

Rib-banded tank

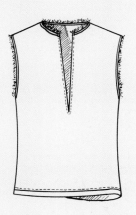

Split neck sleeveless
pullover

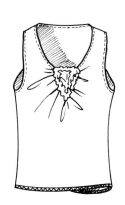

Medallion front tank

Spaghetti tie beaded cami

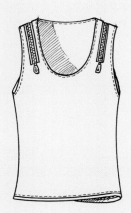

Zipper tank

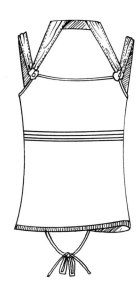

Halter neck tank

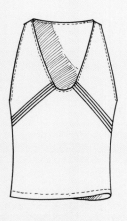

Deep U-neck tank

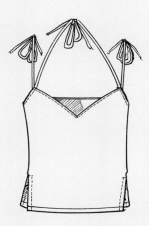

Spaghetti strap cami

Stapless self tie

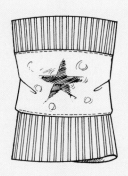

Graphic tube top

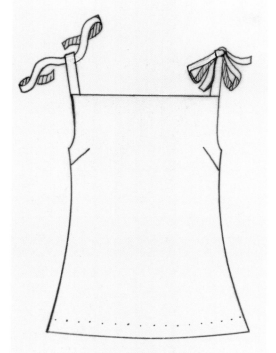

Spaghetti strap ties side darts

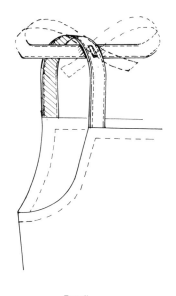

Detail

Smock blouse gathered empire waist

Off-the-shoulder raglan sleeve

Gathered v-neck raglan short sleeve

Puff sleeve blouson ruffled hem

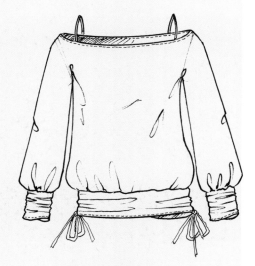

Off-the shoulder long sleeve gathered cuffs waistband

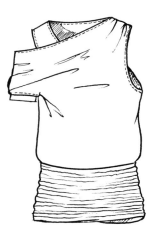

Asymmetrical opening crystal pleated waistband

Short sleeve asymmetrical tie wrap

Fitted sun ruffled lace trim

Back view

Detail

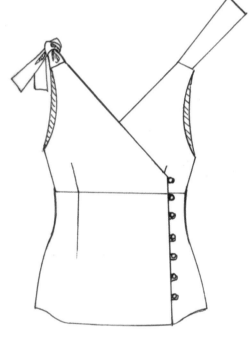

Asymmetrical button closure sun

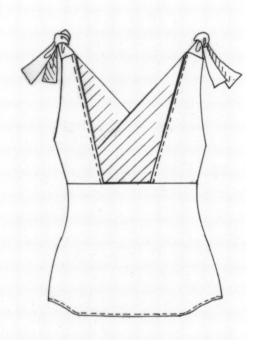

Back view

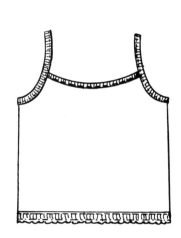

Banded rib tank

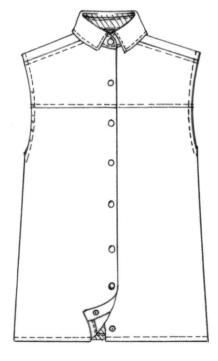

Sleeveless shirt snap closures

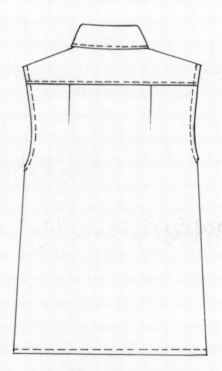

Back view

Ribbed pullover

Peasant blouse

Set-in sleeve top-stitching

Knit turtleneck

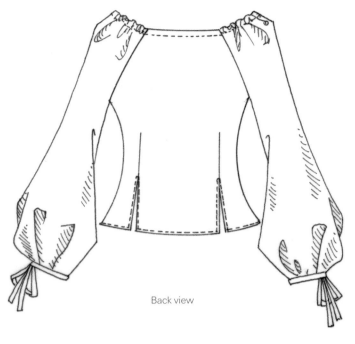

Back view

Dolman sleeve top-stitching

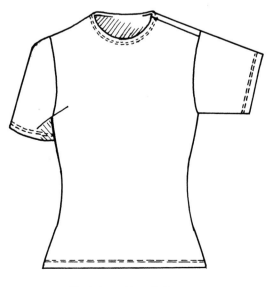

Short sleeved top-stitching

Pintuck detail tuxedo

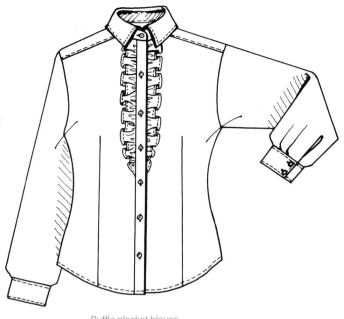

Ruffle placket blouse

Hidden placket pocket shirt

Banded collar shaped shirt

Pintuck yoke

Camp shirt

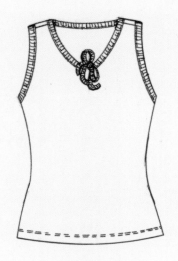

Sleeveless ribbed trim

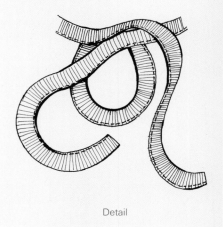

Detail

Button front printed cropped

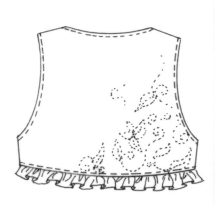

Back view

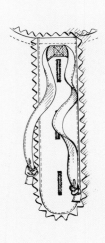

Detail

Puff sleeved yoke

Back view

Sleeveless smock

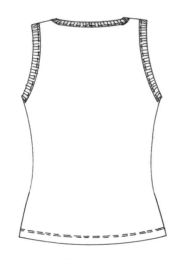

Back view

Knit turtleneck raglan sleeve

Rolled cuff cardigan sweater

Cable-knit cardigan

Bow tie blouson pullover

Fringe poncho

Knit vest with cable feature

Turtleneck turned up sleeve

Popcorn-stitch knit cardigan

Military

Western style

Bishop sleeve fold cuff

Peplum bell sleeve

Long sleeved polo

Pocket T

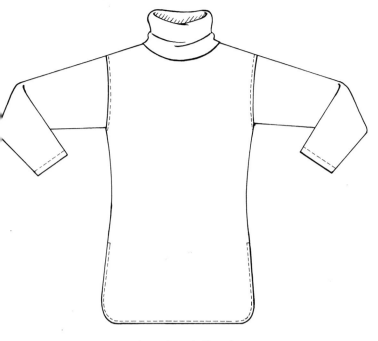

Long sleeve turtleneck

Two pocket placket

Fur-trimmed parka

Back view

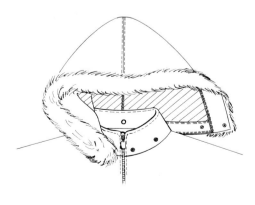

Detail

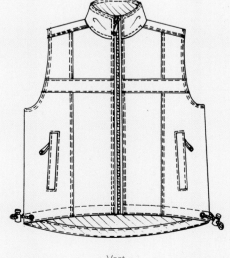

Vest

Gathered yoke double
button cuff

French cuff multibuttoned

Tab roll-up sleeve

Fitted princess seams
welt and flap pockets

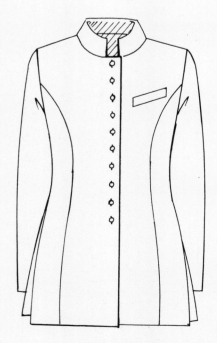

Nehru jacket

Double breasted
peak lapel fitted

Pea coat

Back view

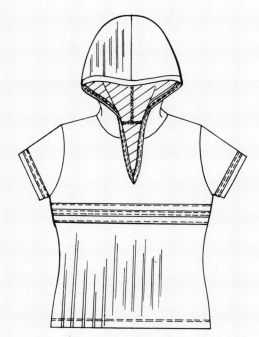

Ribbed hoodie

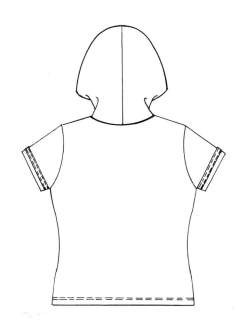

Back view

Fur-trimmed jean jacket

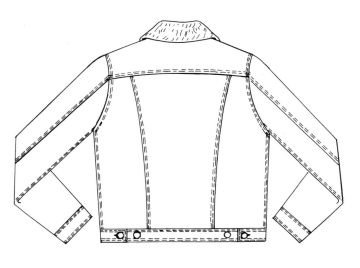

Back view

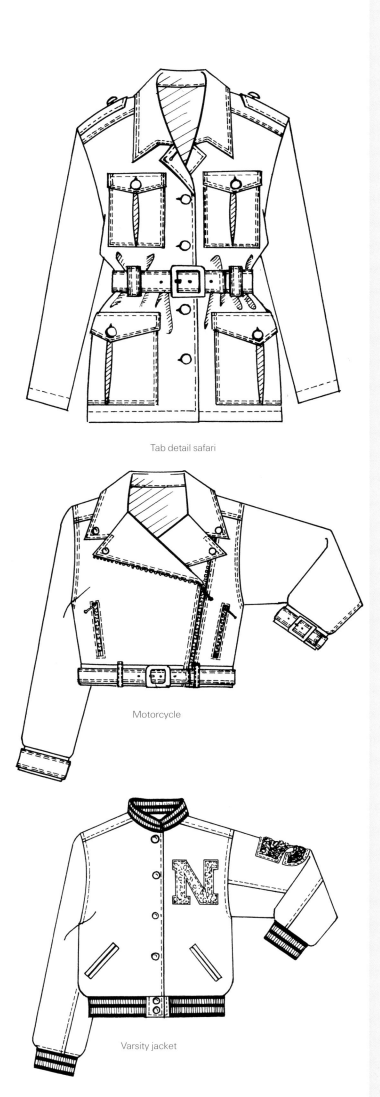

Tab detail safari

Motorcycle

Varsity jacket

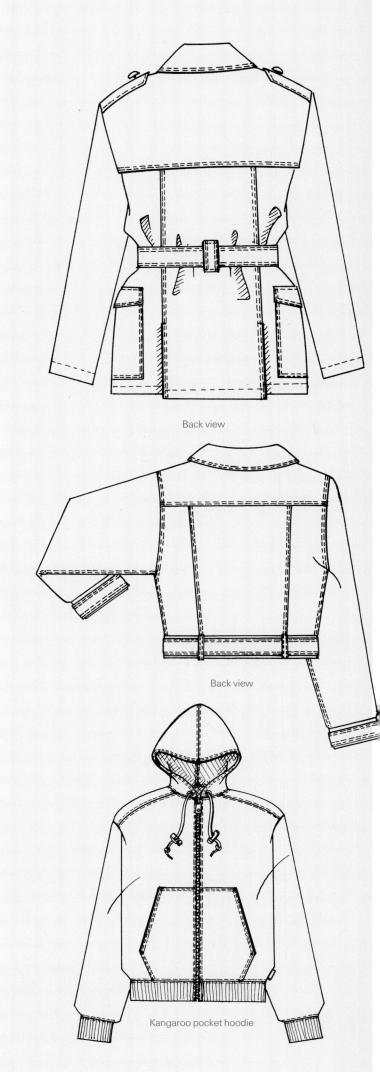

Back view

Back view

Kangaroo pocket hoodie

Piping-trimmed jacket

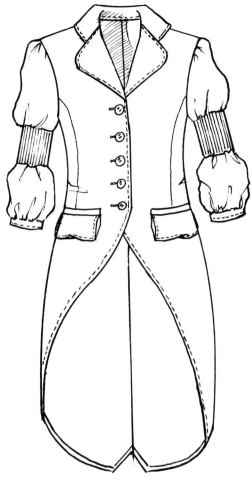

Edwardian morning coat

Racing jacket

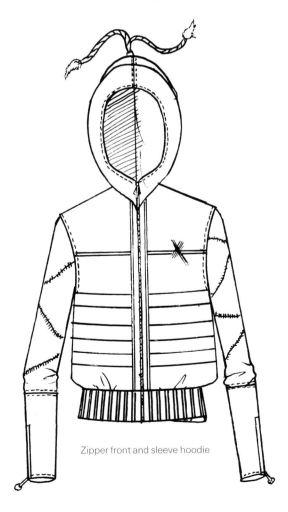

Zipper front and sleeve hoodie

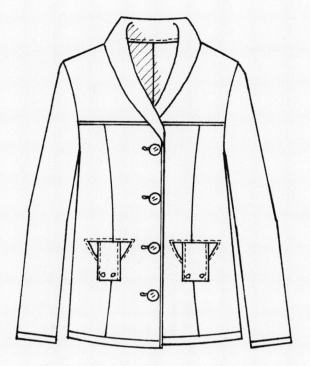

Tailored tab pocket shawl collar

Princess seam short blazer

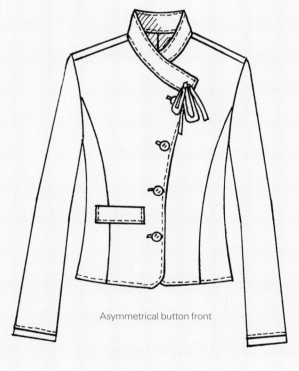

Asymmetrical button front

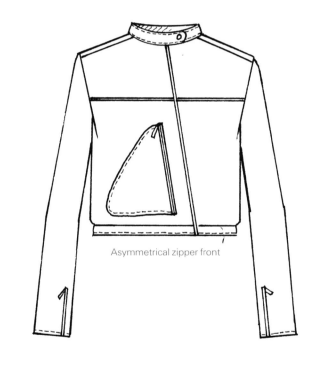

Asymmetrical zipper front

Scarf tie capelet

Double-breasted fitted top-stitch

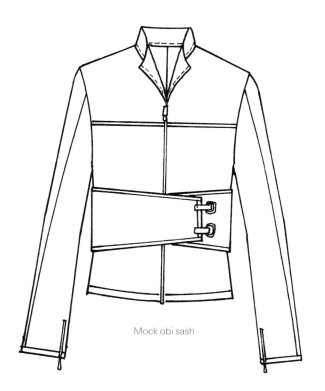

Mock obi sash

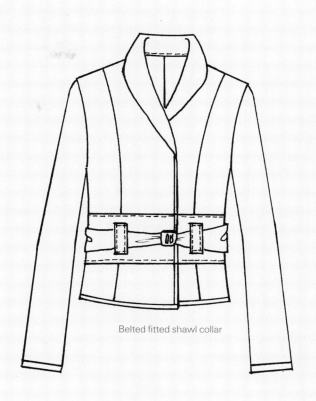

Belted fitted shawl collar

Stand collar with clips banded rib trim

Welt pocket cropped blazer

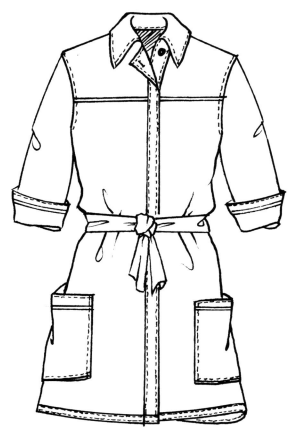

Dressmaker coat

Flight jacket

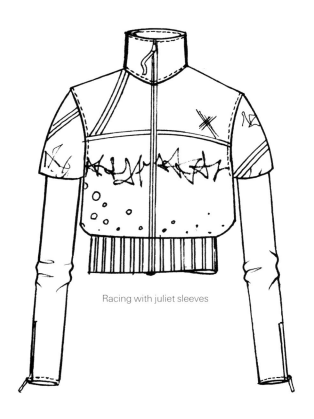

Racing with juliet sleeves

Bomber jacket

Fur trimmed lapel
and hem tie closure

Double-breasted round collar

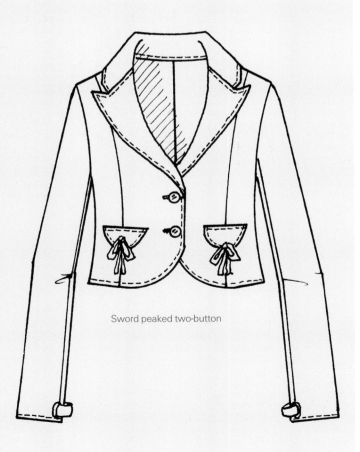

Sword peaked two-button

4-button D-ring belted pockets

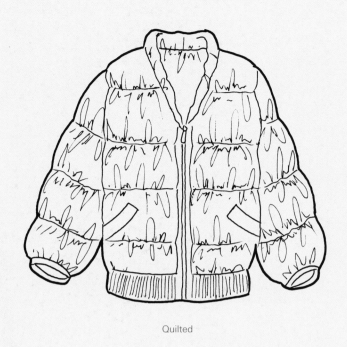

Quilted

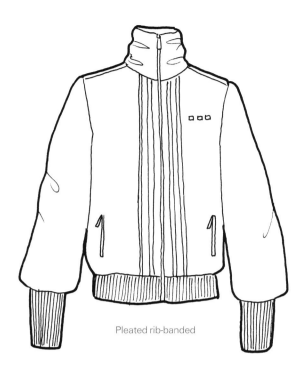

Pleated rib-banded

Fitted cloverleaf collar

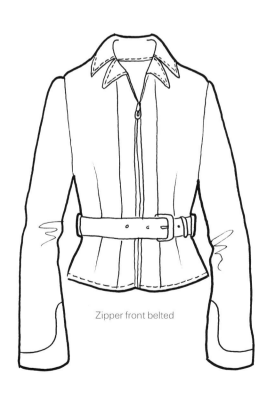

Zipper front belted

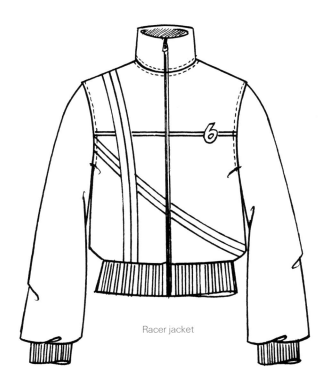

Racer jacket

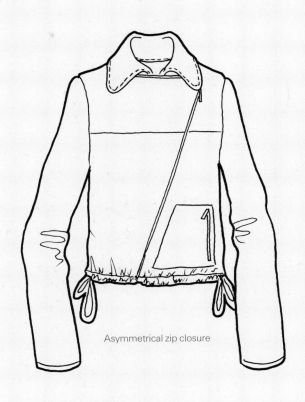

Asymmetrical zip closure

Zipper front

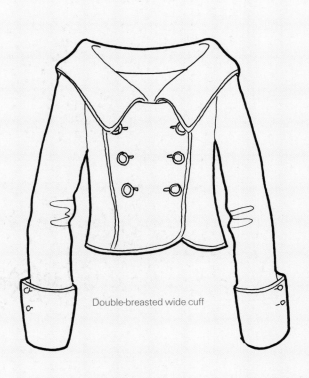

Double-breasted wide cuff

Daytona racing

Fitted two button stand collar

Cropped shawl collar zipper

Draped hooded belted

Zipper front stand collar racer

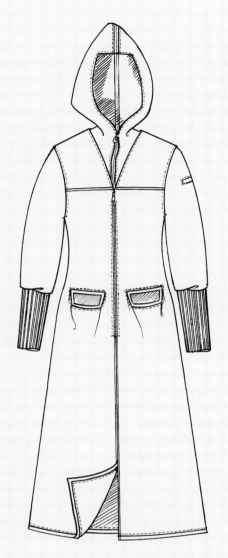

Zipper front rib-cuffed hooded

Coachman's pocket coat

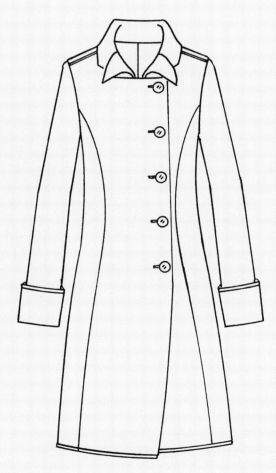

Asymmetrical button princess

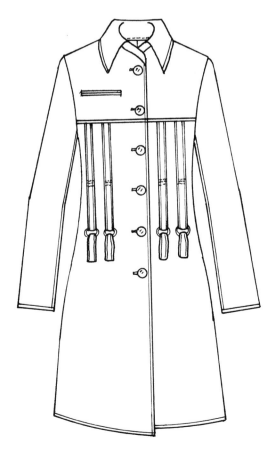

Banded tab retail coat

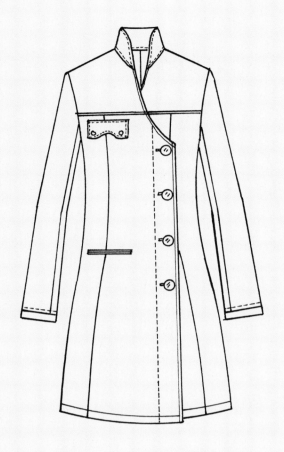

Asymmetrical closures yoke princess

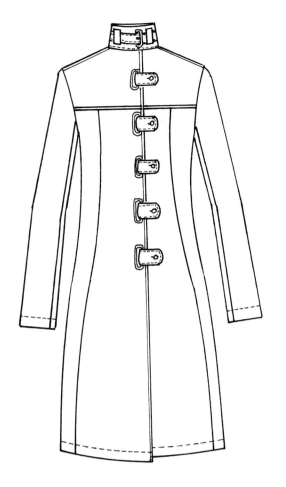

Band collar tab closure princess

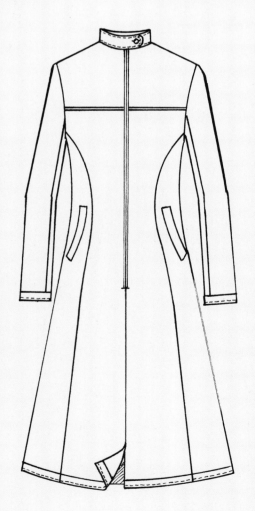

Zip front band collar princess

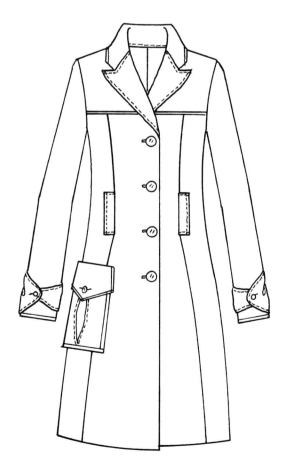

Peak lapel cargo pocket princess

women´s flats/coats

Notch collar tie detail princess

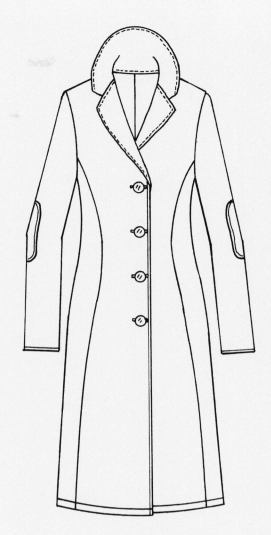

Patch elbow high collar princess

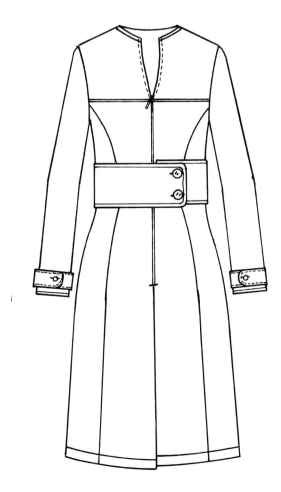

Zipper front obi-belted princess

Novelty equestrian

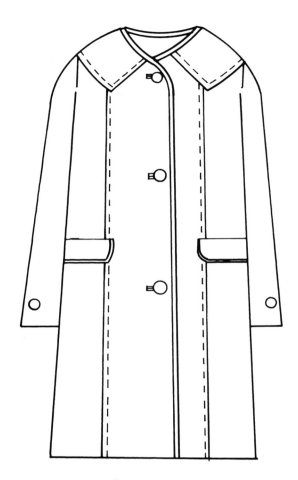

Three buton car coat

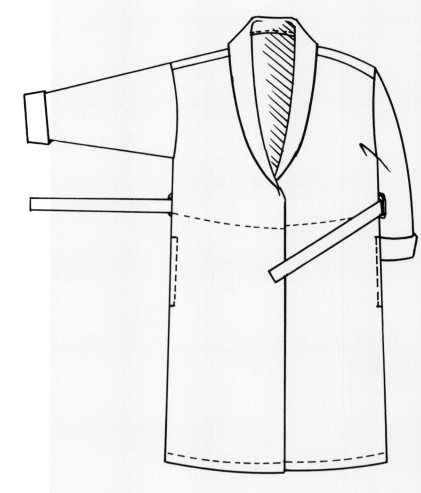

Belted lounge coat

Double-breasted notch collar car coat

Piped shoulder loop closure fitted topcoat

Yoke detail tie closure riding cape

Caped walking coat

Side button shawl collar jacket

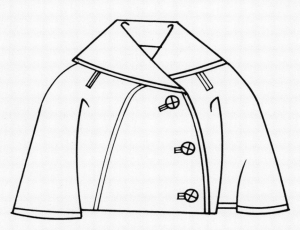

Shawl collar capelet

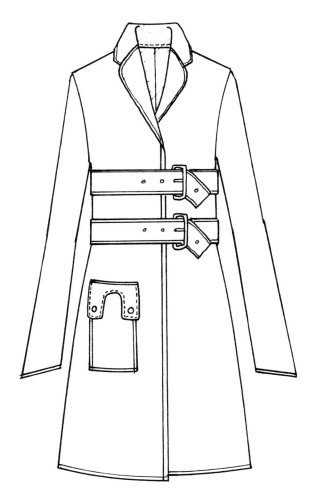

Double belted polo coat

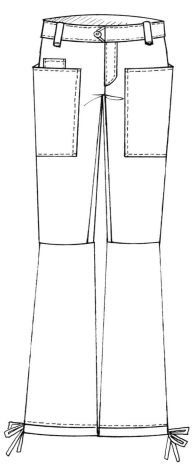

Patch pocket flared jeans

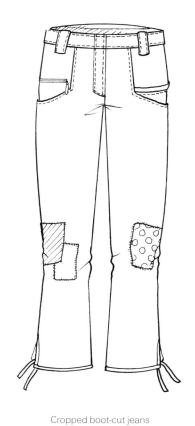

Cropped boot-cut jeans

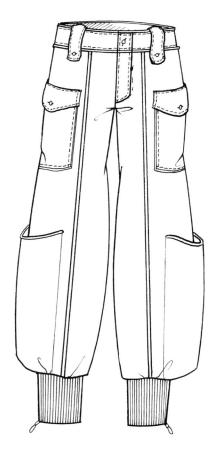

Urban cargo pants

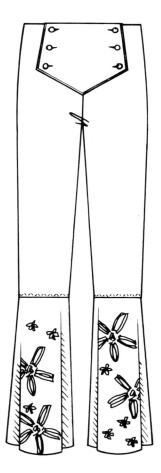

Sailor panel bell bottoms

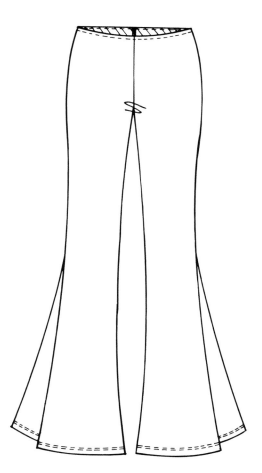

Low-rise bell bottoms

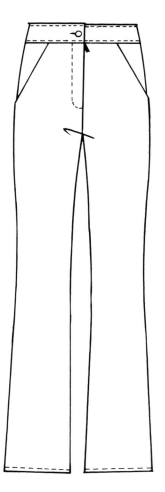

Boot-cut trousers

women's flats/pants

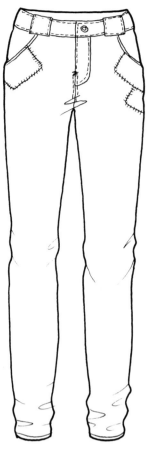

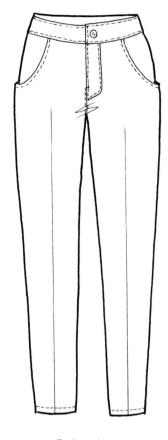

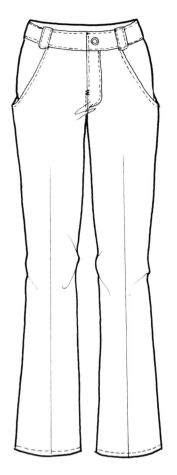

Slim leg jeans

Basic cut jeans

Boot cut jeans

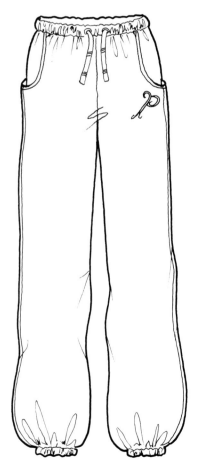

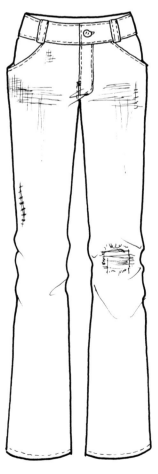

Logo detail sweatpants

Distressed boot cut jeans

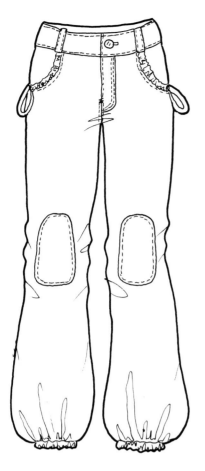

Jean style sweats

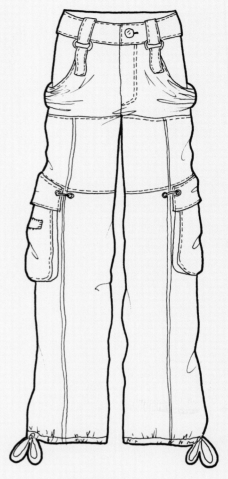

Cargo pocket parachute jeans

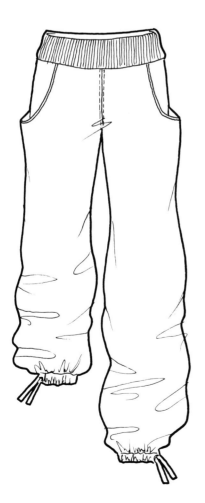

Rib banded yoga style sweatpants

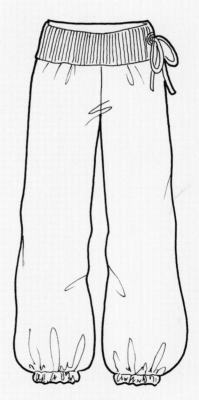

Drawstring cropped sweatpants

women's flats/pants

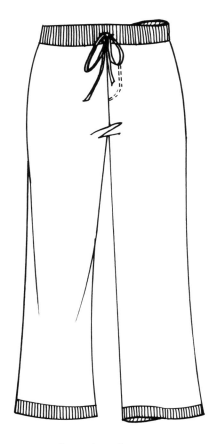

Drawstring pullon pants

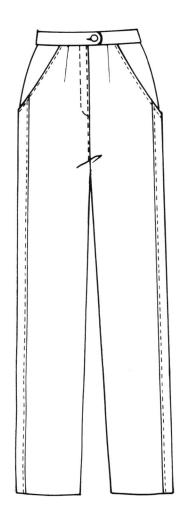

Extended tab trousers

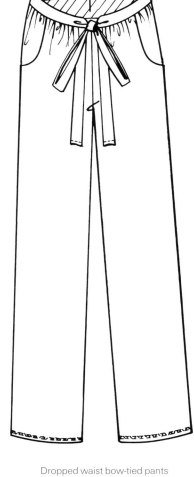

Dropped waist bow-tied pants

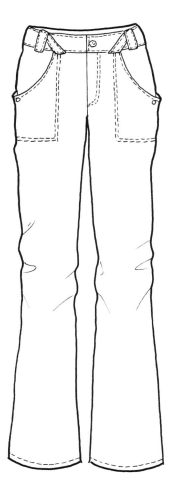

Boot cut jeans

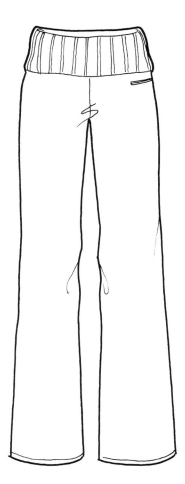

Yoga pants

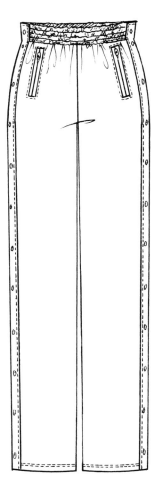

Side snap warm-up pants

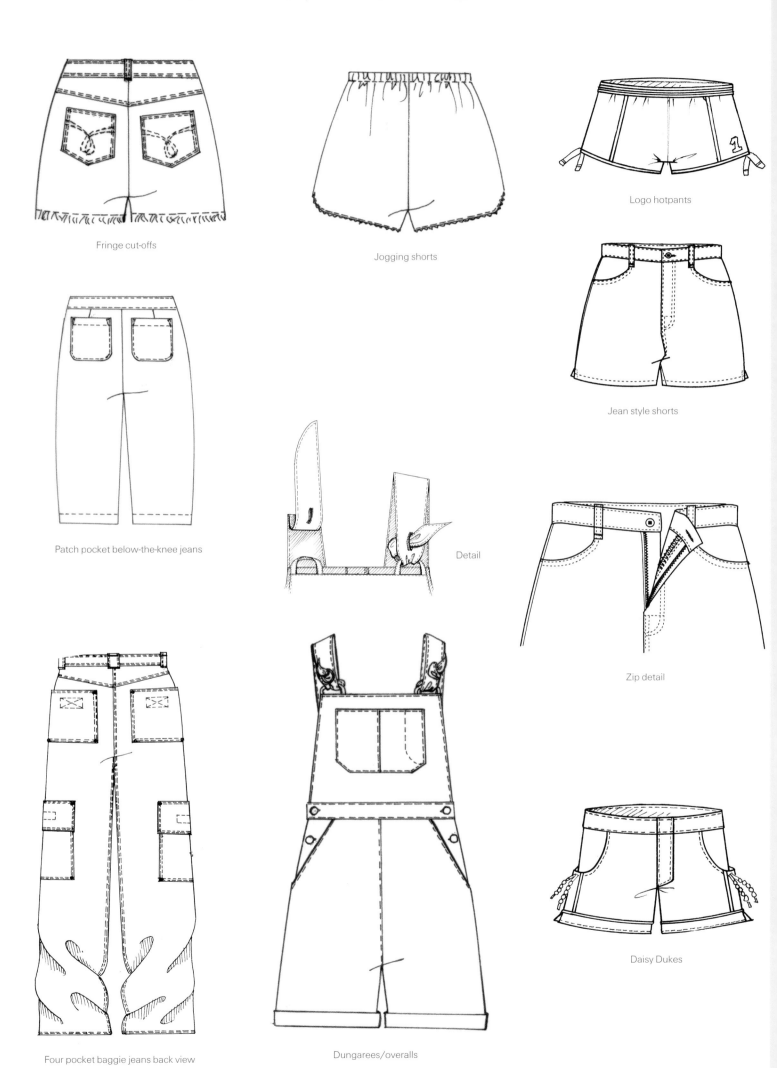

Fringe cut-offs

Jogging shorts

Logo hotpants

Jean style shorts

Patch pocket below-the-knee jeans

Detail

Zip detail

Four pocket baggie jeans back view

Dungarees/overalls

Daisy Dukes

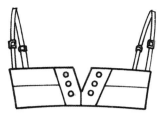

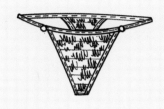

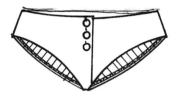

Retro two piece swimsuit/lingerie

Thong and underwire bra combo

Button detail two piece swimsuit

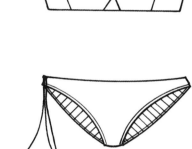

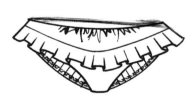

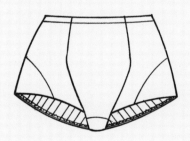

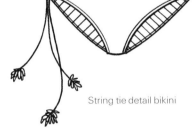

Ruffle-trimmed two piece swimsuit

Girdle style retro swimsuit

String tie detail bikini

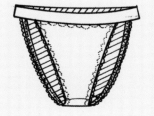

Strapless bra lace trimmed thong

Comfort mock wrap bra and thong

Tanner's two piece swimsuit

Satin edge retro bra front/back

Lace panties front/back

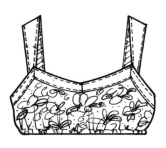

Retro bra swimsuit top front/back

Lace-up corset front/back

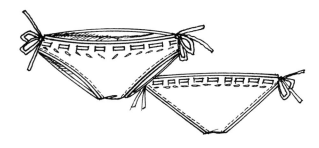

Swimsuit bikini bottoms front/back

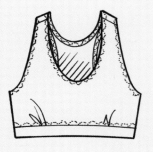

Racer back sports bra

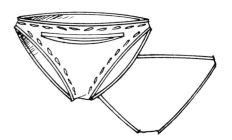

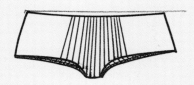

Strapless top boy-cut bottoms swimsuit

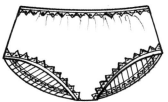

Lace trimmed underwire bra/panties

Sports bra/ trainer briefs

High-cut two piece swimsuit

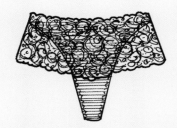

Lace strapless bra and thong

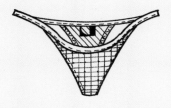

Full underwire bra/thong

Seamless bra/ribbed panties

Ribbed bra and brief

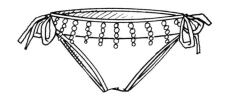

Beaded fringe bikini

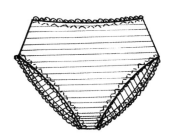

Bra- cut swimsuit

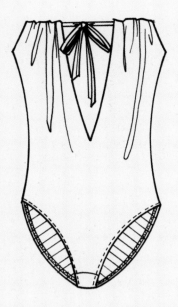

Pull-on strapless v-tie swimsuit

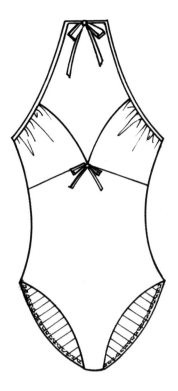

Spaghetti tie halter swimsuit

Underwire body suit

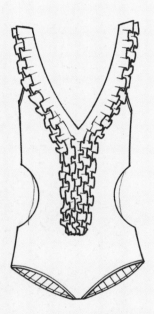

Ruffled deep-v boy leg swimsuit

String tie swimsuit

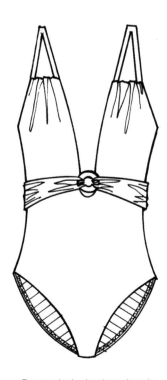

Deep v cinched waist swimsuit

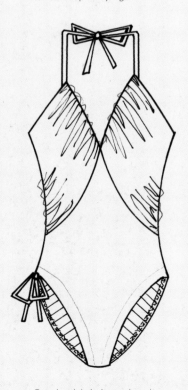

Spaghetti tie halter swimsuit

Tie-back halter swimsuit

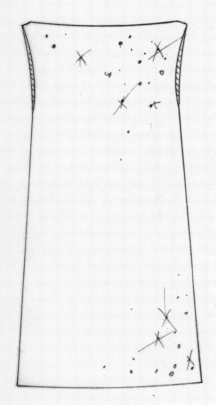

Beaded sheath

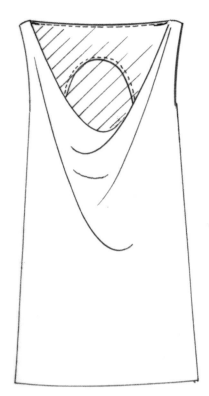

Cowl back (back view)

Empire with ruched trim

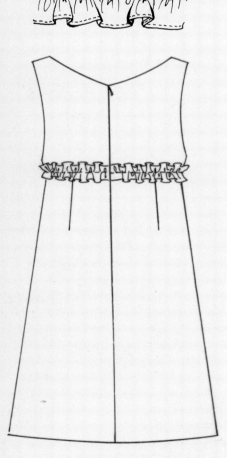

Empire with ruched trim.
Back view with detail.

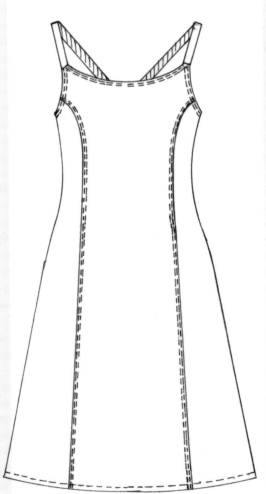

Princess seam sundress

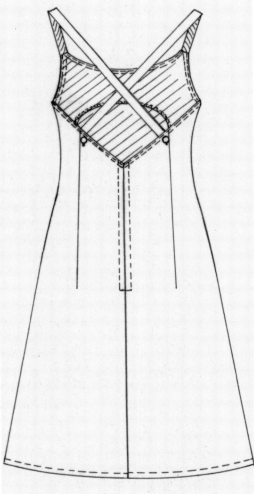

Back view

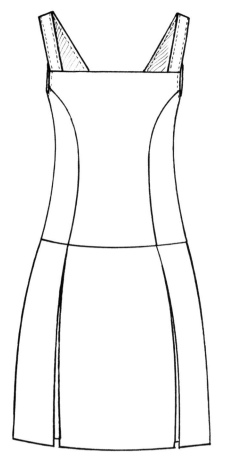

Sleeveless sundress inverted pleats

Back view

Empire flared skirt sundress

Empire flared skirt sundress. Back view.

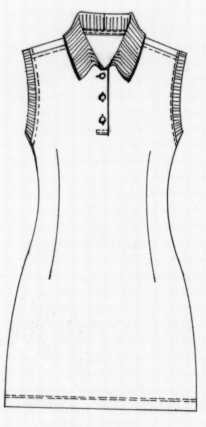

Ribbed collar placket fitted

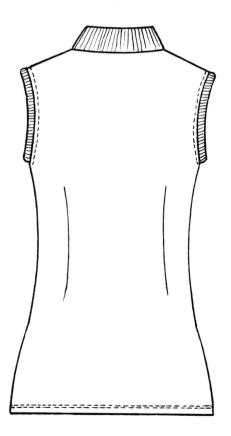

Back view

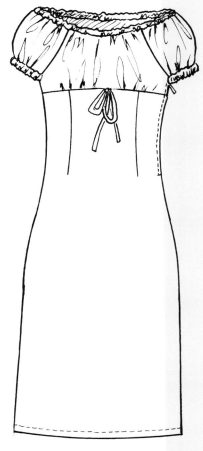

Empire baby doll

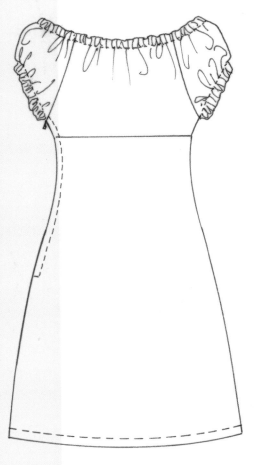

Back view

V-neck layered cocktail dress

Back view

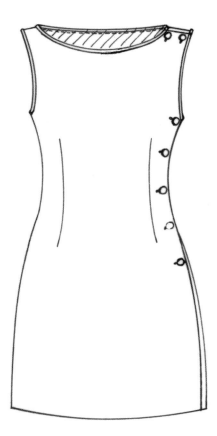

Side and shoulder button sheath

Spaghetti strap asymmetrical ruffle sun

Back view

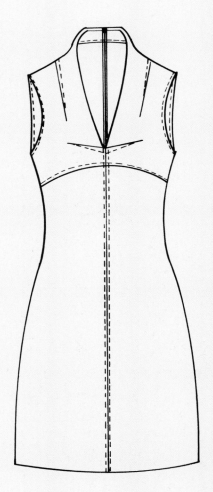

Deep v-neck dart construction Empire

Keyhole neckline sheath

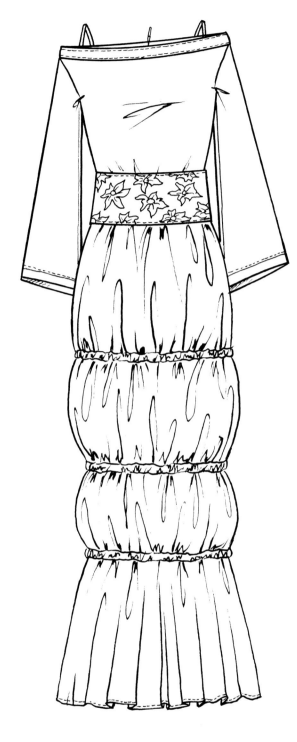

Modified obi ruched

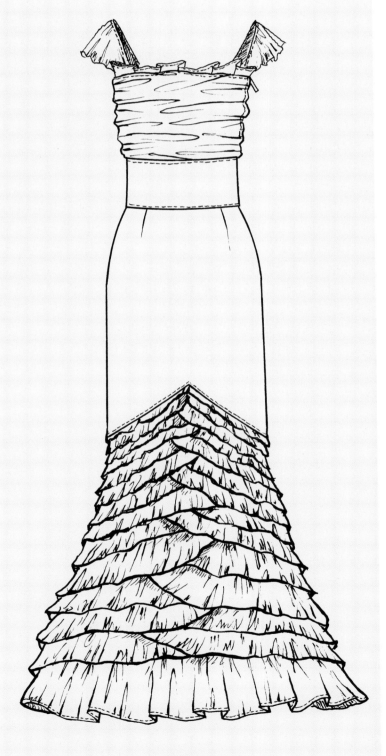

Retro layered flounce

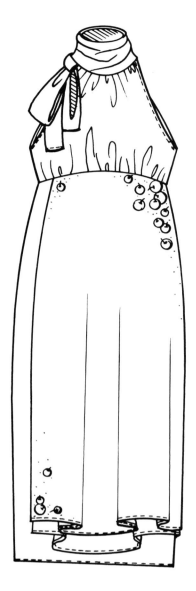

Bow detail mock apron cocktail dress

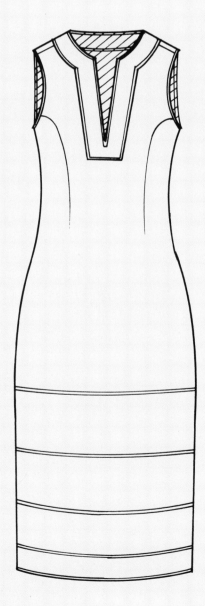

Slit neckline sleeveless princess seam

String tie halter neck wide waist

String tie halter, beaded waist full skirt

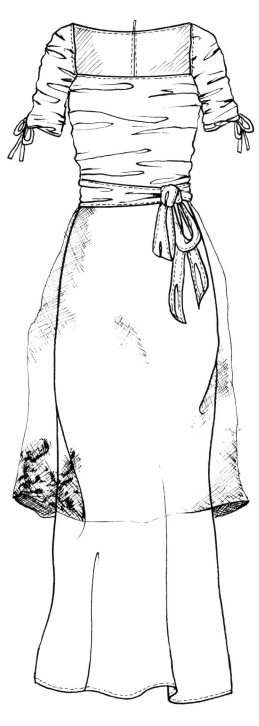

Square neck cinched waist apron dress

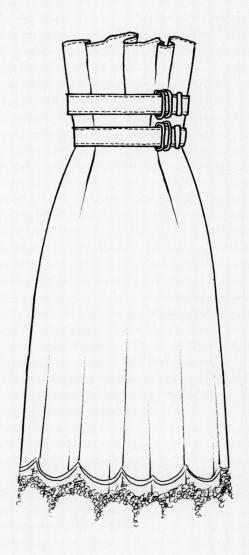

Strapless belted waist scallop hem

Mock wrap lace -trimmed

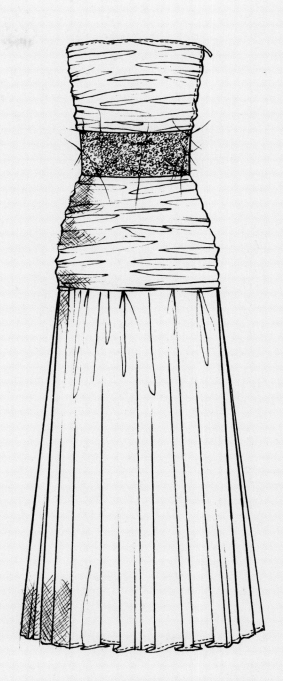

Ruched cinched waist beading and embroidery detail

Drop-v halter tiered skirt

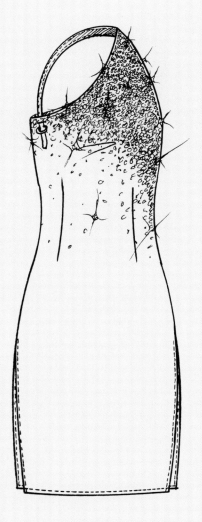

Beaded asymmetrical closure cocktail

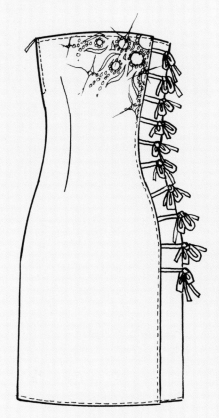

Strapless fitted beading side bows

Beaded waist strapless cocktail

women's flats/dresses

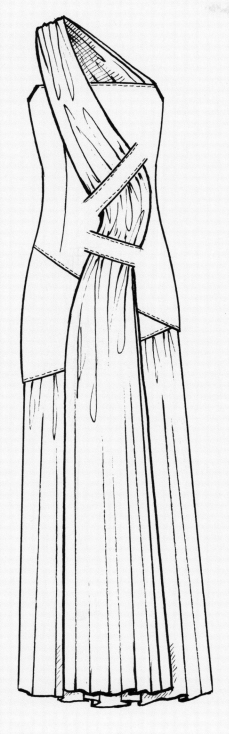

Grecian-inspired sash gown

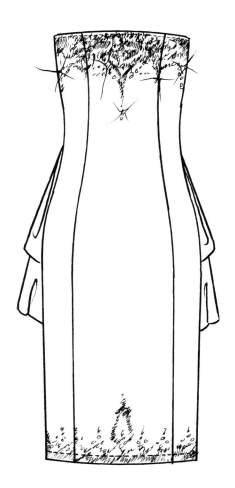

Strapless beaded cocktail

index

index

index

index

Issey Miyake gown by Ruben Alterio